Implementing Amsterdam

Immigration and Asylum Rights in EC Law

Edited by
ELSPETH GUILD
and
CAROL HARLOW

• HART •
PUBLISHING

OXFORD – PORTLAND
2001

Hart Publishing
Oxford and Portland, Oregon

Published in North America (US and Canada) by
Hart Publishing c/o
International Specialized Book Services
5804 NE Hassalo Street
Portland, Oregon
97213-3644
USA

Distributed in the Netherlands, Belgium and Luxembourg by
Intersentia, Churchillaan 108
B2900 Schoten
Antwerpen
Belgium

Hart Publishing is a specialist legal publisher based in Oxford, England.
To order further copies of this book or to request a list of other publications please write to:

Hart Publishing Ltd, Salter's Boatyard,
Folly Bridge, Abingdon Road, Oxford OX1 4LB
Telephone: +44 (0)1865 245533 or Fax: +44 (0)1865 794882
e-mail: mail@hartpub.co.uk
WEBSITE: http//www.hartpub.co.uk

British Library Cataloguing in Publication Data
Data Available
ISBN 1-84113-116-4 (hardback)

Typeset by Hope Services (Abingdon) Ltd.
Printed and bound in Great Britain on acid-free paper by
Biddles Ltd, www.biddles.co.uk

Contents

Table of Cases

1. INTERNATIONAL COURT OF JUSTICE

2. EUROPEAN COURT OF HUMAN RIGHTS

3. EUROPEAN COMMUNITY COURTS

European Court of Justice

Court of First Instance

4. NATIONAL COURTS

Australia

Belgium

France

Germany

Netherlands

United Kingdom

Table of Legislation

1. INTERNATIONAL

2. COUNCIL OF EUROPE

3. EUROPEAN UNION AND COMMUNITY

Directives

Regulations

Decisions

4. NATIONAL

France

Germany

United Kingdom

Contributors

Nicholas Blake is a founder member and former chair of the Immigration Law Practitioners Association. He has written and lectured extensively on asylum law, EU free movement law and human rights law in the immigration context. He is now a member of Matrix Chambers London and has appeared in many leading cases in the UK including the case of *R* v. *Secretary of State for the Home Department ex p Adan and Aitsegur* and cases before the ECJ and the ECHR.

Pieter Boeles, is an attorney at law since 1975. He was one of the founders of Everaert Immigration Lawyers in Amsterdam, a law firm presently consisting of 14 attorneys specialised in immigration law. Since 1996 he is a part-time professor of law at the University of Leiden, where he was one of the founders of the Institute of Immigration Law. He has written a number of books on immigration law (in English: Fair Immigration Proceedings in Europe; Kluwer Law International, 1997) and he has published many articles and comments. He is Chief Editor of a Dutch case law journal, member of the Dutch Standing Committee of Experts on Immigration and Criminal Law and member of the editorial board of the European Journal of Migration and Law.

Gisbert Brinkmann is an official at the German Federal Ministry of Labour and Social Affairs, since 1994 he has been head of the division of International and European Legal Affairs. Before beginning work with the Ministry in 1979 he had been a lecturer at the (then) Centre of European Governmental Studies at Edinburgh University since 1975. He is co-editor of a journal on European labour and social law and is the author of numerous publications on constitutional law, human rights, international public law, German and European migration law, in particular freedom of movement. He received a Dr.jur. from Tübingen University and a M.P.A. from Harvard University.

John Crowley is a Research Fellow at the Centre d'Études et de Recherches Internationales of the Fondation Nationale des Sciences Politiques in Paris. He holds a doctorate in political science from the Institut d'Études Politiques de Paris. His recent publications include *Sans épines, la rose. Tony Blair: un modèle pour l'Europe?*, Paris, Éd. La Découverte, 1999; "The politics of belonging : some theoretical considerations", in Adrian Favell & Andrew Geddes (dir.), *The politics of belonging: migrants and minorities in contemporary Europe*, Aldershot, Ashgate, 1999, pp. 15–41; "Some thoughts on theorizing European citizenship", *Innovation*, 12(4), 1999, pp. 471–488; "France: the archetype of a nation-state", in Louk Haagendoorn, György Csepeli, Henk Dekker & Russell

Farnen (eds), *European nations and nationalism. Theoretical and historical perspectives*, Aldershot, Ashgate, 2000, pp. 67–106.

Deirdre Curtin is Professor of the Law of International Organisations and Director of the Europa Institute at the University of Utrecht. She is also a member of the Standing Committee of Experts on International Immigration, Refugee and Criminal law (Meijers Committee). She has published extensively on issues relating to the institutional law of the EU, access to information and human rights matters. Recent publications include *Postnational Democracy. The European Union in search of a Political Philosophy* (Kluwer, 1997).

Guy S. Goodwin-Gill is Professor of International Refugee Law and Rubin Director of Research, Institute of European Studies, University of Oxford. From 1994–1999, he was also Professor of Asylum Law, University of Amsterdam. He served in the Office of the United Nations High Commissioner for Refugees (UNHCR), principally as a Legal Adviser, in various countries from 1976–1988, since when he has been engaged in teaching, research and the provision of advice on international law and refugee and migration-related issues. He has been Editor-in-Chief of the *International Journal of Refugee Law* (Oxford University Press) since its first issue in 1989, and in November 1997 he was elected President of the Refugee Legal Centre (a non-governmental organization providing advice and representation to refugees and asylum seekers in the United Kingdom). His recent publications include *The Reality of International Law: Essays in Honour of Ian Brownlie,* (with Stefan Talmon, eds.), Clarendon Press, Oxford, 1999; *The Refugee in International Law,* Clarendon Press, Oxford, second edition, 1996; Russian translation published 1997; *Codes of Conduct for Elections,* Inter-Parliamentary Union, Geneva, 1998; *Free and Fair Elections: International Law and Practice*, Inter-Parliamentary Union, Geneva, 1994 (also in French, Spanish, Khmer and Indonesian); and *Child Soldiers*, (with Ilene Cohn), Clarendon Press, Oxford, 1994 (also published in French and Spanish).

Kees Groenendijk is Professor of Sociology of Law at the University of Nijmegen (The Netherlands) and Director of its Centre for Migration Law. He is chairman of the Standing Committee of Experts on International Immigration, Refugee and Criminal Law (Meijers Committee). His recent publications include *Temporary employment of migrants in Europe* (1995), *Nederland en zijn islam* (The Netherlands and its islam) (1996, with others), Regulating ethnic migration: the Aussiedler (1997), *Security of residence of long-term migrants, Law and practice in European countries* (1998, with E. Guild and H. Dogan), and Immigration, immigrés et législation sur la nationalité aux Pays-Bas 1945–1998 (1999, with E. Heijs).

Elspeth Guild is the academic coordinator of the Centre for Migration Law, University of Nijmegen, and a partner at the London law firm, Kingsley Napley. She also teaches at Sciences-Po in Paris. She is the UK expert to the European Commission's network on implementation of Community law on free movement of workers. Among recent reports which she has written or collaborated upon are: A Case Study on Accession to the European Union: Hungary and Free Movement of Workers, for the ILO (forthcoming) and the Impact of the Amsterdam Treaty on Justice and Home Affairs Issues for the European Parliament (3–2000). She has written or edited six books in the field of European Community law and free movement of persons, including the human rights dimension.

Cristina J. Gortázar Rotaeche is Professor of Public International Law at the University Pontificia Comillas of Madrid (UPCO, Spain). She is also Lecturer in Asylum and Refugee Law. Director of Masters' Programme on Immigration at the University Institute on Migration Studies (UPCO) and coordinator of the Faculty Section on Public International Law and International relations. She is the Spanish National Expert in the Odysseus Network (Academic Network for Legal Studies on Immigration and Asylum in Europe). She has published several books and articles on immigration and asylum lawrelated issues; among others, "Derecho de asilo y "no rechazo" del refugiado" (Right of Asylum and non refoulement, UPCO/Dykinson, 1997).

Carol Harlow is Professor of Public Law at the London School of Economics and has been Visiting Jean Monnet Professor at the European University Institute. She teaches and researches in the areas of constitutional and administrative law and European Public Law. She is the author with Richard Rawlings of Law and Administration and Pressure Through Law and co-editor with Paul Craig of Lawmaking in the European Union.

Johannes van der Klaauw has a Masters in Theology/Comparative Religion and a Bachelors in Philosophy from the University of Leiden, the Netherlands. From 1989 until 1995 he headed the Amnesty International European Union Office in Brussels as the Organization's EU Representative, and from 1992 also as its Director. In 1995 he joined the UNHCR Regional Office in Brussels as Senior European Affairs Officer. He is responsible for the liaison with the EU institutions, particularly regarding the harmonisation of asylum policies in Western Europe, capacity – and institution – building in the field of refugee protection in Central and Eastern Europe, the EU Stability Pact for the Balkans and the Common Foreign and Security Policy.

Gregor Noll, LL D (Lund), is a lecturer at the Faculty of Law, University of Lund, Sweden. He has recently finalized his dissertation on the legality of the asylum acquis in the European Union (forthcoming august 2000 with Kluwer Law International). Gregor Noll teaches international law at undergraduate and graduate level and has been lecturing extensively on subjects related to flight, refuge and return. He has published articles on burden-sharing, gender and persecution, the return of rejected asylum-seekers as well as the democratic legitimacy of refugee law.

Steve Peers is a Reader in Law at the University of Essex, Colchester, United Kingdom. He has written extensively on EU immigration and external relations law and is the author of EU Justice and Home Affairs Law (Longman, 2000); The Amsterdam Proposals (ILPA/MPG, 2000); EU Social Law (Blackstone, forthcoming); and International Agreements of the European Union (OUP, forthcoming).

Jens Vedsted-Hansen is Professor at the University of Aarhus Law School, Denmark. He received his Master and Doctor degrees in law from the University of Aarhus in 1980 and 1997, respectively. He was granted a research fellowship in 1980 at the University of Aalborg, Faculty of Social Sciences. In 1983 he became assistant professor at the University of Aarhus Law School, and from 1984 to 1995 he was associate professor of public and international law. He worked at the Danish Centre for Human Rights as a research fellow from 1993 until 1997, by which time he joined the Faculty of Law at the University of Copenhagen as associate professor of administrative law. Since 1999 he has been professor of law at the University of Aarhus. His publications and research interests include administrative law, social welfare law, immigration and refugee law, and human rights law. He served as a member of the Refugee Appeals Board 1987–94, and was coordinating the legal part of a comparative Nordic research project on temporary protection of refugees 1995–98.

Introduction: Freedom, Security and Justice for All

PIETER BOELES

The ambitious and promising overture of the new Title of the EC Treaty on visas, asylum, immigration and other policies related to the free movement of persons is in contemporary terms, a mission statement. According to the first sentence of Article 61 EC, the purpose of measures harmonising law in immigration and asylum must be: "to establish progressively an area of freedom, security and justice". This is the goal which the harmonisation is meant to serve and therefore the touchstone for the adequacy of the texts to be drafted and the prevailing source of inspiration for judicial interpretation.

Article 61 EC is obviously referring to Article 2 TEU, where five objectives of the Union are enumerated:

(1) to promote economic and social progress and a high level of employment and to achieve balanced and sustainable development, in particular through the creation of an area without internal frontiers, through the strengthening of economic and social cohesion and through the establishment of economic and monetary union, ultimately including a single currency in accordance with the provisions of the Treaty;

(2) to assert its identity on the international scene, in particular through the implementation of a common foreign and security policy including the progressive framing of a common defence policy, which might lead to a common defence, in accordance with the provisions of Article 17;

(3) to strengthen the protection of the rights and interests of the nationals of its Member States through the introduction of a citizenship of the Union;

(4) to maintain and develop the Union as an area of freedom, security and justice, in which the free movement of persons is assured in conjunction with appropriate measures with respect to external border controls, immigration, asylum and the combating of crime;

(5) to maintain the full *acquis communautaire* and build on it with a view to considering to what extent the policies and forms of co-operation introduced by this Treaty may need to be revised with the aim of ensuring the effectiveness and the mechanisms of the Community.

It seems reasonable to interpret the meaning of these objectives in the context of their mutual coherence. This is not, however, the only context to be taken into account. The objectives mentioned in Article 2 TEU cannot be isolated from the goals of the Union formulated in the Preamble and in the common provisions of the TEU (Article 1–7). Article 6(1) and (2) TEU especially deserves to be mentioned:

"(1) The Union is founded on the principles of liberty, democracy, respect for human rights and fundamental freedoms, and the rule of law, principles which are common to the Member States;

(2) The Union shall respect fundamental rights, as guaranteed by the European Convention for the Protection of Human Rights and Fundamental Freedoms signed in Rome on 4 November 1950 and as they result from the constitutional traditions common to the Member States, as general principles of Community law."

On the other hand, the Preamble to the EC Treaty and the general provisions of Articles 1–16 EC are relevant as well, whereas Title IV is part of the Treaty establishing the European Community and must, therefore, primarily be interpreted within the context of that Treaty. Particularly relevant are Articles 2 and 3 (on the purposes and activities of the Community) and Articles 12 (prohibition of discrimination on grounds of nationality within the scope of application of this Treaty) and 13 (action to combat discrimination based on sex, racial or ethnic origin, religion or belief, disability, age or sexual orientation).

In this introduction, I will attempt to analyse the content and meaning of the concept of an "area of freedom, security and justice" in these contexts. The leading question will be, for whom is this area meant to be maintained and developed? For EU citizens only? For third country nationals who have a right to legal residence in a Member State? Or for everyone? I will try to answer this question in a step-by-step approach: first, I will look at the normal meaning of the words "area", "freedom", "security" and "justice". Next I will denote the possible meaning of each word in the light of the text of the TEU and the EC. In the final part of my research, I will point out what the consequences may be of a given interpretation for the rights of individuals under a harmonised European immigration and asylum law.

NORMAL MEANING OF "AREA", "FREEDOM", "SECURITY" AND "JUSTICE"

The word "area" as such is rather a neutral concept, as it does not pretend to do more than designate any delimited part of space. I will, therefore, not elaborate on that at this stage. However, the words "freedom", "security" and "justice" have a much wider connotation. I suspect that this is equally true for all the languages of the Member States.

- "Freedom" means not to be bound by any limitation; to do what one wishes to do. Where absolute freedom is an impossibility, we have learnt to put the word in perspective. We give freedom its practical meaning by specifying the limitations to be removed: freedom from governmental interference, freedom from tax duties, etc. We may discern a psychological connotation: for the well-being of humans it often appears to be more important to feel free than to be free. The feeling may be absolute, even if there are limitations ("singing in the rain"). Freedom does not exist in the same measure for all people. However universal the longing for freedom may be, in a more precise and technical meaning "freedom" is always related to specific limitations to be removed or prevented, and those limitations are normally linked to specific persons or groups of persons. This observation does not apply when we are talking of "fundamental freedoms". Those freedoms are still specified by the limitations to be removed or prevented, but they are rights that belong to everyone.

- "Security" in its most absolute sense pretends the exclusion of any probability for certain "things" to happen. If we use the word in physical scientific reasoning, we have no special feeling towards these things. But if we use the word in the sense of "safety", it is related to a threat of unpleasant events. "Security" does not say much if we cannot specify the threat that is supposed to be eliminated. As we all know, there normally is no such thing as an absolute guarantee that unpleasant occurrences will never take place. Security, in social terms, is more a goal or a wish than a fact. The psychological connotation, therefore, often tends to override the technical meaning of the word. "Security" may indicate a feeling of freedom from worry or fear. This unveils connection with the concept of freedom. "Security" will normally—if not always—be linked to persons or groups who are to be protected. One will have to specify what kind of security is meant and to whom it will apply.

- "Justice" is probably the most complicated concept of the four. It may refer to (parts of) the organisation of law enforcement and, generally, to law and order But above all it has an abstract and idealistic content: justice comes into being when injustice is prevented or solved. What is just and what is unjust? Legal practice and political parties would not flourish if all people had the same view on this matter, particularly when their own interests were involved. However, in the total of clashes between legal interests and visions one golden rule for negotiating a mutually acceptable solution appears to emerge and survive: one should not do to others that which one does not want to be done to oneself. It is a basic rule of common sense, which inevitably leads to the fundamental principles of equality and non-discrimination. The different connotations of the word "justice" may lead to misunderstandings between people who think that they are talking about the same concept. Some may have the equality and non-discrimination "justice" in mind and others may at the same time talk about "justice" in the sense of enforcement of law and order. Those two views may be hugely different. It is the difference between a universal and a more limited concept. The pretence of non-discrimination and equality can hardly be limited to certain privileged persons or groups of persons, as that would imply the acceptance of inequality and discrimination. But the pretence of law and order is bound to practical limitations, and therefore normally implies the definition of a region, territory or a group of persons where or on whom law and order is to be enforced. The two approaches may come together when the primary goal of maintaining law and order in a certain area is the prevention and combating of injustice, in other words, when the rule of law prevails.

MEANING OF "AREA OF FREEDOM, SECURITY AND JUSTICE" IN THE CONTEXT OF THE EC TREATY AND THE TEU

So far my amateurish exercise in language exegesis is, hopefully, sufficiently recognisable to serve as a starting point for further discussion. What can now be said about the meaning of an "area of freedom, security and justice" in Title IV?

"Area"

It seems apparent that the boundaries of the "area" are none other than the external borders of the common territory of the Member States of the Union. It is the same area as mentioned in Article 2 TEU and Article 14(2) EC: an area that should have no internal frontiers and where an internal market (see Article 3 EC) is to be created. However, it would be too narrow to define the "area" in strictly territorial terms. It is neither logical nor advisable that the fundamental purposes of freedom, security and justice could be renounced whenever external relations and activities of the European Community/European Union are at issue. These purposes are also governing treaties between the Community and third countries and even external actions (like in Kosovo) under the Second Pillar (see Article 11(1) TEU). Further, they are relevant in the relationship between Member States or the Community and persons who are abroad and apply for visas or other types of permission concerning admission or residence. It seems, therefore, adequate to read "area" as "jurisdiction"—which is wider than "territory".

"Freedom"

If we look at the word "freedom" as it appears in different places in the texts of the EC Treaty and the TEU, we see clear references to the concept of fundamental freedoms. According to the preamble of the EC Treaty the contracting parties were "resolved . . . to preserve and strengthen peace and liberty". In the third paragraph of the preamble to the TEU, and in Article 6 TEU, mention is made of "principles of liberty, democracy, respect for human rights and fundamental freedoms and the rule of law". This offers a solid basis for believing that "an area of freedom" refers to a place of liberty, where fundamental freedoms are respected. Precisely by not specifying to what and to whom this "freedom" refers, the drafters of the Treaty of Amsterdam (ToA) suggested a general and fundamental denotation of freedom which—by its nature—should apply to everyone within the jurisdiction of the Member States, the Community and the Union.

However, this is not the only reference to "freedom" we find in the EC Treaty and the TEU. There is also the freedom of movement of persons, which is one of the four freedoms mentioned in Article 3 EC, referred to in Article 2 (fourth paragraph) TEU, in the heading of Title IV and in Article 61(a). It is likely that we should include this connotation in the concept of the "area of freedom" as well. This is also the opinion of the Council and the Commission who consider freedom in the sense of free movement of people within the Union as a fundamental objective of the Treaty. This raises—amongst others—the question, to whom the freedom of movement must be deemed to apply. Before the ToA entered into force, it was commonly assumed that freedom of movement applied only to nationals of the Member States and their families. It is my opinion that this view was not necessarily supported by the text of the EC Treaty even at that time and that the view is inconsistent in itself. It is hard to indicate how the Council could ever be competent to make regulations and directives granting free movement rights to family members, irrespective of their nationality, if the freedom of movement was to be reserved for EC nationals only. The mere argument that their rights are derived from those of EC nationals is neither compelling nor convincing. I would advocate an interpretation according to which the Community had always the competence to regulate free movement of persons irrespective of their nationality, and according to which it was only the first goal set by the Treaty to realise free movement of workers, self-employed persons, companies and providers (recipients) of services with the nationality of the Member States. The basis for the competence of the Community would have to be found in the text of Article 3 EC, where the freedom of movement of persons has always been mentioned without any specification as to the nationality of those persons. Also, in Article 14, second indent, the freedom of movement of persons has never been limited to citizens of the Member States, although it could have been done at several occasions (in Luxembourg, 1986, in Maastricht, 1992, and in Amsterdam, 1997). Even Article 39 EC, which has existed since 1957, does not restrict the freedom of workers as to their nationalities. It is true that Article 43 EC prohibits restrictions on the freedom of establishment of nationals of a Member State, and that Article 49 EC prohibits restrictions on freedom to provide services within the Community in respect to nationals of Member States, but these prohibitions do not necessarily imply that nationals of third countries would not be entitled to any freedom of establishment or freedom to provide services at all, or that the Community institutions would not be competent to regulate or control such freedom on the basis of Article 3. I understand that it is not very likely that I will convince many readers, as I seem to have the ECJ against me on this interpretation. But there may be good grounds for taking a fresh look at this theme since the ToA has entered into force. Whatever the value of the above-mentioned arguments may be for the situation before 1 May 1999, it seems impossible to understand how Article 61 EC could ever speak of "measures aimed at ensuring the free movement of persons" in accordance with Article 14, if this movement was only to be set apart for nationals of the Member States. So, at least under the ToA, we will have to assume that the freedom of movement within the internal market, mentioned in Article 14, must be established for all persons. This does not mean, however, that there would be no difference in legal position between EC citizens and third country nationals. I will deal with that below.

Is this all to be said about the concept "freedom"? I do not think so. Though the concept of the "area of freedom, security and justice" must be understood in the context of the EC Treaty and the TEU, it would be a mistake only to allow interpretations if they can be deduced from what has been written elsewhere in those Treaties. In their Action Plan of 3 December 1998, the Council and the Commission have stated that the ToA opens the way to giving "freedom" a wider meaning: "It is also freedom to live in a law-abiding environment in the knowledge that the public authorities are using everything in their individual and collective power (nationally, at the level of the Union and beyond) to combat and contain those who seek to deny or to abuse that freedom". The Council and the Commission have also mentioned the respect for privacy and in particular the protection of personal data. The area of freedom, security and justice has an autonomous, dynamic meaning in itself, and is waiting for further interpretation by the ECJ. There may be more freedom in this area than we can imagine now. But it should at least include the fundamental human freedoms and the freedom of movement: freedoms applicable to both EC citizens and third country nationals.

"Security"

According to the Preamble to the TEU, security is sought by means of a common foreign and security policy and by means of co-operation in crime fighting.

In the tenth paragraph of the Preamble to the TEU, the contracting parties declare to be "resolved to implement a common foreign and security policy including the progressive framing of a common defence policy . . . thereby reinforcing the European identity and its independence in order to promote peace, security and progress in Europe and the world". This is repeated in the second paragraph of Article 2 TEU and in Article 17, first paragraph EC. In Article 11(1) TEU the objectives of a common foreign and security policy are elaborated. They are:

—to safeguard common values, fundamental interests, independence and integrity of the Union in conformity with the principles of the United Nations Charter;
—to strengthen the security of the Union in all ways;
—to preserve peace and strengthen international security, in accordance with the principles of the United Nations Charter, as well as the principles of the Helsinki Final Act and the objectives of the Paris Charter, including those on external borders;
—to promote international co-operation;
—to develop and consolidate democracy and the rule of law, and respect for human rights and fundamental freedoms.

Security for whom? Here, we are apparently dealing with security for all people in the common territories of the Member States and this means security from external threat. The third paragraph of Article 11(1) TEU probably extends the pretence of "international security" even to people outside the Union. Within the common territory of the Member States, the quoted provisions of the TEU offer no room for discrimination as to inhabitants enjoying safety. Foreign and defence policies must safeguard common values, alongside values with universal pretensions like democracy, the rule of law, respect for human rights and fundamental freedoms. So, the Union must also care for the security of third country nationals within the area, of course leaving unimpeded the responsibility of individuals under national and international law.

However, the crime-fighting co-operation under the Third Pillar could—at least at first sight—be said to be designed especially for the safety of the "citizens" (or the "peoples") of the Union. In the last paragraph of the Preamble to the TEU the contracting parties have reaffirmed their objective to facilitate the free movement of persons "while ensuring the safety and security of their peoples, by including provisions on justice and home affairs in this Treaty". The first of these provisions, Article 29 (ex Article K.1) starts as follows:

> "Without prejudice to the powers of the European Community, the Union's objective shall be to provide citizens with a high level of safety within an area of freedom, security and justice by developing common action among the Member States in the fields of police and judicial cooperation in criminal matters and by preventing and combating racism and xenophobia."

Are third country nationals excluded from the intended "high level of safety" from criminal acts? This would not make sense. I cannot believe that genuine safety for the citizens of the Union could be established if the same security were not to be offered to third country nationals who are also present in the area. It just would not work. It is a basic principle of criminal law, that all people suspected to have committed a crime should be treated equally before the law. Further, it is no idle element of Article 29 TEU that the prevention and combating of racism and xenophobia are a major goal of police and judicial co-operation. Apparently, the Council and the Commission are of a similar opinion, as they state in their Action Plan that "Freedom loses much of its meaning if it cannot be enjoyed in a secure environment and with the full backing of a system of justice in which all Union citizens and residents can have confidence" and that "the full benefits of any area of freedom will never be enjoyed unless they are exercised in an area where people can feel safe and secure".

In Article 61 EC the goals of freedom of movement of persons and security are connected in different ways. The Action Plan pays particular attention to the linkage, made in paragraph (a): "Freedom in the sense of movement of people within the European Union remains a fundamental objective of the Treaty, and one to which the flanking measures associated with the concepts of security and justice make their essential contribution". No less important is the association of measures in the fields of asylum and immigration with "safeguarding the rights of nationals of third countries" in paragraph (b). It refers to safety and security for third country nationals by protection against persecution, torture, inhuman and degrading treatment or punishment. It refers to safety and security by respect for fundamental rights and freedoms, which also must include the right of access to an impartial court when the rights of third country nationals are violated in the "area".

"Justice"

The general notion of "justice" did not appear in the TEU or the EC Treaty before the ToA. Since Maastricht, there was co-operation in the fields of "justice" and "home affairs", but there the word "justice" was apparently meant as an indication of a field of tasks and interests normally linked to a ministry of justice or—in some countries—to a ministry of home affairs. In their Action Plan, the Council and the Commission put emphasis on the aspect of law enforcement, when speaking of a "law-abiding environment" and "bringing to justice those who threaten the freedom and security of individuals and society". When they refer to "a system of justice in which all Union citizens and residents can have confidence" and when expressing their ambition "to give citizens a common sense of justice throughout the Union", they may have had something more in mind than merely law and order, but the text is not very clear in that respect. In any case, it would be highly unlikely that the universal sense of justice as denoted by concepts like equality, basic rights and the rule of law could not be considered a relevant aspect of the notion of "justice" in the European Union. That would not be consistent with the weighty references in the EC Treaty and the TEU to non-discrimination, fundamental rights and the rule of law. In Article 6 TEU the rule of law and the respect for human rights and fundamental freedoms are mentioned as founding principles of the Union. Certain rights of a Member State under the TEU may, according to Article 7 TEU, even be suspended if those principles are seriously and persistently breached by this Member State. The principle of non-discrimination, a general principle of

Community law, is laid down in Articles 2, 3, 12 and 13 EC. So, there are strong reasons to conclude that "justice" is not only meant in the more limited sense of "a system of law enforcement" but also in the universal sense of the word—as the opposite of "injustice"—and including equality, the rule of law, and respecting human rights and fundamental freedoms. "Justice" in this universal sense cannot be set apart for EU citizens only, and must apply to everyone within the jurisdiction of the Member States, the Community and the Union.

CONSEQUENCES OF THE UNIVERSAL CHARACTER OF FREEDOM, SECURITY AND JUSTICE FOR THIRD COUNTRY NATIONALS

If an area of freedom, security and justice is a jurisdiction within which the universal aspects of freedom, security and justice must be guaranteed to everyone, the question arises as to how this can be reconciled with the dissimilar legal positions of EU citizens and third country nationals and what it means for the right of Member States to control immigration.

The first thing to realise is that the core rights of nationals *vis-à-vis* their country of nationality are not affected by Title IV. Only nationals have an inherent right of abode in the Member States. People still have no fundamental right to enter any country. The European Community has expanded the rights of nationals of Member States to enter and to stay in other Member States (with their families) and it has, since Maastricht, also expanded their political rights. But Article 17 EC stresses that "citizenship of the Union shall complement and not replace national citizenship".

This is the departing position: third country nationals have no inherent right of access or residency in the territory of Member States. Member States have the right to control immigration. On the other hand, if we accept that all human beings are holders of fundamental rights and freedoms and have a natural claim to security and justice by birth, we must accept that Member States may not infringe such rights and claims of the people who fall within their jurisdictions further than necessary for the achievement of their legitimate purposes. The same model applies when the competence of Member States in this field is transferred to the European Community. This is in line with the standpoint of the Coordinator's group in the Palma Document, and with the plea by the Commission for a balanced and integrated approach. Restrictions in the securing of freedom, security and justice to third country nationals are permissible only when they are necessary and proportionate to achieve a legitimate goal.

Thus, we have to answer the question, what legitimate purposes may be pursued by immigration control? In the case-law of the ECJ and the European Commission of Human Rights, two purposes of an immigration policy have been found legitimate: (a) the protection of the economic well-being of the country, including the protection of the domestic labour market; and (b) the protection of the interests of public order and the prevention of crime. In the Netherlands, the protection of the system of social security and social care has become a major goal of immigration legislation, which could be seen as a component of the wider purpose of serving the economic well-being of the country. These are well-known reasons that are normally invoked for justifying an immigration policy. Other reasons that have been mentioned are demographic developments or the political need to reassure a public concerned about large numbers of immigrants. Reassuring the public may not, however, amount to a racist immigration policy, which would not be a legitimate aim.

If we assume that every decision to grant access or residency to a person is the result of a conscious weighing of the interests of the individual and the legitimate purposes of immigration control, then we may state that every such decision marks a deliberate change in the position of the immigrant: by granting the permission to enter or to stay, he/she is—to a certain extent—elevated to the same position as a national. The national labour market, the social security system and economic well-being, which the state seeks to protect in favour of its population, are now also protected in favour of the newcomer. The more similar this permitted position is to the inherent position of a national, the less justification remains for different treatment. Once a third country national is granted access to the labour market, the economy or the social security system, the receiving state wishing to terminate this can no longer rely on arguments which would have been sufficient for initial refusal. The longer the period of legal residence of an immigrant, the less justification remains for making distinctions between this immigrant and a national. This is especially important where public order is concerned: nobody can deny that nationals of Member States may be involved in serious crime. If nationals have a right to be prosecuted and judged in the territory of a Member State and to remain living on this territory with their families after serving their penalty, this right must also be granted to long-term immigrants.

This leads to a sliding scale of immigrants' positions between two extreme poles: at one end the position of a candidate immigrant who never obtained any permission to enter or to stay; and, at the other end, a position which is similar to that of a national. In the creation of an area of freedom, security and justice, each of these positions may lead to a different outcome when a fair balance between legitimate state's interests and legitimate individual interests is sought. It would go beyond the scope of this introduction to elaborate on all these various positions, but we cannot afford to overlook the position of the candidate immigrant. Precisely this position at one of the two extreme poles enlightens the impact of the area of freedom, security and justice. To what extent do freedom, security and justice apply to candidate immigrants, and what is the effect if they enter or stay illegally?

Candidate immigrants are brought under the jurisdiction of a Member State once they apply for permission to enter or stay, and thus invoke the internationally recognised right of states to grant or refuse such permission. Merely by applying, they enter the area of freedom, security and justice. *Freedom*: The Member States must acknowledge their potential and conditional right to free movement within the Union, and respect their fundamental freedoms and their right to privacy (for instance when they are listed in a computerised information system). But candidates may also be held responsible themselves for respecting the freedoms of others. *Security*: Member States must safeguard candidate immigrants from torture and inhuman or degrading treatment or punishment (for instance when they apply for asylum) and protect their right to life (for instance if they apply for medical treatment in a Member State). But candidates—especially if they have a criminal record—may also be held responsible for the security of others. *Justice*: Candidate immigrants must have access to national courts of a Member State to fight a negative decision on their application, or to fight a decision to list them in a computerised information system for the purpose of being denied entry. They must be able to invoke their potential and conditional right to free movement and their fundamental rights and freedoms in fair proceedings before an impartial and independent court.

This picture does not change radically when candidate immigrants enter or stay illegally on the territory of a Member State. Member States may take measures against them to discourage or punish illegal stay or to remove them from the territory, but they may only do this in so far as necessary within an area of freedom, security and justice and proportionate to a legitimate goal.

CONCLUSION

The concept of an "area of freedom, security and justice" is embedded in the conceptual sphere of the TEU and the EC Treaty but also has an autonomous, dynamic meaning. The word "area" is best understood when read as "jurisdiction". "Freedom" encompasses fundamental freedoms, freedom of movement and, as far as it is within the power of governments to provide such, freedom from worry and fear. "Security" not only means safety from external threat and from criminal acts but also protection against persecution, torture and inhuman or degrading treatment or punishment. "Justice" certainly refers to a system of law enforcement, but above all to a system in which injustice is fought by respecting the rule of law, fundamental rights and freedoms and the principle of non-discrimination.

The full benefit of these values must be guaranteed to everyone within the jurisdiction of the Union, the Community and the Member States. As far as restrictions are made in connection with the circumstance that an individual has no (perfect) right to entry or residence in a territory of the Union, these restrictions are justified only if they are necessary and proportionate to achieve a legitimate goal. The longer an immigrant has stayed legally on the territory, the less justification remains for making distinctions between this immigrant and a national. Even candidate immigrants within the jurisdiction must be granted freedom, security and justice, though they have no recognised right to entry or residence at the moment. They must at least be able to invoke their potential and conditional right to free movement and protection of their fundamental rights and freedoms before an independent and impartial court.

1

Differential Free Movement and the Sociology of the "Internal Border"

JOHN CROWLEY

INTRODUCTION

Implementation of the Treaty of Amsterdam (ToA) is neither straightforward nor automatic. It depends, at crucial points, on inherently unpredictable political bargaining. Its meaning will thus evolve not just organically, as any body of law expressed in routine judicial practice must, but as a result of outside impulses. Furthermore, its meaning is itself contentious. Quarrels, uncertainties and more or less deliberate ambiguities, readily apparent in the process leading up to the Treaty and the public debates surrounding it, are also easily discernible in the text itself. Where judicial intervention is significant, it will play a major role in elaborating what *in fact* the Treaty will come to mean. Such intervention is somewhat more predictable than its political counterpart, but nonetheless leaves much, at the time of writing, still within the realm of speculation.

These points are familiar. There is a large body of literature on European developments in the 1990s, written by people more competent than myself, and that I shall make no attempt here even to survey. Suffice it to note that even the most Euro-enthusiastic commentators admit the mysteries of European integration: to the extent that they believe it is, as Tertullian reportedly said of Christianity, "*quia impossibile*"—because it is impossible. Such faith is a rather peculiar intellectual posture. I have suggested elsewhere that it is in a sense strategic, serving to fudge the distinction between European integration as a "sociological process" and as a "political project";[1] and, as a consequence, that a degree of tactical skepticism is requisite for an analytically coherent approach to the issue.[2] Such considerations are not directly relevant here. My concern is not European integration in any general sense, but one small aspect of it: immigration. "Tactical Euro-scepticism" does however inform my approach to frontiers in a world—"Schengenland"—supposedly devoid of them, at least

I wish to thank Katia Novikova for her assistance in the background research for this chapter.

[1] J. Crowley, "European integration: sociological process or political project?" (1996) 9 *Innovation—The European Journal of Social Sciences* 149.

[2] J. Crowley, "Some thoughts on theorizing European citizenship" (1999) 12 *Innovation—The European Journal of Social Sciences* 471.

internally. On the one hand, their "removal" is deeply ambivalent because it always was, to some extent, a pretence. The intention was, as indeed the contradictions within the treaties reveal, to *reconfigure* frontiers so as, in some respects, to *reinforce* them. It is therefore arguable whether supporters of "free movement of peoples" should support the kind of "free movement" created by current European processes. On the other hand, quite apart from political tactics and normative issues, European thinking on the relations between "frontiers" and "free movement" is deeply confused. A more subtle sociological consideration of "boundaries", to use a generic term that deliberately does not refer to legal distinctions, leads to rather different ways of asking the questions.

FREEDOM OF MOVEMENT IN THE EUROPEAN TREATIES

At a very general and abstract level, "free movement" is central to the current form of the European project. The single market was intended both to express the idea of Europe and to contribute to its economic dynamism: in the context of the perceived "Euro-sclerosis" of the early 1980s, even left-leaning pro-Europeans were convinced that free movement of goods and capital would, if correctly regulated, provide significant efficiency gains. The development of what is now known as the "first pillar" of the Union since 1986 has been primarily driven by the need to create the conditions in which such regulated free movement might be feasible. Free movement of persons was partly an adjunct to this (labour being a third "factor of production"). However, the level of labour mobility between European countries, which is affected by a whole series of obvious cultural factors, remains quite low; and priority was in fact given to free travel rather than to free settlement. Movement of persons thus had a symbolic character, as an expression of what the Maastricht Treaty came to define as European "citizenship". Whether one has to wave one's passport at a border post is not, in most cases, a matter of vital economic concern, even to business travellers (especially if special "EU passport" lines exist); it can however be regarded as expressing, and thereby making tangible, an identity and a legal status that would otherwise remain vacuous.

A closer look at the current status of free movement in the treaty texts, however, points to a somewhat more complex picture.[3] While the content of the treaties is no doubt familiar to most readers, it is nonetheless useful to summarise the main points in the way that suits my purpose here. The establishment of a "common citizenship" is one of the resolutions expressed in the preamble to the TEU, with the objective, as stated in Article 2, of "reinforcing the protection of the rights and interests of the nationals of the Member States". This status, as defined in the EC Treaty (Part II) implies for citizens of the Union free

[3] I refer to the consolidated version of the TEU and the GC Treaty, ignoring for these purposes the distinctions between the various historical "strata" that make up the currently valid text.

movement and residence, subject to the conditions deriving from the Treaty or its application (Article 18). Furthermore, quite apart from the status of citizenship, the Treaty states the objective of an "internal market" defined as "an area without internal borders in which the free movement of goods, persons, services and capital is assured according to the provisions of the present Treaty" (Article 14.2). Article 61(a) EC specifically sets a deadline, five years from the entry into force of the ToA, for the promulgation of measures designed to ensure such an internal market as it applies to movement of persons (in association with other measures on external borders, asylum, immigration and crime). The Preamble to the TEU in turn refers back to this in stating the Member States' "determination to promote their peoples' economic and social development "in the context of the realization of the internal market". In addition, the EC Treaty explicitly provides for free movement of workers (Articles 39–42). Restrictions to such movement may derive only from considerations of public order, public safety and public health, and from the right of Member States to limit certain public sector positions to their nationals. The general principle of free movement is thus hedged in three ways: by the distinction between citizens of the Union and "third-country nationals", by the distinction between workers and others, and by other considerations that may legitimately restrict freedom of movement.[4]

These considerations, while vague, assume major significance in the treaties, and are repeated at many points. Although the preamble to the TEU offers a commitment to the realisation of the internal market, and therefore by implication to free movement subject only to such regulation as is necessary to ensure it, it also places an explicit restriction on such free movement when stating the Member States' resolve to "facilitate free movement of persons, while ensuring the safety and security of their peoples, by the establishment of an area of freedom, security and justice". To *facilitate* is not to *guarantee*: taken in isolation, this passage clearly makes "security" a first principle of equal weight to "freedom of movement" rather than a subsidiary consideration that may justify pragmatic restrictions to it. Of course, the principles of freedom, liberty, democracy, human rights, basic liberties and the rule of law are explicitly enshrined in the same preamble, and reaffirmed in TEU Articles 6(1) and, with specific reference to the European Convention for the Protection of Human Rights, 6(2); and the commitment of Member States to them is stated without qualification. Issues of "security" are therefore subsidiary to them; but it is equally true that "freedom of movement" cannot be construed, in the context of the treaties, as a fundamental right, but rather one derivative from economic efficiency (without distinction on the grounds of nationality) and from the symbolism of "ever closer union" (for citizens of the Union only). The way in which the internal market and "Schengenland" are juxtaposed in Article 2 TEU strengthens this impression. On the one hand, the first objective of the Union is to "promote economic

[4] For a more detailed survey, see E. Guild, "Competence, discretion and third-country nationals: the European Union's struggle with migration" (1998) 24 *Journal of Ethnic and Migration Studies* 613.

and social progress . . . in particular by the creation of an area without internal borders"; on the other hand the fourth objective is "to maintain and develop the Union as an area of freedom, security and justice, in which the free movement of persons is assured". "Appropriate measures" to control external borders, to regulate asylum and immigration, and to prevent and combat crime are explicitly given the same status as free movement in the arrangement of this "area"—hence the way in which the post-Amsterdam agenda is formulated in Article 61(a)EC, as quoted previously.

This tension between an "area without internal borders" and an "area of freedom, security and justice in which the free movement of persons is assured" encapsulates the ambivalence of the current European project. On the one hand, the latter area is not merely compatible with, but actually premised upon, the existence of internal borders: Articles 29–42 TEU, on police and judicial co-operation, make this clear, and even refer revealingly to "cross-border" crime (Article 30(2)(d)).[5] The shifting status of borders within the EC Treaty—often traceable, of course, to the "strata" that compose it—similarly points to a latent contradiction. One of the objectives of the Community is to abolish, "between the Member States, barriers to the free movement of goods, persons, services and capital" (Article 3(1)(c)). Are borders necessarily "barriers" in this sense, as the idea of the "internal market" implies? Conversely, does the absence of borders necessarily signify the absence of "barriers"? Finally, are "barriers to free movement" never justifiable? Critics of European integration have an easy task in pointing to the confusion rampant in current debate on these issues.[6] That borders are not necessarily barriers is central to the way in which external borders are conceived in "Schengenland": as potentially highly permeable lines that require active defence. That many barriers have nothing to do with borders in the territorial or jurisdictional sense is at the heart of the wide range of provisions in European law against discrimination, in the broadest sense.[7] Finally, that certain kinds of free movement are detrimental, and deserve regulation or even prohibition, even within the limits of a uniform territorial jurisdiction, is a general assumption almost too obvious to be stated. These points are exceedingly trivial: it is a sad comment on the degree of current European ideological confusion, far beyond legal technicalities, that they need to be made at all. Nonetheless, the conjunction of two parallel, unco-ordinated, and to a considerable extent incompatible, discourses on borders and free movement has very real consequences in contemporary Europe. *Pace* one interpretation of the objective of "ever closer union", the "territories of the Member States" still exist, and are likely to remain in existence for some time: indeed, the treaties

[5] "Cross-border" issues arise again in Art. 65 EC.

[6] A good statement of the view that the European idea is fundamentally and deplorably anti-political, partly because of a widespread failure to understand what a "border" is: J. Laughland, *The Tainted Source* (London, Little, Brown,1997).

[7] Thus, the absence of discrimination on the grounds of nationality is the first implication drawn by Art. 39(2) EC from the principle of free movement of workers (Article 39(1))—which at least suggests that it is the most significant "barrier" to it.

refer to them at many points. But such territories are, by definition, limited by borders, which have both geographical and jurisdictional content. The EC Treaty explicitly recognises this in Article 62(1), which calls on the Council to take measures aiming, following Article 14, to "ensure the absence of any control of persons, whether citizens of the Union or third-country nationals, when they cross internal borders". But Article 14, as already quoted, *abolishes*, at least rhetorically, internal borders. If Article 14 were seriously implemented, internal borders would no longer be there to be crossed, rendering Article 62(1) otiose. Conversely, if Article 62(1) means anything, it is that free movement (subject to the requisite caveats about security) is compatible with the existence of internal borders.[8]

At least with respect to immigration within the current European context, such confusion reflects a deeper ambiguity about the whole notion of "freedom of movement". The obvious limits to such freedom, particularly with respect to third country nationals, and the absence of any general commitment to it at the external borders of the Union, do not mean that it is a sham. "Fortress Europe" and the internal market are not contradictory (except, possibly, at the level of abstract principle): they are different, and complementary, aspects of the same thing. That the "front view" and the "back view", so to speak, are very different does not imply that there is no object of which they are both views. It does mean, on the other hand, that there is no single organising concept, such as "freedom of movement", that can account for both. What I wish to pursue in the rest of this chapter is a more complex idea of "boundary processes" that can take in both perspectives, with particular empirical reference to the current immigration and asylum issues in France.

THE DIFFERENTIATION OF FREEDOM OF MOVEMENT

A feature of contemporary European immigration policy, expressed at the level both of the Member States and of the Union, is the combination of two tendencies that are, in somewhat different ways, both complementary and contradictory. On the one hand, as we have seen, a general principle of free movement is enshrined in positive law and has steadily been extended by successive treaties. Furthermore, it is strongly underpinned by abstract considerations that are thought to justify it as being more than simply a contingent set of legal arrangements. On the one hand, there is a possible inconsistency in supporting both free trade in general terms and restrictive immigration policies.[9] Certainly, genuine

[8] The existence of internal borders is further recognised, in a different context, in Art. 77.

[9] "Possible" because one could argue that most migrants are forced to move, often in rather indirect ways: high levels of immigration might thus be a symptom of unjust international arrangements rather than the statistical expression of individual freedom. The argument is, however, an awkward one to follow through, since given an unjust system, migration could still be regarded as a genuine individual choice, albeit one that is structurally constrained.

free-traders tend to support immigration on grounds of economic efficiency (which is not incompatible in this case with individual freedom)—one needs only to read *The Economist* and *The Wall Street Journal* to get the point. On the other hand, "tearing down (internal) borders", at least in the sense of removing visible controls at the territorial limit of state jurisdiction, is regarded as having powerful symbolic significance—it may give, as I suggested earlier, tangible content to the otherwise very abstract idea of "integration" based on some kind of "common belonging", especially when combined with reinforced controls at the *external* borders of the Union. It is no coincidence in this respect that the abolition of border controls and "European citizenship" are closely associated. In a word, the free movement of people expresses the process of "geographical fusion" that T. H. Marshall makes central to the first phase of the development of citizenship. Unless one regards Europe as a potential nation, such a view may give rise to the kind of confusion analysed earlier: Marshall's framework, though often used as a reference in "post-national" theorising, in fact presumes a strictly national context.[10] Furthermore, a world without borders might in principle permit the development of forms of membership not based on belonging, rather than the displacement of belonging from national to European level. The abolition of internal borders is indeed sometimes defended in precisely these terms. Nonetheless, however ambiguous the relations between freedom of movement and European identity may be, the conjunction of these considerations is at the centre of the current immigration and asylum configuration.

Free movement, however, is limited from the outset—in principle and not simply in practice. On the one hand, even for those who enjoy it to the fullest extent—citizens of the Union moving for employment-related purposes—it is restricted. On the other hand, a series of considerations, quoted earlier, draw a distinction, among citizens of the Union, between nationals of a Member State and non-nationals present on its territory. For example, quite apart from the familiar differences of political rights, the latter may, and the former may not, be deported. As a consequence of this limited and non-uniform character, in other words, "European citizenship" is a misnomer: as currently defined, citizenship of the Union does not correspond to any of the traditional dimensions of citizenship. It is not a relation between a person and a nation, or a state, or a political community. It is best described as a (limited) set of rights attached to legal membership of existing states but extending beyond their territorial jurisdiction on the basis of reciprocity.[11]

The status of citizenship is obviously *intended* to be much more than that, and its symbolic import perhaps exceeds its practical content. The reason for its inclusion in the Treaty of Maastricht was, consistently with the whole institutional dynamic of the early 1990s, to put political integration on a par with economic integration. However, while the latter was expressed clearly enough by

[10] J. Crowley, "The national dimension of citizenship in T. H. Marshall" (1997) 2 *Citizenship Studies* 165.

[11] As indeed the aims of the Union as quoted previously make quite explicit.

the single market, the former was and remains obscure.[12] The problem as generally defined is citizens' failure to identify with Europe, which the elections of June 1999 starkly underlined. Citizenship could be seen as contributing to such identification, along with such things as patriotic symbols (the flag, the anthem, etc.), political participation, greater democratic accountability and, indeed, a single currency. The problem is that "Europe" here is indeterminate, since the subject and nature of identification are different in each case. At the very least, Europe means an idea (itself ambiguous as to its historical, cultural and ideological scope), a system of institutions, a set of states, and a group of people. As a matter of fact, it seems that many citizens of the Union have little awareness of their new status and attach little significance to it. Indeed, when such awareness does exist—as, say, in Catalonia, Scotland or Northern Italy—it relates as much to identity fractures within Member States as to Europe *per se*. My focus here is however conceptual rather than empirical. The current form of European "citizenship" would be important if it entailed any commitment, or even bias, towards a specific path of future political development. In fact, precisely because it is hardly a form of "citizenship" at all, it has no such implications. Is Europe likely to become (or is it desirable that it should become) a nation, a unitary state, a federal state, a confederacy, a co-operatively regulated free-trade area, an entirely novel political entity, a more or less problematic combination of some or all of the above? The current status of citizenship—as of other European institutions—leaves all this entirely open. For strong theoretical reasons, any idea of citizenship implies a basic, irreducible principle: that all citizens should, *as citizens*, be equal.[13] What constitutes citizenship in terms of obligations, rights and other features, is of course historically and geographically variable, as Marshall and others have shown. But whatever the content, citizens are necessarily equal in respect of it, so long at least as some conception of citizenship exists. In respect both of political authority and of free movement, "European citizenship" conflicts with this basic principle. Its symbolism in many ways plays on this, through the idea that the absence of border controls might contribute to the perception of a "European identity". (I do not propose to discuss here how empirically significant might be such matters as the cover of one's passport and where and when precisely one has to wave it. Suffice it to note that the Schengen principle paradoxically undermines the symbolic significance of border controls even as it enshrines it. At the internal borders of the Schengen area, citizens of the Union have no privileged position.)

The key point, however, is not that freedom of movement is incomplete, even for citizens of the Union. It is rather that the kind of free movement that the legal framework, briefly discussed earlier, is designed to promote is inherently

[12] J. Crowley, "European integration: sociological process or political project?" (1996) 9 *Innovation—The European Journal of Social Sciences* 149.

[13] J. Crowley, "Some thoughts on theorizing European citizenship" (1999) 12 *Innovation—The European Journal of Social Sciences* 471.

differential.[14] Certain kinds of movement are "good", others are "bad": the whole point of "Schengenland" is to reduce the degree of control, or more accurately of ostentatious monitoring (of which passport checks are emblematic), on "good" movement, while increasing the capacity to control "bad" movement. "Good" movement involves genuine tourists, legitimate business people, economically useful migrants, and so on; "bad" movement involves drug traffickers, illegal aliens, bogus asylum seekers, pimps, Mafia "wiseguys", and so on. Relaxing "border controls" does not mean relaxing control of the border; indeed, once freedom of "good" movement has been promulgated, "border controls" are a singularly ineffective way of controlling the border. The fact that this sounds gratuitously paradoxical is an indication that we need a sociologically more sophisticated view of borders.

It may seem self-evident that "borders" and "immigration control" are intimately connected. After all, immigration is most appropriately defined in legal terms as entry into a country, by a non-resident, for the purpose of residence, which obviously involves crossing frontiers or borders. Indeed, progressively minded commentators are often—understandably—concerned to stress this definition in political debate, as a counterweight to explicitly or implicitly xenophobic descriptions of, say, French-born people—often in fact French citizens—as *immigrés*. Furthermore, a presumptively very tight connection is at the heart of current debate about immigration, which is regarded as a risk or pressure to be controlled by reducing the permeability of the border. The "problem" of immigration, in other words, is often implicitly defined as illegal immigration, defined as the clandestine or otherwise fraudulent crossing of borders. While both these points are important, closer consideration shows that the border does not *in fact* have a privileged position in either immigration politics or immigration policy, and furthermore that there are strong *theoretical* reasons not to expect it to.

The desire to promote "good" movement of persons (which, as we shall see, may equate to movement of "good persons"), of which current European developments are exemplary, has nothing to do with inability to restrict migration or indifference to it (which acted in combination before state borders began to harden in the latter third of the nineteenth century). It is a conscious decision, or set of decisions, that tend to pass almost unnoticed, presumably because they are not politically controversial.[15] Yet this framework severely limits the relevance of the border as a control point for a potentially very large volume of movement, involving business travel and tourism as well as entry for settlement. Indeed, the removal of visa requirements for settlement makes this distinction arbitrary as far as EU nationals are concerned. Furthermore, the reconfiguration

[14] D. Bigo, *Polices en réseaux* (Paris, Presses de Sciences-Po, 1994).

[15] In France, for instance, it is striking that the Front National's policy of "national preference" takes an explicitly European form: e.g. (illegal) attempts by FN-run local authorities to offer special bonuses to the parents of "good" babies extended to EU nationals. I suspect that this is not entirely sincere, but it at least shows that there is judged to be little political benefit in generalised xenophobia—even with respect to traditional foes such as the Germans and the British.

of borders between European states cannot be interpreted simply as a displacement to the external border of the European Union. A degree of differential freedom of movement is extended by the absence of visa requirements for business and tourism to, roughly speaking, all OECD nationals—although the distinction between visitors and settlers is maintained in this case.

The reduced significance of the border is not, however, simply a consequence of freer movement of people. It is rather that differential freedom of movement creates new logics of control that for practical, institutional reasons are located elsewhere. The border in its conventional territorial configuration is thus eroded relatively—and not just absolutely—as a site of control. With regard to illegal immigration, clandestine or otherwise fraudulent border crossing is dramatic and newsworthy: stowaways die in a hermetically sealed ship's hold, twenty-five Pakistanis are found in a mini-van at Dover, Turks die of exposure in an Alpine snowstorm. Maybe paradoxically, this puts a human face to abstract misery, but thereby defuses and depoliticises it by pinning the blame on a convenient culprit: the organiser of illegal migration, who grubbily makes money from it. Be that as it may, the emphasis seems hardly justified by the statistical evidence, at least in Northern Europe, where most illegal residents are found to have entered the country legally (with a visitor's visa or without being required to have a visa at all), and often, indeed, to have been legally resident at some time. In this sense, tighter controls on migration generally and the high political profile of illegal migration inevitably shift the spotlight away from the border. Some of the alternative sites are external: consulates and airline check-in desks, in particular; others are internal. In principle, the whole territory could be a site of control by spot identity checks, although in practice the process tends to be highly differentiated, focusing on a combination of target groups and target areas. On the other hand, identity checks are also be conducted at sites not directly connected to immigration control (such as the gateways to welfare benefits), and indeed are often more systematic in such cases—although the effectiveness of controls is limited by restrictions on exchanges of information between state agencies governed by civil liberties concerns. Furthermore, even to the extent that the border remains the juridical point of control, it increasingly becomes "control at" rather than "control of". In other words, precisely because restrictive immigration policies are associated with enhanced freedom of movement, the border is differentiated and selective.[16] Thus, in airports, which for logistical reasons tend to exhibit these tendencies in unusually pure form, passengers are increasingly "sorted" by destination, provenance and legal status (and to a lesser extent by class of travel or "frequent-flyer" status) for the purposes of control. What "freedom of movement" most tangibly means for the business traveller is not having to stand in the same queue as the people just off the flight from Kinshasa, Bangkok or Casablanca. Indeed, as anyone who

[16] G. Lahav, "Immigration and the state: the devolution and privatisation of immigration control in the EU" (1998) 24 *Journal of Ethnic and Migration Studies* 675.

travels frequently will have noticed, many large European airports have been reconfigured in recent years to write this "triage" as tightly as possible into their architecture. Ideally, the "good" and the "bad" should not meet or mix, or even be aware of each other's existence. No doubt this is one reason why their occasional, sudden juxtaposition is so "ugly":[17] even people who have no objection in principle to illegal aliens being deported often react strongly to seeing them handcuffed at the back of the plane they are travelling in.

Some aspects of the processes that have just been sketched in very broad outline are peculiar to Europe—i.e. primarily to relations between EU Member States and, to a lesser extent, to relations between the European Union as such and the rest of the world. However the contention in this chapter is that the reconfiguration of borders, and their subsumption in a broader field of border and boundary processes, has a wider significance. The implementation of the ToA is in this sense typical of broader processes of reconfiguration of the contemporary state, which may affect migrants with particular sharpness but are, in many cases, of quite general application. On the one hand, it is misleading to regard the control of access to territory as being the most important aspect of concern over immigration, even in xenophobic discourse. Many people who cannot be suspected of any kind of immigrant friendliness would probably admit, if pushed, that illegal immigrants are useful—so long as they stay in their place. So long, in other words, as their legal status is precarious, as they are not a burden on the welfare state, as they do not make any claim to be "integrated" into the society in which they live, and as they can be ultimately be deported if they cease to be useful. The informal domestic economy is perhaps the most familiar site of this ambivalent inclusion/exclusion. The specific "place" that such constraints define is territorially "within" the state, but in most other respects outside both it and the society. On the other hand, features of the contemporary state that have little to do with territory lead to new forms of boundary control. For instance, the gateways that control access to social rights via the labour market or welfare mechanisms are by their very nature multiple, shifting and heterogeneous. Furthermore, while such mechanisms of control are often designed at least in part with restrictive immigration policies in mind—and to that extent are inseparable from border controls in the narrow sense—this is accidental: the logic of localised boundary control is in fact an essential feature of any administrative construction of rights, of any set of *entitlements*. Even when not "about" immigration, therefore, they nonetheless impact powerfully on immigrants. Their effects, however, extend far beyond foreign legal or illegal residents to constitute a defining feature of contemporary governance and of perceptions of statehood and nationhood.

The reduction of straightforward, ostentatious forms of control, combined with sharply differential freedom of movement and the desire to increase the effectiveness of selective control, raises difficult practical issues. Unless one is

[17] With apologies for the gratuitous Sergio Leone reference.

able, unostentatiously, to check everyone, all of the time, it becomes necessary to decide, *a priori*, whom to target. Indeed, constraints on administrative resources push in this direction quite apart from the implementation of differential free movement. Yet so long as nationality, which is a strictly legal construct, is a primary criterion for distinguishing legitimate from illegitimate movement, there is no obvious way to make such *a priori* distinctions. Similarly, the enhancement of crime prevention, in the absence of a range of traditional techniques, requires either systematic generalised surveillance, or much more effective targeting principles. While new technological developments may facilitate systematic surveillance, or at least lower its cost, its efficiency is inherently limited by the sheer volume of information that it is likely to produce. Targeting will always be more effective. The effective control of differential free movement thus necessarily implies efficient techniques of *suspicion*.[18]

THE USUAL SUSPECTS . . .

The profound significance of current immigration issues—exemplified in France by the new question of the *"sans papiers"* (people without identity papers)—is that, for the general reasons just stated, it is embedded in the social structure instead of being neatly compartmentalised on its margins. The number of illegal aliens in France is quite small: between 300,000 and 500,000, according to most estimates.[19] While the absolute number may seem large (how many football stadiums. . .?), it is only about 10% of the number of legal aliens, and the related flow is tiny compared to the 80 million foreign visitors to France each year. There are many reasons for the political resonance the issue has attained in France during the 1990s, among them party politics, effective mobilisation techniques, humanitarian concern and, in some ways most importantly, the perception, in certain sections of the Left, of the illegal alien as the ideal vehicle for the critique of the nation state.[20] One important feature, however, has been the inchoate perception that anyone, potentially, might be an "illegal alien".

This perception fed on specific legal issues as much as on a general feeling of solidarity. Thus, one effect of the reform of immigration regulations enacted by the Balladur Government in 1993 (known by the name of the then Interior Minister, Charles Pasqua) was to remove the entitlement to legalisation previously enjoyed by certain categories of illegal aliens, particularly the parents of French children. Yet this did not affect the general legal principle, enshrined in

[18] J. Crowley, "The politics of belonging: some theoretical considerations", in Adrian Favell and Andrew Geddes (eds), *The Politics of Belonging: Migrants and Minorities in Contemporary Europe* (Aldershot, Ashgate, 1999), 15–41.

[19] The fact that some 140,000 requests for legalisation were filed under the programme announced in 1997 gives some credence to such estimates.

[20] For an overview, see J. Siméant, *La cause des sans-papiers* (Paris, Presses de Sciences-Po, 1998).

the case-law of the Conseil d'État,[21] that deportation orders cannot be enforced if their enforcement would result in family break-up. French citizens, of course, even if minors, cannot be deported, although their parents may remove them from France voluntarily. Thus the operation of the law created the perpetually illegal status of a significant group of people.[22] Other technical changes in the conditions for renewal of residence permits—including the ten-year permit created in 1984 and previously renewed unconditionally—gave rise to a further group who lost their legally resident status by operation of law. Some could in principle be deported, while others, for the reasons just mentioned, "enjoyed" the paradoxical status of secure illegal residence.

The point that "the law giveth, and the law taketh away" residence status is fairly obvious, but such legislative jeopardy made it tangible in a new way. The climate that led to the restrictions in both immigration and nationality law in 1993—strongly influenced by the threat to the mainstream Right from the Front National—was also significant in defining the social meaning of the new rules. The desire to enhance the capacity to detect and deport illegal aliens, new concerns about endemic violence in deprived urban areas (usually termed *banlieues*, or suburbs, in both political discourse and academic literature), and a series of terrorist incidents related to the civil war in Algeria, significantly deepened the general climate of suspicion surrounding immigrants. New rules and practices concerning identity controls, a significant redeployment, from 1990 onwards, of police and military intelligence towards urban surveillance, and the militarisation of routine policing in the context of the *"Vigipirate"* anti-terrorist plan, were the defining features of the 1993–97 period. (While certain changes have been made, as we shall see, since the Left's return to office in 1997, the current climate is on the whole quite similar.) The effect is to associate, if not actually to fuse, the three targets of suspicion: illegal aliens, terrorists and habitual criminals. Anyone who might belong to any of the groups is thus a prima facie suspect. In this way, the general technical requirement of differential surveillance—which the distinction between free "good" movement and prohibited "bad" movement necessarily entails—acquires a clear social meaning. Any young, visibly North African male, might be an illegal alien, a terrorist or an habitual criminal: a spot-identity check has a fair statistical chance of turning up something. The effects of such systematic suspicion on those who suffer the consequences do not need to be spelt out. To sum up: there is perhaps no *inherent*

[21] Particularly the *arrêt* of 24 November 1978 striking down several ministerial instructions (*circulaires*) from 1974 suspending family migration; and the *arrêt* of 8 December 1978 striking down a decree of 10 November 1977 which had placed restrictions on family members' access to the labour market. While the instructions (which had in any case been withdrawn in 1975) were merely declared *ultra vires*, the decree was regarded as contravening general principles of equity, held specifically to include the entitlement to a normal family life.

[22] Until 1993 it was possible for an alien parent to request naturalisation for a child born in France while retaining his/her own nationality. In that year, a separate reform of nationality law removed the option. The families that had previously made use of it were of course not affected by the change.

difficulty in the idea of an area of "freedom, security and justice"; once, however, "security" has been defined by reference to a protean threat attached, even vaguely, to a group of people not susceptible of precise legal definition, the erosion of freedom by considerations of security becomes depressingly likely.

The logic underlying the processes of differential suspicion is powerful enough to operate well beyond the limits of repressive state activity. For instance, any administrative procedure involving the assessment of eligibility prior to the allocation of some good is liable to be configured, often in quite subtle ways, by the modes of suspicion (meaning here presumptive ineligibility) that frame it.[23] A convenient French example is the way in which applications for residence permits are processed in practice. My own observations at the Paris Préfecture de Police point to sharp differentiation in the treatment of various classes of foreigners. This has three rather different strands. (1) Immigration law clearly distinguishes a "fast-track" group comprising those with some strong claim to be admitted—particularly expatriates with an employment contract concluded prior to entry. Others (e.g. students, or applicants for family reunion) are prima facie suspicious. (2) The administrative procedures put significant demands on cultural capital. A high level of competence in French and familiarity with bureaucratic jargon again demarcate a de facto "fast track". (3) Officials bring preconceptions about "good" and "bad" foreigners to the job. These usually derive from available public discourse, and define yet another informal "fast track", cutting across the previous two. The second strand is easily forgotten, yet the legal and political norms (categories (1) and (3)) give a poor picture of the actual process and of the kinds of inequalities that arise. Inability to cope with the procedures is generally regarded as proof of ineligibility, because, however arbitrary, they become exemplary of "the way things are done here", and the bewildered foreigner's invariable "but why?" clearly marks him as alien. There is no reason other than French bureaucratic convenience, for instance, why the standard proof of residence should take the form of an electricity bill in one's name at the relevant address (it is not a legal requirement)—and good reasons for some *bona fide* applicants to be unable to comply. But to attempt to provide proof in some non-standard form—or, worse, to miss the point of the requirement or to deny that it matters—is to invite both ridicule and hostility, unless of course the official is complicit in some kind of prior, taken-for-granted "commonality". The procedures themselves thus become a kind of self-referential norm that is never made explicit, still less justified, but nonetheless determines both the social meaning of legal residence and its factual distribution: non-compliance designated as such leads to a lethal combination of shoddy service (a kind of punishment for not playing the game) and technical ineligibility. A direct consequence is that it is very easy—quite probably regardless of conscious prejudice on the part of the agent involved—to deny access to

[23] I borrow here from J. Crowley, "The politics of belonging: some theoretical considerations", in A. Favell and A. Geddes (eds), *The Politics of Belonging: Migrants and Minorities in Contemporary Europe* (Aldershot, Ashgate, 1999), 15–41.

claimants whose "face doesn't fit" (perhaps only because they are not submissive enough) simply by applying the rules with painstaking thoroughness.

Of particular importance in this respect is the welfare state. A close look at the way in which it actually works suggests that, as in the previous example, processes of differential inclusion and exclusion are necessarily embedded in it for reasons that are not reducible to the possibly xenophobic prejudices inscribed in law or brought to their desk by the employees. Suspicion is *both* a technical requirement and a background condition. The bureaucratic implementation of welfare necessarily involves distinctions based on criteria of eligibility implemented under pressure of time, as well as discretion in handling difficult cases. Almost regardless of their content, both these features will affect, both practically and symbolically, those claimants who are most vulnerable by marking them as targets for official suspicion—possibly making rights that are in principle entrenched effectively meaningless. There is indeed abundant research suggesting that welfare take-up is often lower than average among those who most need it, even when they are technically eligible. From this point of view, challenges to the welfare rights of immigrants or minority groups tend to reveal in amplified form what is going on generally.

For instance, all countries have rules restricting certain benefits to permanent residents, which is understandable (though not of course unexceptionable) both on abstract grounds of fairness and because abuses—so-called "benefit tourism"—do exist. What, however, do such rules actually mean? They mean two things which, combined, produce a much more complex picture. (1) All claimants are required to prove residence, in ways that may be arbitrary and difficult to comply with (see the previous comments on residence-permit application). There is therefore an unacknowledged "fast track". (2) Some claimants, who are regarded prima facie as suspicious, for whatever rational or irrational reason, are told that their (officially sanctioned) proof is inadequate, and that they must provide more. The obvious problem that such rules create is that illegal residents, who may be made such by the operation of law rather than any fraud on their part, are excluded from benefits that, on grounds on fairness, should be theirs. Less obvious, but in some ways far more important precisely because it seems to lie beyond the confines of normative analysis, is that translating the rules into a bureaucratically streamlined algorithm (something that, for the reasons sketched earlier, can in fact never function as such) inevitably causes significant inequalities between claimants. More generally, the whole climate of financial crisis has highlighted fraud, which is recognised to be widespread even by those who are not sanctimonious about it. But the technical efficiency of a "clampdown" requires it to be targeted, and differential suspicion has, again, major substantive consequences. The group of people who "might be" ineligible is large, and its limits are drawn in a very indeterminate way.

Not only is anyone who "might be" an illegal alien the object of suspicion, but in addition anyone associating with someone who "might be" such an alien is inevitably dragged in. A striking feature of recent tendencies in immigration control is that the changing nature both of geographical borders and of the "territory"—social rather than geographical—to be protected against trespass, which implies a multiplicity of points of entry, and therefore of control, makes a wide range of agents "auxiliaries", in some sense, of boundary control. Welfare officers have just been mentioned. Employers and airline employees are familiar examples of agents who have increasingly strict obligations, with penalties attached, to contribute to immigration policy. An interesting aspect of recent French debate has been mobilisation against the principle that *everyone* might be drafted in as an auxiliary to the "border police". The Balladur (1993–95) and Juppé (1995–97) Governments sought to "get tough" on illegal immigration in a number of ways, including more systematic identity checks (in the context, as previously noted, of anti-terrorist measures), tighter surveillance of the informal economy, new legal rules and administrative techniques to prevent people of uncertain status from entering French territory,[24] efforts to enforce a higher proportion of deportation orders,[25] and, by no means trivially, a rhetoric of "toughness". Between 1993 and 1995, Interior Minister Charles Pasqua, whose reputation for toughness had been established during his previous tenure of the office (1986–88), was the face and voice of the new policy. From 1995–97, his successor, Jean-Louis Debré, attempted to fill the same role. His comparative lack of credibility led him to be particularly ostentatious, and made him, even more than Pasqua, a left-wing hate figure. He was notably responsible for the order given to riot police to smash in the door of the church of Saint-Bernard in Paris, which a group of illegal residents claiming legalisation had occupied during the summer of 1996.

FROM ILLEGAL ALIENS TO "SANS PAPIERS"

In 1997 the Government attempted to introduce a series of changes to immigration rules, designed to deal with illegal migration, which, as a result of the Saint-Bernard affair and a series of other mobilisations, had then a very high political profile. Given the position and style of Debré, strong opposition was inevitable, especially as the changes failed to address key issues such as the entrenchment of secure illegal status for certain categories of aliens. It is interesting, however, that what achieved greatest political prominence was not substantive reform, such as further restrictions on renewal of residence permits, but an apparently rather trivial technical issue. One clause in Debré's Bill made changes to the existing system of "accommodation certificates" (*certificats d'hébergement*).

[24] On the various kinds of "holding areas" and the legal and administrative issues surrounding them, see F. Julien-Laferrière, "La rétention des étrangers aux frontières françaises" (1996) 23 *Cultures & Conflits* 7–43; and, more generally, D. Bigo (ed.), "Circuler, enfermer, éloigner. Zones d'attente et centres de rétention des démocraties occidentales" (1996) 23 *Cultures & Conflits* 24.

[25] For a variety of reasons, such efforts were largely unsuccessful. On average, only about one-quarter of deportation orders are enforced (for instance, in 1996, despite the climate of "toughness", 12,330 deportations out of 43,861 orders).

Anyone requiring a visa to visit France must prove either adequate funds for self-sufficiency during the stay or access to free accommodation.[26] Such access was, at the time, established by a certificate, issued by the local mayor to the French resident with whom the visitor planned to stay, and stating that the proposed accommodation was in fact adequate. The amendment to the law intended by the Government would have placed on any person to whom a certificate had been issued an obligation to register the departure of the visiting alien. The purpose of such a change was obviously to facilitate targeted surveillance of over-stayers (since most illegal aliens are known initially to have entered France legally).

Reform of the system of certificates was not in itself politically controversial. There had been, for several years, widespread criticism on the Left of the way in which xenophobic mayors used the differential issuing of certificates in discriminatory ways to implement a kind of informal "municipal immigration policy". This was unquestionably *ultra vires*, but could be corrected legally only by the intervention of the *Préfet*, which is in practice discretionary and in addition was strongly circumscribed by the decentralisation reforms of 1982, or by judicial review, which is too lengthy to be of much use to people planning their summer holidays. Test cases were successfully brought by interested voluntary bodies, and local political pressure proved effective in some cases, but no general solution was available. However, the Debré Bill did not address these issues at all. As a result, it was seized on, as a symbol, by a broad coalition of left-wing groups, and produced an unprecedented level of mobilisation in February 1997. What was being rejected was, explicitly, the idea that people receiving foreign guests should be made auxiliaries of immigration control (though in a sense, via the traditional system of certificates, they already were to a certain extent) and, more generally, the increase in social surveillance, *affecting potentially everyone*, implied by such mechanisms for combating illegal immigration. There was, furthermore, a widespread feeling that the local difficulties caused by mayors' abuse of their power to issue certificates would be aggravated by the creation of an additional administrative procedure. In view of the success of the Front National in the municipal elections of 1995, which gave it unprecedented

[26] Since the mid-1980s visa requirements have been considerably tightened in France as in other European countries. In view of the fairly limited significance of clandestine entry into France (directly, at least: entry from Spain and Italy of aliens who had entered one of those countries clandestinely by sea seems to be a more extensive phenomenon), visa restrictions have come to be viewed as an effective and discreet method for the management of migratory flows. Such restrictions indicate, like internal controls at such places as welfare gateways, that the territorial borders of the state are of comparatively limited significance in the contemporary governance of migration—and that, therefore, the disappearance of ostentatious border controls is not necessarily, in itself, "A Good Thing". The issue is particularly important with regard to nationals of Algeria, Tunisia and Morocco, many of whom have business and/or family reasons to visit France. Between 1993 and 1997, partly as a result of the closure of several consulates in Algeria for security reasons, delays in obtaining visas and rejections of applications (which did not then have to be justified) increased considerably, and became a significant diplomatic issue between France and all three countries. For example, 47,000 visas were granted to Algerian nationals in 1996, compared to 507,000 in 1990.

control of several large towns, such concerns had particular resonance at the time. Finally, the episode also entrenched the term *"sans papiers"* as the standard description of illegal aliens. Originally used to apply only to those people who, as explained earlier, had immunity from deportation but no clear legal status—and therefore could be regarded as deprived of a residence permit to which they were morally, and in a sense even legally, entitled—the phrase has, since 1997, come to refer to anyone claiming legalisation on the basis of effective membership of French society or of moral entitlement to asylum. The two categories are obviously different in a number of respects, and their conjunction is in itself interesting. The phrase *"sans papiers"* has given rise to complex normative arguments, which cannot be dealt with here, but has also shaped, by its very existence, the policy debate. An "illegal alien" rhetorically invites deportation, and if legalised is so only at the discretion, and for the purposes, of the state; a person *"sans papiers"*, on the other hand, is a natural candidate for legalisation as of right.

While clearly directed against the Government, the mobilisation of 1997 proved politically effective. Having lost the support of part of his own majority, Debré attempted to rescue his Bill by shifting responsibility for accommodation certificates from the mayor to the Préfet, and did indeed succeed in getting the legislation on the statute book. As a result of the snap election of May 1997, however, the issue became moot. A Socialist-led coalition came to office committed, in principle, to abrogation of the Pasqua (1993) and Debré (1997) legislation. Its alternative policy, while still undeveloped in detail, was framed by the notion of the *"sans papiers"*: the idea that certain illegal aliens have an entitlement to legalisation. The difficulty is to determine *which* aliens and on *which grounds*, and with *which policy consequences*.

The Minister of the Interior in the new Socialist Government, Jean-Pierre Chevènement, took a number of measures in June 1997 within days of taking office. First, a series of administrative changes relaxed the handling of visa applications and the criteria for exceptional leave to remain to be granted to illegal aliens.[27] Secondly, a legalisation programme was announced, targeted at those aliens who had entered France legally and whose family circumstances were indicative of membership in French society (including, but not limited to, the category of "secure" illegal aliens as defined earlier). Thirdly, in a bid to frame reform of immigration policy in terms of rationalisation—implying the possibility of cross-party consensus—rather than the left-right "pendulum" characteristic of the period from 1977–97, an independent report was commissioned from the academic expert Patrick Weil. In view of the very recent political controversy over the Debré Bill, this move was tactically crucial: the Socialists could afford neither to alienate their core supporters by doing nothing, nor to give the

[27] As a result, to take just two figures, the number of visas issued to Algerian nationals increased to 57,000 in 1997 (a significant change given that the new policy applied only to six months of the year), and the number of deportation orders dropped to 25,700 (though effective implementation remained below 30%).

opposition the opportunity to depict them as "soft on immigration".[28] None of these measures required legislation.

The Weil report,[29] published in July 1997, advocated a rationalisation of immigration policy based on the recognition that certain kinds of immigration are "good" and that generalised suspicion directed against migrants is contrary to the French national interest.[30] By clearly stating both the possibility and legitimacy of state control of migration, Weil sought to create the conditions for cross-party agreement on the issue. There is certainly much to be said for such a positive approach, especially in a context where, as recently as 1993, the French Interior Minister could define his policy objective as *"immigration zéro"*—in grotesque defiance of the facts. In fact, the most positive aspects of the Weil report were ignored by the Government. The law eventually promulgated in May 1998 makes a series of (generally welcome) technical changes rather than any general restatement of immigration policy.[31] What are important for my purposes here, however, are the implications of the distinction between "good" and "bad" immigration which, at least tacitly, are at the heart of the Weil report. Of course, there is no obvious way of avoiding such a distinction, short of dropping any attempt to regulate migration. Within the Amsterdam framework, in particular, the idea of "bad migration" is necessarily central. Furthermore, the recognition that there is such a thing as "good migration" is undoubtedly valuable in terms of political rhetoric. But, as a consequence, the practical alternative to generalised suspicion is not the absence of suspicion, but *differential suspicion*. The effects of differential suspicion depend on the detailed structure of the institutions and practices designed to implement it; there is no general, theoretical ground for regarding it as more, or less, socially destructive than generalised suspicion. However, in a context where "bad migration" is defined primarily by reference to geographical origin, where such origin can be framed in racist terms with some degree of plausibility, and where immigration status is

[28] P. Weil, the author of the most comprehensive study of post-war immigration policy, *La France et ses étrangers—L'aventure d'une politique de l'immigration 1938–1991* (Paris, Calmann-Lévy, 1991), was not a non-political figure. A leading figure in the Socialist youth movement in the 1970s, and an associate of Chevènement (then very much on the left of the party), he had been a member of the staff of the Secretary of State for immigration in 1981–82. Having withdrawn from active politics, however, and not having been prominent in the *sans papiers* movement, he was not obviously partisan. He had, indeed, been nominated by the right-wing government to serve on the official Haut Conseil à l'Intégration, a consultative body set up in 1990 to advise on immigration-related policy. On his role, see also P, Weil, "*Le chercheur et la décision politique*" (1998) 1 *Critique Internationale* 44.

[29] P. Weil, *Mission d'étude des législations de la nationalité et de l'immigration*, Report to the Prime Minister (Paris, La Documentation française, 1997).

[30] The report also made recommendations on reform of nationality law which the Government, on the whole, took on board.

[31] The two most important points are the creation of a category of political asylum, which drops the requirement, deriving from the standard interpretation of the Geneva Convention, of persecution by the state of which the refugee is a national; and a new requirement for refusals to grant visas to be motivated, which offers opportunities for judicial review.

central to a wide range of social controls, differential suspicion is at the very least deeply problematic.

In addition, differential suspicion as a technique of social control is often ineffective as well as normatively indefensible. The development of the 1997 legalisation programme neatly illustrates some of the problems. The initial intention, as mentioned earlier, was to identify the *sans papiers*—those in some way "deprived" of legal status—and to legalise them. Conversely, other illegal aliens could be judged to have no entitlement to legal status, and would indeed be easier to deport once thus identified. There was no intention to grant a general amnesty; nor, indeed, was such an amnesty an explicit demand of the *sans papiers* movement. In an attempt to reduce the degree of administrative discretion, and the proportion of rejected applications (which would inevitably raise great practical difficulties), the Chevènement *circulaire* (ministerial instruction) of June 1997 laid down very detailed criteria for eligibility. It very soon became apparent, however, that no criteria could be detailed enough to deal with the infinite variety of human circumstance—something that, as discussed earlier, was entirely predictable on theoretical grounds. Furthermore, some voluntary organisations involved in the *sans papiers* movement deliberately encouraged ineligible applications in order to protest against the narrowness of the criteria. Because the Government needed, politically, to be seen to be "firm but fair"—to borrow a British cliché—, the option of disregarding the ostensible criteria was not envisaged; indeed, the existence of rejected applications became regarded as an indication of the thoroughness, and even the fairness, of the whole process. According to a preliminary report issued by the Interior Ministry in October 1997, 144,000 applications had been received, and 77,000 legalisations had been effected. The balance was then pending: some applications had not yet been adjudicated, and in other cases appeals against rejection had yet to be heard.

However, the legalisation process did nothing to pre-empt the *sans papiers* movement. On the contrary, the combination of criticism of the criteria and protest against the treatment of specific persons completely undermined the attempt to reduce eligibility for legal status to a tidy bureaucratic algorithm. Officially, the legalisation procedure ended on 31 May 1998. The results as published showed that some 70,000 applications had been rejected, particularly among the "unattached" persons (those neither married to, nor the parents of, French citizens or legal residents) who did not meet the 1997 criteria, but had nevertheless sought legalisation. Within the logic of the Government, this should have been the end of the story. In fact, it was merely the beginning of a new phase. The Prime Minister declared that it would be invidious to use the information provided by applicants to deport those who had not been legalised, thereby effectively entrenching the absurd status of secure illegality which was the cause of the problem in the first place. Furthermore, those groups that had been most successful at mobilising and achieving media recognition were often able to negotiate special collective procedures. The Interior Ministry responded in July 1998 by setting up an ad hoc commission with responsibility for reviewing rejected applications. By introducing ever more exhaustive procedures for examining individual cases, and ever greater sensitivity to human circumstances, this made a nonsense of the initial claim to solve the issue by applying strictly impartial *a priori* criteria. Furthermore, by making discretionary legalisation effectively conditional on collective mobilisation, it undermined the whole idea of implicit "entitlement". What the term *"sans papiers"* has now become in French political debate is a straightforward synonym of illegal alien. The attempt to define a special group, with a status not reducible to their lack of a valid residence permit, has broken down. The whole principle of ever finer distinctions between "good" and "bad" immigrants is thereby called into question. Indeed, former Interior Minister Charles Pasqua caused considerable surprise by suggesting that the only valid method of legalisation (to which he was of course opposed) was a collective amnesty on the basis of public policy, not individual entitlement. My discussion suggests that this idea, while superficially paradoxical, is in fact correct.

A FORTRESS WITHOUT WALLS?

Implementing the ToA involves, among other things, implementing a form of free movement which is differential to an unprecedented degree. This rather trivial fact—which no one would disagree with, since it is the explicit premise of the "area of freedom, security and justice"—has some unexpectedly significant consequences. A sociologically sophisticated perspective on borders, frontiers and boundaries shows that such an area, assuming differential free movement, *cannot*, as it claims, be devoid of internal borders. On the contrary, it is necessarily structured by a range of internal boundary processes, which correspond to diverse institutional patterns of entitlement. These inherently give rise to forms of differentiation corresponding to the assessment of eligibility, but they are considerably sharpened by the background distinction between "good" and "bad" movement of people. The recent politics of immigration in France illustrate the salience of the new issues of internal control, and the difficulties of dealing with them. The increasingly discretionary treatment of illegal aliens and the growing significance of political bargaining (as distinct from the impartial application of legal rules)—even in the context of a less restrictive policy—are not, in the final analysis, anomalies, but an expression of the deep logic of a highly differentiated "area of free movement". The problem with current European immigration policy, of which the treaty framework is one important dimension, is not that it erects, in any straightforward sense, a "Fortress Europe". Such a project might be abhorrent, but would not necessarily be absurd so long as the walls were carefully constructed and scrupulously defended. The problem is rather that in trying to combine freedom for some and restriction for others, the edifice is fundamentally unstable. Implicitly, the ultimate model is one of a fortress without walls. Perhaps no one would explicitly defend such a thing, and it is certainly in many ways deeply uncomfortable: the society of perfect surveillance, the fortress without walls *par excellence*, is a recurrent science-fiction nightmare. In any case, it is probably unachievable in practice. But this simply means that aspects of the current European dynamic are profoundly incoherent in both normative and empirical terms. The apocryphal Dubliner could not direct the tourist to O'Connell Street because "he wouldn't have started from here". Perhaps the same applies to a coherent framework for free movement in Europe: implementing the ToA may not be the best way to start.

2

The Developing Right of Citizen Access to Information on Asylum and Immigration Decision-Making

DEIRDRE M. CURTIN

INTRODUCTION

The term "transparency" is a "catchword" much bandied about by politicians of all hues and shades. It evokes the image of a clear pane of glass through which the sunshine (or the light) can beam in an unrestrained fashion. It is a notoriously imprecise term and is to be understood more as the expression of a political objective than anything else. "Transparency" as a topic within the EU system of governance has however featured prominently in various institutional debates over the course of the past five years, including those on giving content and meaning to EU citizenship, the substance of democratic accountability, the role and influence of parliaments, both national and European, flexibility or "enhanced cooperation", and certainly not least, those enabling more "citizen participation" in the various levels of governance in the European Union. Access to information on decision-making processes affects the quality of citizens as political beings. Without effective open decision-making processes, political responsibility, political control and the true exercise of political rights and duties are all inhibited or impaired.[1] The general argument is essentially that all citizens, in their capacity as democratic citizens, are entitled to know what is done in their name and that this principle should apply in a general fashion irrespective of whether concrete measures of application have been adopted with a specific recourse to a judicial remedy.

Citizen access to public documents is considered highly appropriate to ensure that a lively public debate takes place with the possibility of participation and deliberation by citizens and their organisations on issues of public relevance and concern. In other words public access can be considered an essential part of a citizen's freedom of information and as a condition *sine qua non* for the will

[1] See P. Alston and J.H.H. Weiler, *The European Union and Human Rights: Final Project Report on an Agenda for the Year 2000* (European University Institute, Florence,1998), para. 203.

formation process so crucial in a democracy.[2] The underlying implication is moreover often that public access to government documents must be considered in terms of a fundamental human right.[3] This right of citizen access to government information exists alongside the role of parliaments in a democracy in ensuring an open and informed debate on matters of public concern.

The decision-making process in matters of justice and home affairs within the European Union has been very largely executive-driven and there has been tremendous resistance to granting not only parliaments but also individuals and public interest groups access to information in this field of activity. The latter is witnessed by the fact that the vast majority of cases to have come both before the courts of justice in Luxembourg as well as before the Ombudsman have concerned documents relating to justice and home affairs. Issues such as the right of citizen access to the minutes of Council and K.4 committee meetings, to access work programmes in the field of immigration and asylum policy-making, the failure of the Council to maintain and make publicly available a list of the measures agreed in the context of justice and home affairs (a register in effect), access to the agendas of the "EU-US Senior Level Group" as well as documents relating to the establishment of the EUROPOL Convention have all arisen and have, to some extent, been teased out in the pre-Amsterdam period.[4] In other key cases in other (EC and CFSP) policy-making fields, such as *Rothmans* and *Hautala*,[5] issues were raised (access to committee documents and to foreign affairs documents) which are of direct relevance to justice and home affairs decision-making. For example if the argument of the Commission had been accepted in *Rothmans* that comitology documents were excluded from the remit of the pre-Amsterdam access rules then this would have had enormous detrimental implications for access to EC documents as such (and thus also to documents in immigration and asylum post-Amsterdam). From the very beginning, the Council has argued that justice and home affairs concerns delicate matters which frequently fall under the protection of the *public interest* in the Member States and has adopted a highly restrictive approach to granting access to documents requested. Public interest in the Council's equation does not seem to include the angle of democratic citizens knowing what is being done in their name.

[2] See, on the link between access to information and the will-formation process in a democracy, J. Habermas, *Between Facts and Norms: Contributions to a Discourse Theory of Law and Democracy* (MIT Press, Cambridge, 1996). See further, D. Curtin *"Civil Society" and the European Union: Opening Spaces for Deliberative Democracy?* (European University Institute, Florence, 1999); and, in the Dutch context, B.W. Biesheuvel *et. al.*, *Openbaarheid openheid. Rapport van de commissie herorientatie overheidsvoorlichting* (The Hague,1970).

[3] See, further, R. Davis, "Public access to Community documents: a fundamental human right?" (EIOP, 1999), No. 8, http://eiop.or.at/eiop/texte/1999–008a.htm. See, however, E. Barendt, "Fundamental freedoms", in J. Korthals *et. al.*, *Information law towards the 21st century* (Deventer, 1992), 13; and I. Mackay, "The public's right to information", in Korthals, ibid. 167.

[4] See further for details of these and other cases before the courts and complaints made to the Ombudsman, T. Bunyan, *Secrecy and Openness in the EU* (Kogan Page, London, 1999).

[5] Case T–188/97 *Rothmans International* v. *Commission* (unreported) 19 July 1999; Case T–14/98 *Hautala* v. *Council* (unreported) 19 July 1999.

An additional problem in the context of the European Union has been the limited role which parliaments, both the European Parliament and national parliaments, have been enabled to play in the process of EU decision-making. This has of course been particularly striking in the context of decision-making in the field of justice and home affairs. Prior to the Treaty of Amsterdam (ToA) the European Parliament was not even properly and systematically informed about all facets of such decision-making processes.[6] Moreover, the role which national parliaments could play is by its nature a limited one and depends on the specific constitutional positioning of the parliament *vis-à-vis* the government in the national constitutional legal systems. Some national parliaments, such as the Dutch Tweede Kamer and the English House of Lords, have managed, within the constraints imposed by their national legal systems, to exert the function of ensuring some (public) debate before the decision-making process at the EU level were completed.[7] One of the problems has however been that these parliaments, both national and European, have struggled to ensure that they were indeed properly informed prior to the completion of the decision-making process. More often than not the information they received was not timely and was not complete, or was in a language incomprehensible to many of the parliamentarians supposed to exercise a control function. In fact once some particularly active citizens started using the access to information provisions introduced for their benefit by certain EU institutions as early as 1994 in a systematic and focussed fashion, they often received documents and information that parliaments had not received directly from the responsible decision-making instances.

A systematic approach to obtaining almost all documents within justice and home affairs which accounts for a huge 47% of all applications for citizen access (compared to, for example, only 13% for internal market matters), is explained by the historic fact that decision-making in this field has always been highly secretive and almost impossible to document. Moreover, it is no insignificant field of activity: recent statistics have shown that almost *one-third of* all paper and all meetings of the Council and its committees relates to justice and home affairs.[8] Nor can it be said either that in terms of individuals' rights and interests the decisions which have been taken in the past in this field of policy activity do not matter for the future. The example of highly secretive Schengen Executive Committee decisions being incorporated in one fell swoop into EU and EC measures shows graphically that this is not the case. The aim in particular of those who adopt a systematic approach to the request of documents in

[6] See, further, E. Guild, "The constitutional consequences of lawmaking in the European Union" in P. Craig and C. Harlow, *Law-making in the European Union* (Kluwer Law International, London, 1997), 65, 72.

[7] See further, House of Lords, *Enhancing Parliamentary Scrutiny of the Third Pillar*, 6th Report, HL 25 (1997–98).

[8] See House of Lords, *Dealing with the Third Pillar: The Government's Perspective*, 15th Report, HL 73 (1997–98).

this field of the EU's activity is to bring certain matters out into the public arena and make them the subject of public debate and knowledge. It should not of course be necessary to have to use the instrument of individual access applications in order to get copies of reports and documents in a legislative decision-making process.

What one indeed saw happening in the pre-Amsterdam period in particular in the field of decision-making in justice and home affairs was that citizen right of access to information, novel as that was, outstripped (by far) the provision of information to parliaments in the same context. The stage post-Amsterdam is however set for some shifting tensions.[9] The European Parliament has potentially at least acquired a much more decisive role with regard to decision-making on matters of asylum and immigration which will henceforth take place within the auspices of the European Community as such. Once the pinnacle of co-decision in these matters has been achieved, at some point in the future, then there can obviously be less substance to the current reality of largely secret decision-making by the Council of the European Union and its underbelly of committees, working parties and other associated bodies. Even within the so-called "rump" Third Pillar, where decision-making in the field of police and judicial co-operation will still take place, a clearer, albeit advisory, role has been marked out for the European Parliament. Some national parliaments remain assertive when faced with the suspicion that their effective control over decision-making is dwindling as a consequence of the onward march of European integration. For the first time some have successfully marked down their claim also to control (asylum and immigration) decision-making in the context of the European Community where the European Parliament has not yet been granted the right of co-decision. This is healthy progress on a linear democratic progression, albeit still with many gaps and lacunas evident. This evolution in terms of parliamentary control must however be seen alongside real progress in the ToA itself with regard to the constitutional underpinning of (citizen) access to information on decision-making processes in the European Union. In its potential the reach of citizen access to information is likely to continue to be much broader and relate to an earlier moment in the decision-making process than the information conveyed to parliaments by either the institutions themselves or national governments.

This chapter begins by the shaded inclusion of the Schengen *acquis* in the EU legal order in the ToA itself. It will then proceed to analyse the position with regard to citizen access to information on immigration and asylum policy areas from the date of entry into force of the ToA. In so doing it will highlight on a selective basis those issues which are likely to be key issues from the perspective of the nature of decision-making in these areas and which require resolution in the legal instrument to be adopted pursuant to the specific provisions of the

[9] For a brief summary of the main changes introduced by the ToA in this respect, see, further, J. Monar, "Justice and Home Affairs in the ToA: Reform at the Price of Fragmentation" (1998) 23 *EL Rev*. 320–35; and E. Tezcan, "*La Cooperation dans les domaines de la justice et des affaires interieures dans le cadre de l'Union Europeenne et le Traite d'Amsterdam*" CDE (1998) 5–6, 661.

ToA.[10] It will relate these issues to the various institutional actors in the policy-making process. Moreover, it will discuss these future developments in the light of the *status quo* before the ToA, in particular in the light of the not insignificant body of case-law on the subject. Finally, the special role to be played by non-governmental organisations and public interest groups both in terms of access to information and in terms of participation in the policy-making process itself will be very briefly referred to from the perspective of inculcating more deliberative democracy into the (asylum and immigration) decision-making process as part of a longer-term agenda.

OPAQUE "LEGAL PRACTICE" IN THE TREATY OF AMSTERDAM: THE INCORPORATION OF THE SCHENGEN *ACQUIS*

The principle of legal certainty requires that law-making procedures should be transparent and that laws affecting basic rights and freedoms should be accessible to citizens. Legal certainty thus goes hand-in-hand with the maximum degree of openness. Article 1 TEU lays down the paramount principle, namely that "This Treaty marks a new stage in the process of creating an ever closer union among the peoples of Europe, in which decisions are taken as openly as possible and closely as possible to the citizen". That maximum degree of openness is expressed in terms so fundamental that they can be considered an "object and purpose" of the ToA itself, within the meaning of Article 18 of the Vienna Convention on the Law of Treaties. The Schengen *acquis* is relevant to the daily life of all EU citizens, touching as it does on fundamental rights and freedoms of individuals. It will be a crucial element in developing the area of freedom, security and justice envisaged in the ToA. Yet this golden opportunity to turn both rhetoric and legal commitment into reality has been used by the Member States acting in Council as a demonstration that they are not committed to openness either in terms of decision-making or in terms of producing decisions which are accessible and intelligible to citizens in the European Union.

The incorporation of the Schengen *acquis* into the EU legal order by virtue of a special protocol to the ToA was viewed by many of the drafters as one of the successes of the ToA. At the same time this incorporation has been responsible not only for a considerable extra dose of complexity but also for the aggravation of the opaqueness of related decision-making. The actual decisions implementing the Schengen *acquis* into the EU legal order are full of ambiguities concerning the delimitation of the *acquis* and the associated legal basis exercise.[11]

[10] For a more detailed discussion not specifically related to decision-making in the field of immigration and asylum, see D. Curtin, "Citizens' Fundamental Right of Access to EU Information: An Evolving Digital Passepartout?" (2000) 37 *CML Rev* 7.

[11] Council Decision 1999/435/EC of 20 May 1999 concerning the definition of the Schengen *acquis* (OJ 1999 L176/1); and Council Decision 1999/826/EC determining the legal basis of each of the provisions for decisions which constitute the Schengen *acquis* (OJ 1999 L176).

The two Council decisions in question are dense in content and are characterised by a total lack of accessibility of the information and decisions involved. They merely contain lists with titles of various decisions on the basis of which it is impossible to understand the substance of the decisions taken or the incorporation being made. Only on the basis of an analysis of all the decisions in question (both those incorporated and those not incorporated) is it possible to say anything on the scope of application of both decisions. The paucity of information accompanying the decisions is striking. Remarkably, to my knowledge, these decisions were not provided by the Council to the European Parliament or to national parliaments at any stage during the decision-making procedure. Indeed, national ratification of the ToA was completed in all Member States before a definitive list of the Schengen *acquis* was established, not to say made available to national parliaments in their own language.

The House of Lords—ironically given the UK's opt-out,—was one of the very few (if not only) to examine and hear evidence on the basis of earlier draft decisions which adopted a very similar approach in many respects to the final decisions. It stressed that:

> "To those uninitiated in Schengen and struggling to comprehend the new arrangements agreed at Amsterdam, they are virtually unintelligible. Yet beneath the texts there are important issues of individual liberty and political accountability which the Committee fears may be obscured by the unhelpful presentation, technical jargon and procedural complexity."[12]

In delimitating the Schengen *acquis*, the choice has been made only to include in this exercise those binding decisions which are still in force. In other words the Council in the exercise of its discretion, has chosen not to give a legal basis for some provisions of the Schengen *acquis*, most notably those where the provision in question has no binding legal force. It seems to me that the Council has introduced an additional element to that found in the Schengen protocol. At the same time an explicit provision is made that this assessment by the Council does not have the effect that such provisions no longer apply or would no longer be valid. In other words it has the effect of preserving the legal validity of the non-incorporated provisions and the legal effects of any acts based on them which are still in force after the rest of the *acquis* has been incorporated. It transpires that as a result some provisions of the *acquis* continue to have an independent existence outside the EU treaties after incorporation has been completed. Such parts of the *acquis* have deliberately not been allocated a legal basis within the EU treaties. Yet the Schengen protocol clearly expresses the Member States agreement to incorporate the entire Schengen *acquis* into the EU framework. The process of incorporation should ensure that individuals and Member States' are able to identify the source of their rights and obligations. There is

[12] House of Lords Select Committee on the European Union, *Schengen and the United Kingdom's Border Controls*, 7th Report (http://www.parliamentary.the-stationary-of...199798/ldselect/ldeucom/139/8072801.htm).

thus a clear risk that both the integrity of the *acquis* itself and the principle of legal certainty will be undermined if some provisions of the Schengen *acquis* are applied independently of the EU treaties. Moreover, on what basis has the Council decided that certain provisions of the *acquis* are without binding legal effect? No indication whatsoever is given as to what criteria were applied in this regard. Yet experience with justice and home affairs decisions pre-Amsterdam has illustrated that opinions can differ widely on this matter of binding force.

A final point concerns the long-awaited publication of the decisions which constitute part of the Schengen *acquis*. The *acquis*, as defined by the Council, was formally published in the *Official Journal* only after it had been incorporated and taken effect within the framework of the EU treaties.[13] Not only is this contrary to the usual practice of publishing binding legal instruments before they enter into force, but important exceptions are made even to the principle of publication post-incorporation. The Council has explicitly included a provision that a consequence of not giving a legal basis to part of the Schengen "*acquis*" in this looser sense is that it will in principle not be published in the *Official Journal*. At the same time the Council explicitly reserves its right at a later stage to publish, and I quote, "other parts of the Schengen-*acquis* in particular provisions whose publication appears necessary in the public interest or that the Council considers important for the interpretation of the Schengen *acquis*". In other words the Council itself considers that certain non-binding or otherwise not in force provisions which will not be explicitly given a legal basis remain part of the Schengen *acquis* and may have some significance in future, to the point of, at some indeterminate future date and entirely at the behest of the Council, actually being published in the *Official Journal*. But at the same time precisely these provisions will not have been incorporated in the EU system but retain the nebulous independent existence referred to earlier.

But this is only one aspect of the non-publication of the Schengen *acquis* in the broader sense of the term. The second highly controversial aspect of the first of the Schengen decisions is the provision that another part of the Schengen *acquis* will not be published in the *Official Journal* (but will receive a legal basis?). This is defined in Article 1, paragraph 2 as "the provisions that at the time of the adoption of this decision have been categorised as "confidential" by the Schengen Executive Committee". Such secret provisions, with binding legal effect, have thus become part of the EC legal order, respectively EU legal order, as a result of the entry into force of the ToA. Moreover, as the law now stands this provision takes precedence over national laws requiring disclosure of documents. But we do not even know how many in number these documents are, nor their essential subject matter. Moreover, it is clear that the grounds on which the Schengen Executive Committee may in the past have classified documents as confidential go beyond the evolving EU law on the matter where the ToA can be considered as an important milestone.

[13] See references above at n. 11.

I would query compatibility with, in particular, Article 1 TEU which in my view expresses the "objects and purpose" of the TEU, namely a Union in which, *inter alia*, decisions are taken as closely as possible to the citizens and as openly as possible. As an object and purpose of the TEU it applies arguably since the date of signature of the ToA (2 October 1997), and in any event binds the Member States not to take measures that worsen the position with regard to the previously prevailing legal position. This means at the very least that the process of incorporation of the Schengen *acquis* should have been transparent and the laws resulting from it accessible to citizens. Legal ambiguity and not legal certainty has indeed been the guiding principle for incorporation of the Schengen *acquis*.

With regard to the putative judicial review of the Council decisions effectuating the Schengen incorporation, it can be said that as secondary legislation implementing primary legislation such decisions should not contain provisions which are *ultra vires* the underlying constitutional framework. Whether that is in fact the case is a matter of discussion and interpretation and would in any event have to be resolved by the ECJ as the constitutional arbiter. It is, however, difficult to see how a case could be brought before it, and who would have sufficient *locus standi* (in any event the privileged applicants according to the terms of Article 206 EC). The time limit of two months having by now expired since the publication of the Council decisions in question without the initiation of an action before the Court, it is submitted that no direct action challenging legality can now be initiated before the Court. This does not exclude the fact that in the future the issue could rise in the context of national proceedings and even in an appropriate case be brought before the ECJ in the context of a preliminary reference on the legality of the underlying Council decisions.

ACCESSING INFORMATION ON IMMIGRATION AND ASYLUM MATTERS: SOME KEY ISSUES POST-AMSTERDAM

The general constitutional framework

It follows from the wording of Article 1 TEU, as amended by the ToA, that the principle of open decision-making is at the very core of what the European Union is about "as a new stage in the process of creating an ever closer union among the peoples of Europe" on a par with the principle of subsidiarity. Moreover, it is clear from the wording used that the perspective is entirely that of the citizen and that secret decisions are as far removed *as possible* from the citizen. In fact further consideration of the principle of subsidiarity (see chapter 9 below and the protocol on subsidiarity, point 7) indicate that the existing status quo regarding national laws on openness cannot be taken away. In other words, respect must be shown to "well established national arrangements and the organization and working of Member States' legal systems".

The principle of subsidiarity, read together with the fact that EU citizenship is explicitly designed to be of a *supplemental* nature *only* to national citizenship and not to detract or reduce in any way national citizenship, suggests that the acquired rights in a manner of speaking of a citizen with regard to access to government information under national law cannot be taken away or affected by rules developed in the context of the European Union. Only this reading can be in line with the wording used in Article 1 that the aim is to achieve the greatest *possible* level of openness. The greatest possible level of openness must in any event include the level of openness already achieved at the national level in any and all of the Member States. In other words, this status quo is the minimum level of openness which must be taken as acquired and to which the development of EU concrete rules and principles will have a supplemental function.[14]

One progressive trend received explicit confirmation in the ToA and this relates to the positioning of decision-making in justice and home affairs within the body of an evolving EU legal order.[15] This was evidenced, *inter alia*, by the transferral of decision-making on such a sensitive matter as asylum and immigration to the so-called First Pillar and the increasing "communautarisation" of decision-making in flanking policy fields in the rump Third Pillar. In particular it was striking how the general rules on openness and access were specifically stated to apply across the board to the entire spectrum of decision-making in this previously inter-governmental realm. A black mark was earned however for the construction adopted in the ToA which specifically incorporated the Schengen *acquis* into the EU framework. It proved to be a peculiarly opaque solution which specifically included the possibility of incorporating "confidential" decisions into the body of EU law with no parliamentary or judicial control over that process. This complex and highly specific technique of incorporation must hopefully be regarded as far from a model precedent of so-called "pre-determined" flexibility within the body of EU law and will be dwelt upon in detail in a separate part of this chapter.

Article 255 EC is the specific provision laying down the general terms of the right of access to information in the EC context and providing for its further implementation. Strikingly, this right of access is specifically stated to apply to Union citizens as such and to "any natural or legal person residing or having its registered office in a Member State". The potential recipients of information in accordance with Article 255 EC include thus not only citizens of the Member States but also all third country nationals *resident* in a Member State. The terminology used would seem to apply to both legal and illegal aliens provided

[14] It follows from this reading of the significance of the new Treaty provision that a decision such as that taken by the Dutch Raad van Staat (Council of State) in the *Metten* case will never again be possible. This case gave precedence to the Council's Rules of Procedure over the provisions of the Dutch Constitution. See, further, L.F.M. Besselink, "*De zaak-Metten: de Grondwet voorbij*" (1996), 71 *NJB* 165.

[15] See further, D. Curtin and I. Dekker, "The EU as a 'Layered' International Organization: Institutional Unity in Disguise", in P. Craig and G. de Burca, *The Evolution of EU Law* (OUP, Oxford, 1999), 83.

appropriate residence can be established. These are the primary beneficiaries of the new access provisions to be implemented in a specific legal instrument. Essentially these are meant to be the *general public*, although a breakdown of the applicants who have actually made requests over the past couple of years shows that they are less "general" than might be expected. Academics, for example, account for a massive 43% of those making applications to the Council, followed by 30% from lawyers and 10% from pressure groups.[16] The fact that this is so should not cause too much surprise: how could the so-called ordinary citizen ever attempt to get to grips with the paper mountain and secretive byzantine paths through it in terms of decision-making structures? Only those with a highly specialised knowledge, time, energy and determination will wager the challenge.[17]

A horizontal obligation to provide access to information?

One of the first questions to arise regarding the obligation to grant access to information in the context of EU decision-making is the personal scope of the obligation. Does it extend to all EU institutions and bodies or only to some of them? This is a vitally important question also in the context of future decision-making in immigration and asylum-related policy matters. It is notable that in recent years the European Union has spawned not only numerous functional bodies and agencies in the more classic sense, but also many hybrid new "satellites", some of which have even been qualified as "unidentified international organisations".[18] Article 255 EC is however specifically limited to three named institutions (the Council, the Commission and the European Parliament) and leaves out of account not only four other institutions named explicitly in the Treaty, namely the Courts (of First Instance and of Justice), the Committee of the Regions, the Economic and Social Committee and the Court of Auditors, but also a whole host of other bodies and agencies (for example EUROPOL, the Trade Mark Agency, EURODAC, SIS, etc.)[19] The worry is that all these various

[16] See Second Report on the implementation of Council Decision 93/731/EC on public access to Council documents (General Secretariat, 15 June 1998).

[17] In its recent report the Council also stresses at some length and with only thinly veiled irritation the fact that two applicants alone accounted for 58% of the documents applied for. These applicants attempted, in the Council's words, to put the system to the test.

[18] In particular, EUROPOL and various treaty organs set up by the Dublin Convention and the Schengen Convention which have been conferred with rule-making powers: see, further, D. Curtin, "EU Police Cooperation and Human Rights Protection: Building the Trellis and Training the Vine", in *Scritti in onore di Guiseppe Federico Mancini, Vol. II; Diritto dell'Unione Europea* (Il Guiffre, Milano, 1998), 227.

[19] The Ombudsman in the context of his own initiative inquiry (concluded in December 1997) into the subject lists a total of fifteen institutions, organs and agencies to which a general principle of the public's right of access to documents applied. By now even more can be added to this list (Europol, Eurodac, etc.), as well as (information) "clearing houses" (such as CIREA and CIREFI) which have already been operating for many years (included in their information gathering—tasks is the independent analysis of information in the preparation of country reports).

agencies and bodies do not fit into any overall constitutional framework. What decisions are they taking and who is controlling them? During the pre-Amsterdam period the assumption of public access obligations remained a matter for internal and specific regulation in the absence of general rules adopted by the Community legislature. As the Court stressed in several cases it was a voluntary matter assumed by a certain number of institutions and agencies, each according to their own rules of procedure and with these rules constituting the main legal basis of the individual decisions adopted. No general obligation was thus applied in a horizontal fashion across the spectrum of EU decision-making activity to all agencies, organs, data-banks, etc., operating in the broad EU constitutional framework. Yet most of these agencies and organs have adopted their own access regulations in the pre-Amsterdam period, including, most recently, even EUROPOL.[20]

As a matter of general principle, it is submitted that all the institutions, agencies and other EU bodies with rule-making activities and operating within the broad EU constitutional framework should be covered by the general obligation to provide extensive access to their documents.[21] Account can be taken of the *special rules* needed for a certain number of institutions because of the nature of the tasks carried out (ECJ, European Central Bank, etc.), although this should not in my view amount to a blanket exception to general access rules applicable in principle to all the institutions and organs and decision-making instances of the European Union. Moreover, the principle of open decision-making as formulated as an "object and purpose" of the Treaty in Article 1 TEU applies in my view as and from the date of signing of the ToA in a general and horizontal fashion right across the spectrum of EU activity to all institutions and organs and other bodies operating within the framework of its activity. In practice, therefore, this means that the latter (including, for example, the Court of Auditors, the European Environment Agency, the ECJ, the Trade Mark Agency, Europol, etc.) have been subject to the general horizontal principle of open decision-making since 2 October 1997 implying that their respective (internal) rules on granting citizens access to documents should be interpreted in the light of this

[20] See, *inter alia*, Commission Decision of 19 September 1996 amending Decision 94/90/ECSC, EC, Euratom of 8 February 1994 on public access to Commission Documents (96/567/Euratom). See the Code of Conduct of the Council, Decision 93/731/EC (OJ 1993 L340). See also the recently adopted Decision of 21 March 1997 by the European Environment Agency concerning public access to its documents (OJ 1997 C282/5) (18 September 1997) and similar decisions adopted respectively by the Committee of the Regions (OJ 1997 L351/70) (23 December 1997) and the Economic and Social Committee (OJ 1997 L339/18) (10 December 1997).

[21] A more controversial point relates to the residual power under the general enabling clause, Art. 308 EC for the Council in the future to ensure in follow-up legislation that the general principles and limits laid down in the secondary legislation which will be adopted pursuant to Art. 255 EC on access to the documents of the three named institutions would also be applied more widely (as a separate exercise) with regard to all the other institutions and organs of the Union (or other bodies constituted under the auspices of the Union) not explicitly referred to in the text of Art. 255 as currently worded. This can in my view be regarded as an important general principle in the light of the general principle of equality as well as the very general and foundational terms in which Art. 1 TEU is expressed, even if it seems very far from the political agenda in the early days of the new millennium.

new, Treaty-based emphasis on open decision-making.[22] Any such reading will of course require an active input by the Court(s) themselves should a suitable case be referred to them in due course and in the changed circumstances of the entry into force of the ToA. This approach implies that it is only the *specific* implementation of that general horizontal principle with a legal basis in the EC Treaty which does not apply as a matter of course to other institutions and bodies than those explicitly named in the text of Article 255 EC itself.

A vertical obligation to provide access to information?

A related issue of *vertical* transparency arose during the pre-Amsterdam period, namely the extent to which the documents of *organs and committees* established by institutions in order to assist them in the exercise of their tasks were covered by the obligation of public access as voluntarily assumed. It is well known that there are many different instances of decision-making even within one, supposedly unitary, "institution". In the vast majority of cases, Council decisions are not really taken at Council level at all but by a whole host of *committees and working parties* which prepare the decision-making of the Council. This is a particularly important phenomenon in the field of justice and home affairs. In a significant number of cases those committees actually take important decisions in highly sensitive areas, which are then "rubber-stamped" by the Council as "A" points on their agenda. Who are the national civil servants on these committees? What is on their agenda? What documents are they discussing? What decisions are they reaching far way from any glare of publicity? It must be said that the practice of the Council has progressed in the pre-Amsterdam period in this regard from almost total obscurity to some sustained shafts of light into otherwise darkened rooms. For example, it has granted public access to the documents of many committees.[23] Moreover, the Europa Server and the web page of various Council Presidents contained, during the pre-Amsterdam period, some information on the composition and meetings scheduled of various Council committees, in particular those operational within the framework of justice and home affairs policy making.[24] Nevertheless, such voluntary and active supply of information is partial, limited and, at times, almost inevitably tailored to the institutions' perspective. The Council itself has, in defending its restrictive policy on access, gone to extraordinary lengths to defend secrecy: for example, in complaints made to the Ombudsman concerning its refusal to grant

[22] In my opinion it cannot be excluded that, for example, certain provisions of the highly restrictive decision by the European Investment Bank could be *ultra vires* the new Treaty provision or, at the very least, require a different reading than simply a textual one of the provisions in question. See OJ 1997 C243/13 (9 August 1997). See, further, European Parliament Report and resolution on openness within the European Union, No. A4–0476/98, in European Parliament Minutes of 12 January 1999, at http://www.europarl.eu.int/plenary/en/default.htm.

[23] See, Council report on access for 1997/1998.

[24] Ibid.

certain documents of the Secretariat-General relating to justice and home affairs, it argued in justification that the Secretariat-General of the Council is a separate "institution" to the Council itself and therefore that the Council could not grant access to its documents.[25] This is essentially a variant of the "authorship" argument defended by the Commission with such vigour before the Court of First Instance (CFI) in the *Rothmans* case and has both horizontal and vertical aspects in its implications.

The Commission has persistently attempted to shield its "comitology" committees in particular from the requirement of public access since it felt that such committees could not be considered as part of the structures of the Commission as such. In so doing it distinguished the position of such committees from what it referred to as consultative committees and expert groups which assist the Commission in its formulation of policy initiatives. The Commission considers the documents of these latter committees to be Commission documents as such and consequently to be covered by the general rules applicable to the Commission. It similarly has little problem, in its own analysis, with so-called scientific advisory committees in the sense that such committees are now subject to new rules which make more provision than in the past for transparency as well as publication of details of names of members, agendas and minutes and opinions which are all to be made public. This analysis can however be queried as recent research has emphasised the extreme opacity of decision-making by such scientific committees in general.[26] In any event it is felt that the best approach even to such committees is probably to consider them as part of the Commission in practice and subject to exactly the same access rules as Commission documents.

"Comitology" committees are essentially those committees with delegated (largely Commission) tasks leading to the adoption of measures *implementing* legislative tasks.[27] Such committees have not had any structural relevance to decision-making in justice and home affairs in the pre-Amsterdam period. Post-Amsterdam, with the new competences acquired by the Commission in the field, *inter alia*, of asylum and immigration in the medium to long term, this is likely to change. Despite the fact that the Commission chairs the meetings of "comitology" committees and produces their agendas and minutes, the Commission has traditionally considered such committees to be independent of the Commission as an institution and their documents not to be Commission documents but

[25] It previously argued that the Presidency of the Council was also a separate institution to that of the Council itself. See, further, Bunyan, above at n. 4.

[26] See C. Joerges, K.H. Ladeur and E. Vos, *Integrating Scientific Expertise into Regulatory Decision-Making. National Traditions and European Innovations* (Schriftenreihe des Zentrums für Europäische Rechtspolitik, 1997) 23; Baden-Baden, Nomos and C. Joerges, "The impact of European integration on private law; reductionist perception, true conflicts and a new constitutional perspective. Private governance, democratic constitutionalism and supranationalism" (1997) 3 *ELJ* 378.

[27] See, further, K. Bradley, "Comitology and the law: through a glass, darkly" (1992) *CML Rev* 693. See also R.H. Pedler and G.F. Schaefer (eds), *Shaping European Law and Policy: The Role of Committees and Comitology in the Political Process* (1996).

documents of *independent* committees. The Council, on the other hand, took the opposite view that such documents were indeed *Commission* documents. This difference in opinion led ultimately to a case before the CFI: *Rothmans* v. *Commission*.[28] The reasoning bears some analysis in the light of the many ad hoc committees which could be established in the future to assist the Commission (or other institution) in the performance of its tasks in the general justice and home affairs policy-making fields and where analogous authorship arguments could be used to deprive applicants of access to key information. The Commission had refused to grant the applicant access to minutes of one such "comitology" committee (the Customs Code Committee) which contained the opinion of the committee, the individual position of Member States and the voting results. The Commission reasoned that whereas these minutes are technically drawn up by the Commission, which is responsible for the secretariat of the Committee, they are formally adopted by the Committee itself and are thus not to be considered as Commission documents subject to an access obligation. The Committee itself was the author of such minutes, in the Commission's view, and any request for access had to be made directly to the Committee itself. In other words the Commission attempted, for the purposes of the relevant access rules, to draw a distinction between the person in possession of a document and the author of a document arguing only that the latter were subject to an access obligation. In effect, therefore, the Commission tried to construe an *additional exception* to the access rules, a tactic not endorsed by the CFI.

After an analysis of the relevant legal provisions underpinning the establishment and functioning of such committees, the CFI concluded essentially that from an organisational and administrative point of view the committees "come under the Commission itself". The alternative approach focussing on authorship of documents would, moreover, in the view of the CFI, not be compatible with "the very objective of the right of access to documents". In such circumstances the Court held that for the purposes of the Community rules on access to documents the Commission was responsible for ruling on applications for access to documents of those committees, such as the minutes at issue in *Rothmans*. Reading between the lines the Court seems to have been influenced by the fact that the links between these committees and any institution *other than* the Commission were tenuous and moreover the comitology committees themselves could not be categorised as "another Community institution or body" within the meaning of the Code of Conduct. In other words their independence was not established for the purpose of the access rules and the Court would not accept that they could simply fall outwith the scope of an access obligation in such circumstances. Interestingly, although the Court's (subsequent) judgment does not refer to it, the new Council decision laying down the procedures for such committees in exercising implementing powers conferred on the Commission[29] provides in exactly the same sense as the Court's judg-

[28] Case T–188/97 *Rothmans International* v. *Commission* (unreported) 19 July 1999.

[29] Council Decision 99/468/EC of 28 June 1999 (OJ L184/23).

ment, a factor which may *sotte voce* have influenced the outcome. This Council (comitology) decision for the first time explicitly and categorically provides that "the principles and conditions on public access to documents applicable to the Commission shall apply to the committees" (Article 7(2)).

Given the complexity and specificity of the decision-making throughout the EU policy areas, it can be considered to be of primordial importance in the post-Amsterdam era that the principle of *vertical* open decision-making applies, at the very least, *within* the three institutions named in Article 255 EC. In other words all committees and organs and other bodies operating under the auspices of those same institutions should be covered by the text of the implementing legislation to be adopted. These latter "subsidiary bodies" should fall as a matter of course within the scope of application of the legal instrument to be adopted in due course. At the same time it is desirable that other bodies (working parties, etc.) in which the institutions in question *participate* should also, as a matter of principle, fall within the scope of application of the general principle. In the field of justice and home affairs there are, for example, numerous working parties, etc., in the field of external relations in which the Council in particular participates and the agendas, etc., of which are co-authored by the Council and or its Presidency. A prominent one which has already been the subject of a complaint to the Ombudsman is the EU-US Senior Level Group.[30] Such instances should be included as a matter of definition within the scope of application *ratione persona* of the principle of access to documents in the secondary legislation to be adopted.

Does the obligation to provide access extend to (partial) information or only to "documents"?

The first substantive issue which logically arises for consideration is how far an obligation *ratione materia* to provide public access to information should reach. What "objects" should it cover? The initial approach of many of the institutions was to limit this right of access specifically to *documents*[31] which is a narrower approach to that taken in several national legal systems which provide a (wider) right of access to "information". The decision in *Hautala* v. *Council*[32] represents a significant recognition of the fact that despite the specific limitation in many pre-Amsterdam access decisions to "documents", the right is essentially to "information" not covered by one of the specific exceptions. Moreover, the Court ruled that the institutions in question have a duty to "extract" such information from given documents in the event of certain parts having to remain

[30] See, further, Bunyan, above at n. 4.

[31] See, for example, Council Decision 93/731 EC on public access to Council documents (OJ 1993 L340/43) and Commission Decision 94/90 EC on public access to Commission documents.

[32] Case T–14/98 *Hautala* v. *Council* (unreported) 19 July 1999. This case is subject to appeal by the Council to the ECJ.

confidential, subject to the application of the principle of proportionality. The question whether access may be sought (and granted or refused) to a whole document as well as to "part of a document" has proved an important and contentious point in practice. For example, in the case involving the Swedish Union of Journalists the applicants argued that an institution is obliged to block out certain pieces of information in a justice and home affairs document and to provide access to the rest of a document (or to extract "information" from a document) but this point was not dealt with by the Court in its judgment. The issue of partial access to documents (or information) has also been adverted to in justice and home affairs cases arising before the Ombudsman and was finally the subject of explicit judicial consideration in the *Hautala* case.[33] The Court held that the Council was wrong in deciding not to allow partial communication of its documents and was indeed obliged to adapt its documents, in appropriate circumstances, by deleting certain passages, so that access could be granted to the *information* contained in the documents in question. The CFI in *Hautala* accepted that the Council Decision on access did not explicitly require the Council to consider whether partial access to documents may be granted, but it emphasised that "the basis on which the Council" adopted the said decision, namely Declaration No. 17 and the Code of Conduct, stress the principle of "the widest possible access to documents". In these circumstances, and taking expressly into account the fact that the basis for such a right should be sought in the *democratic principle* (the principle that exceptions to general principles should be construed narrowly as well as the principle of proportionality), the Court concluded that the Council is obliged to examine whether partial access should be granted to the information not covered by the exceptions. In that connection, the principle of proportionality would allow the Council, in particular cases where the volume of the document or the passages to be removed would give rise to an unreasonable amount of administrative work, to balance the interest in public access to those fragmentary parts against the burden of work so caused. The Court thus, in those particular cases, gave priority to the Council's desire to safeguard the so-called interests of "good administration" above the citizens' right to information. The Court did not further reason this conclusion and its putting to one side of the citizens' interest in the face of what is, after all, merely a matter of administrative convenience which could be solved in a different manner is regrettable.

This is also at issue in the *Kuijer*[34] case in the context of justice and home affairs pre-Amsterdam. This case raises specifically the question of citizen access to documents of the Centre for Information, Discussion and Exchange on Asylum (CIREA). The Council refused the applicant access to reports, analyses and evaluations drawn up by CIREA relating to third countries where a large number of asylum-seekers originate from or reside, as well as certain related

[33] See above at n. 5.
[34] Case T–188/98 *Kuijer v Council* (unreported) 6 April 2000.

documents supplied by the Member States. This case raises difficult questions with regard to the application of certain exceptions to the general principle of access (relations with third countries, public interest), but even if it would appear that the disclosure of certain aspects of the CIREA reports could undermine the protection of the public interest (international relations), the Council could, since *Hautala*, be regarded in violation of its duty to provide access to those part of the documents not covered by relevant exceptions. The principle of proportionality, the principle of good administration as well as the principle that the widest *possible* access to documents should be granted all plead strongly in favour of the principle of partial access to documents. This has been confirmed by the CFI in *Hautala* in the strongest possible language. After all if a document is not drafted in such a manner that genuinely confidential parts can be removed then it is not the citizen who should bear the consequences of the institution's failure to adapt its administrative practice to the requirements imposed by an evolving culture of openness.

Does the obligation to provide access extend to documents "incoming" to an institution?

With regard to pre-Amsterdam access to *incoming documents* (in other words documents with a different author), the status quo is that there is no right of access and in practice it seems that no access will be granted by the various institutions concerned to documents emanating from or produced by third parties, whether they be Member States, private individuals or other EU institutions or organs. Access can only be obtained with regard to documents "drawn up" by the institution in question. In the Code of Conduct adopted by the Council and the Commission the sensitive question of information supplied to an institution by a third party is dealt with. It explicitly states that: "where the document held by an institution was written by a natural or legal person, a Member State, another Community institution or body of any other national or international body, the application must be sent direct to the author".

The Commission practice has for example been to grant a right of access only to documents "originating with" the Commission. It emerges from the figures produced by the Commission for the year 1998 that this was a significant category of refusal of access (29.8%) and that it considered such requests as "inadmissible".[35] In practice therefore this category of refusal functioned as an extra exception to the principle of access to documents since its consequence is that incoming documents are completely excluded from the scope of application of the general rule.[36]

[35] See Discussion Paper on public access to Commission documents, Secretariat Directorate C (23 April 1999) 25; text on http://www.statewatch.org (Statewatch home page).

[36] In a decision of 30 June 1998 concerning one of multiple Statewatch complaints the European Ombudsman (EO) stressed that Art. 2(2) of Decision 93/71/EC is not presented in the form of an

In the post-Amsterdam period it will need to be considered whether the phrase used in Article 255 EC, namely "documents of" three named institutions, covers *incoming documents* to the three institutions and not only documents produced by those institutions themselves.[37] It can nevertheless be reasonably argued that the phrase which was ultimately included in the final text ("EP, Council and Commission documents") is capable of bearing the construction that it *implicitly* refers to *incoming* documents held by the institution in question and should not simply be limited to the much more restrictive interpretation of documents "originating from" the institution in question. The argument in favour of a wider interpretation gleans some support from the wording (and inclusion) of Declaration No. 35 to the European Community. This Declaration enables the Member States to request to the Council and the Commission that their documents not be disclosed. It specifically states that "Member States will be allowed to request the Commission or the Council not to communicate to third parties a document originating from that State without its prior agreement". The underlying premise is that incoming documents are in fact covered by the general principle of paragraph 1, otherwise the wording of the Declaration makes no sense whatsoever! It seems therefore that incoming documents are prima facie covered by the general principle of access to documents expressed in paragraph 1 of Article 255 EC.[38] It is submitted that the issue whether "incoming documents" to the three institutions in question are to be covered in the secondary legislation to be adopted under Article 255 EC can in any event be simply and effectively resolved as a matter of definition by indicating that both documents "produced by" and "considered by" the institutions and its subsidiary organs fall within the scope of definition of "documents of" the institutions in question. This was not the thrust of the Commission's initial draft regulation which was leaked into the public domain even before its adoption by the Body of Commissioners.[39] But precisely the public influence and deliberation which could take place as a result of this fact led to it being amended in this regard before finally being adopted by the Commissioners themselves.[40] This must surely constitute an excellent illustration of the benefits

exception to the general rule of public access. He did not take a formal position on the matter of incoming documents in this particular decision but did stress that to include documents of which the Council is a joint author would considerably broaden the scope of this *de facto* exception. The EO concluded that neither the express wording of Art. 2(2) nor the relevant case-law on the subject supported the Council's position that documents of which it is a joint author fall outwith the general right of access. See, further, *Statewatch Bulletin* (1998), 8.2 and 8.5.

[37] Initially in the version of the Draft ToA produced by the Dutch Presidency in May 1997 the wording was very restrictive indeed and stated that Art. 255 EC (draft) was limited to documents "originating from" the institutions in question. This wording compared poorly with earlier proposals that the phrase should rather be the much wider documents "held by" the institutions in question. The latter phrase clearly would have covered incoming documents to the institutions (i.e. not originating from those institutions) but the path of ambiguity on this point has clearly been preferred.

[38] See further on this point, Curtin, above at n. 10.

[39] See the full text on http://www.statewatch.org.

[40] See the version adopted by the Commission on 27 January 1997.

of allowing the public access to preparatory documents at the earliest possible stage in the decision-making process.

A more general question relates to the status of *security classifications* given to documents and to what extent documents bearing such classifications are in general excluded from the scope of application of the access rules in question. In this regard it must be noted that several of the decisions of institutions specifically state that regulations on confidentiality are to remain unaffected by the access regulations. For example, in the Council Decision,[41] Article 8 states that "This decision shall apply with due regard for provisions governing the protection of classified information". This general rule implies that documents bearing such security classifications do not fall under the general principle of access to documents. This applies both to incoming documents with such classifications, as well as to documents originating within the various institutions themselves. In other words there is no explicit procedure to revise classification in the light of an access obligation, although individual institutions may do so in practice. The practice of the institutions (Council and Commission) has, on the whole, been to grant access to some documents bearing the "restricted" ,"secret" and "confidential" classification. The real problem lies in knowing that such documents exist in the first place rather than necessarily being denied access in practice.

The problem is however more extensive in security terms in that many of the "incoming documents" have been classified by the Member States or third parties. The practice of the European Union in that regard is to accept the original security obligation and no procedure is provided for revision over the course of time. The status quo is that it is only after a period of 30 years have elapsed that any fresh consideration of the matter (under the Archives Regulation[42]) takes place. Council Regulation (EEC) No. 354/83 lays down rules concerning the opening to the public of the *historical archives* of the European Community and the EAEC[43] and provides that as regards "documents and records received from a Member State or from another institution, the institutions shall abide by the classification established by the originator". It can safely be assumed that if the institutions have this obligation concerning documents at the historical archives then they have it prior to that, namely before the documents concerned are transferred to the historical archives.[44]

An additional problem is the fact that the confidentiality regulations currently in place are extremely fragmentary, with each separate institution, organ, agency, clearing-house and data-bank deciding its own specific rules on the question of confidential information. A recent example involving Europol is

[41] Council Decision 93/731/EEC of 20 December 1993 on public access to Council documents (OJ 1993 L340/43).

[42] Council Regulation (EEC) No. 354/83 of 15 February 1993 concerning the opening to the public of the historical archives of the EC and the EAEC (OJ 1993 L43/1).

[43] Ibid.

[44] See also, in this sense, P. Dryberg, "Current issues in the debate on public access to documents" (1999) 24 *EL Rev* 157,169.

illustrative of the scope and gravity of the problem. Europol is an international police body which will collect, hold (analyse) and exchange highly confidential information on a broad range of individuals, many of whom are neither convicted criminals nor suspects.[45] Far-reaching "confidentiality regulations" have been agreed by the Council as an "A" point on its agenda (in other words, decided in all its details by Council "committees" and passed without debate at ministerial level), with no prior public discussion whatsoever. According to the terms of the ToA its officers will get "operational powers" but they have been granted *total immunity* from legal proceedings "in respect of acts performed by them, including their words spoken or written, in their official capacity" even *before* the ToA entered into force.[46] Moreover, with regard to Europols' own system of files for intelligence and analysis (containing highly sensitive information including data relating to racial origin, religious or other beliefs, political opinions, sexual life and health) it was initially provided (in implementing regulations) that incoming information for these files from other international organisations (Interpol, Schengen Information System) as well as from any third countries (non-EU countries) will have minimal safeguards. Basically the third party or third state will assess itself "as far as possible the information and its source".[47]

It is submitted that the question of confidential information bearing security classification should be treated as in principle subject to the general rules on access to documents and subject only to the limits of one of the specific exceptions included in the secondary legislation to be adopted (see, further, below). In other words a security classification as such (either by an institution or by a third party) should not, post-Amsterdam, be capable of constituting an *automatic* disqualification from access. This is different to the pre-Amsterdam *status quo*, but in the light of the fundamental nature of the principle and the principle that the *greatest possible* access will be granted, it cannot be considered acceptable that existing secondary legislation and other internal rule making by the respective institutions could provide an automatic exception to the general principle, with no specific provision for judicial scrutiny or review of classification over time.

[45] Council Act of 18 July 1995 drawing up the Convention based on Article K.3 TEU, on the establishment of a European Police Office (Europol Convention) SN 3549/95 (OJ 1995 C316) (27 November 1995).

[46] OJ 1997 C221.

[47] Moreover, these regulations, which were rubber-stamped by the Council as an "A" point, contained the extraordinary provision that "information which has been obtained by a third state in obvious violation of human rights will be marked by Europol". In other words, the information in question was not to be "removed" but simply "marked" and retained and, if necessary, used or passed on by Europol! This provision was subsequently (after some publicity) not included in the Council act as finally adopted. See, further, *Statewatch Bulletin*.

Does the obligation to provide access extend to an institution's "internal" documents?

With regard to the question which *internal documents* of affected institutions fall under the general scope of the access regulations, the pre-Amsterdam status quo is that all internal Council and Commission (and other?) documents fall within the material scope of application of the relevant access regulations, unless covered by one of the exceptions explicitly provided for in the Code of Conduct. This applies to all types of preparatory documents and those not intended for publication, regardless of the medium. For example, with regard to the Commission, this would include "summary records of meetings, internal departmental memo's etc. and even the minutes of Commission meetings", as well as documents relating to the institution's internal organisation and administration and preparatory documents forming part of the legislative process.[48] All these kinds of documents have been released in practice both by the Council and by the Commission prior to the entry into force of the ToA.

An exception to the general principle of a citizens' right of access to documents could be considered in the post-Amsterdam regime in order to take account of the fact that it may also be in the interest of each of the individual institutions' (the Council, the Commission and the European Parliament) specific role in the decision-making process to enable them, during the course of that decision-making process, to keep certain documents internal to that institution confidential. This basically was the reasoning behind the discretionary exception in the original Code of Conduct that access could be refused on the ground of the institution's own interest in the confidentiality of its own proceedings. In the draft discussion paper which reveals the Commission's preliminary thinking on this subject it not only recommends keeping this exception but *in addition* proposes an exception for certain "internal documents" in the future draft regulation it intends to propose under Article 255 EC. It envisages that the scope of this exception would be limited to "contributions to internal proceedings" and defines this essentially as "documents of a purely internal nature" embracing "summary reports of meetings, briefing notes, departmental opinions, mission reports, notes containing officials, personal thoughts or opinions etc.". In so doing it attempts to draw a distinction with what it terms "preparatory documents forming part of the legislative process (the framing of Commission initiatives and decisions)": this category would cover both related preparatory and explanatory documents and other factual information. Such documents would fall within the scope of the general principle of access, whereas "documents of a purely internal nature" would not. Moreover the idea behind the formulation of this distinction seems to be that this latter category of documents would constitute an automatic and mandatory exception to the general principle of access and that there would be no requirement on the

[48] See Commission Discussion Paper, above at n. 35, 8.

Commission or other affected institutions to carry out the balancing of interests test as currently required with regard to the discretionary exception in accordance with the relevant case-law of the CFI. In the draft Commission regulation which has now been formally proposed the exception in question is specifically worded so as to complete.

It may well not be considered unreasonable that each institution should feel that it must have a certain margin in the interests of efficient decision-making—that is indeed the thinking behind the provisions of certain national legislation, for example in Denmark and Sweden where some restriction on the disclosure of internal documents exists. Thus, for example in Sweden, access is given only to "official" documents: this is the case only when a document reaches its final form and has not been sent outside the department in question. The Swedish legislation excludes from the definition of "official" document preliminary outlines or drafts and memoranda which have not been filed. Under both the Swedish and Danish legislation documents however lose their internal character if they have been submitted to another authority (for example another ministry or third party).

The problem in the context of EU decision-making and in the Commission's views as expressed in its draft regulation lies in considering that the interest in efficient decision-making is capable by its very nature of prevailing *as a matter of course* over the citizens' interest in obtaining access to documents. In other words it is suggested that a balancing of interests test must always be included. Moreover, a considerable difficulty lies in drawing a precise line as to what must be considered an "internal document" of an institution falling within the scope of any putative exception. It is, after all, an exception which must be considered not only in relation to Commission documents but also to Council documents and European Parliament documents, three very different institutions, each with a distinct role and function in the EU decision-making process. Further, "documents forming part of the legislative process" may well be too narrow to cover in a satisfactory and realistic manner all the various types of rule-making which now takes place in a fragmented and very diffuse European Union. For example, with regard to the policy area of justice and home affairs, it is suggested that an increasing proportion of rule-making does not take place as part of a "legislative process" in any formal sense but rather as a matter of implementation by various instances operating (in general) under the auspices of the Council.[49] The tendency is more and more towards operationalisation of previously taken decisions. Europol is a striking instance of that very phenomenon. Moreover, given the manner in which the EU decision-making procedure operates in practice, and in particular the fact that the content of so many important decisions for citizens as well as related practices take place in the working party and "subsidiary organ" structure, it cannot be considered acceptable to limit the citizens' access to those documents written for the purposes of external use (or at least distributed outside the institution itself).

[49] See, further, Bunyan, above at n. 4.

One senses that part of the motivation leading the Commission to propose an exception limited to "working documents in the form of contributions to internal proceedings" is the desire to protect civil servants and to enable them to express their own opinions as part of an ongoing internal process without fear of being exposed and held to account (or ridicule) in that regard. This may well be a laudable objective in itsel,f which deserves to be treated with some sensitivity; nevertheless, it must be remembered that we are dealing with proposed secondary legislation for (at least) three institutions and that this particular interest must always be weighed against the citizens' interest in obtaining "the fullest possible" access. I would suggest that there are (other) ways of protecting the interests of civil servants less damaging to the citizens' interest in access than the absolute exception envisaged by the Commission in its draft discussion paper. In the first place, access could be granted even to those "contributions to internal proceedings" if that could be considered important from the perspective of the will-formation process of citizens in the context of a democratic rule-making procedure (broader than a legislative procedure). That could emerge as part of the balancing of interests process suggested above and would take account of the fact that it is important to guarantee citizens access to information at the earliest possible moment, where an institution has not yet taken a definitive view and when alternative solutions can still be chosen. Secondly, this test would apply only where the rule-making in question had not yet been completed: where the process had been completed it is suggested that access should always be granted to the "working documents" in question, if requested. The interest of the particular civil servant(s) could be adequately protected by the institution in question removing any reference to named civil servants (including of course contact numbers, etc.). It is submitted that this approach is in line with the recent approach of the CFI in the *Hautala* case which placed emphasis on the citizens' primary right to (partial) information.

Revamping the exceptions to the obligation to provide access: a specific exception for justice and home affairs?

The approach in the pre-Amsterdam decisions on access to documents which the respective named institutions have adopted on the basis of their internal rules of procedure with regard to the exceptions is to elaborate a *list* of possible exceptions along the fairly classical lines found in similar legislation in various Member States. In other words, a list of exceptions including elements such as public interest, international relations, security, and exceptions relating to more private or commercial interest (privacy, intellectual property rights, etc.). This is the so-called obligatory non-discretionary list. In addition a number of the decisions in question contain a discretionary, non-obligatory and highly controversial exception relating to the specific institution's interest in "the confidentiality of its own proceedings" as a ground for denying access. The inclusion of this exception was originally one of the reasons that the Netherlands (unsuccessfully) challenged the legal basis of the Council Decision on access. In the earlier practice and cases before the CFI this exception figured prominently but, probably as a result of these successful cases, the more recent practice of the institutions reveals considerable reticence in relying on this particular general exception. For example, the 1998 figures for the Commission reveal that the Commission relied on this exception in order to refuse documents in only three cases (5.9%). The institutions originally intended this exception, it seems, as a way of safeguarding the internal workings of the institutions in question, in particular internal documents expressing personal opinions of civil servants and other documents relating to its own internal use. The problem for the institutions has been that since the *Carvel case* the institution is required to weigh up the interest of the institution in question in maintaining confidentiality of its proceedings against the interest of the person seeking the document. In practice the experience seems to be that this can be an extremely difficult test to apply and is time-consuming. The Council for example interpreted this ruling to mean that the balancing of interests test has to be performed in respect of every single document.[50]

This difficulty as experienced by the institutions in the aftermath of the initial case-law of the CFI may indeed explain why the recent practice of the institutions has placed considerable emphasis on the non-discretionary list of exceptions and, in particular, the exception in the *public interest.* Again, if one looks at the Commission figures for 1998 it transpires that of all the replies to (admissible) requests, a huge 52.9% (27) were refused on some aspect related to the public interest. It is not surprising therefore that this exception has received quite some judicial attention in recent years.[51] The first striking point is how broadly this exception has tended to be construed by the institutions in question. In particular they have argued that the defence of the public interest is not limited to the list between brackets in the decisions, but that these are merely examples of the public interest and that the public interest may embrace more. The Council, for example in interim proceedings in the *Carlsen* case,[52] argued against disclosure of the opinions of its Legal Service on the grounds that the public interest in the maintenance of *legal certainty* and the *stability of Community law* could be damaged. Neither of these grounds are mentioned in the relevant access Decision on access or the Code of Conduct as interests which can be invoked under the heading of public interest. The CFI nevertheless accepted the reasoning of the Council, pointing out that the list of interests mentioned between brackets are simply specific examples of public interest but that access may also be denied under the *general notion* of public interest. The

[50] T. Brunmayr, "The Council's Policy on Transparency", in: V. Deckmyn and I. Thomson (eds), *Openness and Transparency in the EU* (Institute of Public Administration, Maastricht, 1998), 73.

[51] Case T–124/96 *Interporc*; Case T–610/97 *Carlsen and others* v. *Council* [1998] ECR II–485; Case T–105/95 *WWF UK*; Case T–83/96 *Van der Wal* v. *Commission.*

[52] Case T–610/97 *Carlsen and others* v. *Council* [1998] ECR II–485.

Council admitted in this case that it refuses, according to long-standing practice, access to the opinions of the Council's Legal Service irrespective of the specific content of the position and of the stage the matter has reached, and the Court seemed to consider this practice of automatic refusal of this category of documents as acceptable. The Commission, on the other hand, does not automatically refuse such documents but rather examines on a case-by-case basis having regard to the particular content of the legal opinions before deciding whether or not to grant or refuse access. It is submitted that this is, in any event, the correct approach. In the later cases of *Interporc* and *Van der Wal*[53] the CFI added that before deciding on a request for access to documents the Commission must consider, for *each* document requested, whether, in the light of the information in its possession, disclosure is in fact likely to undermine one of the interests protected under the first category of exceptions.

With regard to the exception of "public interest", attempts have also been made to rely on this exception in order to exclude entire *policy areas* from the access rules. The Council in particular has often argued that justice and home affairs concern delicate matters which frequently fall under the protection of the *public interest* in the Member States and should be similarly protected under EU law. It is striking that public interest in this equation does not seem to include the angle of the citizens of a democracy knowing what is being done in their name. In any event the CFI gave short shrift to the idea that justice and home affairs were excluded from the access rules in both the *Carvel* and *Swedish Union of Journalists* cases.[54] Furthermore, in *Hautala*[55] the Court accepted that documents relating to security and foreign affairs issues also fall under the general scope of the access rules and were not as a category excluded on public interest grounds.

In the perspective of post-Amsterdam implementation, the Commission, in its draft discussion paper on public access to Commission documents, considers that the existing system of exceptions (mandatory and one discretionary exception):

> "operates relatively well. It has been applied quite restrictively and on increasingly legitimate grounds. The only real difficulty has arisen with the application of the discretionary exception, since the CFI required the institution to balance the interest of the public in gaining access to a document against the interest of the institution in maintaining the confidentiality of its deliberations, given that applicants are not required to justify their requests."

The Commission does not favour a "radical reform of this system" but rather specific changes to the *status quo* such as including under the heading of public interest the "stability of the Community legal order", etc. More noteworthy is the statement that "specific exceptions might also have to be provided for the

53 See Case T–124/96 *Interporc*; and Case T–83/96 *Van der Wal*.

54 Case T–174/95 *Svenska Journalist, Jorbunded* v. *Council* [1998] ECR II–2209.

55 Case T–14/98 *Havtala* v. *Council* (unreported) 19 July 1999.

sectors of justice and home affairs, common foreign and security policy and fraud prevention". Moreover the Commission advocates the retention of the protection of the confidentiality of the institutions' proceedings as a discretionary exception. I do not share the Commissions' analysis with regard to the exceptions to the right of access and believe that a fairly radical albeit focussed reform of the existing list system is where the European Union should move in the post-Amsterdam implementation period. In the first place the real problem lies not with the discretionary exception (although this is highly objectionable in the way it is worded, implying that the institutions can have an interest in their own proceedings which can pre-empt the citizens' right of access), but in particular with the public interest exception.

In the second place the problem is not that one must apply a balancing of interest test in the context of the discretionary exception but rather that no balancing of interest test is applied in the context of the so-called "mandatory" list of exceptions. In the third place, post-Amsterdam, the emphasis has shifted in one absolutely fundamental respect: we are no longer dealing with a system of internal regulation by institutions enabling them to impose, at their complete discretion, a system of absolute secrecy in some instances, but rather with a system where the general and fundamental principle is of the "greatest possible" level of openness. This latter level can never in my view include the option of mandatory exceptions but must include necessary exceptions in a more tailor-made fashion and always incorporating a balancing of interests. Finally, specific exceptions cannot, in my view, be provided for entire policy areas such as "the sectors of justice and home affairs" and "common foreign and security policy". Not only would this constitute an enormously retrograde step compared with the existing status quo but it would be contrary to the specific wording of the ToA, not to mention its spirit.[56]

Only those interests which are sufficiently weighty should prevail over the citizens' right of access to documents. The difficulty lies in isolating those areas of EU policy-making where there may be a genuine interest which by its very nature may, in certain circumstances, be so imperative that it should prevail over the general interest of the citizen in obtaining access to documents. In practice these interests are most likely to arise in the context of policy making in the fields of foreign and security policy and police and judicial co-operation where, by their

[56] Little concrete thinking has taken place to date about how the system of exceptions to the right of access could be reformed in a genuine fashion which attempts to take account of the specificity of the EU system of governance and its interaction with citizens. A different approach to that taken in the specific access decisions under the pre-Amsterdam status quo is to attempt to think about the nature of the European Union as such, very different to that of its component Member States, and to carve out relevant and acceptable exceptions in general terms. In this spirit, four possible exceptions will be suggested, all phrased in general terms, in the spirit of launching a genuine debate about what kind of exceptions should be contemplated in the changed situation post-Amsterdam See, further, Standing Committee of Experts on International Immigration, Refugee and Criminal Law, *Proposal for a European Parliament and Council Regulation Laying Down the General Principles and Limits Governing Citizens' Right of Access to Documents of the European Parliament, Council and Commission and the Explanatory Memorandum* (Utrecht, 1999).

very nature, policy making is likely to involve certain considerations relating to external and internal security and relations with third states where confidentiality of documents may be appropriate. But there should in any event not be an automatic exception with regard to policy making in these fields: the Treaty itself clearly shows that this was not meant to be the case. Rather, an exception should be contemplated which would apply only where the interest of the European Union in not permitting access to certain documents is sufficiently weighty that it would take priority over the interest of the citizen in obtaining access to the documents in question. The reason why the balancing of interests should be expressed in this manner is to underline the fact that the burden of proof placed on the institutions in question is a heavy one and that they have a serious duty to discharge if they invoke it. At the same time, the wording of such an exception would be designed to take into account the fact that there will indeed be circumstances which fully warrant reliance on this exception but this will only exceptionally be the case. It could in any event not be used as a matter of course every time a citizen requests access to documents pertaining to the policy-making fields of foreign and security policy or judicial and police cooperation.

CONCLUSION

Much information is not sought by interested citizens because they are unaware of its existence. The obligation on institutions to make information available to the general public on request at the same time entails, in my view, the obligation to make known the information they have in their possession. Interested citizens must be able to know what public information the institutions possess and where and how it can be found. It is in my view the task of the institutional actors in the formal political process to themselves make this information available and in principle freely available. The role of commercial publishers in this regard must clearly also be considered but here it is a matter more of a supplemental role where such publishers charge commercial rates for information to which some clear added value in terms of information provision is present. But the *raw materials* in terms of the basic information itself must be provided by the institutions themselves. This should in the first place include the establishment of a *public register* where, as a rule, documents that have been received and drawn up by a public authority (including all its preparatory instances) must be registered. This would include documents which the public authority in question estimates initially to be "secret" or "classified" (i.e. not falling within the rules on access to documents but under one of the specific exceptions to the general rule of openness). It could, for example, be put behind special "walls". Only in this way can it be guaranteed that public activities are open to the citizens (and their representatives) in such a way that they can choose the information they wish to obtain, without having to rely on public information services (the information that public authorities choose to give about their work).

The danger of a resulting information "overload" is clearly present. Already today citizens, public interest groups and national parliaments all experience difficulty in sifting the information they do receive and evaluating it to know what is important and when precisely action, at what level, is required. Could any increase in the requirement to provide information not lead to a paradoxical "disempowerment" of citizens by simply swamping them with information which they can impossibly sift in a meaningful fashion? Would this risk not be exacerbated considerably by any active information policy going in the more radical direction of *Lexcalibur?* My view is that it is in precisely this context and with this perspective in mind that a putatively significant role can be carved out by the more specialised issue-oriented non-governmental organisations (NGOs) as a kind of well-informed "early-warning" mechanism helping to stimulate and focus public deliberations on related areas. "Active" citizens per se can also have a pivotal role to play in this context of the more widespread dissemination and filtering of information with the aim of assuring more concrete possibilities for political participation in the deliberative process itself.

It is well known that for many people membership of an NGO provides a vital means through which they can express their sense of citizenship and demonstrate an active concern for fellow citizens and society at large. Civil society in this sense is used as a convenient shorthand term to refer to the organisations of non-profit interest groups which form to assert interests and causes outside state-based and controlled political institutions, which constitute networks of action and knowledge and which can be regarded as constituting in some sense a civic *space*.[57] It embraces, but is not restricted to, NGOs, and some element of "public interest" as opposed to the defence of a purely private (commercial) interest is required.[58] The perspective is that the "civil society sphere" has a potentially significant role to play in widening and expanding the scope of the public debate at the EU level. This is seen as a supplementary role to that of parliaments (the European Parliament and the national parliaments). Once information on decision-making processes is more genuinely accessible, there is arguably a role for the *formalisation* of political participation by citizens, but further consideration of this issue is beyond the scope of the current chapter.

The challenge is to de-mystify and move to the public domain deliberations on variegated issues of policy making of real and fundamental concern to the citizens and resident aliens in the Member States of the European Union. The fate of the Schengen *acquis* and the manner of its incorporation into the EU legal order is a poor precedent. There was no effective parliamentary control possible at any stage due to the technique of diplomatic negotiation and its status as part of the overall "package" of the ToA. By the time the full implications of the wording agreed upon and signed (and even ratified by some Member States)

[57] For further consideration of the historical and philosophical usage of the term "civil society", see CURTIN, *Civil Society and the European Union: Opening Spaces for Deliberative Democracy?*, above at n. 2.

[58] Closer study reveals a terminological jungle; see ibid.

there was nothing to be done by either civil society or parliaments other than to vent their frustration at such arcane practices relating to fundamental areas of concern to individual rights and liberties. With regard to the more general decision-making and the post-Amsterdam rule-making laying down the general rules applicable right across the wide spectrum of EU activity, the trumpet has been clearly sounded by civil society and the battle lines drawn. The idea is that in order to influence policy, public opinion needs to be aroused and channelled: the task of the "citizen association" or "civil society" sector is the repoliticisation of issues which otherwise would be reduced to technical considerations in order to improve the prospects of (bureaucratic) agreement. The classic instrument of "leaking" documents to alert journalists has been used to full effect. For example, the draft of the Commissions draft regulation on access to documents was been placed on the Internet even before the Commissioners could agree upon it. Some Commissioners indeed spent their turn of the century Christmas and Millennium vacations in their respective countries being subjected to some (public) discontent as to the unsatisfactory and minimal content of the draft they would be asked to sign in January 2000. The result? The draft regulation that the Commissioners finally formally adopted on 27 January 2000 was much improved with some of the most objectionable restrictions removed. Such timely input by "civil society" can materialise only if documents one way or another enter the public domain. Once the formal legislative process has been started then the role of the parliaments (the European Parliament and the national parliaments) rightly moves to the fore. But parliaments can also only fulfil their intended constitutional function if they are in possession of the right documents or information at the right time. They should not however be dependent on active "civil society" in order to receive that information but should automatically receive the requisite information from their legislative partners in order effectively to fulfil their pivotal role.

3

Primary Immigration: The Great Myths

ELSPETH GUILD

INTRODUCTION

The European Union has enjoyed a rather tortured relationship with primary economic immigration over the last ten years at least. While on the one hand it has sought to improve labour mobility among the Member States on the grounds that primary migration improves prosperity, it has maintained a discourse against primary economic immigration from outside the Union. This discourse has not necessarily been supported by the actual actions of the Member States as regards the admission of persons for employment[1] or indeed the Union's own actions as revealed in its championing of a new international framework for the movement of workers.[2] It is this dichotomy which I will investigate here.

In its 1997 Action Plan for Free Movement of Workers,[3] the Commission stated:

> "Historically, cross border mobility in the EU has been low. Presently, around 5 million European citizens reside in another Member State. Less than 2 per cent of the

[1] For example, each year from 1991–96 the United Kingdom admitted between 45,000 and 58,000 foreign nationals for work purposes (excluding persons admitted for family reunion and some other work-related categories of admission—in 1998 the figure approached 90,000); over the same period the numbers of persons apply for asylum in the United Kingdom moved from a total of 44,000 in 1991 to 29,640 in 1996. However, from the press reports, one would be led to believe that asylum was the main ground for admission to the United Kingdom (HMSO, *Control of Immigration: Statistics United Kingdom 1996*, Cm 3737 (London 1997)). For more general figures on EU countries but less clarity on the specific question, see SOPEMI, *Trends in International Migration, Annual Report 1996* (OECD, Paris, 1997).

[2] The General Agreement on Trade in Services (GATS) is one of the foundation agreements of the World Trade Agreement. Among other things, it provides an international framework for the movement of natural persons from one member country to another to provide services, which in the terminology of the WTO includes establishment of a commercial presence, a concept not foreign to Art. 43 EC. The European Union and its Member States were among the most vocal supporters of the GATS and to no small extent responsible for its successful conclusion: see J. Jackson, *The World Trading System, Law and Policy of International Economic Relations* (MIT Press, Cambridge, 2nd ed. 1997).

[3] European Commission, *An Action Plan for Free Movement of Workers, Communication from the Commission*, COM(97)586 final (Brussels, 1997).

working age population in the EU consists of people from one Member State working in another. Low mobility is a consequence of a number of factors, including high levels of unemployment, social and cultural barriers, practical obstacles to movement and lack of information on opportunities."

It then goes on to set out the four main strategies it will pursue in order to improve labour mobility in Europe. It states:

"This Action Plan fulfils a commitment in the Action Plan for the Single Market [1985] to present a package of measures to overcome the remaining barriers to the free movement of workers and to improve the prospects for labour mobility in the EU."

When it comes to labour mobility from outside the Union, the position becomes much less positive. In the 1994 Communication on Immigration and Asylum Policies[4] the Commission stated:

"In addressing migration pressures, the Union and its Member States must, of course, honour their international obligations and basic traditions of respect for human rights, fundamental freedoms and social justice. That will mean retaining their traditional openness for refugees, for other persons in need of international protection and for those whose admission is justified for humanitarian reasons. That openness should not, however, deter the Union from seeking to address the underlying causes of migration pressures. In the case of illegal immigration the economic situation in the country of origin is often the major underlying cause. If the economic situation in the country of origin had provided the person concerned with sufficient opportunities, he/she might not even have considered emigrating."[5]

The framework of the Union for primary immigration is to remove any possibility not only that an intra-Member State migrant citizen might be illegal but to promote positively migration as an important element. The purpose is to open European labour markets to all EU workers, thereby contributing to the overall goals of peace and prosperity and complementing the development of the Single Market for goods, services and capital.[6] The other face of primary immigration, that from third countries, is presented as primarily illegal (with the underlying assumption that it should remain legally defined as such), the result of pressures which need to be addressed in such a way as to diminish the movement. A comprehensive approach to migration pressure requires co-ordination of action in the field of foreign policy, trade policy, development co-operation and immigration and asylum policy by the European Union and its Member States.[7] In other words the whole panoply of international relations of

[4] European Commission, *Communication on Immigration and Asylum Policies*, COM(94)23 final (Brussels, 1994).

[5] The parallel between the reasons why people within the Union do not move and why people from outside the Union do move is noteworthy. This indicates either a lack of imagination or a supposition that people within the Union behave fundamentally differently from people outside the Union.

[6] European Commission, *An Action Plan for Free Movement of Workers, Communication from the Commission*, COM(97)586 final (Brussels, 1997).

[7] European Commission, *Communication on Immigration and Asylum Policies*, COM(94)23 final (Brussels 1994).

the Union and Member States should be focussed on reducing migratory pressure from outside the Union.[8]

Part of the extreme segmentation of the EU's policy on primary migration results from the roles of the different national ministries involved in various aspects of policy development. The justice, interior and home affairs ministries have been the lead agencies in the development of extra EU immigration discourses.[9] Their job is to control the population and regulate who is allowed to be present on the territory. This function has become increasingly limited as their power of control has been circumscribed both by the introduction of immigration rights by EC law which the national authorities are obliged to honour,[10] and the gradual extension of the principles of administrative law into the area which limits the discretionary power of the authorities.[11] These processes have coincided with an increasingly shrill rhetoric about the need to control illegal immigration, for compensatory controls at external borders and within states[12] and even the construction of an internal enemy in the form of migrants.[13]

On the other side, the industry, trade and foreign affairs ministries have been responding to the globalisation of the market place by adapting national and Community law to a new regulatory regime for trade in goods and services based on reducing obstacles both within the Union and abroad.[14] The Union has accepted the principle as enunciated by Samuleson that:

> "there is essentially only one argument for free trade or freer trade but it is an exceedingly powerful one, namely: Free trade promotes a mutually profitable division of

[8] S. Hyett considers this issue in respect of the subsidiary issues around the General Agreement on Trade in Services: "It is true that the GATS also deals with other matters, such as the movement of persons to the territory of another member for the purpose of the supply of services. However, these matters are included as ancillary provisions to the supply of services. If one were to hold that on account of ancillary provisions an agreement does not come within the scope of the EC's trade policy powers, quite a few of the agreements concluded by the EC under these powers would rest on a shaky legal basis. The tail should not be allowed to wag the dog" ("The Uruguay Round of GATT: Some General Comments", in N. Emiliou and D. O'Keeffe, *The European Union and World Trade Law After the GATT Uruguay Round* (Wiley & Sons, Chichester, 1996), 91–105).

[9] This was through the creation of the intergovernmental mechanisms, most importantly the former Third Pillar of the European Union, created by the Maastricht Treaty and providing an important venue, not regulated by the rules of the European Community in which the Member States interior, justice and home affairs ministry officials could discuss and agree policy in the fields of immigration and asylum. See M. den Boer, *Taming the Third Pillar, Improving the Management of Justice and Home Affairs Co-operation in the EU* (EIPA, Maastricht, 1998); A. Pauly, *De Schengen à Maastricht: voie royale et courses d'obstacles* (EIPA, Maastricht, 1996).

[10] D. Martin and E. Guild, *Free Movement of Persons in the European Union* (Butterworths, London, 1996).

[11] P. Boeles, *Fair Immigration Proceedings in Europe* (Martinus Nijhoff, The Hague, 1997).

[12] House of Lords Select Committee on the European Communities, *Community Policy on Migration*, 1992 Session, HL 19 (1992–93).

[13] D. Bigo (1999) 24 *Culture & Conflits*.

[14] J. Cox, *The Single Market Rules and the Enforcement Regime after 1992* (Earlsgate, 1993); L. Gormley, "The Community Customs Code", in N. Emiliou and D. O'Keeffe, *The European Union and World Trade Law After the GATT Uruguay Round* (Wiley & Sons, Chichester, 1996), 124–36.

labour, greatly enhances the potential real national product of all nations, and makes possible higher standards of living all over the globe."[15]

Traditional trade obstacles in the forms of discriminatory tariffs and quantitative restrictions have come under concentrated attack. In these areas free trade and *laisser faire* are elided. However, new obstacles to trade in the form of consumer and environmental protection have become increasingly accepted as both necessary and in the general interest of Europe.[16] A third form of obstacle to trade, important to this chapter, remains much more contested: the protection of labour standards.[17] Free trade, however, has consequences far beyond the movement of goods. So long as a market remains primarily national and the movement of goods across borders is the exception to the rule, national borders and national political choices remain essentially co-terminus. The globalisation of the market place, however, has raised questions about the ability of the national state to fulfil one of its traditional functions—control of the economy.[18] Once a policy is adopted which promotes as a norm not just that goods move across borders but that technicians needed to install, repair, etc., need to go with them the territory covered by trade policy and national control diverges in another traditional field of nation state sovereignty—movement of persons across borders. As Hart points out, the global economy is rapidly becoming "denationalised", but governments continue to govern on the basis of national goals and frontiers. Over the past decade, governments have quietly begun to forge a new world order to accommodate the disjunction of a world where political frontiers bear little resemblance to economic activity. They appear to have taken a number of steps "some consciously, some less so to create a post-cold war order centred in the World Trade Organisation". Hart prophetically adds, "Making the new order work effectively will not be easy".[19]

This disjunction between political frontiers and economic activity entailing the movement of persons represents a substantial challenge to the EU's primary immigration policy. Finding the balance is no simple matter. There are three immediate challenges:

(1) the approach of ministries, particularly in the fields of justice and home affairs, to refute the existence of the disjunction in their interest to retain control;

[15] P. Samuelson, *Economics* (McGraw Hill, New York, 1980).

[16] M. Shapiro, "The European Court of Justice", in P. Craig and G. De Burca, *The Evolution of EU Law* (Clarendon, Oxford, 1998); G. Majone, *Regulating Europe* (Routledge, London, 1997).

[17] The opening of what was intended to be the Seattle round of negotiations of the WTO in November 1999 highlighted the controversy over this aspect of international trade. US President Clinton's address at the opening with strong reference to this issue was considered by some to be instrumental in the failure of the round.

[18] Z. Baumann, *Globalization: The Human Consequences* (Columbia University Press, New York, 1998).

[19] M. Hart, "The WTO and the Political Economy of Globalization" (1997) 31(5) *Journal of World Trade* 75.

(2) the approach of labour and social affairs ministries trying to come to terms with the question of transnational labour standards when the objects of those labour standards, persons, are moving;[20] and
(3) the approach of trade and industry ministries at the forefront of the creation of the supranational system of governance to expand their regulatory capacity to encompass the new phenomenon.[21]

The tension among these interests highlights the difficulty which Member States and the European Union have in translating the principle of free trade to the area of services and persons. In effect, two sets of attitudes inform discussion of globalisation: one informs those enthused by its possibilities and the other those who alternatively deny it or bemoan the threat it poses to national values and to various other objectives ranging from social justice to environmental protection. These competing visions strongly colour people's attitudes towards the stresses and strains flowing from the changes in the technology and organisation of production. One vision is grounded in concepts of individual responsibility and is philosophically committed to the ideal of equality of opportunity; the other is grounded in ideas of collective responsibility and is committed to the ideal of equality of results. When it comes to the role of government, for example, the equality of opportunity perspective sees a relatively small role for government involving largely negative prescriptions. Government's principal function is to guarantee and protect the right of individuals to pursue their interests. The equality of results perspective insists on a much larger and more activist role for government, dedicated to the promotion of equal results and the removal of obstacles to their achievement.[22]

In terms of an EU primary immigration policy, this has two important consequences. First an approach to primary immigration informed by the pro-globalisation perspective, i.e. that free trade or freer trade means greater prosperity, requires a diminution in protectionist measures which inhibit the movement of persons for economic activities. Secondly, an anti-globalisation perspective on primary immigration means that the protection of the EU labour market is the way to achieve greater prosperity and therefore the greater the regulation of

[20] European Commission, Non-Paper, *The Trading System and Internationally Recognised Labour Standards* (Brussels, 1996).

[21] "Globalisation affects not only the financial markets, where it is a long-standing reality, but also mass lifestyles, as it impacts on the production and consumption of goods, the progress of technology and the diffusion of information. It has created everywhere the conditions for a universal, single market, in some ways resembling the regional European one. Of course, the social tensions deriving from this fact are enormous, but enormous as they are, they lack any political or institutional context in which they can find mediation and reconciliation, as would betoken an acceptable level of economic democracy. Globalisation, therefore, exposes the existing mechanisms of government, whether these are the institutions of states or those of universal institutions of international economic co-operation, to two kinds of pressure: internal and external". A. Tita, "Globalization: A New Political and Economic Space Requiring Supranational Governance" (1998) 32 *Journal of World Trade* 47.

[22] European Commission, Non-Paper, *The Trading System and Internationally Recognised Labour Standards* (Brussels, 1996).

movement of persons for economic purposes in order to inhibit that movement from outside the defined territory is a benefit. At the moment, it is the unresolved conflict between these two perspectives which creates the most basic incoherence in EU policy on primary migration: on the one hand transborder movement of nationals of the Member States for economic purposes is a benefit to be pursued (i.e. a manifestation of globalisation which is wanted; on the other hand the movement of third country nationals for economic purposes into the Union is unwanted) i.e. a manifestation of globalisation which is unwanted.

This is the context of the policy challenge which the transfer of competence to adopt rules on primary immigration to the European Community has created. I will look at that challenge in the following manner:

(1) examine the scope of the Community's new power in the field;
(2) consider the treatment of primary immigration in Community law and in the TEU's pre-ToA Third Pillar;
(3) analyse the Commission's proposal on primary immigration for third country nationals which was made just as the ToA was signed;
(4) set out the international framework on primary migration looking at the European regional level and international instruments;
(5) conclude with some remarks on resolving the contradictions in the Community's primary immigration policy.

THE NEW COMPETENCE OF THE EUROPEAN COMMUNITY FOR PRIMARY IMMIGRATION

The ToA extended to the European Community a power to adopt measures in relation to primary immigration. By primary immigration I mean here immigration which is unrelated to international protection, which is dealt with by G. Goodwin-Gill in chapter 6, or family unity which is considered by G. Brinkmann in chapter 10, but which is, potentially at least, long term. I will focus on primary immigration as immigration related to economic activity. For this reason I will not deal with students, retired persons or the economically inactive. This somewhat arbitrary exclusion of some categories of primary migration is not random. What is under consideration here is the extension of a Community law power which has already been exercised in respect of the primary migration of nationals of the Member States. The starting point for the Community in this regard was and continues to be that the right to move arises from the intention to exercise an economic activity.[23] Although the Community has extended the scope of the right of primary migration within the Union to

[23] The particularity given to Art. 3 EC (the activities of the Community which include at (c) an internal market characterised by the abolition, as between Member States, of obstacles to the free movement of goods, persons, services and capital) in the original EC Treaty by Arts. 39 to 49 EC (free movement of workers, self-employed and service providers and recipients according the Court's jurisprudence) was exclusively related to economic activity.

include students,[24] pensioners[25] and the economically inactive,[26] this extension is still based on the economic ability of the individual to support him or herself without burdening the social security or assistance scheme of the host Member State. The discussion on whether Article 18 EC, citizenship of the Union, and its interpretation by the ECJ changes this economic foundation of Community migration rights is still open.[27] For the purposes of looking at the extension of the power of the Community to regulate primary immigration from one limited to Community nationals[28] to one in principle unlimited by nationality restrictions, I shall focus on economic primary immigration.

The new power is found in Article 63(3), which states:[29]

> "The Council acting in accordance with the procedure referred to in Article 67, shall, within a period of five years after the entry into force of the ToA,[30] adopt:
>
> . . .
>
> (3) measures on immigration policy within the following areas:
> (a) conditions of entry and residence, and standards on procedures for the issue by Member States of long term visas and residence permits, including those for the purpose of family reunion;"

The power is to adopt measures on immigration policy. The policy in respect of which the measures are to be adopted includes the conditions of entry and residence and the standard on procedures for the issue of long-term visas and residence permits. There is specific reference to family reunion but not other areas. Access and restrictions thereon to economic activities are fundamental conditions of the entry and residence rules which the Community is charged with adopting.

The measures are intended to cover three geographic spaces: consular authorities of Member States in third countries when an individual applies for a long-term visa; the external border of the Member States when the individual comes to cross it (conditions of entry); and the internal territory of each Member State (the conditions of residence). The external control is as regards the standards on procedures for the issue of visas. The personal scope of the measures which may be adopted is not specifically defined. It must include everyone who does not have a stronger right under some other provision of Community law. In other words in the hierarchy of norms, those persons who are able to rely on rights arising elsewhere from the Treaty must be entitled to do so, for instance

[24] Directive 93/96/EEC.

[25] Directive 90/365/EEC.

[26] Directive 90/364/EEC.

[27] See Case C–85/96 *Martinez Sala* [1998] ECR I–2691; and S. O'Leary, "Putting Flesh on the Bones of European Union Citizenship, Martinez Sala" (1999) 40 *EL Rev* 68.

[28] Including a derived right which extends, for instance, to third country national family members or third country national employees.

[29] I will not deal specifically with the position of Ireland, the United Kingdom and Denmark which have negotiated separate protocols to the Treaty which permit them to remain outside the legal scope of the new Title.

[30] 1 May 1999.

Community nationals and their family members of any nationality, or third country nationals protected under specific agreements between their states and the European Community.

Unlike most other provisions in the new Title, Article 63(3)(a) is not subject to a five-year implementation deadline from entry into force of the ToA. Nonetheless, in the Joint Action Plan of the European Commission and Council on how best to implement the provisions of the ToA establishing an area of freedom, security and justice, two institutions most intimately involved with the production and adoption of Community legislation state "in these last two fields, although the ToA does not request action to be accomplished in a five year period, efforts should be made towards an improvement of the situation in due time".[31]

As Community law in its interpretation is teleological it is important first to consider the objective of the power. It is to be found in Title IV EC: "Visas, Asylum, Immigration and Other Policies Related to Free Movement of Persons". Article 61 states that:

> "In order to establish progressively an area of freedom, security and justice, the Council shall adopt:
>
> . . .
>
> (b) other measures in the fields of asylum, immigration and safeguarding the rights of nationals of third countries, in accordance with the provisions of Article 63."

Article 63(3) EC comes within the objective of Article 61(b) part of the measures needed to secure the area of freedom, security and justice. The objective of an area of freedom, security and justice has been considered in some depth by P. Boeles in the introduction of this book. Over the period of negotiating the ToA, the intention that this field should come within the ambit of the area of freedom, security and justice was consistent. In a Presidency Introductory Note,[32] near the beginning of the Intergovernmental Conference (IGC) the following wording was proposed to start the new Title:

> "In order to further develop an area of freedom, security and justice in which free movement of all persons is ensured, the Community shall adopt appropriate provisions as provided in this title within the following areas: the removal of controls at internal border and the crossing of external borders as provided for in Article B; asylum policy, immigration policy and policy regarding nationals of third countries within the Community as provided in Article C; coherent action in relation to the abuse of drugs as provided for in Article D; strengthening co-operation between customs authorities as provided in Article E.[33]

[31] Council Document 13844/98 of 4 December 1998 (OJ 1999 C19).

[32] CONF/3976/96 of 11 November 1996.

[33] The areas included with reference to immigration and asylum were: removal of controls at internal borders; the crossing of external borders; asylum policy; immigration policy; and policy regarding nationals of third countries within the Community.

The actual wording of the provision changed very little during the negotiations. In the Presidency Note of November 1996 it read "harmonisation of conditions of entry and residence, and of procedures for issuing residence permits, including those for the purpose of family reunion".

In order better to understand what at least one of the Community institutions considered to be the framework of the new power at the time of the IGC negotiations, I will look later in this chapter at the Commission's detailed proposal submitted during the period of the negotiations and covering primary immigration. But for the moment, I would like to consider the extent of the power. First, it is an extremely open-ended power, the personal scope of which is limited only by the personal scope of other free movement provisions of Community law. Secondly, its geographic scope is not limited to the territory of the Member States but includes activities undertaken at consular posts abroad. To this extent it acknowledges the transfer in reality of the Community border checks to third countries for all those persons whose countries figure on the Visa Regulation list.[34] Thirdly, its material scope is also defined by exclusion, it covers everything relating to conditions of entry and residence, standards on procedures for the issue of long-term visas and residence permits which are not otherwise covered by Community law. Therefore, in terms of a permissive Title, which creates power to take action but gives little guidance on what action to take, this provision stands out as particularly devoid of indication as to how it should be exercised. The search for guidance on how to exercise the new power must begin where the powers do: at the edge of existing Community law. Therefore, the starting point for this consideration is the situation which existed before the entry into force of the ToA.

PRIMARY IMMIGRATION WITHIN THE UNION BEFORE 1 MAY 1999

I will examine the Community's powers in respect of primary immigration from two perspectives: first the nationality of the individual seeking to exercise a primary immigration right or possibility within the territory of the European Union; secondly whether the individual is seeking to exercise a primary immigration right or possibility between Member States or from outside the Union into the territory.

Within the EC Treaty

1. *A Community law right to primary immigration both within the Union and from outside the Union: citizens of the Union and their third country national family members for economic reasons or where economically self-sufficient*

[34] Regulation (EC) No. 574/99 OJ L 72 of 18 March 1999.

The initial EC Treaty established three types of primary immigration rights which are foundations of the Community: the right of free movement of workers;[35] the right of establishment—that is to say of free movement for the self-employed whether natural or legal persons;[36] and the right of free movement of service providers[37] and recipients of services to go to seek services in another Member State.[38] In respect of the first category, workers, there was substantial discussion about the extent to which the wording of the Treaty could include third country national workers already within the territory of the Member States. The ECJ's decision in *Awoyemi*[39] clarifies the current limit of the concept of "workers" to Community nationals. Under the Treaty provisions, all nationals of the Member States, nationality being a matter of declaration by each of the Member States,[40] are entitled to exercise economic rights in any of the three categories in any other Member State.

The right is individual to each national of a Member State and exercisable in any Member State with the sole exception of the state of his/her nationality in respect of which Community law on free movement of persons does not bite.[41] The direct relationship between the Community and the individual entitles the individual to rely on the right to defeat an interference with it by a Member State unless justified on the basis of public policy, public security or public health, all concepts the interpretation of which is strictly guarded by the ECJ.[42] Therefore the personal scope is clear: a right to economic primary immigration for all Community nationals moving within the Union.

This right is also the basis of a derived right to third country nationals in specific circumstances. For natural persons it extends to a wide circle of third country national family members as defined by Community law.[43] For legal persons it extends at least to a right to send third country national employees already lawfully employed in one Member State to another Member State to carry out services.[44]

35 Article 39 EC.

36 Article 43 EC.

37 Article 49 EC.

38 The extension to service recipients was the result of a clarification by the ECJ of the scope of Art. 49 EC (Joined Cases 286/82 and 26/83 *Luisi & Carbone* [1984] ECR 377).

39 Case C–230/97 [1998] ECR I–6781.

40 Case C–192/99 *Kaur*; a challenge on the question of the compatibility of a citizenship declaration by a Member State with Community law is currently pending before the Court of Justice.

41 The situation is wholly internal to the Member State and therefore outside the scope of Community free movement law: Case 175/78 *Saunders* [1979] ECR 1129 (workers); Case 204/87 *Bekaert* [1988] ECR 2029 (establishment); Case C–41/90 *Hoefner* [1991] ECR I–1979 (services). An exception exists where the individual has exercised a free movement right in another Member State and is returning to his/her home Member State: Case C–370/90 *Singh* [1992] ECR I–4265.

42 Case 30/77 *Bouchereau* [1977] ECR 1999.

43 Article 10 of Regulation (EC) No. 1612/68.

44 Case C–43/93 *Vander Elst* [1994] ECR I–3803. See J. Onslow-Cole, "The Right of Establishment and Provision of Services: Community Employers and Third Country Nationals", in E. Guild (ed), *The Legal and Social Consequences of Free Movement of Persons in the European Union* (The Hague, Kluwer Law International, 1999), 63–73.

Community nationals and their third country national family members are entitled to exercise these rights even where they come from a third country.[45] The Community national does not already need to have moved him or herself to one Member State in order to exercise the free movement right together with family members in another Member State other than that of his/her origin. The same is not true of legal persons. Here they must have already established a base in one Member State. Also unclear is the extent to which their right to provide services creates an entitlement to send personnel engaged outside the territory of the Union to another Member State to carry out service provision. Therefore there is a divide: for natural persons who are Community nationals the right to economic primary immigration applies both as regards movement between Member States and from outside the territory of the Union into any Member State (except that of their nationality). For legal persons who enjoy Community nationality by reason of the place of establishment and the genuine exercise of economic activities there[46] while they have a right to exercise economic primary immigration rights through the deployment of personnel, this may be limited as regards the deployment of third country national personnel from outside the Union into the Union. They have a right, however, to deploy such personnel between Member States.

2. A Community law right to primary immigration both within the Union and from outside the Union: citizens of the countries with agreements with the Community: EEA; CEEC and P&C Agreements

In accordance with agreements settled by the Community with third countries or groups thereof, nationals of those countries may enjoy economic primary immigration rights to varying degrees. For example, nationals of Iceland, Liechtenstein and Norway enjoy primary immigration rights with Community nationals which are coterminous.[47] Nationals of the Central and Eastern European countries (CEECs) also enjoy primary immigration rights by virtue of agreements, but these right are limited to self-employment (and service provision). Between 1991 and 1996 the European Community concluded agreements with ten CEECs, all of which provide a right both to natural and legal persons to move to and between Member States for the purpose of self-employment. The wording of the right mirrors that for Community nationals in Article 43 EC.

[45] This follows from the *Saldanha* judgment (Case C–122/96 [1997] ECR I–5325), where a UK national resident in the United States could claim EC Treaty rights and the Commission's proposals for amendment of Regulation (EC) No. 1612/68.

[46] For limitations of legal persons, see Case 81/87 *Daily Mail* [1988] ECR 5483.

[47] EEA Agreement 1992.

Country	*Date of signature*	*Entry into force*
Bulgaria[48]	03.03.1993	01.02.1995
Czech Republic[49]	04.10.1993	01.02.1995
*Estonia[50]	12.06.1995	01.02.1998
Hungary[51]	16.12.1991	01.02.1994
*Latvia[52]	12.06.1995	01.02.1998
*Lithuania[53]	12.06.1995	01.02.1998
Poland[54]	16.12.1991	01.02.1994
Romania[55]	08.03.1993	01.02.1995
Slovakia[56]	04.10.1993	01.02.1995
Slovenia[57]	10.06.1996	01.03.1999

* For individuals a right of establishment is delayed in these Agreements.

All of these agreements, known as the Europe Agreements, have entered into force. Implementing legislation providing the modalities for the exercise of the right have been adopted in at least three countries to my knowledge (Germany, the Netherlands and the United Kingdom). A court in a fourth (Belgium) has held the right of establishment in the agreements to be directly effective.[58] Although statistics on the take-up rate of CEEC nationals to self-employment in the Member States are not available, anecdotal evidence from lawyers engaged in the field across Europe indicates low numbers. It would appear that this experiment with primary immigration has proved uncontentious even though it is founded on the principle of a right to move for economic purposes given to the alien. Legal persons in successor states of the former Soviet Union through the Partnership and Co-operation (P&C) Agreements settled by their states with the Community enjoy primary immigration rights limited to the sending of key personnel to the Union.[59] These rights are in character the same as the rights of Community nationals in that they apply on the basis of nationality[60] and are similarly worded in order to give a right to the individual (natural or legal). The right may be relied upon in all the Community courts, and appears to apply both

[48] OJ 1994 L358.
[49] OJ 1994 L360.
[50] OJ 1999 L000.
[51] OJ 1993 L347.
[52] OJ 1998 L26.
[53] OJ 1998 L51.
[54] OJ 1993 L348.
[55] OJ 1994 L357.
[56] OJ 1994 L359.
[57] OJ 1999 L51.
[58] E. Guild, "Waltzing towards Accession: the Case of the Central and Eastern European Countries" (1998) *European Business Law Review* 34.
[59] For a fuller consideration of this aspect of the rights of third country nationals in Community law see S. Peers' analysis in ch. 12 below.
[60] I.e. result of an international agreement between their states designed to privilege nationals of the contracting parties.

where the individual is seeking to enter the territory of the Union for the first time and where he/she is seeking to move from one Member State to another in exercise of the primary immigration right.

3. *A Community law right to primary immigration limited to the territory of the Union*[61]

Article 49 EC, second paragraph contains a power to extend the right to provide services throughout the territory of the Member States to third country nationals who have already established themselves in one Member State. The power was introduced by the Single European Act in 1987. The Commission introduced in 1999 a proposal for a directive to give effect to this power.[62] It applies without differentiation on the basis of nationality of the service provider. The requirement is that the service provider is established within the territory of the Union. It is therefore a limited power to extend the primary immigration provision of Community law regarding service providers to third country nationals again limited to primary immigration across internal borders of the Union. In other words, there are three fundamental limitations: first the type of economic activity must be service provision. The defining feature of service provision (as differentiated from establishment) is that the persons providing the service does not have a stable and permanent establishment in the member state, though the service provider is not barred from providing itself with some infrastructure.[63] The duration of the service provision is not the defining feature.[64] Secondly, the person must be established in another Member State which means that there is a stable and permanent establishment there. Thirdly, the right to economic migration is limited to the fifteen Member States (plus the three EEA States). The right has yet to become effective as the Community institutions have yet to adopt the Commission's proposal.

[61] The Council may, acting by a qualified majority on a proposal from the Commission, extend the provisions of the Chapter (on freedom to provide services) to nationals of a third country who provide services and who are established within the Community.

[62] Com(99)3 (Brussels, 1999).

[63] Case C–55/94 *Gebhard* [1995] ECR I–4165.

[64] For a fuller discussion of the difference, see European Commission, *Guide to the Case-law of the European Court of Justice in Articles [49] et seq of the EC Treaty: Freedom of Establishment* (Brussels, 1997); and *European Commission, Guide to the Case-law of the European Court of Justice in Articles [49] et seq of the EC Treaty: Freedom to Provide Services* (Brussels, 1997).

Within the TEU

4. The former Third Pillar policy proposals consisting of: a resolution on limitations on admission of third country nationals to the Member States for employment (20 June 1994);[65] *and a resolution relating to the limitations on the admission of third country nationals to the territory of the Member States for the purpose of pursuing activities as self-employed persons (20 November 1994)*[65a]

Moving away from the European Community (the First Pillar of the European Union) to its former sister Pillar, "Co-operation in the Fields of Justice and Home Affairs",[66] in this intergovernmental forum the Member States reached agreement on two relevant resolutions: the first on limitations on admission of third country nationals to the Member States for employment (20 June 1994); the other on limitations on the admission of third country nationals to the territory of the Member States for the purpose of pursuing activities as self-employed persons (20 November 1994). Both these resolutions I have discussed in some depth elsewhere.[67] For the history of their negotiation, Peers has recently published an excellent analysis.[68] The first, on employment, was designed not to cover third country nationals resident in one Member State and moving to another. It was specifically limited to third country nationals (natural persons) coming to the Member States from outside the territory of the European Union. Of course, in the hierarchy of the European Union, it could not be used as a tool to limit the rights created by Community law for persons exercising primary migration rights.

As regards the form, a resolution was an intergovernmental agreement binding as such and to such an extent only. It was not an act upon which an individual could rely to establish a right. At most an individual could seek to use its provisions as interpretative guidance to national law. Nonetheless, the Member States in the resolution state that they will "endeavour to seek to ensure by 1 January 1996 that national legislation is in conformity" with the principles laid out. No independent assessment has been carried out as to whether or not these endeavours were successful. The general criteria were:

(1) Member States were to refuse entry to their territories of third country nationals for the purpose of employment;
(2) Member States would consider requests for admission to their territories for the purpose of employment only where vacancies in a Member State could

[65] OJC 274 of 19 September 1996.

[65a] OJC 274 of 19 September 1996.

[66] Following the entry into force of the ToA this has now been entitled "Provisions on Police and Judicial Co-operation in Criminal Matters" and its contents have been substantially altered.

[67] E. Guild and J. Niessen, *The Developing Immigration and Asylum Policies of the European Union, Adopted Conventions, Resolutions, Recommendations, Decisions and Conclusions* (Kluwer Law International, 1996), 321–31, 370–77.

[68] S. Peers, "Building Fortress Europe: The Development of EU Migration Law", (1998) 35 *CML Rev* 1235.

not be filled by national and Community manpower or by non-Community manpower lawfully resident on a permanent basis in that Member State;

(3) third country nationals may be admitted on a temporary basis and for a specific duration where (a) an offer is made to a named worker or named employee of a service provider and is of a special nature in view of the requirement of specialist qualifications, (b) an employer offers named workers vacancies where the competent authority considers that the grounds given by the employer are justified. Special let out clauses apply to seasonal workers, trainees, frontier workers and key personnel in intra-corporate transfers.

As regards self-employment, the Member States adopted a resolution on 30 November 1994 with specific reference in the preamble to their new commitments under the World Trade Organisation Agreement (WTO) which is clearly a reference to the new framework of service provision in the General Agreement on Trade in Services (GATS), an integral part of the WTO Agreement. The Member States agreed to "endeavour to seek to ensure by 1 January 1996 that national legislation is in conformity" with the principles they set out in the resolution. No independent research is available on the degree of conformity achieved. The resolution was only to apply to natural persons not covered by Community law, admitted for family reunion, covered by GATS or admitted for employment or studies. The principles were:

(1) associates actively involved and whose presence was necessary in pursuing a company or firm's aims and in its management might be authorised to establish themselves in a Member State;
(2) self-employed persons might be admitted if they establish that their activity will produce benefits (add value through investment, innovation, transfer of technology, job creation);
(3) persons seeking to take employment should be excluded;
(4) authorisation should be obtained before the individual comes to the territory of the Union.

Some suggestions of types of documentation which might be required were provided.

Generally in respect of both resolutions, while they may have played a useful role in settling some fundamental principles among the Member States as regards the creation of categories of primary migration in the areas of employment and self-employment, they lack sufficient precision to be transposed into Community law in implementation of Article 63(3)(a) EC. It would be difficult, for instance, to categorise either of the resolutions as "measures" as they lack substance and clarity. Further, in terms of a coherent policy on economic primary migration, they need considerable development in order to fit into the Community legal regime. Among the striking aspects of the resolutions was that they inserted a discretion into the admission of third country nationals even where a right previously existed. To this extent, in terms of the tension of globalisation referred to above, they may be seen as protectionist measures designed to maximise state authorities' control over the admission and residence of persons for primary immigration purposes to the territory of the Member States.

In conclusion, the position before 1 May 1999 exemplifies the dichotomy of policy on primary immigration set out at the beginning of this chapter. On the one hand there is a high degree of autonomy for primary migration accorded to nationals of the Member States. In the exercise of that autonomy the role of the state authorities is diminished to a very small space. In respect of third country nationals a differentiated position obtained depending on the nationality of the individual. Some third country nationals enjoyed the same degree of flexibility and autonomy from state control over primary migration as Community nationals; others enjoyed autonomy only for specific types of economic activity; others enjoyed autonomous rights based not on their nationality but on their association with a Community national either legal or natural. A final group of persons enjoyed no specific primary immigration rights under Community law and were the object of the full extent of the opposing perception of globalisation expressed by the interior, justice and home affairs ministries within the Third Pillar: that movement of persons for economic purposes has, prima facie, a negative impact on prosperity and should be discouraged. Each exception should be exactly that: an exception based on the specific arguments and grounds put forward by the applicant in the particular case against a norm of exclusion and refusal. Therefore the framework for their treatment is highly discretionary and reserved to the relevant state authorities whose expertise is to assess the public good.

THE GRADIN PROPOSAL

The Commission introduced a proposal for a convention on rules for the admission of third country nationals to the Member States just over a month after the signature of the ToA.[69] While clearly it had been in preparation for a substantial period before that date, its appearance, like that of its sister document (the Joint Action on temporary protection) indicated the intentions of the Commission in its new role as guardian[70] of the competence for third country nationals at that time about to be inserted into the EC Treaty. For this reason it deserves detailed attention from the perspective of contents and the balance between Community, Member State and individual.

The draft convention includes fairly detailed guidelines on admission of migrants for employment, self-employment, study and training. They are drafted in such a way as to provide a framework, but do not exclude national

[69] OJ C337 of 7 November 1997.

[70] The right of initiative is shared with the Member States for the first five years after entry into force of the ToA (1 May 1999), but becomes exclusive to the Commission after that.

discretionary powers which render migration such a risky business. As the Commission stated in the preamble:

> "these common rules on admission, with the exception of those concerning family reunification as well as those applying to persons recognised as long term residents, confer no right of residence and the Member States retain their discretionary powers to take actual decisions as to the admission of nationals of non-member countries."

Authorisation of admission for employment remains discretionary at the Member State's choice. A third country national *may* be granted admission for paid employment where a job vacancy cannot be filled in the short term:

(1) by a citizen of the Union; or
(2) by a third country national who is legally resident in the Member State and already forms part of the regular labour market in that Member State; or
(3) by a third country national who has been recognised as a long-term resident.

In the field of self-employment, the Commission's proposal leaves discretion in the hands of the Member States. The Member States *may* admit a third country national in this category. The requirements to be fulfilled are that the third country national has "sufficient resources to undertake in the relevant Member State, the activity for which they submit their admission application" and "the business generated by the person admitted will have, during the period of validity of the initial residence authorisation, a beneficial effect on the employment in the Member State". Both of these requirements are subjective. The first, as regards resources, is, according to the Explanatory Memorandum, intended "to ensure that [the third country nationals] genuinely intend to engage in the activity for which they seek admission and have the economic capacity to do so".[71] Implementation measures are provided for under this provision.

As regards the "beneficial effect on employment" the Commission is fully aware of the difficult subjective nature of this requirement. According to the Explanatory Memorandum, the second purely economic condition is designed to ensure that the admission of third country nationals brings in value added for the economic capacity of the country where they settle. It should be seen in the most objective light possible. Consequently, if within the two years corresponding to the minimum residence authorisation available, at least one other person is recruited, whether full time or part time, or use is made of service companies (accounting, data-processing or maintenance services), or work is regularly given to subcontractors, there will be practical evidence for assessing value added in terms of employment.[72]

The draft does not make reference to the Community's obligations under the GATS which provides a framework for movement of persons for service

[71] Explanatory Memorandum, XII.
[72] Ibid. XII.

provision. Within the GATS' definition of service provision is included the Community law concept of establishment.[73]

In terms of the tension set out at the beginning of this chapter, the Commission's proposal appears to try to find some middle solution. Discretionary control of primary immigration is left to the Member State authorities. The principle is established that beneficial primary migration should be permitted as a normal rule rather than an exception.

The differentiation between the stated benefit of movement of persons for economic purposes which informs Community law and the discretionary limitation of third country nationals not otherwise privileged by an agreement between their state and the European Community is most noticeable. Indeed, in leaving the field to national discretionary control subject to some general guidelines, the Commission did not build in the guidelines for which it had so fervently argued in the WTO negotiations—standards on liberalisation of the regulation of movement of persons for service provision. One of the achievements of the GATS is a requirement for transparency: rules on admission of service providers must be published and public. This is a critical first step towards limitation of discretionary control. Only once rules which limit absolute discretion have been adopted can they be published. Therefore a transparency requirement forces the adoption of rules. Once rules have been adopted and published, in the EU legal framework, departure from those rules requires justification and reasons if it is to be lawful. The failure to act in accordance with published rules in most, if not all, Member States will give rise to the possibility of a legal challenge against the state. A transparency requirement, however, is not specified in the Commission's proposal.

Nonetheless, in the Commission's own view:

> "Since the Convention constitutes a legal framework of rules on admission, the detailed rules for applying [them] will be laid down by implementing measures. These will deal, in particular, with the compulsory procedure to be followed for filling a vacancy so as to ensure that the practical conditions specified are not satisfied [i.e. there is available labour within the Union]. What this provision imposes, therefore, is not so much an obligation as to the result to be attained by the authorities responsible for examining applications as to the manner in which they proceed."[74]

As a guide for measures regulating primary migration it is not particularly interesting or fresh. It follows with little innovation the approach of the Member States in the Third Pillar, fleshing out some general principles, in this case principles in favour of labour migration which are closer to the reality of what in fact the Member States do in practice.[75] However, unlike Community law regulating primary migration, it gives no right to the individual to some

[73] See further on this, E. Guild and P. Barth, "The Movement of Natural Persons and the GATS: A UK Prespective and European Dilemmas" (1999) 4(3) *European Foreign Affairs Review* 395.

[74] OJ 1997 C337.

[75] K. Groenendijk and R. Hampsink, *Temporary Employment of Migrants in Europe* (Reeks Recht & Samenleving, Nijmegen, 1995).

certainty of his/her position when embarking on a move of country. The control-centred approach of the interior, justice and home affairs ministries in which the state retains discretionary control over the admission or rejection of individuals is untempered by a thread which could give rise to a legitimate expectation on the part of an individual. The need for certainty,[76] which the globalisation process has demanded from international trade law, is missing.

After putting in place a scheme such as the Commission's proposal suggests, is an international enterprise in the service industry, for example a computer software company, going to be in any better position to know whether or not its employees will be admitted to a Member State to carry out a services contract for it? On balance it will not, as the discretionary control which the Member States retain will be more than sufficient to render the Community measure irrelevant to the enterprise; the real power will rest with the national administration. In other words a common immigration policy meeting the needs of the globalised market place is not being serviced by a proposal of this kind. What is being served by this mechanism is the retention at national level of control over primary immigration. It accommodates both those Member States and ministries within Member States which favour globalisation of trade and those opposed to it, by leaving them to fight it out at the national level. So, the power which the Community is given in this scenario is not genuinely exercised. What is happening is that power is being returned to the national level whence it came. There is nothing particularly exciting about this scenario. The status quo is maintained. But something more insidious is also happening in this framework: a legitimation of national discretion. One of the defining features of immigration law in Europe over the past two decades has been the slow and sometimes painful move from a very wide discretion by state authorities to rule of law in the field. Slowly, lawyers and migrants through the courts have forced the publication of secret immigration rules, required authorities to provide reasons for negative decisions and found means to access court procedures to review administrative action. This move to limitation of administrative discretion has been very important in improving the lives of migrant workers. The clarity of enforceable rules gives individuals the tools with which to make life decisions. If an individual is entitled to a permanent residence permit he/she can decide whether to invest the energy needed to improve economic possibilities such as seeking recognition of diplomas or undertaking language training. Without this security the investment is too uncertain. By creating a system where the European level reinvests discretionary power in national authorities, the Community reverses the struggle to insert security and foreseeability into the field of migration through the creation of legal rights for migrants.

[76] This is the need for a stable regulatory environment within which to do business at the international level.

THE INTERNATIONAL FRAMEWORK: REGIONAL TO INTERNATIONAL ARENAS

While the European Union was developing its law and policy on primary migration, important developments were taking place in the same area but in larger fields. Two deserve specific reference: the Council of Europe, which I will deal with first, and the United Nations, both through its treaty-making powers and through its agency, the International Labour Organisation. Finally, The WTO, to which I have made reference above, has also created a new framework for primary immigration.

International Treaties relating to Labour Migration: 1949–99[77]

Measure	*UN/International Labour Organisation (ILO)*	*Council of Europe*
ILO Convention 97 on Migration for Employment	1949; parties[78] (EU): 8[79]	
European Convention on Establishment		1955; parties (EU): 10[80]
European Social Charter (original)		1961; parties (EU): all 15
ILO Convention 117 on Social Policy	1962 parties (EU): 3[81]	
ILO Convention 143 concerning Migrant Workers	1975; parties (EU): 3[82]	
European Convention on the Legal Status of Migrant Workers		1977 parties (EU): 12[83]
UN Convention on the Protection of the Rights of All Migrant Workers: not yet in force; not ratified by a single EU Member State	1990 none	

The interest of Europe to regulate either labour migration or the conditions of residence and employment of migrant workers had its main impetus between 1955 and 1977. The EC Treaty of 1957 was subject to transitional provisions on

[77] Excluding for these purposes the European Communities treaties.

[78] "Parties" here means countries which have signed the relevant instrument.

[79] Belgium, 1953; France, 1954; Germany, 1959; Italy, 1952, the Netherlands, 1952; Portugal, 1978; Spain, 1967; United Kingdom, 1951.

[80] Belgium, 1962; Denmark, 1961; Germany, 1965; Greece, 1974; Ireland, 1966; Italy, 1963; Luxembourg, 1969; the Netherlands, 1969; Sweden, 1971; United Kingdom, 1969.

[81] Italy, 1966; Portugal, 1981; Sweden, 1973.

[82] Italy, 1981; Portugal, 1978; Sweden, 1982.

[83] Belgium, 1978; France, 1982; Germany, 1977; Greece, 1977; Italy, 1983; Luxembourg, 1977; the Netherlands, 1977; Portugal, 1977; Spain, 1977; Sweden, 1977; Turkey 1977.

movement of persons which were lifted in 1968. The Council of Europe instruments adopted during the period enjoyed a reasonable degree of support; ratification was normal. The last instrument to achieve any degree of support was the Council of Europe's Convention on the Legal Status of Migrant Workers, for which the decision which led to its creation had been taken in 1966.[84] From the record of ratification, it appears that European states prefer European multilateral instruments to international ones. This may be not least because the European agreements generally limit the benefit of rights for migrant workers to those who are nationals of other contracting parties.

Council of Europe

Like the European Union, the Council of Europe is a regional organisation currently with 41 member States. Most of the original state parties of the Council of Europe are Member States of the European Union (the most notable exception is Turkey). However, the law-making powers of the Council of Europe are substantially different from those of the European Community. It settles international conventions which only become part of national law of the contracting parties according to their own national rules to that effect.

Three times the Council of Europe has opened for ratification instruments which regulate migrant workers. The first is the Convention on Establishment. This Convention relates mainly to the treatment of nationals of other parties residing on the territory of one party. Article 2 provides that the parties should facilitate to the extent permitted by their economic and social conditions the prolonged or permanent residence of nationals of other parties on their territory. It regulates the grounds of expulsion of persons residing on the territory but in the main it provides for equal treatment in a wide variety of fields, such as working conditions and social rights of nationals of one party resident on the territory of another. The next instrument, the European Social Charter, in so far as it relates to migrants, does not seek to regulate movement of persons, but rather their treatment when moving and on the territory of the parties. Again, the key to the rights is equal treatment with workers nationals of the host state in social and economic spheres. The third instrument is the Migrant Workers Convention which, in contrast with the others, includes detailed provisions on the recruitment of migrant workers as well as their treatment on the territory. The regulation of recruitment is premised on the idea that the state will itself be intrinsically involved in carrying it out. Therefore the role of the state is fundamental to the instrument. This limits its use as a precedent for the European Union in drafting an instrument on primary immigration, even though it is signed by most of the Member States, as the nature of labour migration in 2000

[84] E. Guild, *The European Convention on the Legal Status of Migrant Workers (1977) An Analysis of its Scope and Benefits* (Council of Europe, Strasbourg, 1999).

is dominated by corporate control and movement of employees rather than state recruitment. However, importantly the principle of equal treatment in social and economic rights also arises here.

ILO Conventions

As a UN agency, the ILO was most directly involved in the preparation of instruments to regulate movement of labour. The first Convention on migration for employment was No. 97 of 1949, at a time when substantial labour migration was taking place worldwide. Besides a duty to facilitate the departure, journey and reception of migrants for employment, the Convention places a duty on its Parties to assure equal treatment after entry onto the territory. By Annexes to it, the Convention sets standards for government-sponsored recruitment of labour migration. To this extent its subject matter has been marginalised by the occupation by companies of that territory which previously had been the domain of state bodies.

The second ILO Convention, on migrant workers, No. 143, has enjoyed very little support from European states. Only four have become parties. It focuses on the suppression of clandestine or illegal migration whether for employment or otherwise. To this extent it comes within the measures which do not support the non-interventionist theory of the benefits of free trade. The theory is that illegal migration must be excluded so that state-regulated employment is less vulnerable to competition from those not obeying the rules. In variations this argument is a constant one against the "free traders" whether appearing as a "level playing field" argument or a "fair trade" argument. Thereafter, the Convention creates or reinforces existing obligations to ensure equal treatment for migrant workers.

UN Convention on migrant workers

This Convention has enjoyed no support whatsoever from European states. It applies to both "documented" and "undocumented" migrant workers: the first receive a wider group of rights than the latter but the latter are also guaranteed fundamental human rights irrespective of their irregular status. It formally declares the right of migrant workers to those human rights recognised in other international instruments, such as the right to life, etc. It does not deal specifically with the question of recruitment of migrant labour or the conditions of movement. However, like the other instruments under consideration here the right to equal treatment in economic and social spheres for migrant workers is fundamental.

In general, considering the regional and international instruments on labour migration to this point, a number of shortcomings present themselves if they are to be taken as tools towards the exercise of the Community's primary immigration power. Some do not deal with the issue of first access to the territory but only treatment after arrival. Those which do treat the issue of first access to the territory do so on the assumption of a strong state control over the recruitment of labour. This role has been abandoned by the state in Europe and is the basis of the much repeated claims of the early 1970s in Germany and France that those countries were no longer countries of immigration.[85] In fact, the statements had much more to do with the relinquishing by the state of control over recruitment of foreign labour than over the admission or deployment of foreign labour. The "privatisation" of the recruitment of foreign labour, i.e. the withdrawal of the state leaving the field to private enterprise, was coupled with a change in the role of the state from provider of foreign labour to certifier of the need and acceptability of an enterprise's claim for authorisation for foreign labour. Within this changed environment the international and regional instruments of the 1960s and 1970s are not particularly helpful as regards admission to the territory. Their value remains critically the regulation of treatment of migrant workers after their first admission. Here the long-standing and frequently repeated commitment to equal treatment in working conditions, pay, dismissal and social benefits is of great importance.

WTO: GATS framework.

The General Agreement on Trade and Tariffs (GATT) 1947 made no provision for trade in services. As the development of industrialised economies began to move more heavily into the services related industries, not least through the 1970s, the United States and the European Community began to campaign for the inclusion of services in the new round of negotiations which led to the WTO Agreement. They were successful notwithstanding substantial suspicion on the part of developing countries.[86] The result was the inclusion of the General Agreement on Trade in Services (GATS) as one of the integral parts of the WTO.

GATS includes both services which do not involve the movement of persons, such as television services, and those which do involve persons, such as training services. The role of persons may be critical to service provision as there are many forms of service provision where the "product" is produced while being consumed. Stern and Hoekman identify three critical differences which may exist between goods and services, all of which relate to the insertion of the

[85] See, generally, J. Salt, *Current and Future Trends in International Migration in Europe* (Council of Europe, Strasbourg, 1991).

[86] W. Kennett, "The European Community and the General Agreement on Trade in Services", in N. Emiliou and D. O'Keeffe, *The European Union and World Trade Law After the GATT Uruguay Round* (John Wiley & Sons, Chichester, 1996), 136; N. Mukherjee, "Exporting Labour Services and Market Access Commitments under GATS in the World Trade Organisation" (1996) 30(5) *Journal of World Trade* 21.

individual in services: services cannot be stored but are consumed as produced; production and consumption take place simultaneously; and services are intangible.[87]

The concept of an international market in services creates difficulties in particular as regards protection of consumers. Because of the difficulty of assessing and controlling the quality of services before their delivery, traditionally they have been fields of substantial national regulation. Anyone who has used legal services will be aware of the control problems which manifest in the field. The problem of consumer protection in the provision of cross-border services has caused substantial headaches in Community law. It arises frequently in the area of the provision of professional services. Not least in recognition of the special regulatory problems which relate to professional services, the ECJ has permitted the maintenance of national rules of assessment and registration where they are non-discriminatory, suitable for securing the objective pursued, justified by an imperative requirement in the general interest and do not go beyond what is necessary for the purpose, in other words a substantial and unfortunately relative list of characteristics.[88]

Within the GATS framework, service provision can encompass three types of movement of persons: first where the consumer moves to the service provider. The second type of service provision in GATS is the equivalent of the right of establishment in Community law: the establishment of a commercial presence on the territory of another GATS member country. Thirdly, service provision includes the movement of persons from one country to another to carry out service provision which does not involve the establishment of a commercial presence. As noted above, in Community law, the difference between service provision and establishment has only to do with the stability and permanence of the infrastructure of the provider; it is not defined in terms of the duration of the service provision. The Member States, however, in their Annexes to GATS have, without exception, limited permission for persons to be present on the territory to carry out the final type of service provision, i.e. where there is no commercial presence, to three months.

The GATS system is based on a number of basic principles in respect of which either member countries are entitled to retain exceptions listed in the Annexes or to which they may sign up in accordance with sectional annexes. I shall only consider the most important features here. The first principle is access to the market, i.e. access to the territory. Here the basic principle is that member countries will provide to one another most favoured nation treatment (MFN) (Article II of GATS). For measures included in GATS, the best treatment which one member provides to another country must be extended to all GATS member countries. Exceptions and exemptions to the MFN treatment were permitted, but had to be tabled at the time of adoption and could not be added to

[87] J. Stern and N. Hoekman, "Negotiations on Services" (1987) 10 *The World Economy* 1.

[88] Case C–71/76 *Theffry* [1977] ECR 765; Case C–19/92 *Kraus* [1993] ECR 1663; Case C–106/91 *Ramrath* [1992] ECR I–3351; Case C–55/94 *Gebhard* [1995] ECR I–4165.

subsequently. If one applies this principle to the three types of movement of persons within the GATS framework it means that access by persons seeking to use services, to provide services on a one-off basis or to set up a commercial presence are entitled to the best conditions of entry into the territory of the European Union available to any third country national. The exceptions and exemptions which are listed for the Member States are all based on their national laws. As Jackson describes this, "The obligations require each member to accord to services and service suppliers of any other members treatment no less favourable than that provided for under the terms, limitations and conditions agreed and specified in its schedule". This is a bottom-up approach, so that GATS applies only to the tabled or bound sectors established in the schedules.[89] A parallel for the Community is to be found in the CEEC and P&C Agreements where the schedules provide for sectional treatment as regards market access but on the basis of exclusion rather than inclusion. However, for the purposes of the EC's new power on crossing the external border for economic activities in service provision or receipt, the best treatment afforded to third country nationals on the basis of bilateral agreements between the Community and third countries should be the starting point if it is properly to implement its commitments under GATS.

Once inside the territory, the GATS principle is that service imports are entitled to treatment "no less favourable than that [the country] accords to its own like services and service suppliers".[90] This equal treatment provision is expanded to ensure that it covers both direct and indirect discrimination: formally different treatment is permitted only so long as it does not modify the conditions of competition in favour of the services of service providers of the host country. Exceptions and limitations to this equal treatment provision are permitted and contained in the schedule of specific commitments. Again these are submitted for each Member State individually. The question arises, to what does this equal treatment provision attach when considering natural persons as service providers? Is it limited to the service or does it also cover the means by which the service is provided, the individual? This is critically important to the question of labour standards. If the natural person who is carrying out the service is excluded from the benefit of equal treatment with natural persons carrying out the same service but who are resident on the territory then the form of "social dumping" which was much discussed by the Member States in the context of the adoption of the Directive on posted workers[91] is relevant here. What is at issue in both contexts is the extent to which the competitive advantage of a company in bidding for a contract abroad can be based on the differential in wage-related costs between the treatment of its own workers in one country and either the minimum or sectoral standard in a country where the service provision is to be carried out. This issue is increasingly disputed in the field of

[89] J. Jackson, *The World Trading System* (MIT Press, Cambridge, 2nd ed. 1997), 309.
[90] GATS, Art. XVII.
[91] Directive 96/71/EEC.

movement of goods—in the context of the attempted opening of the Seattle round of WTO negotiations in November 1999, US President Clinton's insistence on fair trade which does not undermine labour standards in the destination country was aimed at this question. In the field of movement of persons, the sensitivity is very great. The spectre of immediate competition by foreign employees engaged under conditions substantially less generous than those in the destination country is unpalatable to many national authorities.

Finally, among the principles which I consider to be of use to the Community in determining a primary immigration policy is the GATS transparency requirement. Regulations must be drawn up and published. I have discussed earlier in this chapter the importance which I place on this requirement as the first step towards the limitation of an unfettered administrative discretion.

The overall responsibility for GATS after the entry into force of the ToA and the adoption of the Council's decision on the Schengen *acquis* which "implements" in Community law the rules on crossing external borders and issue of visas[92] as regards access to the territory will need to be reconsidered in the light of the ECJ's Opinion on WTO[93] that the Community shares competence with the Member States on GATS as regards persons.[94] New Article 133(5) EC gives the Community a general power over services in international negotiations and agreements as part of general commercial policy. Once exercised this would bring movement of persons of any nationality for services within the undisputed exclusive competence of the Community.

CONTRADICTIONS OF A PRIMARY IMMIGRATION POLICY

The fact that the Member States (subject to the opt-outs of Denmark, Ireland and the United Kingdom) have chosen to transfer to the Community a power to regulate primary immigration indicates that there is political will that common rules apply to the movement of persons into the territory for the purpose of economic activity. Where does this will come from? In part it comes from the unravelling of the internal market with the abolition of intra-Member State border controls: one Member State's third country nationals become those of the whole unified territory. Accordingly, the question of how third country nationals get access to the territory for economic purposes needs to be addressed as a confidence-building measure. The Member States must be assured that they are all playing by the same rules. At the same time, the globalisation of the market place has its own interests as regards the treatment of natural persons. In so far

[92] OJ 1999 L176.

[93] *Opinion 1/94* [1994] ECR I–5267.

[94] For an excellent discussion of the meaning of this Opinion, see A. Arnull, "The Scope of the Common Commercial Policy: A Coda on Opinion 1/94", in N. Emiliou and D. O'Keeffe, *The European Union and World Trade Law After the GATT Uruguay Round* (John Wiley & Sons, Chichester, 1996).

as the WTO generally is an effort not just to reduce barriers but also to increase the certainty surrounding international trade and therefore to make it more attractive, it is responding to the market place, which has become increasingly intolerant of national borders. The move to negotiate GATS is also the legislative response at international level to the explosion in international trade in services which began in the 1970s. The Member States, and EU's attempt as appears in the schedules to GATS, and indeed in the ECJ's Opinion on GATS, to work around GATS without actually coming to terms with the movement of persons, is not responding to the actual impetus for GATS where three of the four modes of supply of services are acknowledged to involve the movement of persons.

The negotiation of GATS evidences the willingness of states to start the process of establishing clear rules on the movement of persons for economic purposes internationally. One of the main purposes of this is to limit some of the risk of international trade in services: the risk that the national regulatory authorities will seek to prevent the admission of natural persons critical to the service provision itself and thereby place the employer in breach of a contract. The principles of transparency, foreseeability and enforceability of trade rules, whether in the sphere of goods or services, is difficult to attack. Both business and people deserve the respect which these principles embody. The problem, however, is over control of the content of the rules. The WTO principle is that trade rules are the correct domain of international agreements sensitive to the needs of transnational businesses. Similarly, trade, as a concept, is expandable to cover an ever wide sphere of activities—now in the form of GATS touching on the question of admission of natural persons to states. Against this approach are a number of contrary forces. Just as in the case of the European Community, as the ambit of WTO rules begin to bite on matters which in some countries are seen as internal and in others as fundamental to sovereignty their legitimacy is questioned. Where WTO rules start to touch on sovereignty-related issues which form the basic work of national ministries, such as admission and certification of foreign labour, the national response, given legitimacy in the interests of protecting the domestic labour market, is to insert discretionary control into the process, where possible, or to place administrative hurdles in the way of exercise of the new rules which render them ineffective.[95]

The underlying economic and social question remains: is the limitation and exclusion of natural persons seeking to come to the Union for economic purposes in the Community's interests? The Community's own commitment to free movement of persons for economic purposes as a factor leading to greater prosperity is as valuable an indicator of assessment of benefit as any other. The argument may then be raised that such free movement creates greater prosperity for the whole area by relieving the burden of unemployment in one region.

[95] Guild and Barth, above at n. 73.

If the Community is consistent in its international trade policy, the principle that increased trade is beneficial should also then apply to trade in services, including movement of persons (subject to an equal treatment provision to exclude the possibility of social dumping). If the same arguments apply to goods as to services in the international sphere, as they have been applied within the Community sphere, the Community's primary immigration policy would be informed by a principle of most favoured nation treatment for all WTO countries, equal treatment of service providers whether coming to receive services, for what in Community law terms is called establishment, or as personnel to work in an office which constitutes the EU commercial presence of an enterprise based in a third country, or as independent service providers, accompanied by transparency of rules and regulations.

Two fundamental problems bedevil this approach to a Community primary migration policy. First, while Western European states have moved out of collective foreign labour recruitment they have retained discretionary control over the certification of labour migration. The principles of transparency and accountability which, through the application of international human rights treaties, have placed limits on national discretion in the protection of persons at risk of torture, of family life and of security of residence of long resident migrants has left untouched the field of labour migration proper.

Secondly, the new international regulatory framework of labour migration, GATS, is written from the perspective of rights of employers. It is not about workers and does not touch upon their well-being. Without a social rights foundation, the new international framework of labour migration depends on pressure from the corporate world for its implementation. What may be a satisfactory level of predictability for the large corporate sector as regards labour migration is not necessarily acceptable for the individual migrant. Additionally, the tendency is for administrations to apply discretion more favourably in respect of large multinational companies, which are able to exert substantial pressure to secure their choices on movement of personnel internationally, unhampered by adverse administrative decisions, whereas medium to small enterprises lack the bargaining power. This makes the non-discrimination rule of the new framework vital.

The perception of the new framework as designed to facilitate multinational enterprises to the disregard of individual migrants and small employers undermines to a very important extent the legitimacy of the international process. Its positive aspects of transparency, predictability, equality and enforceability are the first victims at national level of contested legitimacy at international level.

When the European Community comes to adopt its measures on primary immigration, a number of lessons could be learned from this history:

(1) The Member States and the Community are already committed through GATS to a liberal regime on labour migration based on the principle of corporate recruitment and deployment of personnel subject to state certification.

(2) The benefit addressed in GATS for economic labour migration is in providing clear rules which are enforceable and mean that states' employers and workers have rights and duties which allow the actions to assess the economic benefits and drawbacks of migration before and when making the move. These choices are not to be rendered meaningless by the arbitrary exercise of state discretion. Community rules in this field urgently need to give life to these principles.

(3) The fundamental shortcoming of the GATS international framework is its silence on the social and economic rights of the individual migrants. This void is already partially filled in Community law through the equal treatment provisions for migrant workers which appear in agreements between the European Community and third countries, notably Turkey, the Maghreb (Algeria, Tunisia and Morocco), the ACP countries (69 states in Africa, the Caribbean and Pacific with which the European Community has an agreement) and the Central and Eastern European Countries. More importantly, however, all the Member States are committed to equal treatment and social rights for workers whether or not migrants in the Council of Europe framework of the European Social Charter, and the majority of Member States are also bound by the more detailed provisions on migrants contained in the European Convention on Establishment and the European Convention on the Legal Status of Migrant Workers (even though those two Conventions are limited by the principle of reciprocity). Eight of the Member States are also committed to the equality provisions of the ILO Convention 97 on migration for employment.

(4) By implementing equal treatment rights in pay and working conditions within the context of a liberal primary immigration law, the Community will also protect both its own workers from the risk of a diminution in labour standards as a result of an influx of workers whose employers are not required to comply with the Community norms, and migrant workers from exploitation.

(5) Where discrimination on the basis of any nationality in pay and working conditions is unlawful in Community law,[96] the issue of labour standards and their enforcement can properly be divorced from the issue of labour migration.

(6) As regards primary immigration for self-employment (establishment) the Community has already experimented with the extension of such a right to CEEC nationals. In the five years since the first right came into force (for Polish nationals) there has been little public concern about "flooding" the self-employed sector with third country nationals. The experiment seems to show that granting primary immigration rights even to nationals of countries whence there is a perceived pressure to emigrate, such as Romania and Bulgaria, does not result in massive movement of persons.

[96] The power to adopt such legislation is found in Article 138 EC.

The fear of insecurity manifests itself in many ways. When it addresses itself against aliens one form is as an expression of anxiety about jobs, pay and working conditions, e.g. "they are taking our jobs, and unfairly competing for work by accepting lower wages". The experience of Europe in labour migration does not bear out these fears. Notwithstanding the anti-immigrant rhetoric to be heard in many Member States, labour migration is continuing and increasing in much of Europe; the Member States have expressed strong support for a new framework to deregulate labour migration and the Member States have all ratified ten agreements with CEEC states giving a right of primary immigration to all their nationals. The reality and the discourse on labour migration have become detached: the reality is a highly active and expanding legal framework for labour migration; the discourse is a focus of insecurity on economic migrants. Such a division between reality and discourse is not helpful to rational policy development. A firmer commitment by Europe's policy makers to providing leadership in explaining the reality is urgently needed.

4

The Dublin Convention and Rights of Asylum Seekers in the European Union

NICHOLAS BLAKE

INTRODUCTION

If the road to hell is paved with good intentions, then the highway to Community harmonisation is littered with the debris of intergovernmental agreements. It is an unpromising start that most of the new architecture of the Community competence in matters of asylum and immigration is to be composed of the builders' rubble of the Third Pillar.

The basic problem with the Dublin Convention of 1990[1] (hereafter the DC) is that it does not really work. Since its coming into force in September 1997 only a few states have been able to use it successfully to return asylum seekers to the first country of arrival within the European Union. Of the 87,772 asylum requests made in the United Kingdom between 1 September 1997 and 30 June 1999, only 4,856 or (5.5%) resulted in requests for transfer; Greece sought transfer in 0.7% of claims made, whilst the Scandinavian countries varied between 13% (Finland) and 29.3% (Denmark). The average success rate of transfer requests has risen from 35% to 55%, while absolute numbers of transfer requests have declined.[2] If it did work as the signatory governments intended, it would probably impose a disproportionate burden on many receiving states at the periphery of the European Union. In the meantime it is certainly inefficient by causing delays in the processing of asylum claims, contradicts the principle of family reunion and is generally ineffective in seeking a just and equitable distribution of such claims. On top of these many claims to a well-deserved redundancy, is the simple fact that it is inadequate as a Community measure. At the end of the process, the successful asylum seeker does not get access to the

[1] Dublin Convention Determining the State Responsible for Examining Applications for Asylum Lodged in One of the Member States of the European Communities of June 1990.

[2] Statistics provided by Matti Heinonen, Senior Adviser to the Finnish Directorate of Immigration, at International Organisation for Migration (IOM) Seminar on the Dublin Convention held in Tallinn Estonia, 26–27 January 2000. The efficiency of the Danish statistics (80% of their requests are successful) is apparently due to a separate border agreement with Germany whereby asylum seekers found within the vicinity of the border with Denmark are returned to Germany automatically for that country to determine the Member State responsible.

European Union but only the Member State to which the application has been referred. One might ask, why is the Dublin Convention a Union-promoted measure if it has no Union-wide consequences; why elaborate inter-state mechanisms if no inter-state status is derived at the end of it? Recognised refugees are supposed to stay in the host state to which they have been arbitrarily assigned until they acquire citizenship of such state according to very unharmonised national rules. Only then, after between six and twenty years, will they be able to move to the country of their intended destination.

In reality, if an Europe free of internal frontiers is ever to be achieved, it is unlikely that effective measures can ever be taken to prevent migration of third country nationals lawfully within the European Union. In the related area of immigration the European Commission has recently suggested in its draft instrument on family reunion for third country nationals in the European Union,[3] that obsession with zero migration, and a refusal to accept as integrated into the Union those who have stayed for many years in the territory of the Member States, is unrealistic and impractical. In the field of asylum especially, it is surely better to regulate the necessary and the inevitable and achieve some fair balance between competing interests, than take unilateral action at state level, without adequate democratic or judicial supervision and inadequate regard to international law principles.

This chapter attempts to examine the principles behind the DC and the compatibility of those principles with international refugee and humanitarian law. It examines the working of the Convention, and highlights what this author believes to be its inadequacies. It suffers from two limitations. First, from the perspective of a UK practitioner I do not attempt to evaluate the operation of the DC in the Schengen system. Not merely has the United Kingdom not put its tentative toe into the Schengen experiment of a frontier free Europe, and continues to opt out of these provisions of the ToA, its domestic law does not afford any significant legal status to international agreements that have not been brought into domestic law by legislation.[4] The DC has not been enacted into English statute law. The seven-year gestation from signature in 1990 to coming into force in September 1997, made no formal difference to the law applied in our courts. Even today it is not a document on which an individual can rely in challenging a decision by the Home Office. This may change if and when it becomes a measure adopted under Article 63 EC. Even then, it is not clear that the instrument as presently drafted gives any rights to an individual. If another Member State agrees to accept responsibility for a claim outside the terms of the DC it is uncertain whether an individual can challenge the legality of the

[3] 1999/0258, CNS 1 December 199, COM (1999) 638, final, Explanatory Memorandum, para. 1.3.

[4] See *J.R. Rayner* v. *Department of Trade and Industry* [1990] 2 AC 418 (the *Tin Council* case) for the exposition of the dualist theory of the common law. For its more debatable application to human rights cases, see R. v. *Home Secretary, ex parte Brind* [1991] 1 AC 696.

decision if the minimal rights of non-refoulement are respected.[5] The fact that the instrument has not been adopted as part of English law or the immigration rules does not, however, mean that it has been irrelevant to the development of public law on removals to supposedly safe third countries. The DC principle of safe third country has for long formed the basis of Home Office policy. Its principles are reflected in statutory restrictions on asylum appeals in certain third country cases[6] to deter asylum seekers from travelling on. The policy of the DC is frequently relied on by the courts in rejecting challenges to Home Office decisions before them.

The second limitation of this chapter is that it focuses on the impact of the DC on the individual asylum seeker and his or her family. I confess that I am an asylum lawyer and not a social scientist. A full evaluation of its utility might require an army of statisticians to examine the Home Office files to determine many relevant questions. Amongst these would be: how many asylum claims could have raised DC issues; how many actually did; how many successful transfers of claims were made; how many ineffective attempts were made; what was the cost to public funds of detaining and supporting the asylum seekers during attempted or actual transfers as compared to processing the claim in the United Kingdom; who bore the cost of removals and what was the fate of the claims sent elsewhere for determination? I do not have this information[7] and I can develop no more than a working hypothesis developed from conversations with immigration officials and statutory agencies that giving effect to third country removals to other EU states since 1997 has been a hazardous and expensive process. In cases where there is no passport endorsed with a visa or residence permit, it appears that the DC has not facilitated or greatly contributed to the successful transfer of claims.

Despite these limitations, an account based essentially on the UK experience does have the advantage that there has been considerable litigation on third country removals to other EU countries that have teased out some of the difficulties in approaching harmonisation piecemeal and without proper regard for and judicially enforced protection of human rights. In the United Kingdom an asylum seeker whose claim is rejected is normally removed subject to a statutory appeal to an immigration adjudicator or judicial review to the High Court. Rejections of asylum tend to be taken seriously in the light of their foreseeable consequences. If a person cannot be expelled then he or she should be given

[5] European Communities Act 1972, s. 2 refers to enforceable Community law rights.

[6] The right of appeal before removal to a special adjudicator afforded under s. 8 of the Asylum and Immigration Appeals Act 1993 was removed by the Immigration and Asylum Act 1996, and the Immigration and Asylum Act 1999 seeks to remove a challenge to the safety of another EU country by way of judicial review by providing a conclusive definition of "safe" country.

[7] Since this chapter was first drafted, some useful statistical information has been made available to me at the Tallinn Seminar (see above at n. 2) that will be published in full in due course. I am grateful to the participants at that seminar, in particular Ingvar Idestrom, principal officer of the Dublin/Schengen Office of the Swedish Immigration Board, and Matti Heinonen, for giving a different perspective on the strengths and weakness of the Convention in its twenty-one-month working life to date.

status of some sort. Perhaps some of the harsher tests for acquiring protection applied elsewhere in the European Union are in part based on the belief that no return to the country of origin will ever be effective. Administrative orders to leave the territory are frequently not enforced. Such indifference to the asylum process diminishes its function and generates cynicism in the general population. In the United Kingdom, rejections of asylum tend to lead to expulsion unless there are insuperable practical difficulties. Prolonged limbo status is discouraged. Where rejection leads to expulsion, then the limits of the possibility of rejection are to be examined in the light of the foreseeable consequences of expulsion both under the Geneva Convention on the status of refugees (GCR) and the European Convention on Human Rights (ECHR).

Where matters of asylum are concerned, effective access to the courts has been and will remain of central importance in developing a body of principled jurisprudence. In the United Kingdom there has been an active community of immigration law practitioners ranging from the state-funded bodies, such as the Refugee Legal Centre, that specialise in advocacy before special immigration adjudicators, through to the private profession responsible for the conduct of litigation in the High Court which has largely been funded on legal aid. This has resulted in a body of case-law as to when it is lawful to remove a claimant to another EU country. This case-law has in various ways engaged with the question at the heart of the criticisms of EU policy made by the UNHCR, academic commentators and the non-governmental organisations concerned with the protection of the interests of the asylum seeker. The core problem is how can the European Union adopt measures for the harmonisation of asylum claims without spelling out who deserves protection, and how can it spell out who deserves protection without altering the meaning of an international treaty such as the GCR? Even the role envisaged for the ECJ, as the apex court in difficult questions of common asylum measures, may be inconsistent with the reference in the GCR itself[8] to the International Court of Justice as being the appropriate forum for the resolution of international disputes. However, in the future it will be the international bodies: the European Court of Human Rights (ECtHR) at Strasbourg and perhaps eventually the ECJ, that will have to grapple with the problems of an effective application of the protection principle. Recent developments in the UK are likely severely to restrict the possibility of legal challenges to removals under the DC.[9]

THE SAFE THIRD COUNTRY CONCEPT AND THE REFUGEE CONVENTION

The DC operates on the basis of the international propriety of the principle of first country of asylum that a return to a safe third country absolves the returning state from examining an asylum claim. This concept, however, is the source

[8] GCR, Art. 35.
[9] Immigration and Asylum Act 1999, s. 11.

of conflict between the interests of the asylum seeker and those of the receiving states. Historically it might have been difficult to talk about a right of an individual to seek asylum, although state practice might well have been generous enough to assume that there was.[10] But history gives way to principle in the modern era. Article 14 of the Universal Declaration on Human Rights (UDHR) recognised the right of everyone to *seek* asylum from persecution. Although this text is pointedly silent on the obligation of states to *grant* asylum, and leaves considerable discretion to be afforded to states as to how and why to grant asylum, it remains unlikely that in 1947 the international community contemplated state parties actively promoting legislation, such as carriers sanctions, visa controls and subordinate agreements, to *frustrate* the seeking of asylum in a particular country. A series of decisions in the common law countries has stressed the reference to the UDHR in the preamble to the GCR[11] when interpreting the meaning of refugee. While the UDHR may not be "hard" international law enforceable in the domestic courts, it is an aid to the interpretation of the policy and purpose of the GCR that is itself a necessary and admissible aid to construction and should surely form an international *principle* to which the state parties promoting the UDHR should respect and take into account when developing policies and practices that give rise to a regional human rights order in Europe.

A person may direct an asylum claim to a particular country for a number of reasons: he or she may have family, friends or a supportive community there, there may be linguistic or historical connections between the place of refuge and the country of origin, or an agent may have selected the end destination for ease of access or known sympathy in that country to the kind of problem faced by the asylum seeker. For receiving states anxious to reduce the flow of asylum seekers, the so-called first country of asylum principle is a statement that any territory through which the asylum seeker has passed can be considered the appropriate one if there was or is an opportunity of making a claim there.

The first country principle is not indicated in the text of Article 1(2) of the GCR defining refugees. Article 31 contemplates that asylum seekers may come either directly or indirectly to a place of refuge without thereby ceasing to be refugees. In the former case, prosecution for irregular entry is prohibited. The UNHCR has argued that "directly" is to be given a broad meaning. An asylum seeker only failed to proceed directly from the place of persecution where she or he had acquired a residence permit or made some other prolonged stay in a country where an effective asylum claim could have been made.[12] Certainly the

[10] See *Re Castioni* [1891] 1 QB 149; *Schtraks* v. *Government of Israel* [1964] AC 556; *Cheng* v. *Governor of Pentonville Prison* [1973] AC 931.

[11] See *R.* v. *IAT, ex parte Islam* [1999] 2 AC 629; following *A* v. *MIEA* [1998] INLR 1 (High Court of Australia); *Ward* v. *A.-G. Canada* [1997] INLR 42 (Supreme Court of Canada).

[12] *R.* v. *Crown Prosecution Service and others, ex parte Adimi* [1999] INLR 490. Those who assist asylum seekers to make a claim are still liable to severe sentences however (*R.* v. *Eyck* (2000) *The Times* 8 February 2000), unless they can advance a defence of necessity. See S. Harrison and F. Webber, in *Legal Action*, January 2000, for a discussion of this case.

mere use of a transit lounge in foreign airports, or passage through foreign borders concealed in a container, is irrelevant to a fair and effective opportunity to claim asylum. The broad meaning has recently been endorsed by the High Court in London granting declarations that decisions to prosecute asylum seekers who had entered the United Kingdom on forged documents was inconsistent with Article 31[13] notwithstanding that they had entered the United Kingdom via third countries, and had not claimed asylum in the transit lounge of the UK airport but had originally intended to travel on elsewhere.

It is well known that states devote considerable resources to ensuring that asylum seekers never reach their territory: criminal intelligence on the interception of false documentation and illegal entry routes and the prosecution of agents prevent departures from places of risk as much as arrivals in places of safety. Left to their own practices, states seek to move from the assertion that return to a country other than the country of origin is not a violation of Article 33 of the GCR, to suggest that self-selection of the appropriate place of asylum is an indicator that the international right is not being relied on at all, but rather an abusive attempt at economic migration. Such an approach tends to define refugees by reference to criteria other than those set out in Article 1. This is clearly a wrong approach.[14]

A person who has protection in another country or a valid residence permit or a valid visa issued that guarantees entry into that country might well be said to have already made an effective choice of place of asylum and there would accordingly be no obligation on another state to examine an asylum claim lodged there in the absence of exceptional factors relating to separation of families. There is in principle no problem with Article 5 of the DC requiring EU states which issued visas or residence permits to take over the examination of the asylum claim. A narrow view of the applicability of the safe third country concept was reflected in the recommendation of the Executive Committee of the UN High Commissioner's programme[15] that an asylum claim need not be considered if a person already had a substantial connection with another country. An old example of a legitimate use of the third country principle was the case of *Miller*[16] where the Court of Appeal concluded that the Home Office was enti-

[13] R. v. *Crown Prosecution Service and others, ex parte Adimi* [1999] INLR 490.

[14] See *Adan* v. *Secretary of State for the Home Department* [1999] AC 293; following on this point the Court of Appeal at [1997] 1 WLR 1107.

[15] Conclusions on the international protection of refugees adopted by the Executive Committee of the High Commissioners programme (1980). Conclusion No. 15(h) states: "A(3) the intentions of the asylum seeker as regards the country in which he wishes to seek asylum should as far as possible be taken into account; (4) Regard should be had to the concept that asylum should not be refused solely on the ground that it could be sought from another State. Where however it appears that a person before requesting asylum already has a connection or close links with another State, he may if it appears fair and reasonable be called upon first to request asylum from that State".

[16] *Miller* v. *Secretary of State for the Home Department* [1988] Imm AR 358, CA. The Executive Committee guidance was considered by the High Court in the case of *R* v. *Secretary of State for the Home Department, ex parte Yassine* [1990] Imm AR 354, where it was held that Chinese asylum seekers who held Venezuelan visas obtained under false pretences could not be returned to that country under the terms of the Immigration Act 1971.

tled to refer a South African asylum seeker of Jewish origin to the state of Israel where he had previously studied and where the law of return would afford him a right to sanctuary. Admittedly, where such a connection existed, the alternative country did not have to guarantee grant of status but admission to the procedures for a fair consideration of the claim to international protection.[17] Nevertheless the broad shape of UK policy before 1990 was based on the existence of an alternative *appropriate* country with which appropriate links already existed. Until 1983, many EU countries might well have been able to refer asylum seekers from the British Commonwealth to the United Kingdom on the basis that in national law these were British nationals of some sort.[18] Long-standing UK practice recognised that family ties and language links might form the basis of an appropriate connection so that travel documents could exceptionally be issued to enable the applicant to claim asylum in the United Kingdom.[19] Past residence in another safe state in the region of origin could well form a basis to make the country of residence an alternative appropriate country of asylum. Thus the draft Action Plan for Afghanistan prepared by the High Level Group of the Member States[20] was based on the proposition that many Afghans arriving in the West had been previously resident in Pakistan and Iran for many years where they had found protection.

The principle behind Articles 6 and 7 of the DC (first crossing of the external frontiers of the European Union) and the broad idea of safe third country under Article 3(5) is not, however, based on the concept of an actual prior appropriate connection; it is based on a contracting state's view that another country *ought* to be the appropriate country if the asylum seeker has passed through or alternatively has been afforded travel facilities by another state enabling the circle of visa sanctions to be broken. With the sharp increase of asylum claims in the 1980s states were examining claims with a view to identifying the route of flight taken rather than the reasons for seeking protection. Returns to supposedly safe third countries (usually the first country reached after flight) were difficult to challenge in the absence of positive evidence that the country concerned practised onward *refoulement* without proper examination of the merits of an asylum claim. In the United Kingdom, a prior readmission agreement with the country concerned was not a formal necessity if the Home Office had reason to believe that the individual would be accepted there.[21] Border guards and the asylum authorities of other countries were not always happy to receive asylum claims just because British domestic immigration law permitted such removals even to countries where the applicant had only changed planes whilst in transit. Asylum seekers thereby became pawns in an international game of shifting

[17] *Alsawaf* v. *Secretary of State for the Home Department* [1988] Imm AR 410, 419–20.

[18] Section 1 of the British Nationality Act 1948 described such persons as British subjects. They still have the right to vote, serve on juries and take Crown employment.

[19] See Home Office Evidence to Select Committee on Race Relations and Immigration, HC 72-iv (1984–85).

[20] *Migration News Sheet*, March 1999; ibid., August 1999, 5.

[21] Immigration Act 1971, Sch. 2, para. 8; see also *ex parte Yasssine*, above at n. 16.

responsibility: either claimants were shuttlecocked on a sequence of journeys between two countries both unwilling to take responsibility, or a chain journey when they were returned down the line reversing the sequence of flight and travelling perilously closer to the country of feared persecution.[22]

In its decision in the case of *Musisi*[23] the House of Lords concluded that, where the right to life was at stake, a high degree of scrutiny of administrative decisions was called for to ensure that the decision was "in no way flawed". Where it was proposed to send an Ugandan asylum seeker back to the supposedly safe country of Kenya, the Home Office decision did not survive that degree of scrutiny when evidence disclosed that refoulement[24] to Uganda had taken place. This decision had two consequences for the development of UK law on removals to safe third countries. First, it confirmed that the prohibition on refoulement under Article 33(1) encompassed indirect as well as direct return: the words prohibiting return *by any means whatsoever* meant what they said. Secondly, detailed examination of Home Office expulsion decisions was called for by the High Court in judicial review both in cases of rejection of claims and in cases of removal to third countries.[25] This decision has formed the basis of most subsequent legal challenges to third country removals in the United Kingdom. Where a right of appeal existed an immigration adjudicator could independently consider whether there was a risk of onward return for a Convention reason.[26] Where no such right of appeal existed the legality of the decision could be attacked on legal grounds only by judicial review, usually on the basis that the decision was insufficiently motivated in considering the evidence of the failures of the asylum procedure in the proposed safe third country.

A reminder of the importance of speedy access to legal advice, and the assertion of the right of the courts to be able to grant suspensive relief in third country cases against the protestations of central government, came in another leading judgment in the United Kingdom. In *M* v. *Home Office*[27] a Zairean asylum seeker was to be returned to Nigeria on safe third country grounds. A late night application for judicial review and a request for a stay (suspensive) order was made on the grounds that Nigeria might be unsafe for such a claimant. The judge ordered a stay on removal. This order was never communicated in time or sufficiently clearly to the border guards. M was placed on a plane to France with

22 A picture portrayed in the Amnesty International Report, *Passing the Buck* (July 1993).

23 [1987] AC 514.

24 Return to a state where the individual has a well-founded fear of persecution on the grounds of race, religion, nationality, political opinion or membership of a social group.

25 The "anxious scrutiny" standards of asylum decisions where there has been no independent right of appeal are thus materially different from ordinary principles of review of administrative discretion. The Court of Appeal has recently declared itself satisfied that its enhanced standards comply with the requirements of Art. 13 of the ECHR with respect to Art. 3 claims: *R.* v. *Secretary of State for the Home Department, ex parte Turgut* (unreported) 28 January 2000.

26 Asylum and Immigration Appeal Act 1993, s. 8. From 2 October 2000 adjudicators will also be able to examine directly the compatibility of removal with Art. 3 of the ECHR: Immigration and Asylum Act 1999, s. 63.

27 [1994] 1 AC 377.

a view to a return to Nigeria. This indirect return became known to the lawyers who applied for a further order against the Home Secretary to stop the journey and return the asylum seeker to the United Kingdom. The Home Secretary argued that the court had no power to do this and took no measures. He was eventually found guilty of contempt of court and fined. The wretched asylum seeker however arrived in Nigeria and was duly returned without more to Zaire where he has not been heard of since.

By 1990 the courts of the United Kingdom had articulated a concept of effective protection that required anxious scrutiny of debatable decisions to expel an asylum seeker. The principle applied to decisions to expel either to the country of origin after prior determination of the claim or to a supposedly safe third country on the basis of admissibility and fair determination there. Such third country cases could be challenged on the basis that there was a risk of refoulement because there was no ratification of the GCR, or no ratification without territorial restriction, or no equivalent system of protection in national law or practice. In addition, many countries that purported to provide protection in theory could in practice be shown to have no system for receiving applications on arrival at the frontiers.[28] Evidence of mass expulsions to places of danger or individual expulsion where an asylum claim is not admitted to undermine the bland assertion that a country is safe because it declared itself to be so. Evidence of direct refoulement of asylum seekers is difficult to obtain. Those who are ill-treated on return may well disappear without notification to the international community. More frequently there may be evidence that border guards would not accept returned asylum seekers back into the territory. Both Council of Europe and EU guidelines advised that substantive asylum decisions be taken by an expert authority centrally[29] with opportunity for access to legal advisers, the UNHCR and effective procedures. Failures to adhere to such standards in the determination of such claims threw doubt on the safety of return.[30] If the evidence supported the conclusion that the asylum seeker would not be admitted to a third country properly or at all, then the consequences of expulsion would either be a swift return to the sending country, or an onward return to a fourth or fifth country where similar difficulties might occur. Either alternative would give rise to the "refugee in orbit" phenomenon, and even where there was no clear evidence of persecution it would be arguably inhuman to continue to apply measures of expulsion that were known to be ineffective and had such

[28] R. v. *Secretary of State for the Home Department, ex parte Mehari* [1994] QB 474 where orders to return an asylum seeker to Italy were quashed. See also R. v. *Secretary of State for the Home Department, ex parte Canbolat* [1997] 1 WLR 1569.

[29] Recommendation R (94) 5 of Committee of Ministers of the Council of Europe. See also Council Resolution on minimum guarantees for asylum procedures: 5585/95, adopted 20 June 1995 (published in E. Guild, *The Developing Immigration and Asylum Policies of the European Union* (Kluwer Law International, The Hague, 1996).

[30] See R. v. *Secretary of State for the Home Department and Special Adjudicators, ex parte Stefan, Ionel and Chiper* [1995] Imm AR 409; *Martinhas* v. *Secretary of State for the Home Department* [1995] Imm AR 190.

damaging consequences for the security of the asylum seeker. A cycle of rejection within or outwith the European Union increases the risk of eventual refoulement to persecution. This could occur directly by border guards of the third country who concluded either that "their" country had no responsibility for the claim or that a rejected asylum seeker for any reason must be an abusive or manifestly ill-founded claimant, or indirectly by the airline burdened with the costs of detaining and removing the unwanted claimant.[31]

THE GENESIS OF THE DUBLIN CONVENTION

According to the Preamble to the DC it was the experience of ineffective removal to asylum seekers to third countries, and the recognition of the dangers and inhumanity of protracted and uncertain disputes between states that led the states of the European Communities to seek agreement on the basis by which states should readmit asylum seekers. It suggests that it was inspired by the humanitarian purpose of precluding chain returns of claimants:

> "Aware of the need . . . to take measures to avoid any situations arising, with the result that applicants for asylum are left in doubt for too long as regards the likely outcome of their applications and concerned to provide all applicants for asylum with a guarantee that their applications will be examined by one of the Member States and to ensure that applicants for asylum are not referred successively from one Member State to another without any of these States acknowledging itself to be competent to examine the application for asylum."

In pursuit of this objective, Article 3(1) provided that Member States "undertake to examine the application of any alien who applies at the border or in the territory to any one of them for asylum". So far so good. Past assumptions about what border guards ought to do were to be replaced with a solemn undertaking to examine applications. UNHCR and others welcomed the founding assumption of an effective right to a determination as providing certainty for asylum seekers. However, the Convention also had a more pragmatic purpose in deterring asylum seekers from choosing the place of intended refuge and making the removal of asylum seekers easier to achieve. These purposes are not expressly articulated in the Preamble and the humanitarian purpose would be defeated if the criteria for identifying the state that was to examine the application were over-rigid. The text of the criteria for identifying the responsible state makes it clear that the concept of most appropriate country of asylum was to be replaced with the concept of first opportunity to make a claim. Those who failed to take this opportunity would be "punished" by denial of access to the procedure in their state of claim, and when their claim was finally determined, suspicion of

[31] See R. Marx, "Non-refoulement, Access to Procedures, and Responsibility for Determining Asylum Claims" (1995) 7(3) *IJRL* 383; see also N. Abell, "Compatibility of Readmission Agreements with the 1951 Convention" (1999) 11(1) *IJRL* 60.

its bona fides would arise by the imaginary assumption that a genuine refugee would not have acted so.

The criteria for selection of the determining state were, in descending priority:

Article 4: state where a spouse or child under 18 (or in the case of such a child a parent) has been recognised as a refugee within the meaning of the GCR;

Article 5: state that issued the applicant with a valid residence permit or visa;

Article 6: state where illegal entry was made from outside the European Union save where the application was made after six months' residence in another Member State;

Article 7: state responsible for controlling the entry across the external frontiers of Member States (whether actual entry was supervised, save where there has been subsequent lawful entry into another state where visa requirements were waived);

Article 8: in all other cases, state of first application for asylum, including any previous applications for asylum that have been refused.

States were free to apply more generous criteria and accept humanitarian obligation for an asylum seeker if they wanted to.[32] But these broader criteria were not defined and states were under no obligation to establish such criteria and apply them. Further, assumption of responsibility for determining a claim did not prevent a Member State returning the asylum seeker elsewhere outside the European Union in accordance with the state's own laws and practices.[33] Thus, despite its Preamble, the DC did not ensure substantive determination within the European Union. National practices determining which were safe third or fourth countries could continue to be promoted outside the DC. Germany had declared by legislative amendment to its Constitution that all its flanking neighbours outside the European Union were safe and asylum seekers could be returned there in the absence of a significant change of circumstances.[34] In theory at least the outcome of a DC exchange application between two Member States could be a transfer outside the European Union to a further country which might return to a fourth and fifth. The problem of refugees in orbit was thus not resolved or removed; the DC merely identified the start of the potential chain of return.

The practical implementation of the DC was then left to an executive committee of participating states.[35] Decisions were taken as to the forms to be used by states requesting a takeover of a claim or a taking back of a claim already made. Critical to the effective operation of the system is information exchange

[32] Article 3(4) enables the state of arrival to entertain the claim under national humanitarian criteria if the applicant agrees. Article 9 enables another state to take the application by mutual consent.

[33] Article 3(5).

[34] G. Noll, "The Non Admission and Return of Protection Seekers in Germany" (1997) 9(7) *IJRL* 415.

[35] Article 18.

between the immigration departments of Member States whereby evidence of previous applications, residence or transit in other countries can be identified. It is intended that fingerprinting, other electronic surveillance and the computerised storing and exchange of information held on Eurodac will identify the previous history of asylum seekers. Once exchanged, this material could be used to undermine the accounts given in substantive applications. Conclusions have been reached on such matters as the periods of time for response, the relevant documents to be relied on, exemptions for public holidays and such like.[36] These decisions and conclusions will enter Community law via the *acquis* of Schengen states for which the DC are integral legal instruments.

Despite the intention that asylum seekers should be processed at the first crossing point into the European Union in the absence of visas, residence permits or close family members recognised as refugees, it seems that migration across Europe from the south and east to the north and west has continued unabated. Only a small proportion of these arrivals has been successfully transferred back within the European Union whether through: lack of executive will to apply it; lack of evidence to convince states of their responsibility; disagreements as to the meaning of terms; domestic challenges to removal; or concern about the safety of certain classes of claimant within the European Union. The arrival of significant numbers of *roma* from Eastern Europe in 1997 caused difficulties of interpretation shortly after the DC had supposedly come into force. It was clear that the bus journey on which these non-visa national asylum seekers had travelled led them to cross the external frontiers of the European Union at Germany. Germany considered that since they were not visa nationals they lawfully entered other countries thereafter and the proviso to Article 7 applied. Further, there were practical difficulties about returning unprocessed *roma* asylum claimants by bus to Germany across a France unwilling to accept them on a transit basis. Until visa controls were imposed on Slovakia, it was easier to process claims in the United Kingdom and bill the ferry company with the cost of repatriation.[37] This was an inglorious start to the UK Government's hopes for the DC. In the end, the text was of little relevance; it was an ability to persuade fellow immigration officers that counted. The DC has no judicial supervision built into it, and the possibility of eventual ECJ competence as an apex court under the consolidated EC Treaty is a long way off.

THE FUNCTION OF INDIVIDUAL CHOICE

The hierarchy of the DC criteria gives little emphasis to the wishes of the asylum seeker as to where he or she seeks asylum. An asylum seeker might well be

[36] For the early decisions of the Committee, see E. Guild, *The Developing Immigration and Asylum Policies of the European Union* (Kluwer Law International, The Hague, 1996), 67–113.

[37] An attempt to impugn the Immigration Carriers Liability Act 1987 on the grounds of EC law failed in the Divisional Court but a subsequent appeal was the subject of a compromise: *R.* v. *Secretary of State for the Home Department, ex parte Hoverspeed* [1999] INLR 591.

expected to want to be with members of his or her close family. Family membership however is narrowly confined by Article 4; the presence of siblings, over-age children, or extended family units of uncles and aunts is not catered for irrespective of any actual dependence on these members in the past. More seriously for EC asylum policy, the presence of the family member is relevant only if the member has been recognised as a full refugee under the GCR. This cuts out first family members who were permanently settled in or may even be citizens of the EC state in question. Secondly, it eliminates family members who have a temporary residence permit or have been permitted to remain without a residence permit being granted at all. This group includes those who have claims for humanitarian protection, whether under Article 3 of the ECHR or under alternative provisions granting lesser protection such as *duldung* status in Germany or "exceptional leave" in the United Kingdom. The common factor is that they are not recognised refugees. This of course has meant that the vast majority of people resident in Europe and recognised as being in need of protection and unable to return to their countries of origin will not qualify. A spouse, a parent or a minor child may therefore end up separated from the rest of the family unit, unless chance results in agents being able to arrange a journey so that the first EC country reached is the place where the relatives are residing. The majority of Member States appear to have recognised the weakness of the family nexus criterion and revisions have been proposed to include family members of asylum seekers and not just recognised refugees. These modest proposals for reform apparently continue to meet opposition.[38] It is left to individual states to give effect to family reunion principles in their national practice and Article 3(5) discretion. But state discretion is not a sound basis for fair criteria. The experience of asylum policy in Europe has tended to be a downward spiral of more restrictive measures without effective democratic, judicial or international restraints. The DC is a measure of state practice designed to remove inconvenient obstacles to shifting numbers.

Contrary to the assumptions of many Member States, choice of the place of asylum is not inconsistent with a well-founded fear of persecution, and not evidence that an abusive claim is being made. The asylum seeker may be very conscious that the claim is so well founded that flight to seek protection is the start of permanent exile from the country of origin. The host country is not merely a transit camp, but a permanent home. The facilitation of integration is an important part of the consequences of recognition of refugee status in the GCR.[39] Integration is achieved if the refugee can stand on his or her own feet as soon as possible, find employment, a home, a profession, an education, participate in the civic life of the host country and make a contribution to its economic, social and cultural well being.[40] This is unlikely to be achieved in countries arbitrarily

[38] *Migration News Sheet*, June and August 1999.

[39] Article 34 GCR.

[40] This point is made in the consultation document issued by the Home Office IND Support Project Team and can be accessed on the Home Office website at www.homeoffice.gov.uk/ind/assd/integration. See paras 2.2 and 2.3 With this in mind the aim of integration is to provide the

selected by the DC criteria with no appropriate links for the claimant. It is difficult to practice a vocation if one does not speak the language of the host state or have a familiarity with its system of public administration. It is difficult to find employment if there is no extended family or support from other members of the same ethnic group available to provide advice and material assistance. It is difficult to integrate and achieve personal security if the perception of one's neighbours is that one is a social security seeking scrounger who should never have been admitted here in the first place.

Past experience of and continuing connections with a country may thus form a sensible basis for choice by a claimant that reduces the period of dependency, ensures swifter and more satisfactory integration, and reduces the economic costs to the host state of the process of examination and integration. Workers and the self-employed pay taxes and social security contributions, those unable to provide for themselves deplete state resources on social assistance. If the modest disposals on social assistance deplete state resources, the costs of detaining an asylum seeker who has no community ties in the host state can be very much more expensive. Asylum claimants, whose wishes as to the preferred country of application are respected, are more likely to co-operate in the asylum process itself. Apart from economic restraints on the ability of the indigent to attend interviews, provide documents, instruct advisers and demonstrate their claim, there is the problem of lack of experience of a community of people from the same ethnic background to know how things are done and what is expected. Such a community may itself be instrumental in providing the confirming testimony which a genuine claimant would be advised to place before the determining authorities. The process of considering claims may be thus speedier and more accurate. If a claim is negative, it may well be that claimants who have community ties and are fairly treated are less likely to abscond than those who consider they are anonymous cogs in an indifferent machine.[41]

THE IMPACT ON BORDER STATES

Apart from the small number of cases under Articles 4 and 5 where family links or prior visas enable transfer of a claim, the primary principles of determination

opportunity for all refugees to be fully included in society and the opportunity to develop their full potential in their new host societies. Britain has also benefited from being a multicultural society. Inclusion in our society does not mean that a refugee is required to assimilate. From the refugee's point of view the need to both integrate (learn the language and procedures of the host state) and be respected as someone from a different cultural background is ground out strongly by ECRE Publication, *Bridges and Fences, Refugee Perception of Integration in the European Union* (2000) and the associated good practice guides on integration of refugees in the European Union at www.refugeenet.org.

[41] Some initial data on a bail project run by the Vera Institute in New York suggests that those who are permitted to build their own community links respond better to enforcement orders than those who do not: unpublished paper at a joint US and European Asylum Law Seminar, Christchurch College Oxford (July 1999).

under the DC are assignment of cases to the first EU country entered, whether lawfully or otherwise. If strictly applied this would shift the burden of EU asylum policy onto states with frontiers close to zones of conflict or flight. Thus Austria, Germany and any new Eastern European additions to the European Union would have the task of absorbing the refugees from Bosnia-Herzegovina, Kosovo and elsewhere in the Balkan theatre of humanitarian catastrophe. Spain, France and Italy would be the nearest port of call for those fleeing persecution in the Magreb or other proximate parts of Africa. The consequence would be that the United Kingdom would only be on standby for the refugee crisis of the Arctic Circle or those who chose to flee by luxury cruiser to a UK port.

It is unsurprising if such an inequitable distribution of responsibility prompts receiving states to develop hard jurisprudence on the particular areas where mass influxes are feared. Arrivals by airport will depend on the random factors of airline schedules, the severity of carriers' sanctions and the efficacy of national measures to turn airline check-in staff into super immigration officers, and above all, the selection of routes for access to the asylum procedure by agents. The misfortune of being a frontier state is not mitigated by EU measures to pay for the cost of asylum reception and determination and compliance with the ECHR. There are no still no binding rules on minimum conditions of reception, minimum standards of procedures, or minimum standards of qualification as envisaged by Article 63(1) EC.[42] There are no Union-wide measures for temporary protection for displaced persons. There is no free movement within the European Union for recognised refugees, that would enable post-recognition migration to mitigate undue burdens on the country of first entry. It is not surprising that Italy and the southern states seek a greater overall policy on burden sharing and equity within the European Union.[43] The dramatic rise of asylum numbers in Switzerland has prompted that country to seek to join the DC system, presumably in the belief that greater co-operation with immigration officers and access to Eurodac will enable greater numbers of return to Italy.[44] The response to date suggests that the Swiss should reconsider membership of the European Union or the EEA if they want the benefits of political co-operation. In the case of Norway and Iceland, however, the Commission has been authorised to conduct accession negotiations, again presumably in response to their fears that exclusion will lead to a rise in numbers of unreturnable asylum seekers.[45]

The recent statistics of the first eighteen months' operation suggest that the northern states are not getting everything their own way. The south is still

[42] For the difficulty this creates for applicants who wish to challenge the safety of countries on the grounds that procedures there do not meet the minimum set out in Third Pillar recommendations, see R. v. *Secretary of State for the Home Department, ex parte Mbanja* [1999] INLR 390.

[43] Information provided by Alberto Colello, Ministry of Foreign Affairs, Rome.

[44] In the first eleven months of 1999 Switzerland received 44,484 asylum claims compared with Germany's 88,500 for a considerably larger country: IGM Secretariat, published in *Migrant News*, January 2000.

[45] *ILPA European Update*, January 2000.

largely used as a zone for transit rather than determination. Loose borders, an absence of stamps in passport, and obduracy on matters of interpretation and evidence may enable the scheme to be frustrated in part until there is greater political satisfaction at an overall settlement. As far as Austria is concerned, there is concern that the prospects of progressive and humanitarian contribution from that nation on questions of EU immigration and asylum policy seem to be further undermined by recent political events. Certainly free movement and acceptance of international obligations towards the homeless and the unprotected must be part of the price to be paid in a materially developed society that wants to participate in the rich club of the European Union.

First entry as a criterion need have no practical relationship to an effective opportunity to seek protection and establish a nexus with the country in question: we have already noted the problems of those who enter concealed in lorries, who are unable to get out at the border and claim asylum until an end destination is reached. A few hours' passage in the transit lounge of an airport does not establish any connection with a country and may not involve any formal encounter with immigration officials. The DC itself recognises that short stays in transit lounges do not amount to entry on the territory,[46] but makes no similar allowance for transit across countries in vehicles. The first entry principle merely has the virtue that it is a principle on which allocation of responsibility can be made if the trail of the asylum seeker's journey can be adequately demonstrated. The DC does depend on acceptance of responsibility and is thus an improvement on previous assumptions that a state ought to accept an asylum seeker back whether or not it agreed. But acceptance of responsibility may itself take many months and defer substantive consideration of the claim. Beyond this the principle neither promotes effective recognition systems, integration of the asylum seeker into the host state, nor achieves an equitable balance amongst EU states.

DISPARITY OF PROTECTION IN THE EUROPEAN UNION

The previous criticisms of the Dublin criteria assume that at the end of the application people in similar situations will be treated the same in whichever EU country their claim is determined. The reality is however far different, and the single most important reason for an overhaul of the Dublin regime before it enters the hard law of the Community. Article 63 EC assumes progress on harmonisation on all fronts, but it is to be doubted whether states have the political will to do this through a binding Community instrument enforceable by the ECJ, if by interstate co-operation and reform of national legislation they can achieve their minimum needs.

Dublin was adopted before even any attempt at harmonised criteria and procedure for protection was identified by the Committee of Ministers acting under

[46] Article 7(2), at least until a common policy for transit visas has been achieved.

the Third Pillar. It has been maintained even in the face of considerable diversity in the application of the supposedly common standards of the ECtHR, let alone joint agreement on countries of origin and measures to provide temporary protection. It is absurd and unfair to deprive asylum seekers of a choice of country of determination at a time when the results of the application depend on significant national differences of approach, as well as varying consequences of the grant of protection *de jure* as a Convention refugee or *de facto* under one of the alternative programmes for temporary protection. Such disharmony is bound to lead to removals that would be inconsistent with some EU states' understanding of their international obligations, and an unlawful administrative reworking of fundamental juridical norms. To maintain deterrence of asylum seekers as a higher priority than the obligation to provide effective protection leads to diminished respect for those obligations. This, in turn, leads to a weakening of the rule of law in the European Union, which is one of the founding values of the European Union and perhaps one reason why asylum seekers are fleeing oppression and persecution in their own countries.

THE JUDICIAL ELABORATION OF PROTECTION

1996 was a year of notable developments in the United Kingdom and Europe in the field of asylum policy. In March the EU guidelines on harmonised criteria for determining asylum claims were published in the *Official Journal*. These were non-binding recommendations to be taken account of by the administrative authorities of the state. In many respects they represented a reasonable attempt to elucidate the meaning of the minimum standards for the interpretation of the GCR. On the vexed but topical issues of persecution by non-state agents, however, the different systems could merely agree to disagree on the lowest common standard.[47] The guidelines could stiffen national judicial application of the GCR; it could hardly be the case that public officials should apply standards less generous than those which officials of the Member States had specially prepared for them. They were however a floor and not a ceiling to standards of protection. Elaboration of the criteria for protection emphasised once more the need for effective judicial and appellate procedures to ensure application of the protection principle. The failure to adopt a regional convention requiring adoption of these standards meant that states that failed to comply could not be categorised as unsafe for that reason alone. Effective procedures must at least mean: proper protection for the asylum seeker during the investigation stage; properly reasoned decisions on the grounds for refusal; opportunity to submit fresh evidence to an independent appellate body; and an effective appeal hearing ensuring that rejection is consistent with both the GCR and the ECHR. The fusion of

[47] Paragraph 5.1.2 d: "where the official authorities fail to act such persecution should give rise to individual examination in accordance with national judicial practice".

the two instruments in a mutually supportive and comprehensive test of protection should ensure an incremental and updating approach to the law applied in the Member State.

Further, the asylum seeker must be able to receive adequate social support during the procedure, and receive a status that provides security and encourages self-sufficiency after it.

In June 1996 the Court of Appeal in the United Kingdom concluded[48] that depriving asylum seekers of benefits pending appeals against adverse decisions was inconsistent with the right of appeal and expressed its concern that such harsh measures undermined the right to seek asylum and put pressure on an asylum seeker to abandon a potentially sound claim. This decision strongly suggests that states adhering to the GCR are obliged to make some provision for the maintenance of asylum claimants pending the determination process.[49] Recognised refugees are of course entitled to equality with nationals in the matter of housing and social security and assistance, but the international rights to such support in other forms of protection status are unclear.[50] There is no doubt that there remains a wide disparity inside the European Union between the regimes for accommodation, access to employment, social assistance and family reunion both before and after decisions have been made on protection. All this makes differences in the choice of the place of asylum real and significant.

In November 1996 the ECtHR in the case of *Chahal*[51] indicated that Article 3 of the ECHR prohibited removal to a country where there were substantial grounds to fear exposure to torture inhuman or degrading treatment was concerned and was wider than the protection provided under the GCR. The subsequent decisions in *Ahmed* v. *Austria*,[52] *HLR* v. *France*[53] and *D* v. *United Kingdom*,[54] established that the principle applied irrespective of the source of the harm, whether through state or non-state agents, or even the absence of essential facilities for the maintenance of life. An expulsion was prohibited where it exposed the migrant to conditions that achieved the minimum level of severity required to engage Article 3. To UK lawyers this jurisprudence is a logical and consistent application of the principle of causal nexus. A government is not vicariously responsible for the wrongs of another state that may not be party to the ECHR or any equivalent instrument; neither does prohibition of expulsion extend the instrument extraterritorially. It is liable because its own acts

[48] R. v. *Secretary of State for Social Security, ex parte JCWI and B* [1997] 1 WLR 275.

[49] See R. Cholewinski, "The enforced destitution of asylum seekers in the United Kingdom" (1998) 10(3) *IRJL* 462.

[50] The ECtHR has not developed the concept of "constructive refoulement" through the imposition of harsh social conditions, although Mr Cabral Barreto has twice suggested in opinions as a member of the EComHR that Article 3 may require something more than mere abstinence from expulsion: see *HLR* v. *France* (1996) 26 EHRR 29.

[51] *Chahal* v. *United Kingdom* (1996) 23 EHRR 413.

[52] (1996) 26 EHRR 278.

[53] (1996) 24 EHRR 423.

[54] (1994) 24 EHRR 423.

create a causal nexus resulting in exposure to prohibited consequences. Inhuman and degrading treatment is inflicted whenever a person is intentionally expelled to conditions of the minimum level of severity. Such conditions may extend to deprivation of essential medical treatment and social facilities necessary for the maintenance of life with a minimum of human dignity.

The dynamic approach of the ECtHR has not yet been accepted by the higher courts in Germany which persist in applying a narrow interpretation of state accountability even to Article 3 of the ECHR.[55] This division of opinion is on top of the unresolved conflict in Europe between the so-called protection and accountability theories underlying differing interpretations of the GCR.[56] For the United Kingdom and a number of Member States, the plain words, context and purpose of the GCR is to ensure surrogate protection for those with a well-founded fear of persecution where the state of origin is unable or unwilling to provide protection; *a fortiori* where no state exists and organised groups inflict harm for reasons of race, religion, nationality, political opinion or membership of a particular social group, a person is entitled to recognition as a refugee. Other states have a more restrictive approach to persecution by non-state agents, and exclude the possibility of refugee status altogether where no recognised state can be said to exist which is accountable for the harm suffered in its territory.[57]

Although return of asylum seekers to other Member States was long assumed to be safe, particularly when the German Constitution guaranteed access to a long procedure before removal, a sequence of cases came before the UK courts closely examining the basis of this assumption. It was held that refusal of admission and mere occasional lapses of procedures at the border were not the same as refoulement.[58] Until the abolition of the right of appeal in 1996, special adjudicators had concluded that such lapses entitled them to disagree that a third country was safe. In *Kerrouche*[59] the application of the exclusion clause under Article 1F to a suspected terrorist claimant was held not to be substantial difference between France and the United Kingdom in practice, although the court added that some margin of appreciation and scope for legitimate difference should be afforded between states as a mater of comity. In *Iyadurai* [60] the court accepted that margin of appreciation may not be the most helpful concept, but nevertheless concluded that differences between states were acceptable; and that

[55] The most comprehensive explanation of German law on the topic has been given by K. Hailbronner. The author in particular relies on the extensive expert opinions given to the Secretary of State in the *Adan* case (see below). The topic is also discussed by Vermeulen *et al.* (see below).

[56] A helpful survey is provided by Vermeulen *et al.*, *Persecution by Third Parties* (University of Nijmegen, May 1999), and the proceedings of the ECRE Conference of September 1999.

[57] According to the UNHCR the case-law in France is developing closer to the position of the common law countries, to which the Netherlands, Belgium and Sweden now adhere.

[58] In R. v. *Secretary of State for the Home Department, ex parte Canbolat* [1997] 1 WLR 1569 mere procedural lapses by border officials were held insufficient to require the Home Office to conclude that the country was unsafe and thus preclude certification of a case under the 1996 legislation.

[59] [1997] Imm AR 610.

[60] [1998] Imm AR 470.

the differences between the United Kingdom and Germany in elaboration of the standard of proof were insignificant in the overall concept of refugee status and did not prevent return to Germany, where indeed statistics showed that Tamil asylum claimants had a higher prospect of success than in the United Kingdom. The courts had identified that a safe third country could be safe only if return of a claimant to that place would not result in return directly or indirectly to the territory where persecution was feared, without prior consideration of the asylum claim. The court added the gloss that the authorities of the safe third country must consider the claim properly.[61] What proper consideration entailed was not spelt out other than the minimal requirements of natural justice to articulate a claim. The judges concluded that as the GRC said nothing about rights of appeal or other minimum procedures, and mere recommendations were not binding, removal to a country without such procedures did not itself amount to a breach of the GCR. Countries did not have to adopt measures identical with those in the United Kingdom, or adopt international recommendations; they had merely to take such steps as to reasonably prevent *refoulement*.[62]

At some point, however, a case raising an indisputably significant difference in interpretation was bound to come before the courts, and it has done so in the cases known as *Adan and Aitsegur*.[63] Ms Adan claimed to be a member of a minority clan set upon by other dominant clans in Somalia where there is no recognised state and a high level of risk of serious harm on the grounds of ethnic origin; in *Aitsegur* the applicant had a cogent fear of reprisals from the armed Islamic groups operating in Algeria against state functionaries and their supporters and it was accepted that the state was unable to provide adequate protection against such harm. The Home Office proposed to send the pair back to Germany and France respectively where it was acknowledged that they were not eligible for refugee status because of the restrictive interpretation of the GCR applied as a result of national jurisprudence. In the United Kingdom it was accepted that if their accounts were well founded they would be granted refugee status. Ms Adan faced the further difficulty that Germany did not consider her eligible for Article 3 ECHR protection either:[64] her claim had been rejected, she had been required to return to Somalia under threat of expulsion and it was unclear whether she could now access any fresh form of the lowest level of humanitarian protection or how stable, supportive and effective such protection would be. In Mr Aitsegur's case, the evidence of *de facto* protection and its inci-

61 *Martinhas* [1995] Imm AR 190.

62 See *Canbolat* [1997] I WLR 1569.

63 [1999] 3 WLR 1274.

64 At the time of writing the ECtHR has requested provisional measures from the UK Government not to return a Tamil asylum seeker to Germany where there is a risk that he would not be able to access effective procedures to reopen his claim. The case may determine when the international obligation of one state breaks the causal connection preventing another state expelling a claimant in circumstances that might result in a return to ill-treatment. In *TI* v. *UK* (Application 00043844198, 7 March 2000) the ECtHR held the application inadmissible on its facts, but left open the issue since the evidence did not support a fresh opportunity to re-examine a claim.

dents was obscure and unsatisfactory. The Court of Appeal decided to focus entirely on the question of the GCR. The national precondition for the issue of a certificate to remove under the DC was that the Secretary State was confident that the person "would not be removed otherwise than in accordance with the Convention" (i.e. the GCR).

The UK Government's submission was that there was no international court charged with the authoritative interpretation of the GCR and that its meaning, therefore, was a matter for each Member State. A reasonable range of differences of approach was inevitable and should be accepted without violation of the international obligation. In the context of removal within the European Union, the Joint Position of 1996 was clear evidence of the reasonable range of permissible interpretations of the Convention. Since EU states had agreed to differ over the eligibility of claimants from persecution at the hands of non-state agents, it was perfectly reasonable for Germany and France, acting in accordance with the Joint Position, to deny refugee status to those who would be eligible for it. There would be no violation of the UK's obligation if the claimants were returned to their countries of origin, although in reality there were lesser forms of protection available if considered appropriate.

The Court of Appeal rejected the Government's submissions. It concluded that the proper meaning of an international instrument brought into domestic law was for the courts to apply the international rules of construction laid down in the Vienna Convention.[65] This was not a matter of executive policy to which a range of meanings could be attached. State practice as evidenced by the EU Joint Position could not be prayed in aid to interpret the instrument. First, it was not an agreement between all the states party to it; secondly, the Joint Position was inconsistent with the judicial interpretation of the GCR in the United Kingdom and indeed many other countries of the world, and in any event the Joint Position was not part of Community law and not said to be binding on the judicial authorities; thirdly, on its face, the Joint Position did not purport to interpret the terms of the Convention but agreed to disagree about what the terms meant. The difference in interpretation was dramatic and would lead to catastrophic consequences for the claimant. A purposive, updating and protective construction of the GCR was called for.

> "It is clear that the signatory states intended that the Convention should afford continuing protection for refugees in the changing circumstances of the present and future world. In our view the Convention has to be regarded as a living instrument: just as, by the Strasbourg jurisprudence, the ECHR is so regarded. Looked at in this light the Geneva Convention is apt unequivocally to offer protection against non-State agent persecution, where for whatever cause the State is unwilling or unable to offer protection itself."

The Court had to explain its previous decisions permitting a certain margin of tolerance in the interpretation of the GCR and the present decision that the

[65] Articles 31 and 32.

meaning of an instrument is ultimately a matter for the court and not the reasonable discretion of the executive. It concluded that there is a difference between application of the Convention where there is room for differing views on the burden of proof or the scope of the exclusion clauses where the text is not dispositive, and the essential meaning of basic scope of the refugee definition. In recent decisions the Court of Appeal has recognised that it may be somewhat difficult to distinguish between interpretation and application, but what is stake is whether there is a disregard of what the national court considers the core values of the GCR.[66] Where the United Kingdom has to consider return under Article 8 of the DC to another Member State that has already rejected the application, if the core values are adhered to then the national court will only intervene in the case of decisions that are wholly unreasonable in their conclusions.[67]

NEW DIRECTIONS FOR HARMONISED ASYLUM LEGISLATION

Although it is merely a decision of a national court, and is now under appeal, I would suggest that the judgment in *Adan and Aitsegur* should inform the foundation of any new EU initiative on a harmonised asylum policy. At the very least it demonstrates that the 1996 Guidelines and the DC cannot be adopted as Community legislation without substantial reworking. Tortuous and technical reasons to exclude claimants from protection are inconsistent with the proper meaning of the GCR, the dynamic interpretation of the ECHR, and the policy and purpose of the European Union in having a harmonised policy to asylum seekers. It is indeed particularly frustrating that there could still be room for debate inside Europe as to the scope of Article 3 in the face of the consistent and constant jurisprudence of the regional human rights court whose rulings are meant to be the foundation of our common system of values and respect for human rights. In short, there cannot be a sensible policy and binding legal measures to distribute the determination of asylum claims, unless the procedures to establish those claims and the support given during them achieve minimum levels of fairness and the criterion for an overall decision on protection is harmonised at the broadest level of protection and respect for human rights that our humanitarian traditions require. None of this is new; the non-governmental organisations (NGOs) of Europe have been saying as much for years but the

[66] R. v. *Secretary of State for the Home Department, ex parte Altun* (unreported) 28 January 2000.

[67] R. v. *Secretary of State for the Home Department, ex parte Dahmas* (unreported) 17 November 1999, CA where a decision of the Danish Refugee Board rejecting an Algerian asylum claim was considered to be unreasonable, precluding a return to that country. The Home Office policy was described as being that "the Secretary of State will determine whether a decision is flawed by reason of some manifest irrationality or serious procedural irregularity, such that it might not be appropriate to issue a certificate in the particular case". See also R. v. *Secretary of State for the Home Department, ex parte Gashi* [1999] INLR 276 for a decision quashing a return to Germany because of an inexplicably high refusal rate for Kosovan Albanian claimants.

undemocratic ways of the Third Pillar, without legislative debate or judicial scrutiny, have served to protect the coteries of interior ministers and their advisers from the great truths of international obligation.

Perhaps the message is getting across. In this respect the meeting of EU Interior Ministers at Tampere did not produce as alarming a conclusion as had been feared. One state party's representative has described its activities:

> "The European Council reaffirmed the importance the EU and Member States attach to the respect of the right to seek asylum. It had agreed to work towards establishing a Common European Asylum System, based on the full and inclusive application of the Geneva Convention, thus ensuring that nobody is sent back to persecution: the Union committed to maintain the principle of non-refoulement. The reference to the principle of non-refoulement was introduced in reply to concerns expressed by NGOs and international organisations that the new system envisaged by the EU could cancel the international right for refugees not to be sent back to persecution."[68]

The goal of a harmonised asylum policy within the ToA remains as necessary as ever.[69] It would be unreal to revert to national policies and ignore the role of EU asylum policy. It is clear that policy informing future legislation is decided between states at an intergovernmental level, whether or not blessed by the European Commission and Parliament. Thus, in the United Kingdom the response to *Adan and Aitsegur* has been to promote a new section in the Immigration and Asylum Act 1999. By section 11(2) a minister may remove an asylum claimant where a certificate is issued on the grounds that another Member State has accepted responsibility. Henceforth in the event of a challenge to such a certificate by judicial review, section 11(1) provides that:

> "A Member State is to be regarded as a place where a person will not be sent to another country otherwise than in accordance with the Refugee Convention."

The challenge for the European Parliament, Commission and Council of Ministers is to adopt binding legislation at Union level on the Member States to ensure that this present piece of parliamentary fiction corresponds to effective reality. But what are the practical options for change?

The most radical proposal would be to set up a super European agency to determine claims to protection made within a Member State. The resources needed to fund such a creature and the methods of judicial review of its decision would be so considerable as to make it impracticable for the foreseeable future. If the logical position is regional protection for claimants who reach the region, the advantages of speed, consistency and high quality decisions based on liberal criteria for protection should at least be a target of alternative procedures. The fully harmonised model suggests that the result of a uniform Union-wide decision would be Union-wide free movement rights at least to the extent of

[68] Unpublished paper by A. Colello, Ministry of Foreign Affairs, Italy, "The European Union and its Immigration and Asylum Strategies" (January 2000).

[69] See "Guarding Standards-Shaping the Agenda" (April 1999), comments on the Treaty of Amsterdam by ECRE, ENAR and MGP.

permitting recognised refugees and their families to work, set up businesses, engage in self-employment and the other activities regulated by directives at present.

Another approach would be to adopt Community legislation under the reformed First Pillar, requiring protection criteria to be based on the most dynamic interpretation of the case-law of the GCR, the ECHR, and other relevant instruments such as the ICCPR and the Torture Convention. A legislative form of an updated and expanded UNHCR Handbook encompassing protection against torture, inhuman or degrading treatment, and temporary protection in humanitarian circumstances could be drawn up. The jurisprudence does now exist and is reasonably clear and cogent, whatever particular states may say about it. The question is essentially whether governments are prepared to accept their minimum international obligations in a comprehensive system of protection or to fritter huge resources in unnecessary and wearying disputes of interpretation. Broadening the EU Guidelines to accommodate broader criteria for protection achieves economy and fair and effective decision-making at an early stage in the determination process. As the JUSTICE/ILPA document "Providing Protection"[70] concluded in its review of asylum procedures, there is a mutual interest in governments and asylum seekers in good quality, well-informed and well-articulated decisions at the beginning of the process rather than shifting the burden onto the appellate systems in Member States and the apex institutions of Europe. If the end result is the same in terms of family reunion, legalised status, access to employment and social security during the period of protection, the precise description in international law may not be of concern to the claimant or the sending state.

Of course, this proposal may seem scarcely less Utopian than a single decision-making body, but the interests of administrative efficiency should at least require careful consideration. Harmonised measures will not and should not work unless we uplift the level of protection to its minimum requirements. Thereafter, there may be room for particular exercise of discretion for individual cases of hardship or compassion. A harmonised country information system and distribution of leading judgments of the relevant judicial bodies on the more difficult questions of the day should cut delays and improve quality of decisions. The current debate, for example, as to the extent to which *roma* from eastern Europe require or should receive protection, is a matter that could be the subject of pan-European information and debate. There is a line to be drawn between mere discrimination and more severe treatment that legitimises flight to seek protection elsewhere. A fair and effective harmonised asylum policy could run consistently with a harmonised human rights-based foreign policy. Recent events in Kosovo and East Timor serve to remind that it is better for all concerned that recalcitrant and rogue states are made to respect their human rights

[70] Justice and ILPA, *Providing Protection* (London, June 1997). The same point has been made by UNHCR, ECRE and many others.

obligations to people within their jurisdiction than for them to rely on the asylum policies of the European Union to empty their states of ethnic and religious minorities. Harmonised intervention early to promote human rights should serve to reduce the incidents of mass evacuation which strain the administrative resources of receiving states. At the end of the day, of course, the asylum seeker must not pay for past failures of the international community to protect rights in country. But protection even for recognised refugees does not have to be indefinite and permanent if there are reasonable prospects of a change of circumstances.

Short of these grand measures of Community architecture, there is a Dutch suggestion to modify the Dublin procedure by assigning the country to determine the claim without first having to remove the asylum seeker.[71] There may be variations on this theme, with the asylum seeker staying in the place where the claim was first made or returning to the place where the claim has been decided as appropriate. This would eliminate delay in examining the substantive claim by spending months debating which country is gong to consider it. Whilst such measures are imaginative contributions to the debate, it is difficult to see how far processes of determination could be effected without an oral interview, opportunities to submit and comment on documents and secure a fair and effective right of appeal for which purposes lawyers would need to be instructed. There may be some scope for video-linked interviews and transmission of documents in the initial decision-making process. As compared with present disharmony, it would be remarkable indeed if the determining country were prepared to have the merits of its decision adjudicated on by the courts of the place where the claimant were situated or the country where the claimant resides accepted the determination decision of the third state and granted residence rights on the strength of it. The concept does however raise the idea of transnational standards and procedures, mutual recognition of decisions and freedom of movement following such recognition. It reduces the scope for purely parochial views about what the criteria for protection are.

At the very least a harmonised asylum questionnaire could be drafted, to be completed in interview after access to specialist advice with a claimant going through standard questions and addressing all eligible claims for protection. This would mirror the harmonised Dublin questionnaire presently completed by immigration officers anxious to secure a transfer of responsibility. Each of these measures may go some way to achieve the proper and consistent application of protection norms that is called for.

It is not the purpose of this chapter to set out in detail the necessary measures of procedural protection, social assistance, effective access to the courts and the like that must form the basis minimum of acceptable procedures. I have attempted to give some indication of where the criteria for substantive

[71] Papers from the Hague Conference on Immigration and the Treaty of Amsterdam (September 1999).

protection should come from. The rights to family life and economic and social rights are equally relevant in shaping the incidents of protection during and after the decision-making process. Family separation and destitution are costly in the long run to the asylum claimant and the host society from which he or she cannot be removed. The happy and efficient social functioning of human beings is not promoted by trauma of separation and exclusion. The constituent elements of the overall package of rights have long been identified by ECRE and other NGOs and are readily capable of support by citation from the case-law of human rights bodies and courts. The point about a harmonised procedure is that safe country decisions are not merely an exercise of national sovereignty to dump unwanted claimants on whatever other territory can be persuaded to accept them, but a constructive effort in international protection, to ensure proper and adequate respect for the rights of asylum seekers. Such a project should receive universal support and would give legitimacy to the measures of expulsion adopted to remove those who fail to qualify or have been demonstrated to have abused the opportunity with fraudulent claims. No such legitimacy can presently be afforded to EU asylum and immigration policies because they do not ensure the protection of those who ought to be protected.

Whatever precise measures the European Union adopts as matters of First Pillar or Community law, harmonisation must address all the relevant issues in a comprehensive package: substantive criteria; effective procedures; reasoned decision-making; access to the courts; proper support during the process; proper implementation of negative decisions; and proper recognition of status for those entitled to protection on a temporary or permanent basis.

5

Abolishing Border Controls: Individual Rights and Common Control of EU External Borders

CRISTINA GORTAZAR

INTRODUCTION

This chapter endeavours to provide a modest contribution to the debate concerning individual rights within the process of European integration. In more detail it views these rights vis-a-vis the measures regarding "common control" of the external border of the European Union after the Treaty of Amsterdam (ToA) came into force.

The effective disappearance of the internal borders within the European Union will mean an area of freedom for all individuals (citizens of the Member States of the European Union, citizens of non-EU countries or stateless persons) in so far as it will provide them with the right to cross these internal borders with no need to submit to any control whatsoever, whenever they do so. However, at the present time, only the citizens of the Member States of the European Union (or those states belonging to the European Economic Area (EEA) will have the right to settle and work within the territories of these states or the EEA.[1]

[1] Although it is a question which goes beyond the scope of this chapter, we believe that the provisions of Art. 18 EC would have to grant the right of movement and the right to settle freely in the territories of the Member States to all the citizens of the European Union (including those not engaged in working activities). Nevertheless, part of the doctrine holds that Art. 18 EC is not directly applicable due to the limitations and restrictions to which it is submitted. We share Mattera's belief that such a thesis confuses the existence of a right with its exercise as all the rights conferred on individuals are limited to certain conditions as regards their exercise. A. Mattera, *Civis europaeus sum. Citoyenneté européenne, droit de circulation et de séjour, applicabilité directe de l'article 8A du Traité CE.* (1998) 3 *Revue du Marché Unique Européen* 21.

However, in Case C–85/96 *Martinez Sala* [1998] ECR I–2691 the ECJ made no ruling on the direct effect of Art. 18, although the question was raised before this Court by the referring jurisdiction and by Advocate-General La Pergola. In fact, the first ruling on the applicability and the scope of Art. 18 was not issued by the ECJ but, curiously, by the European Commission on Human Rights (ECmHR) on the occasion of an appeal made by the leader of Sinn Fein, Gerry Adams, and a British parliamentarian, Tony Benn MP. The ECmHR considers that Art. 18 is not a norm with direct effect (*Adams and Benn* v. *United Kingdom*, Appeal no. 28979/95–30343/96, 13 January 1997, ECtHR). *Cf.* the commentaries in E. Vallejo Lobete "*Las excepciones a las libertades de establecimiento, circulación de personas y servicios motivadas por razón de orden público, seguridad y salud públicas*", *Gaceta Jurídica de la CE*, Series D, February 1999, 167–9.

Despite this, it is clear that the legal regime applicable to third country nationals, traditionally made up mostly of "domestic" norms, has increasingly become affected by Community law and the most outstanding landmark in this regard is the new Title IV of the EC Treaty introduced by the ToA.

The extent of this process of progressive cession of state competence to the European Community, is a matter which depends not only on the technical and legal measures which become feasible (i.e. the new Community competence laid down in the aforementioned Title IV), but, especially, on the political will of the Member States, reluctant to cede sovereignty in matters of deep rooted exclusive "national competence".

As the European Community takes its first steps with its new competence, the road appears complicated. Adapting the policies relative to the legal regime of third country nationals to Community law is not a sudden decision nor is it a uniform one as it will entail different speeds depending on the matter at issue (different decision procedures will be used) and, above all, the measures may not be binding in all EU Member States (with specific positions adopted by the United Kingdom, Ireland and Denmark).[2] Only one factor must be cleared up *ab initio,* as J.D.M Steenbergen so rightly remarks, the new Community regulations must respect individual rights and the rule of law.[3] Thus, some of the existing legal instruments cannot be transposed to the new Title IV unless they undergo substantial changes beforehand.

As has been said before, we should examine the issue regarding the rights of the individual faced with the combined measures to be adopted concerning the crossing of external borders by virtue of the new Title IV EC, as these measures are deemed essential in order to guarantee the free movement of persons as laid down in Article 14 EC.

(PRE-AMSTERDAM) FLANKING MEASURES FOR THE ABOLITION OF INTERNAL BORDERS

Once the Treaty of Rome came into force in the 1960s—years of progress in little Europe—the entry of workers from outside the Community was encouraged and contributed substantially to the reconstruction of the continent.

The economic crisis of 1973 led to a drastic reduction in the demand for workers, but, as the crisis had affected everyone, the migratory flows towards Europe continued to rise. The new restrictions on the entry of third country nationals adopted by the European states were not successful and provoked the apparition or generalisation of clandestine immigration, the underground economy or the fraudulent use of the legislation on asylum.[4]

[2] Protocol on the application of certain aspects of Art. 7A EC to the United Kingdom and Ireland and a Protocol on the position of Denmark (annexed to the TEU and the EC Treaty).

[3] J. Steenbergen, "All the King's Horses . . . Probabilities and Possibilities for the Implementation of the New Title IV EC Treaty" (1999) 1 *European Journal of Migration and Law* 30.

[4] C. Gortàzar Rotaeche, "*Normativa aplicable a los nacionales de terceros estados en la Unión Europea*" (Rules Applicable to Third Country Nationals in the European Union), in *La Inmigración Derecho español e internacional (obra colectiva)* (Bosch, Barcelona, 1995), 62.

Some time later, Article 13 of the Single European Act signed on 17 and 28 February 1986 defined the future internal market as:

> "... a space with no internal borders where the free movement of goods, persons, services and capital will be guaranteed under the provisions of this treaty."

The Single European Act was an invitation made to the Community to adopt the measures required to progressively set up the internal market throughout a period of time which should end on 31 December 1992. The signatories to the Act added statements to the Final Act, which included number 2 on "the free movement of persons" which expressly lays down that:

> "In order to encourage the free movement of persons, the Member States will co-operate, notwithstanding the competence of the Community, specifically as regards the entry, movement and residence of third country nationals."

From the start it was understood that the disappearance of the internal borders would be preceded by the combined control of what would become the external border of the European Community. As regards the free movement of persons, the single external border would mean, among other things, the necessary standardisation of the policy on visas, the right to asylum and, generally, the conditions for the entry of a third country citizen into the European Community. How could this be carried out? The European Commission was not competent in this matter,[5] so the Member States adopted policies merely at government level.

Some agreements were negotiated among the Member States (the Ad Hoc Immigration Group),[6] but the most outstanding work was carried out within the core made up of a group of only some members (the Schengen Group).

The Dublin Convention and other provisions arising from the intergovernmental "15" route

The 1990 Dublin Convention sets up binding criteria regarding the share-out of responsibilities as regards the study of applications for asylum for all the states of the European Union, and its entry in force provoked the derogation of the articles in the Schengen Implementation Agreement which had dealt with this matter.[7]

Although those issues concerning asylum seekers will be studied in another chapter of this book, these are of considerable importance as their crossing of

[5] Ibid., 63–6.

[6] The Ad Hoc Immigration Group prepared two agreements: the Dublin Agreement (Agreement relative to determining the state responsible for examining the applications for asylum submitted to the European Community) and the draft Agreement on the transfer of the external borders of the Community (the draft External Borders Agreement), but that Agreement has not been signed due to the difficulties between the United Kingdom and Spain regarding its application in Gibraltar.

[7] Bonn Protocol, 26 April 1994.

the external borders is of necessity very different from that of other third country nationals. Thus, the measures for control of the external border directly affect the rights of refugees. Therefore, the new Title IV EC must make the criteria for the entry of those seeking asylum much more precise as regards the scrupulous respect for the pre-existing international obligations.

Many different problems arose from the Dublin Convention,[8] and a serious reflection on its content must be carried out before it is incorporated into the norms of Title IV EC. In practice it has become very difficult to set down how the applicant entered irregularly in the European Union; thus, the criterion which makes the state where the applicant has requested asylum responsible (this being the criterion to apply finally) has become customary.

As this is not the place to deal with the technical difficulties and deficiencies of the Dublin Convention, we will confine ourselves to mentioning only some of the main limitations as regards the protection of individual rights. From this standpoint, the most important criticism lies in the fact that nothing is added to the responsibility for examining applications concerning the criteria to follow in order to determine the *status* of refugees. Thus, the asylum seeker whose application is turned down by one Member State which might be applying the 1951 Geneva Convention wrongly has no right to submit an application for asylum in any other EU Member State.[9]

Even more serious are the consequences of Art. 3(5) of the Dublin Convention which includes the possibility of the Member States sending the asylum seeker to a third country. Based on this point, the 1992 London Recommendation regarding a *safe third country* included a concept which is very difficult to reconcile with the previous international commitments of the Member States.

If the concept of *safe third country* is upheld after the adoption of measures on asylum in the framework of Title IV EC, this concept must be accompanied by an undertaking to study the application for asylum fittingly and to provide resources in the event of a possible rejection. On the other hand, the Community rules on the Member States responsibility for the examination of asylum claims must follow the international interpretation of the 1951 Geneva Convention on the Status of Refugees.[10]

[8] Marinho and Heinonen have highlighted this point. As an example: two members of the same family might have visas issued by different states of the European Union, or they may have entered the European Union illegally through different borders; by virtue of the criteria of the Dublin Convention, different states would be responsible for studying their applications. Both the Schengen Executive Committee and the Dublin Committee by decision laid down what situations could give rise to apply the "humanitarian criteria" (whereby any state might accept the petition of another state to examine the application for asylum for humanitarian reasons): these might be medical reasons, old age, pregnancy, minors who might be left unattended, but no account was taken, for example, of the case in which a relative might have received protection as a de facto refugee in another Member State, nor in cases involving non-married couples: C. Marinho, and M. Heinonen, "Dublin after Schengen: Allocating Responsibility for Examining Asylum Applications in Practice 2" (1988) 3 *EIPA SCOPE* 6.

[9] In this regard, see R. v. *Secretary of State for the Home Department, ex parte Adan and others* [1999] 3 WLR 1274.

[10] We do not consider it convenient that the "common position regarding the standardised application of the definition of the term refugee in accordance with Article 1 of the Geneva Convention"

To sum up, the Community instruments which will regulate questions related to asylum (those contained in the Dublin Convention and others such as the concept of *manifestly unfounded applications* for asylum[11] or the concept of *safe country of origin*[12]) must ensure the right of the asylum seeker to a sufficiently guaranteed procedure for asylum.

Draft External Borders Agreement Convention arising from the intergovernmental "15" route (Ad Hoc Immigration Group)

The draft Agreement on the crossing of external borders (the draft External Borders Agreement), deserves at least a mention for the purposes of this study. Although it was never signed, its content has served as the basis for the European Commission draft on a Convention on the crossing of the external borders of the Member States.[13]

The draft Agreement would define the concept of external borders and would lay down the common requirements for crossing them. It would also deal with the conditions for authorising visas and their territorial validity, and propose a common, three-month European visa for citizens from third countries. All other visas for longer periods of time would be an individual state type and be effective only in that state.

In addition, the draft Agreement takes into account the citizens from third countries already residing legally in the European Community and their right to travel within the Community for a period of three months with no need for a visa, although this does not include the right to work or settle in the territory of another Member State.

Schengen *acquis*

The Schengen Group[14] prepared the 1985 Agreement and the Schengen Implementation Agreement 1990 (hereinafter the Schengen Agreement) in order

be transferred to the European Community in its present terms (Common position of 4 March 1996 concerning the standardised application of the definition of the term refugee in accordance with Article 1 of the Geneva Convention of July 28, 1951 regarding the Refugee Statute (OJ 1996 L63/2)). The aforementioned Common position excludes persecution by non-state groups unless the state powers encourage or authorise this. However, the Geneva Convention must be interpreted as also including the persecution "of third persons" even when the state does not wish to or cannot avoid it.

[11] Some of these "manifestly unfounded claims" were refuted by the criterion of the ECHR in the case of *Hatami* v. *Sweden*, 59/1998/962/1177, 9 October 1998, ECtHR.

[12] The safe country of origin concept must not be upheld in a system based on the recognition of individual rights. See ILPA Comments on European Commission Working Paper "Towards Common Standards on Asylum" Sec (1999) 271, 3 March 1999, 6.

[13] Com (93) 684, end, 10 December 1993 (OJ 1994 C11).

[14] At the present time, the Schengen Group, which initially included only the three members of the Benelux countries together with France and Germany, includes all the EU Member States except the United Kingdom and Ireland.

to anticipate the free movement of workers laid down in the Single European Act. The entry into force of the Schengen Agreement was repeatedly postponed, but eventually the articles concerning the activities and competence of the Schengen Executive Committee came into force on 1 September 1993 for the original members.[15]

The decisions taken by the Schengen Executive Committee have not always been made public and this deserves to be criticised due to the situation of defencelessness it provokes as regards the rights of individuals. The controls employed at the external borders were drawn up in a "Common Handbook on External Borders" approved by the Schengen Executive Committee and it includes the list of states whose citizens were obliged to obtain a visa in order to enter all the Schengen states, as well as a list of states whose citizens did not require visas to enter any of the Schengen states and a list of states whose citizens required visas to enter some of the Schengen states.[16]

The Schengen Agreement regulated a variety of issues, ranging from police co-operation to legal aid in criminal matters and included the traffic of weapons and drugs. Among these issues was carriers' responsibility as regards the transfer of aliens without proper documents (Article 26) and the standardisation of visas (Articles 9–20). When the Dublin Convention came into force, Articles 28 *et seq* in the Schengen Agreement regarding the determining of the state responsible for examining the applications for asylum were no longer applied, in order to avoid duplication with the Dublin Convention and because the rules laid down for the Dublin Convention bind all the Member States of the European Union. The Schengen Agreement also set up the Schengen Information System (Title IV) which provides for the creation of a list of persons who are not admissible in any of the Schengen Member States and to which the states would add the names of aliens who had committed acts against public order or national security (Article 96).

The main criticisms of the Schengen Agreement from the standpoint of the defence of individual rights were stated clearly and concisely by the so called Meijers Committee:[17]

(1) The lack of adequate jurisdictional control. No international court was competent to try the cases where the Committee itself broke the Agreement

[15] On 1 March 1994 it came into force in Spain (*BOE* (Official State Gazette) No. 81 of 5 April 1994). As regards the original Schengen Agreement of 1985, Spain began to apply this "provisionally" in 1991 (*BOE* No. 181 of 30 July 1991).

[16] The provisions of the Schengen *acquis* have now acquired a legal basis within Community law or EU law, after the incorporation of the Schengen *acquis* into the framework of the European Union (Council Decision 99/435/EC of 20 May 1999 which defines the Schengen Group (OJ 1999 L176).

[17] "Opinions, Recommendations and Proposals concerning the international implications on ratification of the Implementing Agreement for the Schengen Agreement, as recently modified by the Agreement 29 March 1991, between the Schengen countries and the Republic of Poland, with accompanying Protocol" (Standing Committee of Experts on International Immigration, Refugee and Criminal Law, November 1991).

or other international commitments or had doubts as regards correct interpretation.

(2) The lack of a common definition of "public order". The Schengen Agreement led to an accumulation of the national concepts of "public order" to such an extent that an alien was refused entry when he/she was a threat to the public order of any of the Member States.

As regards what matters here and now, we must review the main flanking measures regarding the movement of persons taking place in the Schengen laboratory. All of these have been incorporated into the EU framework by applying the Protocol by which the Schengen Group is integrated into the EU framework.[18]

(1) Article 5 of the Schengen Agreement, which has been assigned judicial foundation in Article 62(2)(a) EC, it has been laid down the travel documents which allow third country nationals to cross the borders when his/her journey takes up to three months.
(2) Article 17 of the Schengen Agreement, which has been assigned legal basis in Article 62(2)(b)EC, has made it possible to lay down common rules for examining requests for visas.
(3) Articles 10, 11 and 19(1) of the Schengen Agreement, which have been assigned legal basis in Article 62(2)(b) and Article 62(3) EC, have led to the creation of a standard travel visa which allows third country nationals to move within "Schengen territory" for a maximum of three months per semester counting from the first entry. These citizens are obliged to declare entry into Schengen territory on entry or within three working days following entry.
(4) By virtue of Article 20 of the Schengen Agreement, which has been assigned judicial foundation in Article 62(3) EC, third country nationals not obliged to obtain a standard travel visa (i.e. those who do not require a visa for any of the Schengen states) acquire the right to move within the territories of the Schengen states for a period up to three months within six months following the first entry. These third country nationals are obliged to declare entry.
(5) Article 21 of the Schengen Agreement, which has been assigned legal basis in Article 62(3)EC, lays down that third country nationals legally residing in a Schengen state do not require a visa to reside in another Schengen state for a period of no more than three months. They are also obliged to declare entry.
(6) Article 96 of the Schengen Agreement (Articles 92–119 on the Schengen Information System (SIS) await judicial foundation, and thus, in the interim, they form part of Title VI TEU) specifies the reasons why each state may include third country nationals in a list of "not admissible" persons, which means prohibiting entry binding on the rest of the Schengen states.

[18] Protocol annexed by the ToA to the TEU and to the EC Treaty.

As concerns the rest, the residency visas and the residency and work permits are the competence of the states and are valid exclusively for the territory of the state issuing them.

Treaty of European Union

At the Luxembourg Summit in June 1991, Germany proposed that the Member States should attribute the competence required to achieve harmonisation on immigration and asylum policies to the European Community in the new Treaty for modifying the constituting treaties which was being drafted at the time.[19]

Finally, after the TEU came into force,[20] the new European Union acquired certain competence as regards immigration, asylum and the status of third country nationals but almost all of these, except for specific norms on visas, remained within the so-called Third Pillar of the European Union and thus outside purely Community decision-making procedure and outside the control of the ECJ.

Article K.1 TEU on the policy for asylum, immigration and the status of third country nationals defined these matters as areas of "common interest", i.e. although there was an *ad hoc* decision-making procedure, intergovernmental co-operation was upheld.

As an exception to the general situation of the policies on immigration and asylum in the Third Pillar, the TEU placed a part of the policy on visas for third country nationals within the First Pillar (former Article 100C EC).

(1) By virtue of this Article, Regulation (CE) No 2317/95 of the Council of September 25, 1995 by which the third countries whose citizens had to have visas to cross the external borders of the Member States was approved.[21]

The original text had been proposed by the European Commission on 10 December 1993.[22] In the Preamble the use of a regulation and not a directive was justified, as the "list", by definition, left no discretionary power to the Member States, nor did it require flanking measures. The Preamble clarified that the Commission would have liked to draft a "positive list" of third countries whose citizens must not have visas to enter the European Union, so that every "third country" would be included on a list in one way or another, but this was not possible "taking into account the very high number of third countries for which the practice of the Member States differs".[23] Thus, the positive list remained as work pending to be done before 30 June 1996. The draft Regulation also included the principle of mutual recognition of visas issued by Member States by the other Member States. However, this principle would be applied only to

[19] Presidency Conclusions, European Council Luxembourg, 28 and 29 June 1991, SN/1 51/3/9 1.
[20] TEU signed in Maastricht on 2 February 1992, and in force since 1 November 1993.
[21] OJ 1995 L234.
[22] OJ 1994 C11.
[23] Might there not also have been disagreement on the drawing up of the "negative list"?

visas valid in the European Union according to the draft Agreement for crossing external borders.

Nevertheless, the Regulation was adopted and allowed the Member States to maintain their particular lists of states whose citizens were subject to obtaining visas indefinitely. The European Parliament was not consulted after this modification and for that reason the ECJ annulled the Regulation although the ECJ did uphold its effects until the approval of a new regulation to replace it.[24]

Finally, on 12 March 1999, Council Regulation (EC) No. 574/99 was approved determining the third countries whose citizens had to have visas to cross the external borders of the Member States.[25] This laid down that the Member States had to make an effort to harmonise their policies on visas with regard to third countries which were not included in the common list (an identical provision to that laid down in the Regulation annulled) and that in the first semester of the year 2001 the Commission had to draft a report on the state of harmonisation.[26]

(2) In application of the former Article 100C EC, Regulation (EEC) No. 1683/95 of 29 May 1995 on a standard model of visas for stays of no more than three months in the European Union was also adopted.[27] Nevertheless, unlike the standard Schengen visa, the standard model of Community visa is not valid for visiting the whole EU territory, so it is a very watered-down flanking measure to the free movement of persons.

As regards the acts proper to the Third Pillar[28] on the crossing of external borders,[29] the following should be stressed:

(1) On 15 January 1994 the European Commission published its proposal to the Council for approval of a Convention on the crossing of external borders of the Member States in the *Official Journal*, in application of Article K3 TEU. (Com (93) 684, end, 10 December 1993) The content of this Agreement is practically the same as the Draft External Borders Agreement Convention negotiated within the Ad Hoc Group on Immigration, which, as was said before, was never signed. The most outstanding difference with the draft Agreement of the Ad Hoc Group on Immigration is the submittal of the

[24] Case C–392/95 *Parliament* v. *Council* [1997] ECR I–3213.

[25] OJ 1999 L72.

[26] On 26 January 2000 the European Commission tabled a new proposal of Regulation on the issue in which it finally adds a "white list" of countries whose nationals need not have visas to cross the external borders of the Member States to the previous "black list" (COM (2000) 27 fin, OJC 177 E/66 of 26. January 00 modified by COH (2000) 577 fin.

[27] OJ 1995 L164.

[28] The legal nature of certain instruments proper to the aforementioned Third Pillar continued to be unclear.

[29] These and other acts are quoted by L. Garau Juaneda, "*La politica común de extranjería de la Comunidad Europea*" (Common Policy on Aliens in the European Community), in *El Derecho Internacional y las Relaciones Internacionales en el Mundo Mediterràneo* (International Law and International Relations in the Mediterranean World) XVII *Jornadas de la Asociación Espatiola de Profesores de Derecho Internacional y Relaciones Internacionales*, BOE (Universitat de les Illes Balears, Madrid, 1999), 137–8.

Agreement on crossing the external borders to the control of the ECJ in order to interpret its provisions and rule in litigation involving its interpretation.[30]

The proposed Agreement specifies the conditions and requirements for crossing the external borders and the measures for controlling them, a three-month common visa was established and visas for longer periods of time were applicable only in the state issuing the visa. Those third country nationals legally residing in the territory of the European Union are freed from the obligation to obtain visas to travel within EU territory only for a period up to three months. As can be seen, all these issues have been regulated in the Schengen "laboratory".

(2) The Recommendation of 30 November 1994 regarding a model of a normalised bilateral agreement for readmission between one Member State and a third country[31] is especially interesting, together with the Recommendation of 24 July 1995 on the governing principles which must be followed for drawing up protocols on the application of the agreements on readmission.[32]

The competence of the Commission regarding the agreements on readmission with third States varied after the ToA. How is State competence in this matter affected? The Commission could request the opinion of the ECJ by virtue of Article 300(6) EC.[33]

(3) Another interesting document concerning the flanking measures for the disappearance of external borders is the Common Action of 4 March 1996, by which an airport transit visa was set up for citizens from certain countries.[34] As is known, the ECJ had to decide whether this measure should or should not be based on Article 100C EC and it decided that it was a Third Pillar question.[35]

(4) The Recommendation of 4 March 1996 regarding local consular co-operation on visas should also be mentioned. In this Recommendation measures for the exchange of information between consular services concerning possible simultaneous applications for visas or previous rejection by other Member States are laid down. Of course, the Recommendation bears the reminder that the exchange of information must respect the norms on data protection in force.[36]

30 In this regard, Art. 29 of the Draft.

31 OJ 1996 C274.

32 Ibid.

33 ILPA European Update (June 1999), 14. The ECJ, since the *ERTA* case in 1971, has held that the European Community can have implied external competencies, but these normally do not exist until the European Community has exercised its internal powers in the area. As we know, new Title IV EC grants competencies to the European Community on illegal immigration.

34 OJ 1996 L63.

35 Case C–170/96 (unreported) 12 May 1998, ECJ.

36 OJ 1996 C80.

(5) On 30 July 1997 the Commission submitted a proposal for an Act of the Council establishing a Convention concerning the rules for admission of the citizens of third countries into the Member States.[37] This draft regulated the conditions of residence of citizens from third countries, family regrouping and the status of "citizens from third countries who have settled permanently". Very probably its content will be used when adopting decisions on these issues within Title IV EC.

As we have seen, little has been done after the entry in force of the TEU concerning the flanking measures taken to achieve the free movement of persons. We suggest that any relevant progress in the matter has taken place in the Schengen "laboratory" and, of course, this has not been sufficiently orientated towards respect for individual rights.

THE TREATY OF AMSTERDAM

New Title IV EC

If the Single European Act was an important step forward as regards the free movement of persons in so far as it laid down the disappearance of the internal borders, the ToA again made considerable progress as it conferred competence on the European Community to adopt the measures necessary for this. Thus, among other novelties,[38] the ToA created a new Title IV EC (First Pillar) on "Visas, asylum, immigration and other policies related to the free movement of persons". This means that the immigration and asylum policies leave the Third Pillar to become incorporated into Community law.[39]

However, this is not a question of suddenly becoming a Community matter, as during the first period of five years after the ToA came into force the measures for guaranteeing the absence of controls on persons crossing the internal borders, both citizens of the European Union and citizens of third countries and, consequently the "measures regarding the crossing of external borders" will be adopted unanimously and on the proposal of the Commission or a Member State, once the Parliament has been consulted. After the transitory period already described only the Commission will have the initiative (although the Member States may make suggestions) and the Council can decide unanimously that all or part of the areas of this Title begin to be adopted by qualified majority.

[37] Submitted by the Commission in accordance with letter (c), section 2, Art. K3 TEU, COM (97) 387 (OJ 1997 (C337).

[38] For example, the new Art. 13 EC on "non-discrimination" proposes that (within the limits of the competence attributed to the European Community) the Council, unanimously, on the proposal of the Commission and once the European Parliament has been consulted, may adopt adequate measures to fight against all discrimination as regards sex, racial or ethnic origin, religion or convictions, incapacity, age or sexual orientation.

[39] This new Title considerably reduces the matters regulated within intergovernmental co-operation of the Third Pillar (now containing only provisions relative to police and judicial co-operation in criminal matters).

For certain questions, which are of particular interest for this chapter, there will be no transitory period and the decision will be by majority *ab initio* (lists of countries whose citizens require tourist visas, lists of countries which do not require these and a standard model of visa).[40] As regards other matters, after the transitory period, the decision will be by majority with no need for a vote to be taken in the Council (procedures for issuing tourist visas).

Hence, Article 61 EC provides that in order to establish a space of freedom, security and justice, the Council must adopt measures to guarantee the free movement of persons laid down in Article 14 EC and "accompanying measures directly linked to them" and relative to controls on the external borders, asylum and immigration within a period of five years from the entry in force of the ToA, 1 May 1999.

Article 62 EC goes on to enumerate, among other matters, the measures to adopt within the aforementioned period of five years as regards crossing the external borders of the Member States:

(1) The rules on checks to be carried out on persons wishing to cross these borders.
(2) Rules on the issue of visas to persons applying for them for stays no longer than three months. Among these are: the list of third countries whose citizens are obliged to have visas in order to cross an external border and the list of those states whose citizens are exempt from this obligation; the procedures and conditions for issuing visas by the Member States; and the standard model of visa and the rules for issuing a standard visa. Moreover, the conditions on which third country nationals can travel freely in the territories of the Member States for a period up to three months are established.[41]

[40] As can be seen, these are matters already regulated by virtue of the former Art. 100C EC.

[41] In addition, in order to guarantee the free movement of persons, in the five year period following the entry into force of the ToA other measures have to be adopted: criteria for establishing the responsibility of the Member States concerning the examination of the applications for asylum and the minimum rules for temporally protecting those who have moved from third countries and cannot return to their countries of origin. In the aforementioned period of five years from the entry into force of the ToA, many other measures will have to be adopted regarding immigration and the right to asylum in order to obtain the "area of freedom, security and justice", which are not directly related to the establishment of the free movement of persons: (1) minimum rules for sheltering asylum seekers, for granting the status of refugees and for the procedures to be followed by the Member States in order to grant or reject the status of refugees and (2) rules regarding immigration and illegal residence. Finally, some of the measures to adopt concerning immigration and the right to asylum in order to obtain the area "freedom, security and justice" but not directly related to the establishment of the free movement of persons, remain outside the period of five years laid down for those mentioned previously, which means that their adoption could be delayed. These are matters which are more intrinsically connected with state sovereignty: (1) the establishment of a balanced effort among the Member States to shelter refugees and displaced persons ("burden sharing"); (2) rules on the conditions of entry and residence on the procedures for issuing long-term visas, residence permits and visas and permits for family regrouping; and (3) rules which establish the conditions on which citizens from third countries legally residing in a Member State can reside in others.

For an update of the proposals submitted by the Commission or the Member States for the creation of an "Area of Freedom, Security and Justice", see: Communication from the Commission to the Council and the European Parliament Com (2000) 167 fin, 24 March 2000.

Faced with the transfer of some immigration policies to the Community, the first reaction could be one of satisfaction for what, apparently, supposed an achievement in the attempt to better guarantee the rights of citizens from third countries in the European Union under the judicial control of the ECJ.

But this first reaction is soon joined by disappointment and distress. The new Title IV EC has three Protocols (3, 4 and 5) annexed, by virtue of which three of the Member States (the United Kingdom, Ireland and Denmark) state that they will not participate in many of the activities and decisions foreseen in the new Title or, more precisely, they leave the possibility open of participating or not as they wish under "opting in" system.

This distress grows on finding that Article 68 of the new Title IV cuts down the jurisdiction of the ECJ as regards appeals. Concerning the preliminary reference procedure laid down in Article 234 EC, the new Article 68 EC lays down that, instead of any judge or court, only the judges or internal courts of final instance will be able to refer preliminary questions and, moreover, they will only request the intervention of the ECJ if "they consider it to be necessary". This reduction in the jurisdiction of the ECJ does not seem to have been sufficient since Article 68 EC goes on to state that the ECJ will not have jurisdiction over decisions adopted as regards the abolition of internal borders "relative to the maintaining of public order and safeguarding internal security". This final provision, depending on how it is interpreted, could empty of all content the control of the ECJ as regards the matters we are dealing with.

From the viewpoint of the defence of individual rights, this reduction of the jurisdiction of the ECJ in matters related to the new Title IV EC is the most worrying factor among the novelties introduced into Title IV EC by the ToA.[42]

One of the questions of most concern consists in knowing whether the rules arising from compliance with the new Title IV will fulfil the requirements for direct effect, i.e. whether they will be rules which are clear, precise and unconditional. It is crucial for individuals to be able to claim the rights arising from this Title before national judges. Some of the provisions adopted by virtue of Title IV EC as complementary to the free movement of persons should have this direct effect: for example, the measures for guaranteeing the absence of controls on persons crossing the internal borders and those which lay down the conditions whereby the citizens of third countries may travel freely within the territories of the Member States for a period up to three months. It is too soon to speculate about direct effect of future measures.

[42] As K. Hailbronner has stated in "The Treaty of Amsterdam and Migration Law" (1999) 1 *European Journal of Migration and Law* 19: "There are very few possibilities for an individual to directly challenge community legislation before the EC. The limitation of preliminary rulings further reduces the possibility of effective protection against community regulations in violation of fundamental rights".

Integration of the Schengen *acquis* in the framework of the European Union

The ToA facilitates the "reinforced co-operation in the framework of the EU" by virtue of Articles 40 and 43–45 TEU, not present in the Maastricht version. The Council will authorise this co-operation by qualified majority, but if a Member State declares that it intends to oppose this qualified majority for important, explicit reasons concerning national policy, voting will not take place and the Council can decide, by qualified majority, that this matter be referred to the Council, meeting as heads of state or government, to decide on it unanimously.

At the same time, the ToA directly regulates the free movement of persons in the European Union through the Protocol by which the Schengen *acquis*[43] was integrated into the framework of the European Union. Article 1 of this Protocol authorises the members to continue with this reinforced co-operation which will be channelled within the institutional framework of the European Union and the European Community.

This means that all measures destined to facilitate the disappearance of the internal borders in the Schengen framework or in the framework of all the EU Member States will not be adopted anymore outside the European Union and will have a greater or lesser level of control by the European Parliament and the ECJ, as we shall see below.

Logically, one part of the Schengen *acquis* has been integrated into the First Pillar, e.g. the questions related to visas, while others, such as action against drug trafficking, etc., have been incorporated into the new Third Pillar. Some of the most significant questions related to individual rights faced with the single external border arise from the situation of subjects inside one or other of the Pillars.

Of course, the integration of Schengen is applicable only to the thirteen Member States of the European Union participating in the Schengen Agreements, that is to say all except the United Kingdom and Ireland. If Ireland or the United Kingdom wishes to participate in any of the provisions of the Schengen *acquis*, Article 4 of the Protocol requires the unanimous decision of the Schengen members in the Council plus the representative of the state in question. Iceland and Norway, members of the Nordic Passport Union, together with the other Scandinavian countries, despite not being members of the European Union, are associated to the execution of the Schengen acquis. After the entry into force of the ToA on 18 May 1999, an Agreement was made between the Council of the European Union, and the Republic of Iceland and the Kingdom of Norway on the association of these two countries to the execu-

[43] Protocol No. 2 by which the Schengen *acquis* was integrated into the framework of the European Union, annexed to the TEU and the EC Treaty. The Schengen *acquis* is constituted by the original Agreement of 1985, the Agreement of 1990, the Protocols of Accession and the decisions of the Schengen Executive Committee.

tion, application and development of the Schengen *acquis*.[44] Denmark is a Schengen member but does not accept Community competence of Title IV EC and so does not accept the part of Schengen integrated into the First Pillar. Thus, the Schengen obligations integrated into the First Pillar as concerns relations with Denmark will, as before, be obligations under public international law arising from an international treaty.[45] The candidates for accession to the European Union will have to accept the Schengen *acquis* in its totality.

By Council Decision (991/436/EC) of 20 May 1999 the judicial foundation of each provision or decision which constitutes the Schengen *acquis* has been determined in accordance with the provisions of the EC Treaty and the TEU.[46] As regards those questions which most interest us for this chapter, the following should be pointed out:

(1) The rules for Title II of the Schengen Convention on the abolition of controls at the internal borders and the movement of persons together with the decisions of the Schengen Executive Committee in this regard have been incorporated into the First Pillar, generally Articles 62 and 63 EC. The same is true of the crossing of external borders, the policy on long- and short-term visas, the conditions for the movement of aliens, even the sanctions applicable to carriers, although here the form, modality and level of sanctions is reserved for the Member States. Only co-operation between the states in order to pursue those who profit from illegal immigration (Article 27(2) and (3) of the Schengen Convention) has been placed in the new Third Pillar.

(2) "The hot potato" was Title IV of the Schengen Convention, which created the Schengen Information System (SIS) and regulates the protection of

[44] Article 18 of the Agreement of 17 May 1999 Treaty states that it substitutes the Co-operation Convention between the Schengen states, the Republic of Iceland and the Kingdom of Norway concerning the abolition of controls at common borders signed in Luxembourg on 19 December 1996 (Agreement of 18 May 1999 between the Council of the European Union, the Republic of Iceland and the Kingdom of Norway on the association of these two states to the execution, application and development of the Schengen *acquis* (OJ 1999 L176/36). See also Council Decision 99/437/EC relative to certain rules for the development of the Agreement between the Council of the European Union, the Republic of Iceland and the Kingdom of Norway on the association of these two states to the execution, application and development of the Schengen *acquis*: (OJ 1999 L176/36). The Agreement of 17 May 1999 states that it replaces the Co-operation Agreement between the contracting parties of the Agreement and the Schengen Agreement, the Republic of Iceland and the Kingdom of Norway concerning the abolition of controls on persons at common borders, signed in Luxembourg on 19 December 1996.

[45] In a period of six months since the Council decided on the development of a Schengen question within Title IV EC , Denmark will decide whether or not to apply this provision within its internal law. If it does so, it will be an obligation under international public law between Denmark and the other Schengen members (also as regards the United Kingdom and Ireland if they participate). See Art. 5 of the Protocol on the position of Denmark annexed to the TEU and the EC Treaty.

[46] Decision 99/435/EC of 20 May 1999 first defines the Schengen *acquis*, i.e. the 1985 Agreement, the 1990 Convention, the Accession Protocols, the Decisions (99) and declarations of the Schengen Executive Committee (37) and Decisions of the Central Group (six). Of the 142 Schengen Articles of 1990, 43 do not require the assignation of a legal basis, neither do some of the provisions of the Accession Protocols (ILPA, *European Update* (June 1999). See both Council Decisions of 20 May 1999 in OJ 1999 L176.

personal data (Articles 92–119). The list of persons who are not admissible, for example, is used for the crossing of external borders and the admission of aliens (First Pillar) but it is also used for police co-operation (Third Pillar).

The Commission was of the opinion that a double legal base should be assigned to it but in practice this turned out to be impossible; how could double practice be followed in the unanimous or qualified majority procedure for acts with identical content?[47] Two states, France and Spain, consider that it should be included in the Third Pillar and as there has been no agreement otherwise, it is provisionally in the Third Pillar.[48]

(3) Title IV of the Schengen Convention (Articles 126–130) on the protection of personal data has been placed in the Third Pillar, but not totally as it has also been granted judicial basis in Article 95 EC.

(4) Article 136 of the Schengen Convention on border agreements with third countries is granted judicial basis in Title IV EC (Article 62(2)).

As regards the new EC procedures, it should be remembered that:

(1) Concerning the Schengen *acquis* which is incorporated into the First Pillar, the power of initiative will be shared among the states and the Commission during the first five years after the entry into force of the ToA, following which it will be the exclusive competence of the Commission. The Council of the European Union has replaced the Schengen Executive Committee and will decide by unanimous vote for the first five years; subsequently, if passed unanimously by the Council, decisions will be adopted by a qualified majority. The European Parliament will be consulted during the first five years, following which it will make pronouncements in co-decision if the Council so decides.

(2) Regarding the Schengen *acquis* which has been incorporated into the Third Pillar, the power of initiative will be shared by the states and the Commission. The Council will decide by unanimity. The Parliament will be consulted during the first five years and then will make pronouncements in co-decision if the Council so decides.

What is most important is the fact that in either case the ECJ will control proceedings, which did not happen with the old Third Pillar, nor in the Schengen framework before the ToA.[49]

According to Article 35 TEU, the ECJ has jurisdiction under Article 143 EC; states have to accept this by an additional declaration, in which they must state whether they also accept preliminary references from all courts or only from the

[47] Délégation de l'Assemblée Nationale pour l'Union Européenne, *Rapport d'Information sur l'integration de l'acquis de Schengen dans l'Union Européenne* (présenté par M.F. Loncle). AN No. 1257, 21–2.

[48] By virtue of Art. 2(1) of the Protocol by which the Schengen *acquis* is integrated into the framework of the EU.

[49] See C. Galdino (1998) 2 *Revue du Marché Unique Européenne*.

final court of appeal. Eleven Member States (all except the United Kingdom, Ireland, Denmark and France) have made declarations regarding the scope of the ECJ in Third Pillar matters. Of these eleven states, all except Spain have stated that they will permit any court, in any case, to make a reference by virtue of Article 35 TEU.[50]

As we have already seen, until now the two most important flanking measures for the abolition of the internal borders have been carried out in the framework of Schengen and so without the participation of the European Parliament and the jurisdictional competence of the ECJ. These concern the standard visa for stays up to three months valid for all the Schengen territory and the SIS, which allows the Schengen states to include an alien on a common list of persons not admissible into the territory of the European Union.[51]

As in the co-operation "among the fifteen", little has been done as regards "the flanking measures" to achieve free movement of persons, the Schengen *acquis* is not only interesting in its "incorporation" into EU Law after the entry into force of the ToA, but also because it will probably be the model to follow for adopting measures within the new Title IV EC, with, we hope, its defects rectified.

The question could even be asked whether it is possible that only the total abolition of internal controls will be achieved in the Schengen framework and, for this reason, flanking measures have been adopted within this framework. The position adopted by the United Kingdom, Ireland and Denmark regarding the new Title IV EC prima facie does not facilitate the adoption of Community measures among all the Member States.

On the other hand, it is contradictory that the "incorporated" Schengen rules on flanking measures for the abolition of internal borders (it should be remembered that Schengen was originally a "laboratory" test) will be binding on fifteen states (the Schengen thirteen plus Norway and Iceland), while the original Community policy could bind only twelve of the Member States due to the particular positions on only opting in, in turn subject to unanimity for acceptance as adopted by the United Kingdom, Ireland and Denmark.

Data protection, access to information and the common external border

The provisions which might be adopted by virtue of Title IV EC, as well as many others related to Title VI TEU, must guarantee the rights of individuals to know and control the information held regarding them and which might be used, for example, to exclude them from the territory of the European Union.

[50] ILPA, *European Update* (June 1999), 10.

[51] As regards the flanking measures for the abolition of the internal border in the Schengen *acquis*, see L. Garau Juaneda, "*La política commún de extranjería . . .*", above at n. 29, pp 129–31.

With regard to the SIS[52], the *Forabosco* case,[53] which was decided by the French Council of State on 9 June 1999, is of interest.[54] The Government Commission, the Council of State could rule on the legal error committed by Germany when it included Mme Forabosco on the SIS list for a reason which was not among those laid down in Article 96 of the Schengen Convention. Articles 111 and 116 of the Schengen Convention[55] were clear in this regard and confer competence in this matter; but if the Council of State were unsure of the interpretation of the articles it could make a preliminary reference to the ECJ by reason of the new Article 35 TEU. The Council of State ruled that it was competent to evaluate a foreign administrative decision and that the German authorities had made an error of law when they included Mme Forabosco on the SIS list for the sole reason that she had requested and been refused asylum in Germany.[56]

Another question concerns the confidential data used by the Europol Convention, in force since 1 October 1998. As it is a confidential distribution system on criminal acts, direct access by citizens is excluded in principle. The data used by Europol are on persons suspected of having committed a crime or who might potentially commit a crime within the area of jurisdiction of Europol. This final provision must be especially criticised from the standpoint of the protection of individual rights as it potentially converts any person into a subject whose data might be stored by Europol.[57]

[52] Article 115 of the Schengen Convention refers *ex professo* to the Convention of the Council of Europe of 28 January 1981 for the protection of persons as regards the automatic processing of personal data and to Recommendation R(87)15 adopted on 17 September 1987 by the Committee of Ministers of the Council of Europe related to the use of personal data in the police area. All the Member States of the Eureopean Union, and more fully the Schengen States, are bound by the aforementioned Convention of the Council of Europe of 28 January 1981 on the automatic processing of personal data.

[53] *Aff.*: *M. Et Mme Forabosco*, AJDA (20 September 1999), 725–8.

[54] M. Forabosco had married Mariana Stancu, a Rumanian citizen, in September 1996. She applied to the French Consulate in Bucharest for a long-term residence visa and the Consulate rejected her application on 21 March 1997. This rejection was confirmed by the Foreign Ministry on 10 April 1997. The reason? Mariana Stancu had been included in the list of the SIS by Germany owing to the fact that before her marriage she had requested asylum in Germany, and been rejected(!). This reason, obviously, is not among the grounds for appearing on the SIS list, which are listed in Art. 96 of the Schengen Convention.

[55] Article 111 of the Schengen Convention provides for the right of every person to take action in the territories of each participating state before the jurisdictional organ or the competent authority in order to rectify, suppress, be informed or apply for compensation due to a description which refers to the person. Article 116 explains that the Schengen States will be liable for injury to a person through the use of data on the SIS, also if the damage has been caused by the "informing" Schengen State, which *de facto* or *de iure* had filed erroneous data. If the Schengen State against which action is taken was not the "informing" state, the "informing" state would be obliged to return the amounts paid as compensation.

[56] In the *Hamsaoui* case, which was also decided by the French Council of State on 9 June 1999, a Moroccan citizen had been refused a short-term visa as she was on the SIS list but had not been given information on the reasons why she was on this list. The French Council of State followed the opinion of the Government Commission and annulled the decision refusing the visa: ILPA, *European Update* (October 1999), 2–3.

[57] J.D. Janez Torren, "*La protección de los particulares en el àmbito del Convenio Europol. Reflexiones con motivo de su entrada en vigor*", *Gaceta Jurídica de la Comunidad Europea*, B–140 (January/February 1999), 22.

On the other hand, after the entry in force of the ToA, there is now a proposal[58] for rules on the Eurodac Convention and Protocol. This entails a system for storing the fingerprints of those applying for asylum and of aliens in an "irregular" situation as supporting measures for the Dublin Convention. The Eurodac Convention lays down that the fingerprints of asylum seekers over fourteen years of age may be taken, with the aim of avoiding multiple applications in the European Union under different identities. Fingerprints may also be taken of those immigrants who have entered the European Union irregularly in order to know the state through which the asylum seeker entered and thus apply the Dublin Convention, and of those residents who are in a situation of irregularity so as to know when an asylum seeker has entered a state after having applied for asylum in another state which was responsible for examining his application.[59]

The new Article 286 EC provides that all Community acts relative to the protection of persons with regard to the processing of personal data and free movement of these data will be applicable to the Community institutions. This provision corrects the absurd situation whereby the institutions could regulate states' dealings with personal data but not apply this rule to themselves.[60]

The position of individuals when faced with the abolition of internal borders in EC law and EU law combined with the limited access of the individual to Community justice raises serious questions about the deficient protection of fundamental human rights in the European Union. The ECJ excludes the right of the individual to contest Community acts of general scope, such as regulations, other than in exceptional cases.[61] The ECJ has put its opinion on deficient access of private citizens to Community justice on record. Thus, in its report on the functioning of the European Union, it states:

> "L'on peut toutefois se demander si le recours en annulation prévu par l'article 173 du traité CE et par les dispositions correspondantes des autres traités, qui n'est ouvert aux particuliers qu' à l'égard des actes qui les concernent directement et individuellement est suffisant pour leur garantir une protection jurisdictionnelle effective contre les atteintes à leurs droits fondamentaux pouvant résulter de l'àctivité législative des institutions."[62]

A fuller consideration of the issue of human rights is beyond the scope of this chapter but has already raised concerns about differential appreciation of individual rights by the ECJ and the ECtHR.

[58] Com (99) 260 of 26 May 1999.

[59] ILPA, *European Update* (June 1999), 8.

[60] S. Sanz Caballero, "*Los derechos fundamentales en el Tratado de Amsterdam: una reforma tímida pero positiva de los tratados constitutivos*" (1998) 4 *Boletín Europeo de la Universidad de La Rioja* 64–5.

[61] Case C–309/98 *Codorníu* v. *Council* [1994] ECR I–1853.

[62] *Rapport de la Cour de Justice sur certains aspects de l'application du Traité sur l'Union Europénne* (May 1995), 20.

CONCLUSIONS

It seems that the disappearance of border controls, in addition to the measures relative to the harmonised control of the "external" borders, will imply more frequent controls inside the territory of the Member States. This could bring us to a situation which is supposedly not what we desire, and, as a well-known specialist in the matter has pointed out, according to this the border might be found "everywhere" from now on.[63]

What can reasonably be expected of the EC measures on the crossing of external borders? On the one hand, vigilance and compliance with the entry requirements will be taken to extremes for third country nationals and the states will use the common list of persons who are not admissible in order to forbid entry and refuse visas. Nevertheless, this must be done with sufficient flexibility to comply with the obligations derived from human rights under international law regarding asylum seekers and any persons in need of international protection.

Perhaps the way to make the new area of freedom, security and justice open to everyone will depend on improving access to Community justice for the individual, as well as solving the as yet unresolved subject pending for European integration: as a well-known Spanish jurist has said recently, while the European Union lacks a good system for the protection of fundamental rights it will lack "a soul".

[63] Antonio Remiro Brotons has expressed this ironically but acurately: "As regards the other matters, let nobody sit down in the park or throw crumbs to the pigeons thinking he/she is safe from any interference due to his good conduct, especially if he/she is in the vicinity of ports, airports, railway stations or highways. Administrative measures for checking identities as a preventative measure seem to have become generalised to the detriment of those with a suspiciously strange appearance. Taking it for granted that the most dangerous criminals will be dressed to kill, the badly dressed 'velis nolis' will be scapegoats, especially if their bodies and baggage include more than one suspect indicator. Naturally, the Home Secretaries in the respectable European countries have been careful to specify to their agents that race or skin colour are not among these indicators. But. . ." (*Los países de la Unión Europea, tierra de inmigración*, Lecture given to the Congress on Immigration in Spain, Madrid (16–18 October 1997), 5.

6

The Individual Refugee, the 1951 Convention and the Treaty of Amsterdam

GUY S. GOODWIN-GILL

INTRODUCTION

An optimist might well conclude that the European Union is about to have a positive impact on the movements of refugees, asylum seekers and migrants to the region—positive, that is, in the sense that all individuals who claim protection receive a fair and efficient assessment of their cases; that protection is granted to those who need it; that those who have no valid claim to remain are enabled to return to their countries of origin in safety and dignity; and that the European Union, as an international force, contributes effectively to development and democratisation beyond the region, which are central to any longer-term impact on the movements of peoples.

Is such an optimistic outlook justified? The development of a human rights dimension in the architecture of the European Union has been spasmodic, at best. The 1993 Maastricht Treaty included limited references to human rights in the context of the TEU, but the ECJ had no jurisdiction to enforce the commitments to human rights, either under the First Pillar (Common Foreign and Security Policy) or under the Third Pillar (Justice and Social Affairs). The 1997 Treaty of Amsterdam (ToA) has now gone farther, incorporating human rights provisions into the accessions process for new Member States,[1] permitting the suspension of a Member State for systematic breaches of human rights,[2] and providing new legislative competences in human rights, for example, in the area of discrimination.[3]

Article 6 TEU confirms the basic "principles of liberty, democracy, respect for human rights and fundamental freedoms, and the rule of law", and proclaims that the Union "shall respect fundamental rights, as guaranteed by" the

[1] See Arts 6(1) and 49 TEU. References are to the numbering of the consolidated versions of the TEU and EC Treaty: EU, *Consolidated Treaties* (Office for Official Publications of the European Communities, Luxembourg, 1997).

[2] Article 7 TEU; Art. 309 EC.

[3] Articles 136–7 and 141 EC.

European Convention on Human Rights (ECHR). Article 11 of the Treaty integrates an equivalent position of principle into the EU's Common Foreign and Security Council: "to develop and consolidate democracy and the rule of law, and respect for human rights and fundamental freedoms". Article 29, in turn, declares the EU's objective, "to provide citizens with a high level of safety within an area of freedom, security and justice by developing common action among the Member States . . . and by preventing and combating racism and xenophobia".[4]

TREATY OF AMSTERDAM

The ToA moves asylum from the Third to the First Pillar, with the prospect of legally binding instruments of harmonisation being handed down by the Council and a measure of judicial control by the ECJ. All the provisions relating specifically to asylum now appear in a new Title IV, "Visas, asylum, immigration and other policies related to freedom of movement of persons". During the transition period of five years from the entry into force of the ToA (May 1999), unanimous voting is still required on any proposal from the Commission or on the initiative of a Member State, and new measures will be adopted only "after consulting the European Parliament".[5] A non-binding declaration provides that consultations will be undertaken with the Office of the United Nations High Commissioner for Refugees (UNHCR) and other relevant international organisations on matters relating to asylum.[6] The ECJ may give a ruling on a question of interpretation of the Title, but subject to fairly substantial limitations. Thus, only a national court of *final* instance may request such a ruling,[7] and no such ruling may be given in relation to "any measure or decision taken pursuant to Article 62(1)"—that is, measures on the suppression of internal borders—"relating to the maintenance of law and order and the safeguarding of internal security".[8] Indeed, the importance attached by Member States to competence in this field is clearly expressed in Article 64.[9]

The central question is whether greater transparency of decision-making will result, given that the exercise of legislative authority will proceed without effective control (effective in the sense equivalent to that exercised by national parliaments) by the European Parliament or the ECJ. The changes introduced by

[4] See also Art. 2 TEU; Art. 61 EC. *Cf.* Art. 9 of the OSCE Istanbul Charter for European Security (November 1999), which also makes special reference to the eradication of "aggressive nationalism, racism, chauvinism, xenophobia and anti-Semitism".

[5] Article 67 EC. See, generally, K. Hailbronner, "The New Title on Freedom of Movement of Persons, Asylum and Immigration in the EC", in M. den Boer (ed.), *Schengen, Judicial Co-operation and Policy Co-ordination* (Maastricht, EIPA, 1997), 201.

[6] See the Tampere Conclusions, further below.

[7] Article 68 EC.

[8] Article 68(2) EC.

[9] See further below, text to n. 14.

the Amsterdam Treaty offer some grounds for optimism, but the proof will lie in the products; and enough ambiguity remains to give cause for concern.

EU PLAN OF ACTION

Article 2 TEU clearly locates "appropriate measures with respect to asylum" within the "area of freedom, security and justice . . .". So far as refugees are concerned, the Council is required, again within five years of the Treaty's entry into force, "to adopt measures on asylum, *in accordance with the Geneva Convention of 28 July 1951 and the Protocol of 31 January 1967 relating to the status of refugees and other relevant treaties*"[10] in the following areas: (a) criteria and mechanisms for determining Member State responsibility to consider an asylum application; (b) minimum standards on the reception of asylum seekers; (c) minimum standards with respect to the refugee definition;[11] and (d) minimum procedural standards for granting or withdrawing refugee status. The recurrence of the word "minimum" is remarkable; Article 63 EC thus proposes a distinctly limited agenda for Community action, and individual states retain considerable powers.

Secondly, and without specific or formal reference to the refugee or other treaties, the Council is called upon to adopt measures relating to minimum standards for temporary protection for displaced persons "who cannot return to their country of origin and for persons who otherwise need international protection";[12] and also to adopt measures "promoting a balance of effort" between Member States accepting refugees and the displaced.[13] By way of reservation, however, it is provided that this new Title, "shall not affect the exercise of the responsibilities incumbent upon Member States with regard to the maintenance of law and order and the safeguarding of internal security . . .".[14]

At its October 1999 meeting in Finland, the European Council affirmed in the "Tampere Conclusions" that, in principle,

[10] Article 63 EC, emphasis supplied. Despite the outward commitment to the 1951 Convention, in fact the major areas of concern and Community action relate to Arts. 1 (definition) and 33 (non-refoulement) CSR51, rather than the standards of treatment due to refugees in general.

[11] Strictly speaking, "minimum standards with respect to the qualification of nationals of third countries as refugees": Art. 63(1)(c) EC.

[12] Article 63(2)(a) EC; see also K. Kerber, "Temporary Protection: An Assessment of the Harmonisation Policies of EU Member States" (1997) 9 *IJRL* 453.

[13] Article 63(2)(b) EC. The Council is also to adopt measures on immigration policy to cover, among others, conditions of entry and residence, procedures for the issue of long-term visas and residence permits, including those for the purpose of family reunion; illegal immigration and illegal residence, including repatriation of illegal residents: Art. 63(3) EC. Additionally, measures defining the rights and conditions under which legally resident nationals of third countries may reside in another Member States are called for: Art. 63(4) EC.

[14] Article 64(1) EC. Provision is made for the adoption of provisional measures by the Council, in the event of "an emergency situation characterised by a sudden inflow of nationals of third countries".

> "freedom should not . . . be regarded as the exclusive preserve of the Union's own citizens . . . It would be in contradiction with Europe's traditions to deny such freedom to those whose circumstances lead them justifiably to seek access to [Union] territory. This in turn requires the Union to develop common policies on asylum . . . The aim is an open and secure EU, *fully committed to the obligations of the Geneva Refugee Convention and other relevant human rights instruments*, and able to respond to humanitarian needs on the basis of solidarity . . ."[15]

In the matter of a common EU asylum policy, "greater coherence of internal and external policies" is called for, in partnership with countries of origin. In addition, the Conclusions acknowledge that the Council "has agreed to work towards establishing a Common European Asylum System, based on the full and inclusive application of the Geneva Convention, thus ensuring that nobody is sent back to persecution, i.e. maintaining the principle of non-refoulement".[16]

Following the agenda established by Article 63, the Council breaks its strategy down into short- and long-term goals, in pursuit of which it "stresses the importance of consulting UNHCR and other international organisations".[17] The short-term goals include:

- a clear and workable determination of the state responsible for the examination of an asylum application;
- common standards for a fair and efficient asylum procedure;
- common minimum conditions of reception of asylum seekers;
- the approximation of rules on the recognition and content of the refugee status;
- subsidiary forms of protection and an appropriate status to any person in need of such protection.

In the longer term, "Community rules should lead to a common asylum procedure and a uniform status for those who are granted asylum valid throughout the Union".[18]

The present chapter focuses, from the perspective of international law, on just a select part of this programme, namely: the human rights background, which impacts not only on the reception of asylum seekers, but on the treatment

[15] Presidency Conclusions, Tampere European Council (15 and 16 October 1999) (Tampere Conclusions), paras 3, 4 (emphasis supplied); text in (1999) 11 *IJRL* 738–52.

[16] Ibid., para. 13. The European Council also decided in June 1999 to push forward on a European Charter of Fundamental Rights: Decision of the European Council, Cologne (3–4 June 1999), Conclusions, Annex IV. Drafting took place over the next twelve months and a text was expected to be adopted by the Council of Ministers meeting in Nice in December 2000.

[17] Tampere Conclusions, para. 14.

[18] Ibid., para. 15. Also of relevance in the present context is the Council's call for assistance to countries of origin and transit to be developed in order to promote voluntary return: ibid., para. 26. The Amsterdam Treaty likewise confers powers on the Council in the field of readmission, and the Council invites the Community to conclude readmission agreements or to include standard clauses in other agreements between the European Community and relevant third countries or groups of countries: ibid., para. 27. Finally, although not necessarily with refugees in mind, the Conclusions also refer to the desirability of "enhanced mutual recognition of judicial decisions and judgements . . .".

generally of refugees, asylum seekers and migrants; the refugee definition, with reference to the obligations towards those within and outwith the Convention; and procedural standards. The purpose of this chapter is to highlight the very significant substantive content of international legal standards and of obligations freely assumed, and to underline the importance of integrating human rights considerations, from the outset, into the processes of protection policy formulation and legislative drafting at both Community and national level.

THE HUMAN RIGHTS BACKGROUND

The European Union has clearly recognised the applicability of human rights treaties in the field occupied by refugees, asylum seekers and migrants.[19] Most provisions of most human rights instruments draw few distinctions between nationals and non-nationals, and the right to life, or the right to integrity of the person and to human dignity, are guaranteed to everyone without distinction.[20] National constitutions, bills of rights and international human rights instruments thus tend to work more from the particular to the general, being based on the inalienability of certain individual rights. Independent of citizenship, fundamental rights in the strong sense have the anti-utilitarian consequence that they may not be denied by states, even in the general interest.[21] Fundamental human rights ought thus to represent a critical point of departure in both European and international discourse. They stress individual security and autonomy, and are founded upon assumptions regarding human dignity, upon the inhering principle that justice depends on an equal right to equal concern and respect,[22] and upon pragmatic recognition that the effective protection of rights commonly requires that judicial intervention resolve conflicts of interest, or set limits to the scope of discretionary power, in accordance with the rule of law.

The factual situation within which rules operate, change and develop, must still be taken into account, however, together with the interests and entitlements of national or host communities and the frequently conditional or qualified nature of many human rights. In the case of refugee movements and forced migration, many European States have attempted to contain or "regionalise" the movement of persons, that is, to keep those in need of protection and solutions within their regions of origin, beyond the developed world. This objective is pursued through visa and transit visa requirements, sanctions against airlines, socio-economic measures of deterrence, accelerated refugee status procedures,

[19] See above, text to nn. 11 and 16.

[20] The following discussion is covered in greater detail in G. S. Goodwin-Gill, "Migration-International Law and Human Rights", in B. Ghosh (ed.), *Managing Migration: Time for a New International Regime?* (Oxford University Press, Oxford, 2000).

[21] R. Dworkin, *Taking Rights Seriously* (Duckworth, London, 1977), 190ff, 269.

[22] Ibid., 180–83, 272–8; J. Rawls, *A Theory of Justice* (Harvard University Press, Harvard, 1972), ss 29, 51 (duty of mutual respect); Art. 1 of the Universal Declaration of Human Rights 1948 (UDHR48); Preamble to the UN Charter.

and procedural devices designed to avoid the necessity for decisions on the merits in favour of rapid removal to some other country deemed or imagined to be responsible or secure. Within the European Union, the possibility of developing comprehensive, "regionalised" schemes has been increasingly discussed, with the primary goals being both the suppression of extra-regional arrivals and the prompt and summary return to regions of origin of any who slip the net. Human rights and individual rights rarely enter the debate at the point of policy formulation.

Notwithstanding the movement towards closer union, in international law each EU Member State is nevertheless responsible for promoting universal respect for, and observance and protection of, all human rights and fundamental freedoms.[23] The movement of persons between states, driven by many factors, yet takes place in a context characterised by *links*—historical, family, community and commercial ties, among others—and by *obligations*. So far, neither dissuasive nor preventive measures appear to have had much lasting impact on the movements of people. There clearly *are* human rights aspects to traditionally sovereign questions about the reception of non-nationals, and the failure so far to manage these elements has worked to the disadvantage of States and to the serious prejudice of those in search of protection. A strong case can be made for more highly developed institutional arrangements, able and competent to pursue clear strategies while remaining close to and governed by the fundamental principles of human rights protection.

Nature and limits of human rights

Where refugees and asylum seekers are concerned, Europe is committed not only to the ECHR and the 1951 Convention/1967 Protocol relating to Refugees, but also to obligations and principles originating in a multitude of sources. These include major declarations and international agreements, such as the Universal Declaration of Human Rights 1948 (UDHR48), the Convention on the Elimination of All Forms of Racial Discrimination 1965, the Covenants on Civil and Political Rights 1966 (ICCPR66), and Economic, Social and Cultural Rights (ICESCR66), the Convention on the Elimination of All Forms of Discrimination against Women 1979, the Convention against Torture and Other Cruel, Inhuman or Degrading Treatment or Punishment 1984 (CAT84), and the Convention on the Rights of the Child 1989 (CRC89). Treaty-based obligations are complemented by duties deriving from customary international law,[24] with the basic obligation of protection illustrated by Article 2(1) of the

[23] The protection and promotion of human rights are the first responsibility of governments: Vienna Declaration and Programme of Action (1993): UN doc. A/CONF.157/23, para. 1.

[24] On the fundamental importance (obligations *erga omnes*) of the principles and rules concerning the basic human rights of the human person, see the views of the International Court of Justice in the *Barcelona Traction* case, [1970] *ICJ Reports* 3, 32; M. Ragazzi, *The Concept of International Obligations Erga Omnes* (Clarendon Press, Oxford, 1997).

Covenant on Civil and Political Rights, requiring every state party to respect and to ensure human rights to "all individuals within its territory and subject to its jurisdiction".

Human rights are inalienable and fundamental, but not necessarily "absolute". Rights generally must be exercised with due regard to the rights of others; in certain circumstances and within the limits prescribed by international law, governments may restrict their exercise in favour of other community interests. But "not necessarily absolute" does not mean that individual human rights can be overridden or dismissed by group and category. States have a measure of discretion in determining whether and what restrictions may be called for in the light of local circumstances, but the standard of compliance remains an international one, involving elements of necessity and proportionality.[25] Some rights, however, are "non-derogable"; no derogation is permitted, even in exceptional circumstances; they benefit everyone—nationals, foreigners, migrants and refugees—whether lawfully or unlawfully in the state, and regardless of any situation of emergency.[26]

At one end of the spectrum, all persons shall be free from torture, and cruel and unusual treatment or punishment, whether directly, within state territory, or indirectly, in another state, as a consequence of removal or refusal of admission. There is also no obvious justification for differentiating between citizen and non-citizen in the availability of legal remedies, such as habeas corpus, in the provision of a fair trial, or generally in regard to due process.[27] In regulating entry to, residence in, and removal from its territory, therefore, the European Union and its Member States ought also to ensure that their laws and policies comply with these international legal requirements, and that otherwise permissible restrictions are not imposed in a discriminatory manner.

[25] For the jurisprudence of the ECtHR, to the effect that restrictive measures must be in accordance with law, adopted in pursuit of a legitimate aim, and necessary in a democratic society, that is, "justified by a pressing social need and . . . proportionate to the legitimate aim pursued", see *Moustaquim* v. *Belgium* (31/1989/191/291), 18 February 1991, para. 43; *Beldjoudi* v. *France* (55/1990/246/317), 26 March 1992; *Kokkinakis* v. *Greece* (3/1992/348/421), 25 May 1993; *Otto-Preminger-Institut* v. *Austria* (11/1993/406/485), 20 September 1994; *Berrehab* (3/1987/126/177), 21 June 1988.

[26] Such non-derogable rights traditionally include: the prohibitions on genocide, slavery and racial discrimination; the right to life, so far as the individual is guaranteed against arbitrary deprivation; freedom from torture or inhuman treatment; the right not to be convicted or punished under retroactive laws; the right to recognition as a person before the law; and the right to freedom of conscience, thought and religion.

[27] Article 10 UDHR48 declares that "Everyone is entitled in full equality to a fair and public hearing by an independent and impartial tribunal, in the determination of his rights and obligations and of any criminal charge against him". These principles are reiterated in Art. 14(1) ICCPR66 and Art. 6 ECHR. See, generally, G.S. Goodwin-Gill, *International Law and the Movement of Persons between States* (Clarendon Press, Oxford, 1978), 58–87.

Human rights at the border

In its General Comment No. 15 relating to the Covenant on Civil and Political Rights 1966, to which all EU Member States are party, the Human Rights Committee observed that while a non-national generally had no right to enter state territory, "in certain circumstances an alien may enjoy the protection of the Covenant even in relation to entry or residence, for example, when considerations of non-discrimination, prohibition of inhuman treatment and respect for family life arise . . .". Moreover, "Aliens . . . are entitled to recognition before the law. They may not be subjected to arbitrary or unlawful interference with their privacy, family, home or correspondence . . . [and] . . . are entitled to equal protection by the law. . . .[28]

In regard to entry and removal, a protected right will thus be involved if the applicant falls within the international law provisions on children, the family and refugees. For example, no state may return a refugee in any manner whatsoever to a country in which he or she may be persecuted, and this prohibition extends also to measures such as rejection at the frontier, where the effect is to compel the individual to return to or remain in a territory where his or her life, physical integrity or liberty would be threatened for relevant reasons. Moreover, the Convention on the Rights of the Child 1989 endorses the standard of the "best interests" of the child which, in principle and in appropriate circumstances, is capable of prevailing over other considerations, including the legally recognised but competing interests of the state. In a wide range of other universal and regional instruments, states have also recognised that the family should receive "protection by society and the State", and that "special measures of protection and assistance should be taken on behalf of all children and young persons".[29] Together with the principle of the best interests of the child as a primary consideration,[30] this puts in question any state action with respect to children that might either "officially" remove the child from the family environment, or have the effect of leaving the child without care and support.

[28] Human Rights Committee, General Comments, No. 15, 5, 7: UN doc. CCPR/C/21/Rev.1 (19 May 1989). On racial discrimination in an immigration context, see *S.M.L. Patel (Application No. 4403/70) and others* v. *U.K.* (unreported) October 1970 (36 Collection of Decisions 92). The European Commission declared several of the applications admissible on the ground that the action of refusing entry was capable of constituting an interference with the right to respect for family life under Art. 8 ECHR or of raising a related issue of discrimination. Later decisions by the ECtHR have confirmed the protection due to the family and, among others, to "second generation migrants" threatened with removal. On the extent of the family relationship, see, for example, *Berrehab* (3/1987/126/177), 21 June 1988; *Keegan* v. *Ireland* (16/1993/411/490), 26 May 1994; on expulsion of second generation migrants, see *Djeroud* v. *France* (34/1990/225/289), 23 January 1991; *Lamguindaz* v. *United Kingdom* (48/1992/393/471), 28 June 1993; *Beldjoudi* v. *France* (55/1990/246/317), 26 March 1992.

[29] Article 23(1) ICCPR66; Art. 10(3) ICESCR66.

[30] Article 3(1) CRC89.

Human rights and removals from state territory

Many of the human rights aspects to state powers over the entry and residence of non-citizens bear generally on the question of removal. In principle, the state is competent to terminate the lawful residence or the irregular physical presence of non-citizens within its territory, and to require them to depart; in the event of non-departure, the state may enforce its decision through measures of expulsion or deportation. State practice over many decades has established a number of limitations on this sovereign power; for example, it should not be exercised arbitrarily, should respect acquired rights, be implemented in accordance with due process, and carried out with full regard for the dignity and integrity of the individual.[31] The collective or mass expulsion of non-citizens is also widely regarded as unlawful, in view of its necessarily arbitrary and discriminatory character.[32]

Article 3 of the Convention against Torture 1984, Article 13 of the International Covenant on Civil and Political Rights and Articles 32 and 33 of the 1951 Convention all mention expulsion specifically when laying down protection standards for non-citizens generally, or in favour of refugees, or against return to torture. The Human Rights Committee has considered the lawfulness of expulsion against the requirements of Article 13 ICCPR66 (entitlement to a remedy for the purpose of challenging an order of removal) in a number of cases,[33] while the European Court and European Commission of Human Rights have reviewed the exercise of the competence to expel non-citizens more broadly, against a range of ECHR rights including Article 3, Article 8 (freedom from interference with private or family life), and Article 14 (non-discrimination).[34]

Refugees are a class known to and enjoying the protection of general international law.[35] Article 14 of the Universal Declaration of Human Rights 1948 provides that "Everyone has the right to seek and to enjoy in other countries asylum from persecution". By 31 October 2000, one hundred and thirty-nine states had ratified the 1951 Convention and/or 1967 Protocol relating to the Status of Refugees, thereby accepting the definition of a refugee in Article 1 and the

[31] Ibid.; Goodwin-Gill, above at n. 27, 202–5, 228, 262, 280–1, 307–8.

[32] See Protocol No. 4, Art. 4 ECHR; *Conka* v. *Belgium* (No. 51564/99) (expulsion of gypsies) allegedly without any examination of their individual situations; application communicated: ECHR, Information Note No. 12, November 1999, 22. See also J. M. Henckaerts, *Mass Expulsion in Modern International Law and Practice* (1995), 8–49, on the prohibition of mass expulsion, and 50–77 on mass expulsion of migrant workers.

[33] See, for example, *Mafroufidou* v. *Sweden*, No. 58/1979: Selected Decisions of the Human Rights Committee, Vol. 1: UN doc. ICCPR/C/CP/1, 80; *Hammel* v. *Madagascar*, No. 155/1983: ibid., Vol. 2, 11; *M.F.* v. *The Netherlands*, No. 173/1984: ibid., Vol. 2, 179; cited by O. Andrysek, "Gaps in International Protection and the Potential for Redress through Individual Complaints Procedures" (1997) 9 *IJRL* 392, 402.

[34] See also *Abdulaziz, Cabales and Balkandali* (15/1983/71/107–109), 28 May 1985.

[35] G. S. Goodwin-Gill, *The Refugee in International Law* (Clarendon Press, Oxford, 2nd ed. 1996), passim.

fundamental principle of *non-refoulement* in Article 33.[36] This rule, which requires that states parties not to return a refugee to a country in which he or she may face persecution on grounds of race, religion, nationality, membership of a particular group or political opinion, now extends to the protection of those who, if returned to a particular country, would face a substantial risk of torture.[37] Lawfully resident refugees are also protected against expulsion, save on the most serious grounds and subject to lawful procedures and the opportunity for challenge.[38]

Moreover, many European and other States acknowledge *as a matter of fact* that international protection is often due to individuals or groups falling outside or not immediately covered by Article 1 of the 1951 Convention/1967 Protocol, such as those having reasonable fear of prejudice or discrimination in the exercise of fundamental rights, or who flee conflict or serious disturbances of public order. The provisions of human rights treaties, and the protection due to those whose rights are at serious risk of violation if returned, are reflected in the reality of temporary protection.

That refugee protection engages a human rights responsibility has been recognised by different treaty supervisory bodies.[39] In particularly striking fashion, the European Court of Human Rights has ruled that there are no exceptions to the protection required under Article 3 ECHR. The case of *Chahal,* for example, involved an individual whom the United Kingdom wished to expel on grounds of national security. The Court noted that, whereas the state had disputed the principle of non-expulsion if the person concerned would face a real risk of treatment contrary to Article 3 in the country to which he or she was returned, it had accepted it before the Court. However, the Government had further argued that the protection due under Article 3 was not absolute in national security cases, but was subject to an implied limitation, or alternatively that the threat posed by the individual should be weighed in the balance against the interest of the state. The Court disagreed, finding that:

> "the Convention prohibits in absolute terms torture or inhuman or degrading treatment or punishment, irrespective of the victim's conduct. Article 3 makes no provision for exceptions and no derogation from it is permissible . . . even in the event of a public emergency threatening the life of the nation . . . The prohibition . . . against ill-treatment is equally absolute in expulsion cases . . . [T]he activities of the individual in

[36] 1951 Convention (CSR51): 189 UNTS 150; 1967 Protocol (CSRP67): 606 UNTS 267. For details of ratifications, see RefWorld at www.unhcr.ch/refworld.

[37] Article 3 of the 1984 Convention against Torture and Other Cruel, Inhuman or Degrading Treatment or Punishment (CAT84): 1465 UNTS 85 (No. 24841)–114 states parties at 31 August 1999.

[38] Article 32 CSR51.

[39] Human Rights Committee, General Comment 20, "Replaces General Comment 7 concerning prohibition of torture or cruel treatment or punishment (Article 7)",10 April 1992, para. 9. Committee against Torture, *Mutombo* v. *Switzerland*, Communication No. 13/1993, 27 April 1994: (1995) 7 *IJRL* 322; *Alan* v. *Switzerland*, Communication No. 21/1995, 8 May 1996: (1996) 8 *IJRL* 440; *Kisoki* v. *Sweden*, Communication No. 41/1996, 8 May 1996: (1996) 8 *IJRL* 651.

question, however undesirable or dangerous, cannot be a material consideration. The protection afforded by Article 3 is thus wider than that provided by Articles 32 and 33 of the United Nations 1951 Convention on the Status of Refugees."[40]

In summary, therefore, the "relevant human rights treaties" to which the European Union has referred in the ToA and the Tampere Conclusions control and structure sovereign state powers in matters of the admission, removal, treatment and protection of non-nationals.

Human rights and defining refugees

States party to the 1951 Convention relating to the Status of Refugees have agreed that the term "refugee" should apply, first, to any person considered a refugee under earlier international arrangements; and, secondly, to any person who, being outside their country of origin, is unable or unwilling to return there owing to a well-founded fear of being persecuted for reasons of race, religion, nationality, membership of a particular social group or political opinion.[41] Even at the time of its drafting, it was recognised that any definition was likely to provoke disagreements with respect to interpretation and application,[42] and that, given its various limitations, the Convention definition would not cover every refugee. The Conference of Plenipotentiaries therefore recommended in the Final Act that states should apply the Convention beyond its strictly contractual scope, to other refugees within their territory.[43] Many states relied upon this recommendation in refugee crises precipitated by events after 1 January 1951, until the 1967 Protocol expressly removed that limitation, and in theory it may still be invoked to support extension of the Convention to groups or individuals who do not fully satisfy the definitional requirements.[44] In recent practice, however, states have preferred to initiate schemes of supplementary or complementary protection, as a way of dealing with large numbers of asylum seekers fleeing situations of conflict and widespread human rights violations, but equally in order to ensure compliance (minimal though it often may be) with their own obligations towards individuals on state territory and subject to their jurisdiction.[45]

[40] *Chahal* v. *United Kingdom*, No. 70/1995/576/662 15 November 1996, paras. 79, 80.

[41] Article 1A(2) CSR51.

[42] Ad hoc Committee on Refugees and Stateless Persons: UN doc. E/AC.32/SR.3, para. 45 (Mr Henkin).

[43] Recommendation E of the Final Act.

[44] *Cf.* Art. 2 of the Declaration on Territorial Asylum adopted by the Committee of Ministers of the Council of Europe on 18 November 1977, which reaffirms the right to grant asylum to Convention refugees "as well as to any other person [considered] worthy of receiving asylum for humanitarian reasons".

[45] See P. Weis, "The Legal Aspects of the Problems of de facto Refugees", in *Problems of Refugees and Exiles in Europe* (International University Exchange Fund, 1974). The notion of "valid reasons" is expanded at 3–5 and would include: (1) a person's reasonable belief that he or she would be prejudiced in the exercise of human rights, would suffer discrimination, or be compelled to act

Refugees under the 1951 Convention/1967 Protocol are identifiable by their possessing four basic characteristics: (1) they are outside their country of origin; (2) they are unable or unwilling to avail themselves of the protection of that country, or to return there; (3) such inability or unwillingness is attributable to a well-founded fear of being persecuted; and (4) the persecution feared is based on reasons of race, religion, nationality, membership of a particular social group or political opinion. Many states have incorporated this definition, with occasional slight modifications, into their laws and policies, and have often made provision also for the protection of those having other valid reasons for flight,[46] or who are "without, or unable to avail themselves of, the protection of the government of their State of origin".

The criteria for refugee status in Article 1 of the 1951 Convention relating to the status of refugees have the individual asylum seeker very much in mind, even though the notion of lack of protection is clearly wider and invites attention to the general issue of a state's duty to protect and promote human rights within its territory. This is hardly surprising, given the historical evolution of international protection and the gradual extension of a "rights regime" into a system of administrative benefits. It is this dimension which remains at the heart of the concept of international protection, and yet also produces concern among states apparently unable to devise efficient and effective means for the determination of status or the need for international protection.

As it stands, the refugee definition accepted by states party to the 1951 Convention/1967 Protocol necessarily requires the evaluation of complex subjective and objective factors, while the context—interpretation of an international instrument with fundamentally humanitarian objectives—implies certain ground rules. The central question is that of *risk*, as it affects the individual in a particular social and political context.[47]

The importance of a uniform interpretation of the terms of an instrument intended to provide protection to individuals in flight from their own country is actively promoted by the Office of the United Nations High Commissioner for Refugees, which is recognised by states party to the 1951 Convention as having a special role in supervising the application of the Convention.[48] Moreover, the failure of the 1951 Convention to define key terms, such as "persecution" or "social group", has led to increasing reliance on human rights jurisprudence and doctrine to fill the gaps and develop a concept of protection commensurate with the needs of today.

against conscience; and (2) war or warlike conditions, foreign or colonial occupation, or serious disturbance of public order in part or all of the person's country of origin. See also UNHCR, "Note on Consultations on the Arrivals of Asylum-seekers and Refugees in Europe": UN doc. A/AC.96/INF.174, July 1985, Annexe V.

[46] For examples, see Goodwin-Gill, above at n. 35, 21–5.

[47] On the assessment of claims, see ibid., ch. 9, s. 2.2.

[48] See UNHCR Statute, UNGA res. 428(V), 14 December 1950, para. 8(a); Art. 35(1) CSR51. UNHCR, of course, is not a court of ultimate authority, unlike the ECJ or the ECtHR; nevertheless, its views on interpretation ought to be given due consideration in good faith: Goodwin-Gill, above at n. 35, above 216–7.

EU JOINT POSITION

The Joint Position on the harmonised application of the refugee definition, adopted by the Council of the European Union on 4 March 1996, attempts to set out the shared understanding of EU countries of the minimum content imposed by Article 1 of the 1951 Convention.[49] It states that the guidelines on interpretation are approved and that they shall be notified to "the administrative bodies responsible for recognition of refugee status, which are hereby requested to take them as a basis without prejudice to Member States' case law on asylum matters and their relevant constitutional positions". It further affirms that the Joint Position "is adopted within the limits of the constitutional powers of the Governments of the Member States; it shall not bind the legislative authorities or affect decisions of the judicial authorities of the Member States".

Although much of its content is non-controversial, parts of the Joint Position represent a compromise among conflicting jurisprudence. For example, the Joint Position rightly emphasises the essentially individual nature of every asylum and refugee status determination, and the importance of basing findings in the circumstances of the case. It offers a sensible interpretation of "persecution", to include acts which are sufficiently serious by their nature or repetition, which either constitute an attack on human rights to life, freedom or physical integrity, or which clearly preclude a person from continuing to live in his or her country of origin.[50] It also stresses that while persecution or fear of persecution must be based on Convention grounds, the fact that such grounds are genuine or merely attributed to the person concerned is immaterial.

In a number of areas, however, the Joint Position does not reflect common jurisprudence, or the view of UNHCR. For example, paragraph 5.2, in relation to the origins of persecution, provides that fear of persecution by non-state agents should be considered to fall under the 1951 Convention only where it "is individual in nature and is encouraged or permitted by the authorities". This approach is very much in line with the German and French approach, but very much out of line with that of most other EU countries.

At the time of its adoption, Sweden objected formally to this provision of the Joint Position, noting that "In relation to the question of origins of persecution, Sweden is of the opinion that persecution by third parties falls within the scope of the 1951 Geneva Convention where it is encouraged or permitted by the authorities. It may also fall within the scope of the Convention in other cases, when the authorities prove unable to offer protection". Denmark considered making an explicit reservation to paragraph 5.2, but found it unnecessary, given the "non-binding" quality of the Joint Position in relation to both legislative and judicial branches of government.

[49] Joint Position 96/196/JHA of 4 March 1996 defined by the Council on the basis of Art. K.3 TEU on the harmonised application of the definition of the term "refugee" in Art. 1 of the Geneva Convention of 28 July 1951 relating to the status of refugees.

[50] The Joint Position draws strongly on the UNHCR *Handbook on Procedures and Criteria for the Determination of Refugee Status* (Geneva, 1979).

The question of interpretation has already been litigated in the United Kingdom, in the context of appeals against the return of asylum seekers to Germany and France under the so-called "safe third country" rule. In *ex parte Adan*[51] the Court of Appeal ruled that it would afford due respect to the system and practice of the third country in question, but that such country had to apply the 1951 Convention. If the state took a position which departed from the Convention's "true interpretation", it could not be regarded as safe. In the view of the court, the refugee definition did extend to persons who feared persecution at the hands of non-state agents, in circumstances in which the state itself was not complicit. In consequence, the appellants could not lawfully be returned to a country which adopted an interpretation at variance with this view.

The UK Home Secretary promptly attempted to frustrate this ruling by amending the Immigration and Asylum Act, then before Parliament, so as to create an apparently indefeasible presumption that other EU Member States are safe by definition.[52] The issue will likely be re-litigated after the UK's Human Rights Act enters into force in October 2000.

Other provisions of the Joint Position potentially giving rise to variations in jurisprudence include paragraph 6 on "Civil war and other internal or generalised armed conflicts", and paragraph 8 on the "internal flight alternative". In addition, the scope of "particular social group" offers considerable opportunities for both progressive and restrictive approaches to protection. The UK cases of *Islam* and *Shah*, for example, may well serve as a challenge in those states which have opted to restrict the protection available to women as refugees.[53] In these joined appeals by two women who had fled the prospect of violence in their own country, the House of Lords found that the social group of which they were members was not some narrow sub-class, but the very group of "women in Pakistan".[54] The court rejected criteria which have enjoyed some success in other jurisdictions; for example, it dismissed the idea that "cohesiveness" is an indispensable requirement for the existence of a particular social group, for it "foists an impermissible restrictive requirement on the words of Article 1A(2)".[55]

Agreement on universals, such as the criteria for refugee status contained in the 1951 Convention, is undoubtedly easier to obtain than agreement on their

51 R. v. *Secretary of State for the Home Department, ex parte Adan* [1999] 4 All ER 774.

52 See further below on an equivalent problem raised by the Protocol on asylum to nationals of Member States of the European Union.

53 *Islam* v. *Secretary of State for the Home Department*; R v. *Immigration Appeal Tribunal and Secretary of State for the Home Department, ex parte Shah* [1999] 2 WLR 1015; the full text of the judgment is also published in (1999) 11 *IJRL* 446–527, with comments by M. Vidal and G.S. Goodwin-Gill.

54 Lord Steyn commented that, "The idea so incisively put forward by Lord Hoffmann is neither novel nor heterodox. It is simply a logical application of the seminal reasoning in *Acosta*'s case": [1999] 2 WLR 1015, 1026.

55 Ibid., 1025. Or, as Lord Hoffmann observed in relation to any required element of "co-operation", "In the context of the Convention it seems to me a contingent rather than essential characteristic of a social group": ibid., 1033.

application.[56] From the perspective of international law, the "Joint Position" is clearly not a treaty; it has not been ratified or submitted to national parliaments, and in theory it has no decisive value in the interpretation of Article 1A(2) CSR51. It is essentially a political document, in the nature of a set of unilateral statements still to be reconciled; the divergences in interpretation reveal not only the constructive possibilities in different legal cultures, but also the deficiencies in a system of protection which, both regionally and internationally, remains without a body competent to promote consistency by ruling authoritatively on the meaning of words.

While the structural necessity of such a body is clear, its governing doctrine will necessarily also include the texts of the relevant human rights treaties and their jurisprudence. This in turn will affect not only the interpretation of refugee defining provisions, but also the very scope of human rights protection, *beyond* the 1951 Convention/1967 Protocol.

HUMAN RIGHTS, PROCEDURES AND REFUGEES

The Convention refugee definition supposes a dispassionate case-by-case examination of subjective and objective elements. Even though not formally required by the terms of the 1951 Convention/1967 Protocol, the simple existence of procedures for the determination of status can ensure effective internal implementation of international obligations, and provide a basic and important guarantee that refugees will not be *refouled* and that they will receive the treatment due under the relevant international instruments. The same argument is equally applicable to the evaluation of the *human rights* implications of decisions on admission, removal and treatment.

International law in fact has little to say with respect to the procedural aspects of due process, particularly as the responsibility of the state for the fulfilment of its obligations turns essentially on what results in fact. The 1977 UNHCR Executive Committee recommendations offer a very basic agenda, comprising guidance to applicants, the provision of competent interpreters, a reasonable time to "appeal for formal reconsideration" of a negative decision, "either to the same or a different authority, whether administrative or judicial, according to the prevailing system".[57] Even if not binding, they indicate a practically

[56] Besides the divergences of interpretation in relation to asylum claims by women, those by conscientious objectors are also likely to provide a source of difference.

[57] Executive Committee Conclusion No. 8 (1977); Report of the 28th Session (1977): UN doc. A/AC.96/549. *Cf.* Council of Europe Recommendation no. R(81) 16 on the harmonisation of national procedures relating to asylum, adopted by the Committee of Ministers on 5 November 1981. See also Report of the Sub-Committee of the Whole on International Protection: UN doc. A/AC.96/613, paras 37–8; Report of the 33rd Session (1982): UN doc. A/AC.96/614, paras 65–6, 70(4). One of UNHCR's principal objectives has long been the establishment of fair and expeditious procedures for the determination of refugee status, preferably guaranteeing "full access" by those in search of asylum, and with the opportunity for independent review of negative decisions. See various UNHCR "Notes" on international protection, including UN doc. A/AC.96/694 (3 August 1987),

necessary minimum for refugees to be identified and accorded protection in accordance with international obligations.

THE TREATY OF AMSTERDAM AND PROCEDURES

The ToA establishes the Community objective of "minimum procedural standards" for asylum procedures in Member States, in accordance with the 1951 Convention/1967 Protocol and other relevant international treaties.[58] Already in June 1995, the Council had adopted a resolution to this purpose;[59] it embodied preambular references to the refugee instruments, the ECHR, the refugee definition and European practice beyond its scope, and the Dublin Convention. It set out the objective of establishing "equivalent procedures" and "common procedural guarantees", and referred to the minimum standards recommended by the UNHCR Executive Committee and the Council of Europe. At the substantive level, the resolution included recognition of the following nine general principles, each with an individual rights dimension:

- the principle of compliance with the 1951 Convention/1967 Protocol, including the refugee definition, *non-refoulement,* and co-operation with UNHCR;[60]
- the principle that procedures should be regulated by law;[61]
- the principle that every application should be considered individually, objectively and impartially,[62] by qualified and informed personnel;[63]

paras 13, 25–8; UN doc. A/AC.96/750 (27 August 1990), para. 15; UN doc. A/AC.96/777 (9 September 1991), paras 25–6; UN doc. A/AC.96/815 (31 August 1993), para. 19.

[58] Article 63(1)(c) EC.

[59] Council Resolution of 20 June 1995 on minimum guarantees for asylum procedures (OJ 1995 C274).

[60] These are described as "universal principles": Council Resolution of 20 June 1995, paras 1, 2.

[61] Ibid., para. 3. In the *Chahal* case, the ECtHR criticised the then existing procedures in the United Kingdom for dealing with expulsion or removal on national security grounds, insisting that the authorities cannot avoid "effective control by the domestic courts whenever they choose to assert that national security and terrorism are involved" (*Chahal* v. *United Kingdom*, No. 70/1995/576/662 15 November 1996, para. 131). An effective remedy within the meaning of Art. 13 ECHR is therefore required: ibid., paras 145–51. Following this judgment, the United Kingdom terminated removal proceedings against Mr Chahal, and enacted the Special Immigration Appeal Commission Act 1997 to meet the remedies requirement. See also Tribunal civil (Réf.)-Bruxelles, 8 October 1993, *X c/ Etat belge*, to the effect that the right to an effective remedy in the case of breach of fundamental rights constitutes an essential element of the rule of law: RDDE, No. 75, September–October 1993, 454.

[62] Council Resolution of 20 June 1995, para. 4.

[63] See also Council of Europe, Parliamentary Assembly, Recommendation 1309 (1996) on the training of officials receiving asylum-seekers at border points (7 November 1996); Reply from the Committee of Ministers, Doc. 8288 (23 December 1998) (which lists various earlier recommendations, but does not deal substantively with the Parliamentary Assembly's proposals).

- the principle that refugee status determination involves a "shared responsibility" between decision-maker and applicant, who should have an adequate opportunity to present his or her case;[64]
- the principle of due process, including the opportunity to apply for refugee status/asylum at the border, the right to an interpreter, to legal advice, to access to UNHCR, and to a personal interview;[65]
- the principle of written, reasoned decisions;[66]
- the principle of appeal or independent review of negative decisions;[67]
- the principle of entitlement to remain pending decision;[68]
- the principle of recognition of status where the criteria are satisfied, and of recognised refugees' presumptive entitlement to residence.[69]

In addition, unaccompanied minors and women asylum seekers are recognised as requiring further protection guarantees, including "guardianship" and the use of female interpreters and examiners.

In many respects, these standards go farther than, or clarify the generality of, those laid down earlier by the UNHCR Executive Committee and the Council of Europe. However, the 1995 Resolution was itself non-binding, and the quality of the "guarantees" therefore somewhat academic.[70] Moreover, Member States individually continued to retain a considerable margin of appreciation and to benefit from a substantial battery of opportunities for derogation.

Already in November 1996 the European Parliament recognised these deficiencies and expressed its concern for individual rights not covered by the Council Resolution including, among others, freedom from detention, the return of rejected asylum applicants in safety and dignity, decisions within a reasonable time, guaranteed access to asylum procedures for those sent back to third states, and for the accession requirements of future Member States to contain conditions in respect of asylum policy.[71] That these concerns continue is clear from the European Parliament's April 1999 Resolution on the Strategy

[64] Council Resolution of 20 June 1995, para. 5. See also UNHCR, *Handbook*, above at n. 50, paras 195–205.

[65] UNHCR, *Handbook*, paras 7, 11–14, 23. In *Amuur* v. *France*, No. 17/1995/523/609, 20 January 1994, para. 50, the ECtHR ruled that detention or confinement "must not deprive the asylum seekers of the right to gain effective access to the procedure for determining refugee status", and that there is a need "to reconcile the protection of fundamental rights with the requirements of States' immigration policies".

[66] Ibid., para. 15; however, note the exceptions in paras 22, 25, allowing oral communication of reasons in certain cases.

[67] Ibid., para. 8.

[68] Ibid., para. 17; however, note the exceptions in paras 21, 22, 25.

[69] Ibid., para. 29.

[70] As the European Parliament succinctly noted, "non-binding guarantees are not guarantees and must therefore be transposed into Community and national law": Resolution on the Council Resolution on minimum guarantees (OJ 1996 C362), para. B. The Parliament also expressed its view that the Council Resolution and other Council decisions in the field of asylum are "pseudo-legislation and quite wrongly removed from parliamentary scrutiny and checks by the Court, and hence unacceptable as forms of Union legislation": ibid., para. 4.

[71] Ibid., paras. L, M, 9, 23.

Paper on the EU's Migration and Asylum Policy.[72] It pointed out that "the potential offered by the Geneva Convention is not fully exploited at present . . . particularly with regard to the criteria for the definition of refugees and the definition of the persecutor (who may be non-governmental)".[73] With the placing of asylum now in the First Pillar, the European Parliament also called for "the division of powers in this pillar to be respected", and emphasised "the need for open and detailed consultation with the UNHCR and citizens' organisations".

Specifically with regard to asylum, the Parliament noted that "the right to request asylum is a fundamental right which it must be possible to exercise in accordance with the Geneva Convention and the 1967 Protocol, with the legislation of the EU and with the national laws of the Member States",[74] and reaffirmed the principle of non-expulsion or return.[75] On procedures, it called for streamlining, "with a view to making them more transparent . . . and speedy . . ., while guaranteeing a means of judicial appeal or appeal", and for priority to be given to "improving the implementation of existing international conventions on asylum".[76]

As at national, so also at Community level, it is often not clear that the human rights dimensions to legislative proposals have been integrated, fully and effectively, into the drafting process; or that the implications of a Union-wide human rights policy are fully appreciated. In addition to the exceptions and derogations noted above, "opt-outs" were negotiated on behalf of Denmark, Ireland and the United Kingdom, while an additional protocol seeks to deal with the necessarily controversial issue of asylum for nationals of EU Member States. These addenda necessarily have an impact on the refugee definition or description of those in need of protection, and on the strategic goal of harmonised or common procedural guarantees.

Even though the European Parliament itself called on the Council to establish "in a clear and binding manner that every Member State shall consider as clearly unfounded any request for asylum or refugee status submitted by a national of another Member State and shall in any event reject such a request",[77] this issue continues to raise problematic questions of principle. The initiative for the Protocol was led by Spain, in the aftermath of the refusal of a Belgian court to allow the extradition of suspected Basque terrorists.[78] Categorically to rule out the possibility of asylum among Member States appears to be in flat contradiction with Article 3 CSR51,[79] while also constituting an impermissible geo-

[72] Doc. A4–0143/99; Minutes of 13 April 1999.

[73] Resolution on the Strategy Paper, paras G, N.

[74] For proposals for an additional protocol to the European Convention on precisely the right "to seek asylum", see Goodwin-Gill, above at n. 35, Annexe 4, No. 11, 527.

[75] Ibid., para. 13; see also para. 15.

[76] Ibid., paras 16, 17. The Parliament also "opposes any attempt to renegotiate the existing conventions", recommending instead that they be supplemented to meet new circumstances: ibid., para. 17.

[77] Resolution on Council Resolution . . ., para. 7.

[78] "*Extradition et asile: vers un espace judiciaire européen?*" (1997) *Rev belge droit* 69.

[79] "The Contracting States shall apply the provisions of this Convention to refugees without discrimination as to race, religion or country of origin."

graphical reservation to Article 1 CSR51.[80] The non-binding Protocol finally agreed attempts to avoid the impermissible by simply establishing a presumption that all Member States are "safe countries of origin", and allowing for rebuttal, although only in highly exceptional circumstances.[81] This did not satisfy all, however, and Belgium declared that, in any event, it would carry out an individual examination of any asylum request,[82] while the fifteen Member States themselves also recognised that the Protocol "does not prejudice the right of each Member State to take the organisational measures necessary to fulfil its obligations" under the 1951 Convention.[83] Clearly, even a rebuttable presumption can effectively frustrate the object of the treaty—protection of the refugee or protection of human rights—and diligent oversight is called for.

The challenges posed by a "closer Union" raise fascinating questions of "state succession" worthy of a separate chapter,[84] although the Danish, Irish and UK opt-outs may well serve to postpone indefinitely the attainment of a single, territorial "sovereign" entity. Protocol No. 5 to the ToA, for example, provides that Denmark will not take part in the adoption of measures under Title IV (Article 1), though it remains free to decide whether to apply any such measures as may be agreed (Article 7). Protocol No. 3 allows the United Kingdom to continue to apply border checks, notwithstanding Article 14 EC (Article 1), while Protocol No. 4 provides that the United Kingdom and Ireland, like Denmark, shall not take part in the adoption of Title IV measures (Article 1). They may opt in for specific measures,[85] however, and Ireland has indicated its intention (as permitted under Article 3) to take part in the adoption process, "to the maximum extent compatible" with the maintenance of the Common Travel Area with the United Kingdom.[86]

CONCLUSIONS

One question raised or implicit throughout the above review is that of compliance; even where the principles seem clear, their effective implementation depends upon levels of official action that are not always forthcoming.

[80] Further to Art. 42(1) CSR51, no reservations are permitted to Art. 1.

[81] For example, where a Member State derogates from its obligations under the ECHR, or is the subject of suspension under Art. 7 TEU.

[82] Declaration by Belgium on the Protocol on asylum for nationals of Member States of the EU (OJ 1997 C340/144).

[83] The 15 Member States, Declaration relating to the Protocol on asylum for nationals of Member States of the EU (OJ 1997 C340/141).

[84] Should the separate territories of the Member States effectively become one territory for the purposes of international law, then the EU's ratification of the 1951 Convention/1967 Protocol might be appropriate, much as it is suggested that the European Union should become a party to the ECHR. In such circumstances, ensuring consistent compliance among different and differing legal cultures would indeed present a huge challenge to the regime of protection.

[85] Article 8 of Protocol No. 4 enables Ireland to opt in to the whole of Title IV.

[86] Declaration by Ireland on Art. 3 of Protocol No. 4.

Compliance with international human rights obligations is patchy at best, and the reasons for this failing call for serious attention. States are disinclined to legislate on family reunion, for example, or to incorporate international standards into law, policy guidelines or best practice statements. The traditional conception of sovereign state rights to control entry, removal and membership still carries weight, but it is rather the incompleteness and lack of balance in the present regime that militates against effectiveness.

The protection of refugees and asylum seekers post-Amsterdam must be clearly premised both on the specific requirements, voluntarily assumed, of the 1951 Convention/1967 Protocol, and on the foundations of international human rights law, the essentials of which are obligations *erga omnes* and much of which draws its authority from peremptory rules of international law (*jus cogens*). State interests may have their place, but the sovereignty of the state exists within a community of principle.

It is sometimes argued that states' obligations to refugees and asylum seekers are no more extensive than those accepted on ratification of the 1951 Convention/1967 Protocol and, indeed, that states are obliged to extend the full benefit of those treaties to all who, being within their territory or subject to their jurisdiction, qualify as refugees in the sense of Article 1A(2). From these assumptions, it is often inferred that Europe's refugee problems will be more easily resolved if, or once, the 1951 Convention/1967 Protocol is taken out of the picture. These and related misunderstandings need to be cleared up, once and for all.[87]

No provision of the 1951 Convention or of any other international instrument applicable in Europe obliges states to *admit* or grant *asylum* to any refugee, including any person whom such state may in fact have recognised as a refugee. As a matter of *law*, states therefore have a large measure of discretion in how they treat refugees and asylum seekers, so long as they do not return the refugee, "by any means whatsoever", to a state in which he or she may be persecuted, and provided they act consistently with their other international obligations. Although embedded in treaty, the refugee definition and the principle of *non-refoulement* are also parallelled by rules of customary or general international law; that is, the *concept* of refugees as persons entitled to international protection exists outside the 1951 Convention/1967 Protocol, as does the rule prohibiting the return of refugees to where they may be persecuted or exposed to risk of torture; both concept and rule are wider than those in the Convention and Protocol.

Denunciation of these two instruments would leave the general law undisturbed. States might cease to owe Convention obligations to other states party, but their obligations to the international community at large would continue, whether deriving from human rights instruments or customary international

[87] In fairness, it should be noted that both the ToA and the Tampere Conclusions acknowledge the wider legal framework.

law. Their performance would remain to be monitored by the Office of the UNHCR which possesses a *general* competence to provide international protection to refugees, irrespective of the country in which they find themselves and independently of such country's ratification of any treaty protecting refugees. The fact that the refugee concept and the principle of non-return have a wider scope than the 1951 Convention/1967 Protocol is in no small way due to developments in the field of human rights, which may also serve to open a jurisdictional door in favour of the Office of the UNHCHR.

Even within the limited regional context governed by the ECHR, a considerable body of jurisprudence has already developed under Articles 3, 8 and 14, clarifying the limits on the competence of the state to refuse admission to, expel, or remove an individual, where such action violates his or her human rights. Such limits extend far beyond the narrow refugee category to protect, among others, family members, long-resident non-nationals and the seriously ill. Protection against, and remedies for, arbitrary and unlawful administrative action are woven into the tapestry of the rule of law.

Moreover, all European States have ratified the Covenant on Civil and Political Rights 1966 (ICCPR66). Like its regional counter-part, ICCPR66 entitles the individual to protection against torture and cruel, inhuman or degrading treatment or punishment (Article 7), and against discrimination (Articles 2(1) and 14). Lawfully present non-citizens enjoy substantive and procedural protection against expulsion (Article 13), and the Human Rights Committee has recognised that ICCPR66 rights may be violated in actions and decisions affecting the admission, residence and removal of non-nationals.

Article 3 of the UN Convention against Torture and Other Cruel, Inhuman or Degrading Treatment or Punishment 1984 extends the protection of *non-refoulement* in regard to the return of any person "to another State where there are substantial grounds for believing that he would be in danger of being subjected to torture". The Committee against Torture has already applied this provision in favour of non-citizens faced with removal to their country of origin, where existing refugee protection machinery has proven inadequate.

Every European State has ratified the Convention on the Rights of the Child 1989 (CRC89). Among others, CRC89 protects the child against discrimination (Article 2(1)), provides that in all actions concerning children, the best interests of the child shall be a primary consideration (Article 3(1)), and guarantees protection in regard to registration and identity (Articles 7 and 8), against separation from parents (Article 9), and in regard to family reunion (Article 10). Separate provision is also made in respect of children as refugees (Article 22).

The above listing provides a summary reminder of the more important sources of obligation which bear on the regulation of admission to, residence in, and removal from the countries of Europe. In practice, however, international human rights standards and obligations are rarely integrated into legislation, policy and practice at national and regional level. This undoubtedly contributes both to the general lack of credibility attaching to systems of management and control, and to the perennial problems of effective enforcement. An integrated approach to refugee issues will need to recognise this dimension, among others, and to reflect both community and individual rights and interests.

The question still remains whether the transfer of powers from Member States to the Union and their exercise at Community level will lead to more or less "freedom". Ultimately, the question of democratic control—close, informed and unhindered analysis of proposals, keen attention to practical implementation at all levels, amendment, change or other sanctions in the event of violations of rights or principles—remains in need of a satisfactory answer.

In principle, both parliamentary and judicial control are called for in relation to the actions of the executive. The basic premises of European governance—the Statute of the Council of Europe 1949, for example, the TEU and the ToA—include democracy, respect for human rights and fundamental freedoms, and the rule of law. Besides national parliaments, whose effective role is diminishing daily, at least one other potential forum of democratic accountability remains. Perhaps not surprisingly, the Parliamentary Assembly of the Council of Europe has expressed its concern at the threat to human rights flowing from restrictions on asylum, which it sees "reflected and amplified in the ever more intensive efforts by the EU to harmonise . . . asylum and immigration policies and practices".[88] Among the questionable practices, it identified measures to expedite the consideration of applications or to "shift the determination procedure to other countries", restrictive interpretations of international refugee law and the refugee definition, and deterrent measures.[89] It therefore urged the Council of Europe Committee of Ministers to step up the monitoring of Member States' compliance with their international obligations, to initiate action to ensure the incorporation of a right of asylum into the ECHR, and to draw up a European convention on harmonisation of asylum polices, with a view to improving the standard of protection and strengthening solidarity.[90]

The Parliamentary Assembly is also concerned about the possible dangers inherent in the European Council's June 1999 proposal to draw up a charter of fundamental rights of the Union. In order to safeguard consistency in protection and to avoid diverging interpretations, it therefore invited the Union specifically to incorporate the European Convention and its protocols into any such charter, and indeed to accede to the Convention.[91]

It is by no means clear at present whether the refugee and the asylum seeker will enjoy effective rights under Community law, or whether their status will remain precariously contingent on national law and procedures. No one

[88] Council of Europe, Parliamentary Assembly, Recommendation 1440 (2000), 25 January 2000, "Restrictions on Asylum in the Member States of the Council of Europe and the EU".

[89] Ibid., para. 3.

[90] Ibid., para. 6. Among other proposals, the Parliamentary Assembly also urges Member States to recognise that persecution may originate from non-state entities, and that war and violence may be instruments of persecution: ibid.

[91] Council of Europe, Parliamentary Assembly, Recommendation 1439 (2000); Resolution 1210 (2000); Order No. 561 (2000), Charter of fundamental rights of the EU, 25 January 2000.

challenges reserves of sovereignty in quite the same way as the refugee, the asylum seeker and the migrant. It is a challenge indeed to ensure that, in the formulation and implementation of laws and policies aimed at such "groups and categories", the individual survives as a holder of rights. If he or she does not so survive, it will not be for want of international obligations, but because States and governments have elected to act in disregard of commitments freely undertaken.

The draft Charter of Fundamental Rights promulgated in October 2000[92] goes some way towards meeting these objections. Indeed, the specific inclusion of Article 18, entitled simply, "Right to asylum", appears significantly to enhance the individual character of the right, even if its precise formulation opens a potential window of exception in its references to the Treaty establishing the European Community and thereby also to the Spanish Protocol.[93] In addition, Article 51 seems to require very little in the way of *action* by those to whom the Charter is addressed ("the institutions and bodies of the Union with due regard for the principle of subsidiarity and to the Member States only when they are implementing Union Law . . ."). Assuming its adoption in due course, it may be some time before any impact is felt through the EU.

[92] Draft Charter of Fundamental Rights of the European Union: Charte 4487/00; Convent 50, Brussels, 28 September 2000.

[93] I am indebted to Andrew Clapham for this point. Art. 18 provides "The right to asylum shall be guaranteed with due respect for the rules of the Geneva Convention of 28 July 1951 and the Protocol of 31 January 1967 relating to the status of refugees and in accordance with the Treaty establishing the European Community." See also Art. 19, entitled "Protection in the event of removal, expulsion or extradition": "1. Collective expulsions are prohibited. 2. No one may be removed, expelled or extradited to a State where there is a serious risk that he or she would be subjected to the death penalty, torture or other inhuman or degrading treatment or punishment."

7

*Towards a Common Asylum Procedure**

JOHANNES VAN DER KLAAUW[1]

INTRODUCTION

Inter-governmental co-operation in asylum, immigration and external borders prior to the entry into force of the ToA has focused so far on the adoption of a number of flanking measures necessary for the effective abolition of intra-Union border controls. The asylum-related measures agreed upon include only one binding instrument, the so-called Dublin Convention[2] governing the determination of the responsibility for the treatment of an asylum claim, in addition to a series of non-binding guidelines aimed at harmonising the key elements of Member States' asylum procedures. Among the latter are a number of resolutions related to procedural asylum law, such as on minimum procedural standards and on key procedural notions which have been included in Member States' asylum procedures since the early 1990s. The inter-state dialogue conducted within the framework of the Third Pillar of the Maastricht Treaty did not affect Member States' obligations under international refugee instruments and other human rights instruments safeguarding the right of asylum. As long as the Union had no competence to develop and implement Community legislation in the asylum area, Member States remained committed to respect their obligations under international instruments such as the Geneva Refugee Convention and the European Convention on Human Rights. With the newly acquired Community competences under the Treaty of Amsterdam (ToA) in the area of asylum (Article 63 EC), and the new conceptual approach to a common asylum system being an integral element of the new "area of freedom, security and justice", the Community will now develop framework legislation, to be transposed and implemented in Member States' law and practice. These new legislative instruments must be in accordance with international standards of refugee law and human rights law, if Member States' obligations under these

* The manuscript of this chapter was completed prior to the submission by the Commission of a proposal for a Directive on minimum standards for asylum procedures in September 2000.

[1] The views expressed in this article are those of the author and do not necessarily reflect those of the United Nations.

[2] Convention Determining the State Responsible for Examining Applications for Asylum Lodged in One of the Member States of the European Communities. The Convention was signed in Dublin in June 1990 (Denmark signed and ratified in June 1991) and entered into force on 1 September 1997 (for Sweden and Austria, 1 October 1997, and for Finland, 1 January 1998).

instruments are not to be violated. Yet will the future Community law instruments in asylum address the individual rights of the asylum-seeker – whether during examination, review and appeal, or once he/she is accepted as a refugee and to be integrated in society? Or will they bear the mark of intergovernmental co-operation, driven by state interests and resulting in decisions based on the lowest common denominator of increasingly restrictive policies and practices? If these future Community asylum instruments will represent an attempt mainly to approximate existing state administrative and judicial practice, yet this practice contains deficiencies which are subsequently codified in Community standards, national courts may be compelled not to respect these Community rules if their application will run into conflict with state obligations under international refugee and human rights instruments.

One of the future Community asylum law instruments needs to codify the "minimum standards on procedures for granting and withdrawing refugee status" (Article 63(1)(d) EC) in each of the Member States. The Commission is expected to table a proposal for such a measure in the course of the year 2000. Such an instrument should establish the legal basis for what ultimately could become a uniform asylum procedure throughout the European Union. Yet Member States remain divided over the issue of a flexible, gradual process versus a prescriptive approach to harmonise asylum procedures, as well as the timeframe for such a process. According to Article 63 of the EC Treaty, the Vienna Council Action Plan and the Conclusions of the Tampere Summit the adoption of a procedural asylum instrument is one of the essential elements of a future common asylum system. The majority of Member States appear to favour the adoption of an instrument establishing a certain communality and agreed level of standards, rather than a framework law which would require Member States to apply exactly the same procedure. Another issue under discussion is whether the adoption of binding common procedural standards should oblige Member States to establish a single national asylum procedure allowing for the determination of all asylum applications, irrespective of whether protection is sought on the basis of the Geneva Refugee Convention or complementary human rights standards

TOWARDS A COMMUNITY INSTRUMENT IN PROCEDURAL ASYLUM LAW

According to the Tampere European Council Conclusions, one of the cornerstones of the future common asylum systems is a Community instrument laying down common standards[3] for Member States' asylum procedures. Once adopted and implemented, these should contribute to the establishment of a common asylum procedure in the longer term. Introduction of a common asylum procedure will be a critical element in the development of the area of free

[3] Interestingly, Art. 63(1)(d) requires the adoption of "minimum" standards, while the Tampere Conclusions refer to "common" standards. This appears to be more than a semantic issue: the drafters of the Tampere Conclusions reportedly wanted to go beyond minimum levels of protection.

movement and respect of fundamental rights throughout the European Union. It therefore seems imperative that the Community instruments which are to constitute the common asylum system need to be conceived from a rights-based approach, its provisions being in accordance with international human rights standards. In the area of procedural asylum law, however, notwithstanding the existence of a considerable body of "soft law" in the form of UNHCR ExCom Conclusions, the UNHCR *Handbook on Procedures and Criteria for Determining Refugee Status* and Recommendation R (81) of the Committee of Ministers of the Council of Europe, EU Member States so far have adopted non-binding rules and policy recommendations aimed at controlling access to the territory and establishing simplified procedures to screen out a large number of what are considered to be abusive and unfounded asylum applications, not deserving a full examination and adjudication. These resolutions and recommendations have insufficiently taken into account the existing body of principles of international refugee law, since they were basically to respond to the needs and interests of states rather than develop a coherent set of individual refugee rights.

The future Community instrument on asylum procedures constitutes a unique opportunity to establish a catalogue of legally binding principles and rights to be exercised by all those who seek asylum in one of the EU Member States. If developed along these lines, the instrument will be the first of its kind among regional standards. Only as a result of the new competences bestowed upon the Community following the entry into force of the ToA can the Commission come forward with an instrument which Member States subsequently will have to negotiate and, following adoption, have to apply in their national administrations. During negotiations over a Commission draft, Member States may have to be reminded of their commitment to apply asylum procedures in full compliance with the Geneva Refugee Convention, particularly Article 1 concerning the definition of a refugee, Article 33 relating to the principle of "non-refoulement" and Article 35 concerning co-operation with the UNHCR, including the facilitation of its duty of supervising the application of the Convention.[4]

The drafters of a future EC procedural asylum law instrument will undoubtedly draw inspiration from administrative and judicial practice related to the basic features of the asylum procedure in EU Member States. They should also be guided by jurisprudence and case-law developed by the European Court on Human Rights, and opinions on individual complaints on the basis of Article 3 of the Committee established under the UN Convention against torture.[5] This would help avoid the possibility that the implementation of the future Community law instrument will result in state violations of international human rights law instruments. Also, the implementation of the new asylum provisions of the ToA are to be subjected to judicial scrutiny by the ECJ in

[4] EU Resolution on minimum guarantees 1995, para. 1.

[5] There exists an increasing number of significant rulings by the ECtHR related, *inter alia*, to issues of access to procedures, effective remedy/appeal, family reunification and detention: see G. S. Goodwin-Gill at ch. 6 above.

Luxembourg and future rulings of this Court, where appropriate, must be in accordance with those of other regional and supranational judicial bodies if serious conflicts of interpretation of fundamental rights are to be avoided. According to Article 68 EC, the Council, the Commission or a Member State can request the ECJ to give a ruling on a question of interpretation of the related Treaty provision, or a national court or tribunal can request the ECJ to do so in a case pending before it if all national avenues have been exhausted.[6] It should be recalled that the ECJ, in various rulings, has referred to international human rights instruments as guiding standards for EU policies and practices.[7] Article 6 TEU stipulates that fundamental rights, as guaranteed by the ECHR and as they result from the constitutional traditions common to the Member States, are to be respected by the Union as "general principles of Community law". The future Community asylum instruments therefore need to be firmly rooted in principles of human rights and refugee law and aimed at the protection of the rights of the refugee.

Because of the wording of Article 68 EC, few possibilities are expected to be created for an individual to challenge the implementation of a future Community asylum instrument in national law and practice before the ECJ.[8] Yet the transfer of competences in legal and policy development to the Community in this area may affect the fundamental rights of the individual. The judicial protection system of the European Community in Title IV, therefore, is to be considered as insufficient, and the limitations attached to the issuance of preliminary rulings aggravate this situation further.[9] It is not unthinkable that an individual will be prevented from seeking an effective remedy for an infringement of one or more of his basic rights before the ECJ, because of lack of competence of the Court to rule in the individual case, while at the same time the individual may not obtain compensation before a national court since the alleged violation is the result of implementation of a Community law instrument on which the national court is not competent to rule.[10]

[6] Article 68 TEU. It should be noted that a preliminary ruling by the ECJ in response to a request by a Member State, the Council or Commission on the interpretation of a Treaty provision shall not apply to judgments of courts which have become *res judicata*; nor shall the ECJ have jurisdiction to rule on any measure relating to the maintenance of law and order and the safeguarding of internal security. It remains unclear which institution will decide in which situations the Court's competences need to be curtailed: is it the Court itself, the Member States, or the Council?

[7] See e.g. para. 33 of the ECJ (negative) Opinion 2/94 of 28 March 1996 on Accession of the Community to the European Convention on Human Rights: "it is well settled that fundamental rights form an integral part of the general principles of law whose observance the Court ensures . . . the Court draws inspiration from . . . the guidelines supplied by international treaties for the protection of human rights on which the Member States have collaborated or of which they are signatories".

[8] Some observers expect however that courts will make extensive use of referring cases to the ECJ, and have expressed concern over the risk of lengthy procedures in individual cases, including the UK Home Office in a position paper on the Tampere Summit.

[9] See also K. Hailbronner, "The Treaty of Amsterdam and Migration Law" (1999) 1 *European Journal of Migration and Law* 19.

[10] These, however, are situations which the drafters of Art. 68(1) may have had in mind when allowing for national courts (but not the individual!) to seek an opinion from the ECJ.

The transfer of competences to the Community in the area of asylum, including asylum procedures, should ultimately be matched with the realisation of the overriding objective of establishing an area of freedom, security and justice for all persons legally moving and residing in the Union, irrespective of their status. As long as there exists a distance between this objective and the competences given to the Community, Member States will retain a varying margin of discretion in implementing their asylum policies and, by consequence, protecting the individual rights of the asylum seekers. The main reason for this anomaly is that the asylum (and migration) harmonisation process has its origins in an exclusively intergovernment co-operation process, without a focus on individual rights. Following the entry into force of Title IV, including its asylum provisions, it has become imperative for the Union to reconcile state interests with their obligations to guarantee rights of the individual. The Tampere Conclusions include clear political guidelines stating that the future common asylum system needs to be firmly rooted in the full and inclusive application of the Geneva Refugee Convention.[11] However, since the Geneva Refugee Convention does not stipulate the rights of the asylum seeker during examination, review or appeal of his application, the Commission and Member States have to take a fresh look at what should constitute a coherent body of procedural standards governing the protection of the rights of asylum seekers as much as the obligations on the part of the authorities. The Commission has made it clear that in making use of its right to initiate legislative proposals, it will do so on the basis of a sound understanding of the subsidiarity principle, i.e. legislate in areas and on issues in so far as the relevant objectives cannot be sufficiently achieved by the Member States individually.

As regards asylum procedures, this would mean that common (minimum) standards are primarily needed in order to help to ensure that asylum seekers are less likely to select their asylum country purely on the basis of differing conditions for admission and examination of their application.[12] Yet if this were the sole objective of the exercise, there is a risk that a future Community instrument on procedural asylum law will be limited in scope by primarily addressing state interests. The opportunity to establish a comprehensive and sufficiently detailed set of rights of the individual asylum seeker and obligations of the asylum authorities would be wasted. Also, such a modest ambition would fail to contribute to the overall aim of establishing an area of freedom, security and justice

[11] Tampere European Council, Presidency Conclusions, para. 13. Paragraph 15 of the same Conclusions states that in the longer term, the Community should adopt rules leading to the adoption of a common asylum procedure and a uniform status for those who are granted asylum valid throughout the Union. It remains to be seen whether the full and inclusive application of the 1951 Convention will result in the proper and inclusive application of "refugee". According to para. 14 of the Tampere Conclusions, a common asylum system must be based on, *inter alia*, the approximation of rules on the recognition and contents of the refugee status, yet this does not spell out how the refugee definition is to be interpreted and applied in critical matters, such as when persecution emanates from non-state agents, is gender-related, or is based on the social group criterion.

[12] See also the Commission Communication, *Towards an Area of Freedom, Security and Justice*, Memo 98/55 (Brussels, 15 July 1998).

allowing all persons including third country nationals, among whom figure asylum seekers, to exercise their fundamental rights and freedoms. Codification of the rights of non-EU citizens, including refugees and asylum seekers, however, is a matter of controversy, as the recent discussions on the initiative to draw up an EU Charter of Fundamental Rights (whether or not of a binding nature) have already shown. Yet in view of existing non-binding EU instruments on procedural asylum law, a future Community law instrument on asylum procedures should include, as a very minimum, the basic rights of the individual asylum seeker throughout the procedure, coupled with minimum standards for the fair and efficient handling of his/her application.

THE 1995 EU RESOLUTION ON MINIMUM GUARANTEES AND THE 1999 COMMISSION WORKING DOCUMENT

In 1995, as a result of intergovernmental co-operation within the framework of the Third Pillar of the Maastricht Treaty, Member States adopted a Resolution on minimum guarantees for asylum procedures.[13] In drawing up a binding instrument on asylum procedures under Article 63 EC, the European Commission is expected to take as a starting point this non-binding Resolution. It is hoped, however, that the Commission will avoid a codification of the Resolution's reservations and exceptions. The Commission and Member States have agreed on the preparation of an EC directive as the most appropriate Community law instrument to harmonise procedural asylum law. The directive shall be binding as to the result to be achieved, that is a harmonisation of minimum standards to govern the asylum procedure in each Member State, leaving to the national authorities the choice of form and method as to the realisation of this objective.[14]

Prior to the drafting of this directive, the Commission issued a working document[15] in which it outlined the main orientations and key elements of the proposed directive, and included a number of critical questions as to what level of harmonisation Member States wish to attain, which procedural notions they want to preserve and strengthen, and which issues do not, or no longer, need consideration when harmonising asylum procedures.[16] A future directive aimed at establishing common guarantees for asylum procedures needs to be aligned

[13] Council Resolution of 20 June 1995 on minimum guarantees for asylum procedures (OJ 1996 C274/13).

[14] Article 249 EC. Whereas directives are not directly applicable in national practice, the ECJ has ruled that individual provisions of a directive may, exceptionally, be directly effective in Member States.

[15] European Commission working document, *Towards common standards on asylum procedures*, SEC (1999) 271 final, 3 March 1999.

[16] In its working document the Commission "takes the view that it will be necessary to revisit some of the concepts and principles found in the soft law and to propose the removal of some of the exceptions and derogations which weaken these instruments" (p. 7).

with basic principles stemming from international standards, as Article 63 EC and the Tampere Summit Conclusions stipulate.

In drawing up the non-binding Resolution on minimum safeguards, EU Member States made an effort to catalogue the core individual rights and state obligations common to the asylum procedure in each Member State. The Resolution, however, has so far not been implemented fully by EU Member States. A number of its provisions reflect the particular practice of Member States[17] and, through the inclusion of a number of exceptions, codify existing divergences rather than represent a positive example of coherent and forward-looking legislation. Moreover, these exceptions seriously undermine the effectiveness of the general principles underlying the normal asylum procedure. The proposed directive should amend this situation,[18] but given the required unanimity voting rules (as laid down in Article 67), a common set of key principles governed by high standards of protection will not easily be achieved. Member States have indicated that full harmonisation of procedural asylum law will remain a long-term objective, and that the first priority is to achieve consensus on minimum procedural standards, and furthermore approve ways and means to shorten the duration of the asylum procedure. It therefore remains to be seen whether Member States will be willing to adopt standards higher than those representing the lowest common denominator.[19] Since the asylum measures listed in Article 63 EC must be adopted by consensus, there is a risk that a future EC procedural asylum instrument will be based on low protection standards, and be emptied of substance in some key areas as a result of continuing controversy.

In its March 1999 working document, the Commission put forward some interesting proposals, such as the abolition of the concept of "safe country of origin", the adoption of additional safeguards required for the implementation of the "safe third country" concept, a restricted application of the definition of "manifestly unfounded" claims, the reintroduction of the suspensive effect of the appeal in all cases where a negative decision on substance has been taken, and the consideration of the introduction of a single asylum procedure in each

[17] For example, para. 19, allowing for a shortening of the review procedure in cases considered to be "manifestly unfounded", has been modelled on the Danish practice; para. 24, referring to refusal of admission at the border by a ministry or comparable central authority, reflects French practice; para. 25 copies German practice permitting border authorities to reject asylum applicants on "safe third country" grounds without allowing for a review of the decision.

[18] Commissioner Kinnock, on behalf of the EU Commission, commented in the European Parliament, 13 November 1996 session (which adopted the Parliament's comments on the 1995 Resolution following submission of a report drawn up by Ms d'Ancona) that the Commission was concerned by the many exceptions of the text (turning it into "a description of the current situation in Member States and less like an attempt to develop a common approach") and the various derogations related to "what are probably the most fundamental principles of the resolution, particularly the right to appeal and the suspensive effect of the appeal".

[19] The possibility of including a final provision in the new EU asylum instruments allowing Member States to adopt more favourable provisions should not be ruled out, as this has been the case so far with the non-binding asylum instruments. This may help to prevent minimum standards becoming maximum standards.

Member State. From Member States' initial discussions on the Commission working document, it has become clear that there is no political will to abandon existing procedural concepts such as the "safe third country" notion or the use of accelerated procedures for claims considered to be "manifestly unfounded". Procedural guarantees governing admissibility procedures or accelerated procedures need to be reviewed, however. A number of procedural notions are disputed, such as the "safe country of origin" concept: some Member States want to abolish this notion altogether while others want to apply it only on an individual basis, and yet a third group wants to apply the notion in a generic manner having recourse to "safe country of origin" lists.

All Member States favour speeding up procedures through streamlining and limiting the appeal and review to two stages (on substance and on points of law). However, they disagree over the use of strict time limits and their legal consequences. A considerable amount of controversy remains regarding the desirability to harmonise the standard of proof during the examination. Generally, Member States favour the adoption of a flexible step-by-step approach in view of the existing differences in national legislations, by agreeing on a limited number of binding principles, leaving it to the national authorities to determine the details of the administrative and procedural arrangements. Member States have indicated as a priority speeding up asylum procedures by making more effective use of admissibility procedures and accelerated procedures for "manifestly unfounded" applications.[20] Following initial exchanges with Member States on the key questions raised in the working document, and after receipt of the European Parliament's opinion, the Commission is expected to table a proposal for a directive later in the year 2000.

BASIC REQUIREMENTS FOR FAIR AND EFFICIENT ASYLUM PROCEDURES

The future directive needs to be construed around a basic set of standards to be respected in the asylum procedure in each Member State, referring to individual rights for the asylum seeker as well as obligations on the part of the authorities. These standards will have to govern the future common, uniform asylum procedure which the Tampere Summit Conclusions have called for (paragraph 15).

The *principal objective* of a future directive must be to ensure the proper and expeditious identification of those in need of protection during refugee status determination. Fair and satisfactory asylum procedures are to remain a cornerstone of Member States' asylum systems, and the directive must take as a starting point the individual right to seek and enjoy asylum—any suggestion that this could be replaced by political arrangements based on the discretion of adminis-

[20] Interestingly, this emphasis on accelerating procedures for manifestly unfounded asylum applications does not reappear in the Tampere Summit Conclusions.

trations[21] must be dismissed. The directive could include a possibility for collective determination in case membership of a particular group will qualify for (provisional) protection on a prima facie basis.

The general provisions of the directive should refer to international refugee law and human rights law instruments, including the principle of non-refoulement. These provisions should also stipulate that all asylum seekers must have access to the asylum procedure, irrespective of the manner in which they enter the territory, and irrespective of their nationality.[22]

As regards the *scope* of the directive, the directive could usefully address status determination on the basis not only of the Geneva Refugee Convention, but also of those international instruments which allow for the provision of complementary forms of protection, including Article 3 ECHR as well as the UNHCR extended mandate which accepts as refugees those fleeing the indiscriminate effects of violence arising in situations of war, conflict and events seriously disturbing public order. The directive needs to set the standards for a comprehensive procedure which would not prematurely exclude any application for protection, including protection on humanitarian grounds or against generalised violence or armed conflict in the country of origin.

Issues linked to *access to the procedure* and *admissibility* need to be an essential part of the directive. Most contemporary problems related to the implementation of the asylum procedure stem from questionable restrictions to access to the asylum procedure and the improper use of admissibility procedures. The directive needs also to spell out basic standards for border procedures and stipulate that border personnel be properly trained in applying these standards. Derogations from the general principle of admissibility of each asylum claim need to be strictly defined; in so far as these are based on application of the safe third country concept, specific safeguards should be included in order to guarantee that the application is examined in substance by the third country.

Generous criteria for admissibility and examination will be more easily accepted by Member States if, as a natural complement, the directive lays down the basic conditions for ending refugee status or withdrawing asylum or other forms of (temporary) protection. Safeguards similar to those available for recognising refugee status should also govern any procedure conducted with a view to ending refugee status or an alternative form of protection. Examination of the possibility for cessation or withdrawal of status should always be on an individual basis.

The core of the directive must include the *procedural rights* of asylum seekers to be applied during examination, review and appeal. These rights are as follows:[23]

[21] One such attempt was made in 1998 by the Austrian Presidency in its strategy paper on migration and asylum policy, CK4 27 ASIM 170 REV 2. That paper suggested replacing, or at least complementing, the individual right to seek asylum with an institutional offer on the part of the host country allowing for flexibility and a significant administrative margin of discretion.

[22] As regards asylum applications lodged by citizens originating from EU Member States, see below.

- the applicant's right of access to the asylum procedure, to be translated in an effective opportunity to lodge an asylum application;
- the applicant's right to a personal interview in order to assess all the personal circumstances of the application;
- the applicant's right to remain in the territory of the asylum country until a final decision has been taken;[24]
- the applicant's right to appeal to a court or a review body in case of a negative decision.

The obligations on the part of the authorities include:

- the obligation of observing the principle of non-refoulement as laid down in the 1951 Convention;
- the obligation to protect the data of asylum seekers, to be laid down in national law;[25]
- the obligation to undertake an impartial and objective examination of the application by a fully qualified authority;
- the need to communicate decisions to the applicant in writing and in a language he/she understands. In case of a negative decision, the full decision shall also be communicated to his/her legal defence, and provide detailed reasons for rejection;
- at all stages of the procedure, to provide the asylum seeker with access to legal counsel and, where necessary, interpreters and the right to contact the UNHCR (or one of its implementing NGO partners).

Concerning the body responsible for examining and deciding on the asylum application in the first instance, the directive should stipulate that this should be a single, central authority with specialised knowledge, having access to all necessary information, and disposing of sufficient numbers of competent and

[23] For an analysis of these basic principles, see A. Terlouw and P. Boeles, "Minimum guarantees for asylum procedures", in *Democracy, Migrants and Police in the EU: the 1996 IGC and beyond*, Standing committee of experts in international immigration, refugee and criminal law (FORUM, Utrecht, 1997), 90–4.

[24] Paragraphs 21, 22, 24 of the EU Resolution on minimum guarantees do not uphold the suspensive effect of the appeal in "manifestly unfounded" cases or in border procedures where the "safe third country" concept is applied. Also, an appeal against a transfer pursuant to the operation of a Dublin procedure does not have suspensive effect, as can be inferred from para. 1 of the Resolution, to be read in conjunction with Art. 3 of the Dublin Convention. The issue of the suspensive effect of the appeal will be discussed below.

[25] See Art. 286 EC. Directive 95/46/EC on the protection of individuals with regard to the processing of personal data and on the free movement of such data contains a number of general and specific provisions to guarantee the right to privacy with respect to the processing of personal data. Although at the time of adoption (1995) this Directive did not apply to the processing of data of asylum-seekers as this activity was outside the scope of EC law, the provisions of this Directive will be applicable to processing of asylum data with the "communitarization" of asylum law. The Dublin Convention (Art. 15) and the draft EURODAC Regulation include similar provisions addressing the handling of data of asylum applicants for the sole purpose of determining responsibility for examining the application. In June 1999 the European Community was allowed by the Committee of Ministers of the Council of Europe to accede to the latter's Convention on the Protection of Automatically Processed Data (1981) following the adoption of the necessary amendments to the instrument which until then only allowed states to become party to it.

trained staff. The impartial and effective functioning of such a body is a key factor in implementing the asylum procedure and protecting the rights of the asylum seeker. Consideration should be given to geographic specialisation of personnel, which can enhance consistency in approach to particular issues in major countries of origin. Staff should have access to comprehensive, accurate, objective and up-to-date information sources both on conditions in the country of origin and issues specific to the individual circumstances of the asylum seeker. Provision also needs to be made for the establishment of ad hoc task forces dealing with sudden influxes or particularly complex claims. It should be recalled that fair and well-resourced, first instance decision-taking can help to reduce frequent resort to appeals, which at present render the asylum procedure cumbersome and lengthy. Streamlining of the procedure, particularly at the appeal/review stage, and investing sufficient human and financial resources in first instance decision-making will provide the claimant with more security by reducing delays, while also helping to economise on the cost of the procedure.

Since the majority of Member States apply *accelerated procedures* for processing applications considered to be "manifestly unfounded" or clearly abusive, often applying a wide definition of these concepts, the directive needs to include safeguards for the fair implementation of such procedures. The instrument should clearly limit the types of claim to which such procedures need to be applied, as well as differentiate between accelerated procedures to determine the merits of the application in a simplified, shorter manner, and admissibility procedures aimed at deciding whether or not the application is to be examined in the asylum procedure.[26] Accelerated procedures need to be limited to cases where the application is presumed to be clearly abusive or not related to the criteria for refugee status.[27] It should be noted that Member States often apply these procedures on the assumption that the application is lacking in credibility. Yet the issues of credibility are normally so complex that they may more appropriately be dealt with under the regular asylum procedure.

Where the application has been rejected, the asylum seeker should receive a written explanation and be informed of the procedure to lodge an *appeal against the negative decision*. The appeal must have suspensive effect in all cases where the negative decision has been taken on substance. Where the claim has been transferred to another EU Member State determined to be responsible for its examination under the Dublin rules, or a third state on the basis of a proper application of the "safe third country" rule (with full guarantees that the third state will examine the application in substance), the appeal against such a transfer need not necessarily have suspensive effect.[28]

[26] UNHCR Note on international protection (EC/49/SC/CRP 12), 4 June 1999, para. 24.

[27] EXCOM Conclusion 30 (1983).

[28] This proposal as put forward in the Commission working document has not been contested by the UNHCR (see "Towards Common Standards on Asylum Procedures: Reflections by UNHCR on some of the issues raised in the Working Document prepared by the European Commission" (May 1999), para. 27) on the understanding that this is to ensure that the suspensive effect is to be maintained in cases where the appeal is lodged against a negative decision on "manifestly unfounded"

It would be in line with developments in international refugee law if the directive made provision for *special arrangements to meet the needs of vulnerable groups* such as victims of torture, sexual violence, unaccompanied minors, the handicapped, including the mentally disturbed, and the elderly. Although Member States generally do not appear to be favourable to such special procedures,[29] the directive, as a minimum, should lay down the need for skilled staff for interviewing and interpreting, to make provision for processing applications of groups with special needs as a matter of urgency, and allow for independent medical expertise where applications of torture victims or handicapped (mentally disturbed) persons are concerned.

The directive may address the issue of *standard of proof*, since the Commission, in its Working Document, paragraph 20, has made a strong plea for its inclusion as "one of the most important procedural issues". Although the matter has a different standing according to the legal system of the Member States and cannot be regulated by a procedural instrument only, yet needs to be addressed also in the context of the harmonisation of material asylum law, approximation of its procedural aspects may help to reduce present differences in recognition rates (in refugee status or alternative forms of protection). A number of Member States argue however against the inclusion of this issue in a procedural asylum instrument, since the credibility and validity of asylum claims is assessed both on objective and subjective elements, with a considerable margin of discretion.

One unresolved issue is whether the directive should include a reference to *repeat applications* and allow for the reconsideration by a Member State of an application rejected by another Member State, for instance where the applicant argues a subsequent change of circumstances, poor representation due to a deficient asylum procedure or improper application of material asylum law in the other Member State. Full harmonisation of procedural and material asylum law, however, would make insertion of this provision redundant.[30]

Many of the procedural issues listed here deserve close attention during the negotiations on a future Community procedural asylum law instrument. Among these issues are the use of admissibility procedures, accelerated procedures, or border procedures, as well as recourse to notions such as manifestly unfounded, safe third country or safe country of origin. Differences in their

grounds in an accelerated procedure. Articles 21, 22, 24 of the 1995 Resolution allow for abolition of the suspensive effect in such cases.

[29] The 1995 Resolution on minimum guarantees for asylum procedures includes scant references to additional safeguards for unaccompanied minors and women. A separate non-binding Resolution on unaccompanied minors who are nationals of third countries (adopted in Council on 26 June 1997 (OJ 1997 C221/23) lists additional standards, including those related to admission to and during the procedure.

[30] Full harmonisation of criteria for refugee status determination would also remove current obstacles to the effective application of the Dublin Convention mechanism, as recent rulings by courts primarily in the United Kingdom have shown. See *R.* v. *Secretary of State for the Home Department, ex parte Adan and others* [1999] 4 All ER 774, (1999) INLR 362, 386E.

application have resulted in a number of derogations from the common standards for the regular asylum procedure, as laid down in the 1995 Resolution. It is precisely in these matters that the protection of the rights of the individual is at risk, as practice in Member States has proven during the last years. The non-binding procedural instruments adopted by the (then) twelve EC Ministers for Immigration in London in 1992,[31] have contributed to the increasingly restrictive application of procedural asylum law in EU Member States.

ADMISSIBILITY

Various Member States have developed procedures to determine the admissibility of asylum applications, and it can therefore be expected that this issue will be addressed by the proposed EC directive. The concept, however, should be applied in clearly defined circumstances. The fact that the applicant has arrived in an irregular manner is as such no reason to declare the application inadmissible (Article 31 of the 1951 Convention). An application for asylum may be declared inadmissible only if it can be proven that the applicant has already found protection in another country (first country of asylum), or if a third country can be identified which accepts responsibility for examining the application (safe third country). Admissibility procedures should be used only to determine whether or not the country where the claim was submitted is taking responsibility for the examination of the claim, and not as a device to dismiss the application as "manifestly unfounded". The latter concept presupposes an assessment of the substance of the application, and this can be made only once access to the procedure has been granted.[32]

For admissibility procedures to be in accordance with principles of refugee protection, they include guarantees that the third country will give an undertaking to (re)admit the applicant, provide access to its asylum procedure and offer effective protection against refoulement, and ensure that the claimant will be treated in accordance with accepted international human rights standards. The mechanism, based on the Dublin Convention—or its successor instrument, to be developed pursuant to Article 63(1)(a) EC—to allocate responsibility between contracting parties for the examination of an asylum claim, can be considered as a specific variant of an admissibility procedure. Some issues related to the implementation of the Dublin mechanism are interlinked with the operation of asylum procedures and, hence, fall within the scope of application of a future

[31] Resolution on manifestly unfounded applications for asylum, Resolution on a harmonised approach to questions concerning host third countries, and Conclusions on countries in which there is generally no serious risk of persecution (Ministers responsible for Immigration of the Member States of the European Communities, meeting in London, 30 November and 1 December 1992).

[32] It should be noted that some EU Member States, such as Belgium, France and Spain, apply admissibility procedures in which applications are rejected on material grounds ("manifestly unfounded").

EC instrument on procedural guarantees. The Commission has recognised this linkage in its working document,[33] and also in regard to the application of the safe third country concept as included in the relevant 1992 London Resolution. Some of the implementing measures drawn up by the Article 18 Committee, the body supervising the implementation of the Dublin Convention, also have a bearing on the operation of admissibility procedures, as well as the treatment of the application once accepted, yet the guidelines adopted so far do not include specific guarantees to address the specific protection needs of the individual, which has been pointed out by the Commission, the UNHCR and non-governmental organisations (NGOs).[34]

The Commission leaves the question open whether such procedural guarantees linked to the operation of the Dublin mechanism should be the subject of a revised Dublin instrument or whether they need to be covered by a future EC instrument on asylum procedures. The former approach may be desirable in case there will be a complete overhaul of the basic principles and allocation criteria included in the present Convention, yet there has been no agreement so far whether a fundamental revision of the body of the text is desirable. Otherwise, in case the underlying principles of the present Convention remain untouched, procedural safeguards for a fair and effective operation of the Dublin mechanism may have to be included in a future EC directive on asylum procedures.

Another element which is likely to be covered in an admission/admissibility chapter of a future EC directive on asylum procedures is related to an application for asylum lodged by a citizen of an EU Member State in another EU Member State. According to the Protocol on asylum for nationals of Member States of the European Union, annexed to the EC Treaty, such an application should normally be declared inadmissible by the receiving Member State given the level of protection of human rights and the absence of grounds qualifying for refugee status. The Protocol allows for exceptions, *inter alia*, where a Member State decides unilaterally to declare the application admissible on the presumption that it is manifestly unfounded and therefore can be decided on in a fast-track procedure.[35] The text of the Protocol was already foreshadowed by paragraph 20 of the 1995 Resolution on minimum guarantees which states that "there should be no *de facto* or *de iure* grounds for granting refugee status to an asylum applicant who is a national of another Member State", yet on the basis of a particularly rapid or simplified procedure the protection needs of the appli-

[33] EU Commission working document, para. 12.

[34] Procedural guarantees need to be developed for instance in cases of shared responsibility for applications by members of one family who, according to a strict implementation of the Dublin criteria, have been separated, or in cases where the responsible Member States intends to apply the "safe third country" concept in accordance with Art. 3(5) of the Dublin Convention.

[35] Protocol on asylum for nationals of Member States of the European Union, annexed by the ToA to the EC Treaty, sole Art. (d). Regard should also be had to Declarations Nos. 48 and 49 as well as Declaration No. 5 by Belgium.

cant are to be determined.[36] Since, as a rule, access to the asylum procedure should not be denied on nationality grounds (e.g. by using the concept of "safe country of origin"), Belgium adopted a declaration to the Asylum Protocol stating its intention to continue carrying out an individual examination of any asylum request made by a national of another Member State. Although not by way of declaration to the Treaty, a number of EU Member States subsequently made similar statements in response to parliamentary questions or NGO approaches.[37] In 1998, Switzerland asked the Council of Europe Ad Hoc Committee of Experts on the Legal Aspects of Territorial Asylum, Refugees and Stateless Persons (CAHAR) to consider the legal implications of the Asylum Protocol[38] but CAHAR declared itself incompetent to comment on the interpretation of international treaty obligations in the field of refugee protection established outside the Council of Europe.

According to the Asylum Protocol, the receiving state has an obligation to inform the Council (which includes the country of origin among its members!) of its intention to declare an application of an EU national admissible. In order to avoid violation of fundamental principles of data protection, contact with the Council Secretariat should normally be limited to informing the Council—orally or in writing—of the fact that the application has been declared admissible and may mention the country of origin, yet under no circumstances should indications be included which would permit the country of origin to identify the applicant.

In summary, it is recommended that the proposed directive includes a provision limiting the use of admissibility procedures to the situation where the applicant may have found protection in a country of first asylum, or where he/she can seek protection on safe third country grounds. Such a provision should prevent the use of admissibility procedures on nationality grounds[39] or on grounds directly connected with the individual merits of the application, such as those involved in the application of the exclusion clauses of Article 1F of the Geneva Refugee Convention or the so-called "internal flight alternative" notion. Guidance contained in EXCOM Conclusion No. 15 (XXX) of 1979 could be followed in stipulating that applications cannot be declared inadmissible because of the applicant's failure to submit the asylum request within a specified time limit or in compliance with other formal requirements.

[36] Para. 20 of the 1995 Resolution adds that "Member States continue to be obliged to examine individually every application for asylum". This important requirement has been made optional in the Protocol to the ToA and prompted UNHCR, NGOs and asylum experts into severe criticism of the text of the Protocol. See *UNHCR position on the proposal of the European Council concerning the treatment of asylum applications from citizens of European Union Member States*, UNHCR Geneva, January 1997.

[37] Examples are the letter of the Swedish Minister for International Development Cooperation to Swedish NGOs (21 July 1997), UK written answer of Mr. Mike O'Brien to Mr. Stinchcombe, No. 16491, and written answer by Ms Quine to Mr Leigh No. 17217 (27 November 1997).

[38] *The Legal Implications of the Treaty of Amsterdam and the Protocol concerning European citizens' access to asylum—contribution by the Swiss delegation* (CAHAR (98) 6, 24 March 1998).

[39] As far as nationals of EU Member States are concerned, the relevant provision could state that full and unrestricted use needs to be made by sole Art. (d) of the Asylum Protocol.

ACCELERATED PROCEDURES FOR MANIFESTLY UNFOUNDED CLAIMS

Accelerated or simplified procedures have been instituted by EU Member States[40] in order to deal with a growing number of applications considered as manifestly unfounded or otherwise not deserving a full examination of all the circumstances of the claim. Procedural safeguards generally applicable to the normal asylum procedures have been reduced in those special procedures. Also, states are applying a broad definition of "manifestly unfounded" application for asylum, based on the criteria elaborated in the relevant 1992 London Resolution. The Resolution defines such applications as those where there is clearly no substance to the applicant's claim to fear persecution, or where the claim is based on deliberate deception or abuse of the asylum procedure. This definition covers widely varying situations such as those where the application is lacking in credibility by being inconsistent or contradictory, where the notion of "internal flight alternative" can be applied, where the application is based on forged or counterfeit documents, or where the application is aimed at fore-stalling an expulsion order, or has been rejected in another country.

In a number of cases, however, a careful examination of the claim may reveal a well-founded fear of persecution and, hence, the concept of manifestly unfounded claim should not be used in an unreserved manner. While the 1992 Resolution states that indications of bad faith or deliberate deception cannot in themselves outweigh a well-founded fear of persecution, experience has shown that Member States resort rather quickly to declaring a claim "manifestly unfounded" in case of such indications. Should the notion be included in the draft directive, it may be necessary to distinguish clearly between abusive, fraudulent and manifestly unfounded claims, as they raise different procedural issues and have resulted so far in different state practices and procedures. If the term "manifestly unfounded application" were to be reserved to those claims which have no relation to the refugee definition, the notion would be applicable only in a limited number of asylum claims such as those lodged for reasons of economic deprivation, flight from prosecution or immigration purposes. Assessing whether the claim is lacking in credibility generally requires a material examination of the application, in which case no recourse should be had to accelerated procedures.

The lack of documentation or use of forged or counterfeit papers in order to provide identity or travel routes should normally not result in processing the application in an accelerated procedure on the presumption that the claim is unfounded or abusive, since asylum seekers may sometimes be forced to flee persecution without or with false documents.[41] Such applications should be

[40] A minority of Member States so far have not introduced accelerated procedures with regard to manifestly unfounded applications, including Belgium and Italy.

[41] See also UNHCR Comments to the Commission Working Document, paras 25–6, and the 1999 Note on International Protection, paras 22–3.

processed through the regular procedure, provided the applicant presents him or herself to the authorities with a plausible explanation.

The 1992 Resolution allows for the application of accelerated procedures where the applicant has committed a serious offence in the asylum country or is a serious threat to public security, or where the application manifestly falls within any of the situations covered by the exclusion clauses of the 1951 Convention (Article 1F). In view of the relatively broad definition of the concept of manifestly unfounded, as well as the possibility offered by the 1992 Resolution to apply accelerated procedures in situations as complex as those arising from the consideration to apply the exclusion clauses, in preparing a new EC instrument, the notion of manifestly unfounded and the use of accelerated procedures must be reviewed in order to prevent the use of accelerated procedures for applications involving exclusionary measures. Exclusion, as is the case with inclusion, should be regarded as part of a comprehensive examination of all relevant facts underlying the application and, hence, should not be practised as a test of admissibility or as an element of an accelerated procedure.[42]

Moreover, the future instrument should stipulate that the application of the relocation notion (often referred to as "internal flight alternative") involving an analysis of whether it is both safe and reasonable for the applicant to relocate elsewhere in the country of origin, is to be reserved for the normal asylum procedure, and not be used in accelerated procedures precluding the necessary careful and thorough analysis of the substance of the claim. Nor should it be used as a notion to deny access to the refugee status determination procedure in admissibility procedures.[43]

In line with developments in international human rights more generally, the proposed directive could also exclude the use of accelerated procedures for the examination of applications lodged by persons claiming to be victims of torture, or originating from countries affected by war, internal conflict or gross violations of human rights.

The 1992 Resolution allows Member States to use the concept of "safe country of origin" in accelerated procedures, although not as an automatic bar to access to the asylum procedure. While the application of the notion is not, in itself, to be considered discriminatory, nationality must not be invoked in order to deny asylum seekers access to the asylum procedure. Application by asylum seekers of certain countries of origin can be handled in accelerated procedures, provided that the applicant is given the opportunity to rebut the presumption that the claim is manifestly unfounded. It can be expected that Member States want to retain the concept in a future binding EC law instrument, even if some Member States have expressed doubts about its usefulness and the Commission

[42] See also UNHCR Note on the Exclusion Clauses, ExCOM 8th meeting of the Standing Committee (30 May 1997), EC/47/SC/CRP.29; and UNHCR *Handbook,* paras 156–7.

[43] See the UNHCR Position Paper Relocating Internally as a Reasonable Alternative to Seeking Asylum (The So-Called Internal Flight Alternative or Relocation Principle) (UNHCR Geneva, February 1999). See also UNHCR *Handbook*, para. 91.

has given them the option to abandon the concept. It is therefore important that the new directive limits the scope of application of the notion of "safe country of origin", stressing that it can have an evidentiary meaning only and that a general assessment of the situation in the home country cannot prevail over a thorough examination of the risk of persecution in the individual case. The use of the notion cannot be the prerogative of governments by listing countries as "safe", which may result in the exclusion of whole groups from the asylum process, and consequently in a *de facto* reservation to Article 1 A (2) of the Geneva Refugee Convention or to a new geographical limitation. It can be resorted to only if all other elements, including the subjective aspects of the fear of persecution in the individual case, are examined simultaneously in an individual procedure.[44]

The *procedural guarantees* for processing manifestly unfounded applications in accelerated procedures have been spelled out already in ExCOM Conclusion No. 8 (XXVIII) of 1977 and ExCOM Conclusion No. 30 (XXXIV) of 1983.[45] These safeguards refer to the need for a complete personal interview by a fully qualified official, where possible of the authority normally competent to determine refugee status. The sole competence of that latter authority is to take the decision whether or not the application is to be considered "manifestly unfounded". The authorities have an obligation to provide the unsuccessful applicant with a review of the decision before rejection and possible removal—this review possibility can be more simplified in order to reduce the time required for the completion of the appeals process as a means generally to speed up the asylum procedure.[46]

The 1995 Resolution allows for the suppression of the possibility to lodge an *appeal* in cases where the negative decision has been taken in an accelerated procedure with recourse to the notion of "manifestly unfounded" claim.[47] Where an appeal is nevertheless allowed, the suspensive effect need not be respected if a central body different from the first instance authority, but part of the same governmental department, has already confirmed the decision. The same policy can be followed if the rejection at first instance has been based on "safe third country" grounds.[48] In the latter case, the decision will be communicated to the

[44] See G. S. Goodwin-Gill, *The Refugee in International Law* (Clarendon Press, Oxford, 2nd edn. 1996), 348 and fn. 102.

[45] It is worth noting that the latter Conclusion adopts broad criteria for defining who is in need of protection, including not only persons qualifying for refugee status under the 1951 Convention but also those who meet other criteria justifying the granting of asylum.

[46] Neither ExCOM Conclusion 8 (XXVIII), para. (e)(vii) nor ExCOM Conclusion 30 (XXXIV), para. (e)(iii) requires that the simplified or accelerated review of a negative decision based on "manifestly unfounded" grounds should have suspensive effect. The 1995 Resolution allows for the lifting of the suspensive effect of the appeal also in situations where according to the ExCOM Conclusions the asylum seeker should be entitled to await the outcome of the final decision on the territory of the host country. Such wider use of exceptions to the rule have been criticised by the UNHCR and NGOs as one of the main flaws of the Resolution. See UNHCR Press Release, "UNHCR concerned by EU Agreement on asylum procedures" (UNHCR, Geneva, 10 March 1995).

[47] EU Resolution on Minimum Guarantees para. 19.

[48] EU Resolution, paras 21, 24.

rejected asylum seeker in writing upon request only.[49] It is recommended that the new directive reintroduces the possibility of a review or appeal in all cases, including where the application has been rejected in an accelerated procedure as "manifestly unfounded". Also, where application of the Dublin criteria or the "safe third country" concept has resulted in a decision to transfer the claim, the presumption of safety of the third country or even the Member State responsible under the Dublin criteria, should be rebuttable and the possibility to appeal the decision should always be available. The appeal should have suspensive effect in all those cases where the initial negative decision has resulted from a substantive examination of the claim.

In conclusion, the directive should limit the use of accelerated procedures to situations where either the application is manifestly well-founded by demonstrating a clear link with the criteria of the refugee definition, or the application is manifestly unfounded or abusive, e.g. applications based on documents which are demonstrably forged whereas the asylum seeker maintains their genuine character; the asylum-seeker originates from a safe country (a presumption to be rebutted); or the claim involves a repeat or multiple application. The directive should stipulate that claims involving internal relocation, exclusionary measures and complicated credibility assessments should never be channelled into accelerated procedures. The definition of "manifestly unfounded" applications should be narrowed down since it is only on the basis of a limited definition that reduced safeguards and limitations to certain rights in accelerated procedures can be accepted.

BORDER PROCEDURES AND THE "SAFE THIRD COUNTRY" CONCEPT

It has become common practice among EU Member States to make use of special procedures in order to deal with asylum applications lodged at the border. In applying these procedures, the concept of "safe third country" is applied frequently, albeit in various forms (using abstract criteria in law or regular updated lists of countries) and resulting in divergences in the assessment of the "safety" of third states and, hence, in the treatment of asylum applications. There is therefore an urgent need to harmonise the criteria and procedures for the application of the notion. Also, there is a need to review the safeguards to be applied in border procedures, including airport procedures, with a view to strengthening the protection standards in legislative provisions and procedural arrangements in order to avoid rejection at the border of asylum seekers, and subsequent deportation. The future Community instrument on asylum procedures is the appropriate instrument to harmonise these safeguards, taking as a starting point that border procedures, if used to replace the regular procedure for in-country applications, should be governed by similar guarantees and

[49] Ibid., paras 22, 25.

principles. The instrument also needs to include clear and unambiguous criteria for the determination of the "safety" of third countries, and comprehensive safeguards for the application of the notion in the individual case. This is no luxury since the substantive criteria and procedural safeguards included in the 1992 London Resolution and the 1995 Resolution have been interpreted and applied differently by Member States and appear to be insufficiently detailed and incomplete. In practice, the sending state may not seek guarantees from the receiving state that the application will be examined in substance, nor is the applicant always given the possibility to rebut the presumption of safety of the third state in his/her particular case. Moreover, the 1995 Resolution does not guarantee a possibility to appeal the transfer if the application is examined in an admissibility procedure at the border and rejected as "manifestly unfounded" (paragraph 24, to be read in conjunction with paragraph 19).[50] Where the Resolution does provide for such an appeal, its effective use is reduced considerably since the negative decision need not be communicated in writing (paragraph 22).

The 1995 Resolution (paragraph 22) stipulates that the authorities of the sending state must, where necessary, inform the receiving state that the application has been rejected for purely procedural reasons and thus has not been examined as to substance.[51] This requirement, which is also contained in Council of Europe Recommendation R (97) 22 (paragraph 2),[52] so far has not been implemented by the majority of EU Member States, and its inclusion in a binding EC directive is therefore highly desirable.

Rejections at the borders are often legitimised by reference to contractual obligations arising from bilateral *readmission agreements* with third countries, being either countries of origin or countries of "first asylum" where the asylum seeker had already found protection—or could have sought it. These agreements normally do not include provisions covering the specific situation of asylum applicants whose claims have not yet been heard. Without such additional safeguards, returns implemented on the basis of readmission agreements may result in chain deportation of persons with a valid claim for protection, and ultimately in return to a situation of persecution in the home country.[53] The need

[50] The 1995 Resolution has been modelled on the German practice of allowing rejections by border guards on "safe third country" grounds without offering a chance to rebut the reasons for the rejection, since border guards apply "safe third country" lists which are regularly reviewed by the competent central authorities but as such have been accepted as general assessments by the highest judicial bodies in Germany.

[51] Some EU Member States, such as Germany, Sweden and the United Kingdom, notify the authorities of the receiving state that no material examination of the application has taken place, although often only in cases of transfer or return by air.

[52] "States should adopt modalities to provide for informing the asylum-seeker and . . . the authorities of the third country that, when a country is considered safe . . . applications for asylum are generally not examined in substance."

[53] EU Member States adopted a non-binding model for a bilateral readmission agreement in November 1994 (Council Recommendation of 30 November 1994 concerning a specimen bilateral readmission agreement between a Member State and a third country (OJ 1996 C274/20) which includes a clause stipulating that readmission agreements should not affect states' obligations

for revisiting the provisions of a readmission agreement is all the more warranted now that the European Union, following the entry into force of the ToA, has acquired competences to conclude multilateral readmission agreements with third countries as part of its common policy to facilitate the return of persons arriving and residing on EU territory in an irregular manner.[54]

A future EU instrument regulating the protection standards to be respected in border procedures needs to stipulate a number of protection principles as laid down in ExCOM Conclusions 8 ((XXVIII) and 30 (XXXIV) as well as Council of Europe Recommendation R (84) 1 and Recommendation (98) 15—all of which call on states to ensure that no person should be subjected to refusal of admission or rejection at the border, and request states to assure unimpeded access to the asylum procedure for those seeking protection.[55] The 1995 Resolution on minimum standards includes a large number of exceptions to the general procedural guarantees in admissibility or border procedures, which need to be revisited as a matter of priority in order to prevent their codification in a future Community instrument.

In addition, agreement needs to be reached on the role and competences of border guards in deciding on the admissibility of asylum applications lodged at the border. A useful set of standards, as well as indicators for training, have been adopted by the Council of Europe in its Recommendation R (98) 15.[56] This instrument stipulates that officials who first come into contact with asylum seekers, particularly border guards, need to receive specific training on how to recognise asylum requests, undertake initial screening and handle the claim by referring it to the central competent body normally responsible for determining asylum applications. In so far as border guards are entrusted with specific tasks as part of a pre-screening procedure, they should receive appropriate training in international refugee law and human rights law principles, domestic refugee and

arising from, *inter alia*, the Geneva Refugee Convention or the ECHR. However, no further provisions referring explicitly to responsibilities of the sending and receiving state in handling asylum applications have been included in this model agreement, nor in the Council Recommendation of 24 July 1995 on the guiding principles to be followed in drawing up protocols on the implementation of readmission agreements (OJ 1996 C274/25).

[54] The Community's responsibility with regard to the conclusion of readmission agreements is not exclusive and remains to be shared with that of Member States individually. Member States can continue to conclude readmission agreements with third states provided the Community has not already done so with that state or has obtained a mandate for negotiating such an agreement. Countries which have been selected for the drawing-up of action plans by the EU High Level Working Group on Migration and Asylum, including transit countries in the region (such as Morocco, Pakistan or Sri Lanka), as well as Russia, are likely to be part of the first group with which the Community could conclude such multilateral readmission agreements.

[55] This, however, would not exclude a third state assuming the responsibility of examining the claim. The 1995 EU Resolution stipulates, in para. 23, that states should adopt administrative measures ensuring that any asylum seeker arriving at their frontiers is afforded an opportunity to lodge an asylum claim, but para. 25 allows states to consider applying the "safe third country" concept and subsequent return/onward transferral, prior to deciding on admission to their own territory.

[56] The Ministerial Recommendation was preceded by Recommendation 1309 (1996) of the Parliamentary Assembly of the Council of Europe, concerning the training of officials receiving asylum seekers at border points.

aliens law provisions and interviewing techniques in order to detect and understand asylum requests. The role of border guards should be strictly defined to understanding and recording asylum requests and should not include responsibility for a material examination of claims; this is the competence of the central authority entrusted with determining eligibility for refugee status or another form of protection. Border guards must also be aware of the limitations under national and international law on the use of detention. In addition, provisions regulating the conduct of pre-screening procedures at borders should allow representatives of the UNHCR and legal and social counselling services access to all border areas at ports of entry in order to monitor arrivals and have access to asylum seekers who are at risk of expulsion.[57]

The harmonisation of the application of the "safe third country" concept should take inspiration not only from the existing EU soft law instruments (the 1992 London Resolution and the 1995 Resolution on minimum guarantees) but also related international standards, such as Council Recommendation R (97) 22[58] and ExCOM Conclusions 15 (XXX) and 58 (XL). In remedying the current problems resulting from wide variations among European States of the application of the "safe third country" concept, a common list of guarantees, as a minimum, should include safeguards that the asylum seeker will (i) be readmitted by the third country, (ii) enjoy effective protection against refoulement, (iii) have the possibility to seek and enjoy asylum and (iv) be treated in accordance with accepted international standards in the third country.

The analysis of whether an asylum seeker can be sent to a third country for determination of his/her asylum application must always be done on an individual basis. Whether a third country is considered "safe" for an asylum seeker is not a generic question which can be answered for any applicant in any circumstances, e.g. on the basis of safe third country lists. A country may be a "safe" asylum country for applicants of a certain origin, and yet "unsafe" for

[57] All of these requirements and safeguards have also been listed in Council of Europe Recommendation R (94) 5 concerning the arrival of asylum seekers at European airports.

[58] It should be noted that Council of Europe Recommendation R(97) 22 has more liberal wording than the 1992 EU Resolution, in that the former includes the additional requirement that, in order to be qualified as a "safe third country", that country should observe international human rights standards relevant to asylum as established in universal and regional instruments, as well as provide the "possibility to seek and enjoy asylum". The Recommendation also includes the additional criterion of personal circumstances of the asylum applicant, including prior relations with the third country, as legitimate evidence of his/her admissibility to that country. Similar references are lacking in the 1992 London Resolution. During the negotiations on the Council of Europe Recommendation in CAHAR, some EU Member States initially opposed a more liberal text, invoking previously reached agreement on various issues as laid down in the relevant instruments of the EU asylum *acquis*. This led to an unprecedented politicisation and polarisation of the debate. EU Member States subsequently introduced a common position aimed at reducing the protection safeguards in the draft CAHAR text. CAHAR, however, recognising that its composition is made up of a larger group of states than those members of the European Union, and that it has to respect international standards additional to those of the European Union, successfully resisted moves by EU Member States to reduce the protection dimension of the text. As a result, the Council of Europe Recommendation includes more liberal and inclusive wording than the relevant 1992 EU Resolution.

those originating from another country or representing a different social or ethnic group. In addition, existing meaningful links with a country should always be taken into account, as well as other humanitarian considerations in order to decide which country should be responsible for the treatment of the application. In the absence of such links with a third country, e.g. in "mere transit" situations, removals should not be undertaken. Moreover, in transferring an asylum applicant to a third country, the authorities of that country should be informed that no material examination of the application has been undertaken so far. This is to ensure that the receiving state will undertake an assessment of the merits of the claim and to prevent the applicant, when referred to the third country, being assumed to be a rejected case. All these safeguards need to be clearly reflected in the future Community directive.

RIGHT OF APPEAL

Legislating at European level on the right of appeal can help to give impetus to the badly needed simplification and streamlining of the appeal procedures in Member States, in an effort to speed up the processing of asylum claims. The existing multi-layered procedures in place in Member States allowing for protracted review or appeal proceedings unduly hamper the efficient functioning of asylum systems. Streamlining of these proceedings is important both to ensure that the protection needs of applicants are met quickly and to prevent asylum procedures, given their length and complexity, being used as *de facto* parallel immigration channels. Future Community standards could prescribe not more than two levels of appeal—one full appeal on the merits of the negative decision involving considerations of both fact and law, and a second appeal dealing with questions of law only and limited by a leave requirement. A satisfactory functioning of such a simplified and streamlined appeal mechanism, is, however, dependent on the quality of first instance decisions. As little as multi-layered appeal procedures can compensate for structural inadequacies of first instance interviews and decisions, reducing and simplifying the appeal proceedings will not, by itself, improve the substantive examination of asylum claims, if existing lacunae (lacking resources, limitations to guarantees) in determination processes are not addressed adequately.

One of the most controversial elements of the 1995 Resolution on minimum guarantees has been the abolition of the suspensive effect of the review or appeal in accelerated procedures for processing manifestly unfounded claims (where even the mere possibility for an appeal by an independent body may no longer be required) or in border procedures where the "safe third country" concept is applied.[59] Some observers have argued that suppression of the suspensive effect of the appeal constitutes an infringement on state obligations to uphold the

[59] See above at n. 18.

principle of non-refoulement.[60] International standards such as ExCOM Conclusions 8 and 30 and Council of Europe Recommendation R (81) 16 allow for the lifting of the suspensive effect only in well-defined situations, where rejection of the application is based on its clearly abusive nature or the absence of any connection with the protection criteria. Council of Europe Recommendation R (98) 13 on the right of rejected asylum seekers to an effective remedy against expulsion in the context of Article 3 of the ECHR stipulates that the execution of the expulsion order is to be suspended until the appellate instance has assured itself that return will not entail the risk of torture or inhuman treatment and, hence, a violation of Article 3 ECHR.[61] The 1995 EU Resolution on minimum guarantees, however, allows for the lifting of the suspensive effect of the appeal in respect of applications which have been rejected either on a large number of substantive grounds (covered by the wide definition of "manifestly unfounded" claims included in the 1992 London Resolution) or for various procedural reasons which do not respect all procedural safeguards (in border procedures where the "safe third country" concept is applied as defined in the 1992 London Resolution).[62]

A future Community instrument therefore should remedy the existing deficiencies as regards the absence of a suspensive effect of the appeal whenever the negative first instance decision has been taken on substance, and this regardless of whether the decision was taken in normal or accelerated procedures, in-country or at the border. Only at the admissibility stage can the general rule to respect the appeal's suspensive effect be ignored, provided it is assured that the substantive examination will be undertaken by a third state, either within the framework of the application of the Dublin Convention if it concerns a EU Member State, or where a non-EU Member State has given an undertaking that it will examine the application in full and will provide protection and treatment in accordance with accepted international standards.[63]

[60] See, for instance, the commentary by E. Guild on the Resolution on minimum guarantees, in E. Guild and J. Niessen, *The Developing Immigration and Asylum Policies of the European Union* (Kluwer, The Hague, 1996), 435–49.

[61] The Explanatory Memorandum to the Recommendation clarifies that this does not necessarily prevent the lifting of the suspensive effect of the expulsion order where the claim was considered to be manifestly unfounded, i.e. having no link with the refugee criteria of the Geneva Refugee Convention, since the substance of the asylum claim as related to a well-founded fear of persecution on Convention grounds is not necessarily in connection with the rejected asylum seeker's risk of being exposed to torture or inhuman or degrading treatment or punishment if the expulsion were to be enforced.

[62] Where the Resolution allows for derogation of the principle of the suspensive effect, it also stipulates that asylum seekers should have the possibility of applying to a court or independent review body for permission to remain on the territory temporarily during the appeal procedure. Such a procedure, however, will complicate the process and render it costly since it is likely to entail a hearing on the question of suspensive effect in addition to the main appeal hearing.

[63] See above at n. 28.

CESSATION OR WITHDRAWAL OF STATUS

Article 63(1)(d) EC stipulates that a future Community legislative instrument should lay out the minimum standards for the procedure for granting *and* withdrawing[64] refugee status. The debate on cessation has emerged with some regularity in national debates over the situation where particular groups have fled civil war, which has subsequently come to an end.[65] In such circumstances, policy makers, administrative bodies or parliamentarians appear to be ill-at-ease with the public perception that refugee status is permanent and irreversible. The future instrument, as a minimum, may take over the relevant provisions of the 1996 Joint Position on the harmonised application of the "refugee" definition.[66] This soft law instrument follows the guidance provided by the UNHCR *Handbook* and ExCOM Conclusion 69 (XLIII) of 1992 in stipulating that withdrawal of refugee status on the basis of Article 1C of the Geneva Refugee Convention is always to be investigated on an individual basis and that the circumstances in which application of the cessation clauses are considered should be of a fundamental and durable nature and be determined in an objective and verifiable manner. The Commission[67] has suggested that the principle of investigating cessation on an individual basis should be laid down in the future directive on asylum procedures, and that a future Community instrument provide for additional safeguards similar to those available during the procedure for gaining refugee status.

It is, indeed, an essential prerequisite for applying the cessation clauses to consider the individual circumstances, particularly where the clauses are invoked with respect to whole groups of persons, and on the basis of the "ceased circumstances" clauses of Article 1C (5)–(6) of the Geneva Refugee Convention. The future Community instrument should spell out clearly that the cessation clauses should not apply to refugees who continue to have valid grounds for claiming a well-founded fear of persecution or other compelling reasons for continuing to be regarded as refugees. Those persons should be given an opportunity to show that, given the particular circumstances of their case, the change of circumstances does not remove the source of well-founded fear of persecution and that therefore they should continue to enjoy refugee status.[68] There should

[64] Withdrawal is understood as cessation. Another form of withdrawal of status could be cancellation of status when the original positive decision appears to have been made on the basis of false information. Both the Commission and the Member States have indicated, however, that they do not see the need to legislate on the issue of cancellation given its relatively limited occurrence.

[65] For instance in the Netherlands in October 1998 when some groups in Parliament proposed cessation of refugee status of the some 20,000 Bosnians who had been granted such status after they had first been admitted under a temporary protection regime. The proposal was defeated in Parliament following intervention by the Government and the UNHCR.

[66] Joint Position of 4 March 1996 on the basis of Article K3 of the Treaty on European Union on the harmonized application of the definition of the term "refugee" in Article 1 of the Geneva Convention of 28 July 1951 Relating to the Status of Refugees (OJ 1996 L63/2).

[67] Commission working document, para. 24.

[68] See also UNHCR *Handbook*, para. 136.

always be a right of appeal against a decision to implement the cessation clause in the particular case (suspensive effect should not be questioned). The standard of proof that the status can be withdrawn should be high, at least as high as that applying to applications for recognition of Convention status.

The procedural principles and safeguards to be included in the future Community instrument generally should follow the guidance of ExCOM Conclusion 69 (XLIII). The Conclusion highlights the need for "clearly established procedures" in the application of the cessation clauses, allowing for a comprehensive individual hearing of the merits of the individual case, particularly where cessation is to be applied on a group basis in relation to "ceased circumstances" in the country of origin. Cessation of refugee status based on the "ceased circumstances" clause should be clearly distinguished from the application of the "safe country of origin" concept which is merely to be used as a procedural tool to expedite processing of refugee applications.[69] Whether cessation is considered on the basis of a change in the objective circumstances in connection with which the refugee was recognised (Article 1C (5)–(6)), or a change in personal circumstances brought about by the refugee's own act (Article 1C (1)–(4)), the clauses must always be interpreted in a restrictive manner. UNHCR should be given a role in evaluating the impact of changes in the country of origin with a view to determining whether these are fundamental, durable and effective to justify withdrawal of status.[70]

Although the cessation clauses are directly linked to the ending of Convention refugee status, they may also provide guidance as regards the withdrawal of complementary forms of protection, particularly where the "ceased circumstances" clause is considered for application. Complementary protection is often granted precisely on the basis of the prevailing circumstances in the country of origin, for instance in situations of civil war or internal conflict, and it can thus be argued that, in considering the withdrawal of a complementary form of protection, the assessment of the return to stability and security of a country/region which was affected by indiscriminate violence and civil unrest is easier to make than a judgment, with full consideration of individual circumstances, of the fundamental nature and projected durability of changes in the country of origin, required when dealing with cessation of refugee status. These nuances, however, can best be dealt with in administrative and procedural guidelines

[69] Qualifying a country of origin as "safe" may, however, reflect lasting improvements in the human rights situation and a durable absence of persecution which could, in turn, warrant the consideration of applying the cessation clause. See also Note on the Cessation Clauses, UNCHR Standing Committee, 8th meeting, EC/47/SC/CRP.30 (30 May 1997), para. 7.

[70] This is particular relevant if assessing whether cessation can be applied to refugees from civil conflict, i.e. whether the refugee can re-avail him or herself of the national protection of the country of origin, although this may have fragmented subsequently into different parts marked by different levels of security. Even if changes in part of a country can be considered as fundamental, they must have stabilised for a sufficient long period of time before an evaluation is made in respect of the possibility of applying the cessation clauses. See UNHCR Note on the Cessation Clauses, ibid., paras 25–6.

related to complementary status rather than included in a Community instrument setting out standards for fair asylum procedures more generally.

TOWARDS A SINGLE ASYLUM PROCEDURE?

In elaborating common standards for Member States' asylum procedures consideration should be given to their applicability in a comprehensive determination procedure aimed at assessing individually all protection needs in a holistic manner. The central and expert determining authority would measure the applicant's case against all relevant criteria: those of the Geneva Refugee Convention, standards laid down in other international or regional human rights instruments (such as the ECHR), or those of the extended UNHCR mandate. The applicant should be offered a possibility to appeal the decision in case a "lesser" form of protection is offered than the level of protection which he/she believes to be entitled to benefit from. The establishment of a single asylum procedure will avoid having different procedures to be applied consecutively where asylum seekers feel compelled to appeal for a "higher" status by admission into the refugee status determination procedure. Also, the expertise of eligibility bodies and tribunals can be used for the examination of applications invoking reasons of flight other than a well-founded persecution directly linked to the Convention criteria. A broadly comprehensive system would be preferable to a mechanism whereby administrative authorities without specialist knowledge and competence in asylum matters would consider the need for alternative (temporary) protection on an ad hoc, discretionary basis.[71]

Whether the standard of proof required for the grant of complementary forms of protection generally can be lower than the standard required for providing refugee status remains an open question. Determination of protection needs resulting from indiscriminate violence, widespread human rights violations or other forms of repression affecting larger groups of persons are often well-documented and reported, and, hence, there would be less need to examine all the particular circumstances of the individual in an application for complementary protection—as would be necessary for the determination of refugee status. Credibility issues may arise, however, where the applicant, due to lack of documentation or use of forged papers, may not be able to make a convincing case out of his/her asylum story, or where he/she cannot prove otherwise to originate from a conflict-ridden country. It should also be recalled that in considering the applicability of Article 3 ECHR in expulsion cases, the Strasbourg Court of Human Rights has set a high standard of proof in that it requires the applicant to show the existence of "substantial grounds", as well as a "real risk" of being

[71] In its working document, the Commission suggests that a single procedure for asylum and complementary protection issues can be instituted by Member States only once a Community instrument on complementary protection arrangements has been drawn up, including agreement on procedural aspects.

subjected to torture and ill-treatment which would militate against return. European States, however, in allowing asylum seekers temporary leave to remain on their territory on humanitarian grounds generally set a lower standard of proof in that they are satisfied with consistent reports of general patterns of human rights violations which afflict the group as a whole to which the applicant belongs—rather than requiring additional evidence related to personal circumstances and substantiating a subjective fear of persecution.

In the event that Member States could be persuaded to institute a single procedure as part of a comprehensive system which, in principle, would consider any application for protection,[72] the next step would be to consider the adoption of a uniform asylum procedure throughout the European Union. At the Tampere Summit, Member States could not agree on instituting a single asylum system in the short term, which would include such a uniform procedure, yet went as far as calling for the adoption, in the longer term, of a common asylum procedure and a uniform status for those granted asylum which would be valid throughout the Union.[73]

CONCLUSION

A new Community instrument on asylum procedures needs to establish a comprehensive set of protection standards to be applicable in the regular asylum procedure, as well as in accelerated procedures and procedures determining admissibility. Derogations from these principles applied in order to quickly screen out asylum applications undeserving of a full determination procedure should be kept to a minimum and should not be applicable to fundamental principles, such as access to procedures and the right to a fair hearing of the claim. The instrument needs to be built around a set of core rights exercisable by the individual, complemented with a list of obligations to be fulfilled by the state. In negotiating such a comprehensive and consistent set of procedural standards, Member States should refrain from comparing existing differences between, and singularities of, their procedural arrangements which tend to result in agreeing on the lowest common denominator only. Instead they should exercise the political will to adopt a coherent framework encompassing all the relevant procedural concepts and arrangements and based on high protection standards. So far Member States have expressed their intention to stick to a strict interpretation of the language of the asylum provisions of the ToA, which call for the adoption of minimum standards in the key areas of their asylum systems,

[72] The majority of Member States have reportedly responded favourably to the Commission's proposal—as put forward in its working document—to establish, in the medium term, a single, comprehensive procedural framework for examining all the protection issues raised by an individual case, irrespective of whether protection is sought on the basis of the Geneva Refugee Convention or other human rights standards, for humanitarian or other reasons.

[73] See also above at n. 11.

including minimum standards governing their asylum procedures. If Member States continue on the old road of intergovernmental co-operation and consultation, preserving the particularities of their own asylum systems, these minimum standards are at risk of developing into maximum standards, particularly if the rule of unanimous voting is to be maintained during the next five-year transition period in which the various asylum instruments need to be adopted.

Legislative and policy development in asylum will be paralleled by a similar process in migration, particular in the areas of admission, expulsion, controlling illegal entry and combating organised crime. While the Tampere Summit Conclusions call for guaranteeing continued access to, and refuge on, Member States' territory for those genuinely in need of protection, the same Conclusions also call for vigorous measures to stem illegal immigration, reinforce border controls and combat trafficking in human beings.[74] Access to the territory and to the asylum procedure, therefore, risks being undermined if stringent control measures are put in place without adopting sufficient guarantees addressing the situation of persons seeking protection. These guarantees, therefore, need to be built into not only the Community asylum instruments (first and foremost the procedural instrument), but also the framework laws which will regulate admission and rejection at the border.

The real challenge for the drafters and negotiators of a directive establishing common asylum procedures throughout the Union will be in devising new procedural arrangements for dealing with admissibility issues as well as manifestly unfounded or clearly abusive applications, and for streamlining and shortening the often lengthy and cumbersome proceedings, while fully respecting the basic procedural rights and safeguards. The last decade has shown an erosion of protection standards by frequent use of accelerated procedures for an increasing number of asylum applications, the adoption of a wide range of elements defining a "manifestly unfounded" or "clearly abusive" application, and the invention of various devices to screen out asylum applications at the admissibility stage. This process has been given impetus by the development of a number of EU soft law instruments, all of which have been characterised by, although relatively few, significant departures from general protection principles. These must not be copied in the future directive; the Commission and the Member States must have the courage and the vision to devise a common procedural framework for the full and fair determination of all protection needs, based on a comprehensive set of protection standards to be applied without limitations except where procedural notions of a practical nature may be applied. This exercise must put the rights and needs of the individual asylum seeker upfront, if it wants to do justice to Europe's vocation to establish an area in which fundamental rights and freedoms are to be respected.

[74] Tampere Presidency Conclusions, para. 3.

8

Temporary Protection and Burden-Sharing: Conditionalising Access Suspending Refugee Rights?

GREGOR NOLL AND JENS VEDSTED-HANSEN[1]

INTRODUCTION

Where is the linkage between temporary protection and burden sharing, and why do both concepts retain such an importance for understanding the EU's emerging immigration and asylum policies? Within the European Union, thinking on the reform of the protection system revolves around two major changes in the distribution of costs stemming from protection responsibilities. The first affects the relationship between the individual protection seeker and the host state; the second relates to the relationship among Member States. First, cost limitation is to be attained by lowering the protection level of the individual. This is the essence of temporary protection—to limit the time during which a person is to be protected, and following some models, even the material rights enjoyed by that person. Secondly, costs should be spread equitably to all states. This is the essence of burden sharing—to prevent peak burdens on single states and to create predictability for all states by sharing the costs of protection. Regarded thus, both temporary protection and burden sharing improve the predictability of the protection system for the single Member State.

Now, it is quite evident that temporary protection and burden sharing are interdependent. The more states succeed in burden sharing, the less need there is to cut the level of protection. However, this relationship can also be reversed: the less burden sharing states achieve, the more protection is likely to be slashed by burdened states. As we shall see, there is a third factor, interrelated to the two others—the number of protection seekers actually present on the territory of a specific Member State. The fewer protection seekers there are, the less need there is for a burden sharing scheme to avoid peak costs.

[1] While this text as a whole should be seen as the result of a cooperative effort, Gregor Noll has focused on the second, third and fourth sections, and Jens Vedsted-Hansen has focused on the fifth section.

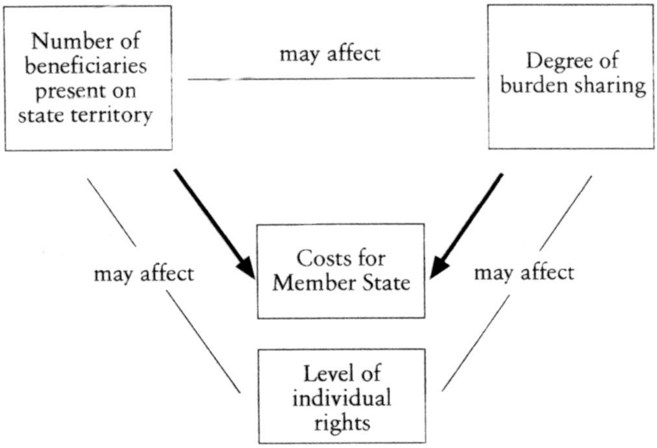

Three factors affecting the costs of protection regimes

The fewer protection seekers there are, the less need there is to slash individual rights in order to keep costs under a certain ceiling. Simplifying, one may claim that the total reception costs of a state are determined by all three factors taken together. Also, given that protection resources are assumed to be finite, each factor affects the two remaining factors.

We have attempted to visualise both functions in the figure above.

Thus, the debates on temporary protection and burden sharing are more than another Eurocrat technicality. After all, they might alter the parameters steering a future European protection system. There are good reasons to assess the emerging *acquis* in both areas against the existing regime based on the Geneva Convention as well as unilateral responses. As expounded elsewhere, ToA[2] represented a singular opportunity to restructure the staggering co-operation in the area of asylum and migration.[3]

In short, in these areas, the ToA is about form rather than substance. At large, Member States consented on procedures and competencies for future deliberations on visa, asylum, migration and other policies related to free movement of persons. Nevertheless, the agenda thus set is binding upon Member States as primary EC law. True enough, the setting of such an agenda predetermines outcomes. What follows presents an analysis of the ToA's effect on the issue of burden sharing and temporary protection. In the second, third and fourth sections

[2] Amending the Treaty on European Union, the Treaties establishing the European Communities and Certain Related Acts, Doc No. CONF 4007/97 (Amsterdam, 2 October 1997).

[3] For a comprehensive overview of the changes introduced by the ToA with regard to refugee and asylum policies, see G. Noll and J. Vedsted-Hansen, "Non-Communitarians: Refugee and Asylum Policies", in Philip Alston (ed.), *The EU and Human Rights* (Oxford University Press, Oxford, 1999), 359–410.

we will track the debate on burden sharing—before and after Amsterdam, while in the fifth section we focus on temporary protection. In the final section, we conclude on the main implications of both debates for a future European protection system.

BURDEN SHARING

The meaning of burden sharing

The core desideratum of any burden-sharing arrangement is the creation of predictability. Like an insurance contract, burden-sharing arrangements allow states to calculate maximum costs in future crisis situations. The insurance parallel suggests that burden sharing cannot be an *ad hoc* affair. Predictability presupposes that principles of distribution are agreed upon in a sufficiently detailed fashion *before* a crisis materialises. From that perspective, a major problem of present approaches to burden sharing is the absence of such predetermined distributive principles.

On the other hand, it can be argued that states would take an unnecessarily cautious approach, if pushed, to predetermine principles of distribution for all conceivable crises of the future. By contrast, a mere negotiating framework, allowing for flexible and situation-adapted solutions, might yield a better, i.e. more generous outcome. This argument, however, leaves out of account that states had ample opportunity to practise such *ad hoc* burden sharing, and that they made insufficient use of this option.[4] The persistent discussions on burden sharing and the tendency towards measures of deflection support this assessment.[5] Moreover, it should be underscored that predetermined principles of distribution represent a minimum common denominator of assistance. Nothing inhibits states from agreeing more generous aid in single cases, exceeding the exigencies of an underlying burden-sharing arrangement. A fixed normative framework prevents states from remaining completely passive when others are struck by a crisis. They are free to do so, however, under a negotiating framework. In the light of these arguments, the ensuing analysis is based on the assumption that regulating burden sharing beforehand is better than negotiating it *ad hoc*.

[4] See G. Noll, "Prisoners' Dilemma in Fortress Europe. On the Prospects of Burden Sharing in the European Union" (1997) 40 *German Yearbook of International Law* 405, 406–411.

[5] The analysis of the receptive unwillingness persisting in Europe is facilitated by looking back to the South Asian refugee crisis of the 1970s and 1980s. At that time, the reluctance by countries in the region to receive refugees could be mitigated by launching an elaborate and predictable burden sharing scheme. It could be argued that a European burden sharing scheme could mitigate the tendency towards ever more deflective policies proliferating among European asylum countries.

Background

On a factual level, there is no equitable sharing of reception burdens in Europe. The largest populations of protection seekers from Bosnia were found in those countries of Western Europe which were either geographically proximate or already hosting immigrant communities from former Yugoslavia. In descending order, per capita, Austria, Sweden, Germany and Switzerland[6] received most of these persons. In total numbers, Germany alone accommodated 58% of all Bosnian refugees hosted by EU Member States.[7] Together, Austria, Germany and Sweden, being the three largest receivers within the European Union, hosted 84% of all Bosnian refugees who found shelter in the European Union.[8]

In terms of solidarity, the Bosnian refugee crisis was a failure. However, it set off comprehensive and protracted deliberations on how to ensure a more equitable distribution in future cases by legal means. These deliberations will be presented in four steps, the first focusing on the 1995 Resolution on burden sharing, the second exposing various facets of burden-sharing in the ToA, and the third focusing on the negotiations following a specific burden-sharing proposal by the European Commission.

Negotiations preceding the 1995 Resolution

Based on the inequitable reception of Bosnian refugees and the difficulties to negotiate even non-binding European instruments, burden sharing was declared to be one of the issues to be examined by the Council in 1994 according to the priority work plan for that year. Accordingly, the German presidency presented an ambitious draft Council Resolution on burden sharing regarding the admission and residence of refugees[9] in July 1994. However, the draft had difficulties in attracting the necessary support and was successively watered down in later compromise drafts.

During the Spanish presidency, a limited consensus on burden sharing had finally begun to develop, and a Council Resolution on burden sharing with regard to admission and residence of displaced persons on a temporary basis on 25 September 1995 was adopted.[10] Let us draw up a brief comparison between the German Draft of 1994 and the 1995 Resolution.

[6] At the time, Austria and Sweden had not acquired membership of the European Union. Switzerland was not and is not a member of the European Union.

[7] Statistical source: UNHCR (1997), as reproduced in European Commission, *Conditions for the Return of Displaced Persons from the European Union* (Luxembourg 1998), 7, table 1.1. By 1997 Germany had received 342,500 Bosnians out of an EU total of 584,017.

[8] Ibid. By 1997 Austria had received 88,609 Bosnians, while the corresponding number for Sweden was 60,671.

[9] Doc No. 7773/94 ASIM 124 (hereinafter the Draft).

[10] OJ 1995 C262/1 (hereinafter the 1995 Resolution). According to the draft list of the *acquis communautaire*, para. I.C., this instrument is also part of the *acquis*. Item Note from the Presidency

The most daring feature of the Draft was to propose a specific distributive key which could be used by Member States.[11] This key was based on Member States':

—percentage of the total Union population;
—percentage of Union territory; and
—percentage of the Union's gross domestic product.

Each of these criteria should be given equal weight. The Draft contained a table of indicative figures[12] for each Member State which were to be revised each five years by joint agreement. The possibility to depart from these figures by joint agreement was expressly provided for in paragraph 8 of the Draft.

The centrepiece of the envisaged redistribution mechanism was contained in paragraph 9:

> "Where the numbers admitted by a Member State exceed its indicative figure under paragraph 8, other Member States which have not yet reached their indicative figure under paragraph 8 will accept persons from the first Member State."

Accordingly, the Draft intended to introduce compulsory resettlement relying on a distributive key. However, a reduction of reception obligations was envisaged with respect to military expenditure triggered by intervention in the refugee-producing crisis[13] and the Convention refugee population already present in a Member State.[14] In terms of *realpolitik*, resistance to the Draft can be explained by the fact that Germany would have been its first beneficiary, with additional reception responsibilities falling upon all other Member States.

Turning to the 1995 Resolution, it is striking to see that the indicative figures have vanished and the stipulated distributive key is devoid of any precision:[15]

to Coreper, Draft list of the "*acquis*" of the Union and of its Member States in the field of Justice and Home Affairs: Doc No. 6437/2/98 REV 3 (20 March 1998).

[11] Draft, para. 7. This solution was obviously inspired by the distributive order in domestic German legislation, which stipulates a distributive key for asylum seekers in deferral legislation. This key may be modified by a unanimous decision of the Länder. See *Asylverfahrensgesetz* [Asylum Procedure Act], s. 45.

[12] Ibid. A look at these figures might help to understand both the German urge and the failing support of other large Member States. In descending percentage order, the figures read as follows: Germany (21.58), France (19.40), Italy (15.83), United Kingdom (14.28), Spain (13.63), Netherlands (3.55), Greece (3.20), Portugal (2.65), Belgium (2.42), Denmark (1.78), Ireland (1.54), Luxembourg (0.12).

[13] Paragrap 9 of the Draft states: "Member States which are helping, by means of particular foreign and security policy measures in the country of origin of the persons referred to in para 1, to control the refugee situation in the State in question, need not admit the full figure assigned to them under para 8. The resulting shortfall should be covered by the other States in proportion to their indicative figures. Measures of this nature include in particular peace-keeping or peace-making initiatives in the framework of the United Nations, NATO or the Western European Union".

[14] According to para. 11 of the Draft, Convention refugees are set off against the indicative figure in para. 8.

[15] With regard to the vagueness of the given criteria, we omit a detailed discussion of their implications. For a critical analysis, see ECRE, *Comments from the European Council on Refugees and Exiles on the 1995 "Burden-Sharing" Resolution and Decision adopted by the Council for the European Union* (March, 1999).

"The Council agrees that the burden in connection with the admission and residence of displaced persons on a temporary basis in a crisis could be shared on a balanced basis in a spirit of solidarity, taking into account the following criteria . . .

—the contribution which each Member State is making to prevention or resolution of the crisis, in particular by the supply of military resources in operations and missions ordered by the United Nations Security Council or the Organisation for Security and Cooperation in Europe and by the measures taken by each Member State to afford local protection to people under threat or to provide humanitarian assistance,
—all economic, social and political factors which may affect the capacity of a Member State to admit an increased number of displaced persons under satisfactory conditions."

In a footnote linked to the first paragraph of this article, it is said that "these criteria are norms of reference that may be supplemented by further criteria in the light of specific situations".

To wit, this statement reveals the self-contradiction contained in the present instrument. In the Preamble, it is correctly stated that "situations of great urgency . . . require prompt action and the development beforehand of the principles governing the admission of displaced persons". However, these principles are developed *ex post facto* by the Council. The 1995 Resolution has been followed by a Decision on alert and emergency procedure for burden-sharing with regard to the admission and residence of displaced persons on a temporary basis,[16] which lays down the procedural framework for Council decisions and monitoring in burden-sharing situations. The *ex post facto* framework clearly fails to provide the necessary predictability for a fair burden sharing. Consequently, a cautious state would rather block access for refugees than trust in the outcome of this ad hoc exercise in the Council.[17]

Who are the beneficiaries of a burden-sharing exercise under the 1995 Resolution? Its personal scope comprises various categories of vulnerable persons "whom Member States are prepared to admit on a temporary basis under appropriate conditions in the event of armed conflict or civil war, including where such persons have already left their region of origin to go to one of the Member States".[18] The categories comprise former camp internees, medical evacuation cases, persons exposed to direct threat of loss of life or limb, cases of sexual violence, and war refugees having come directly from a combat zone to the territory of a Member State. In the 1995 Resolution, an exclusion clause similar to Article 1F(a) and (b) of the 1951 Refugee Convention has been inserted.

[16] OJ 1996 L063, 10.

[17] The importance of a detailed and predictable burden sharing framework seems to have been realised by the authors of the German draft Resolution. See para. 5 of the Draft: The Council is convinced that if Member States are to be able to react promptly in emergencies, they must first devise an appropriate range of measures for the admission of refugees from war or civil war. Such measures must include prior agreement on principles for distributing refugees. Otherwise there is a risk that, in situations in which prompt action is necessary to avert serious danger to human life, decisions which need to be taken urgently will be delayed by the fact that complicated consultation procedures must first be initiated.

[18] 1995 Resolution, Art. 1(a).

It emerges clearly that no State obligation to admit is envisaged. Any decision on admission remains within the discretion of the relevant Member State.

Furthermore, the 1995 Resolution does not apply retroactively, i.e. to persons admitted before its adoption.[19] The responsibility for persons applying for refugee status under the 1951 Refugee Convention will be distributed by the rules laid down in the Dublin Convention.[20] Interestingly and in contradistinction to the 1995 Resolution, the Draft contained a provision allowing for the reduction of a certain state's reception obligations according to the number of persons residing there in accordance with the protection of the 1951 Refugee Convention or the ECHR.[21]

As the remaining personal scope is imprecise and ultimately refers back to the assessment made by each Member State, it is not clear how Member States are to single out a group of persons which could be the subject of burden sharing according to Article 4 of the 1995 Resolution. Finally, it must be recalled that a resolution is a so-called atypical instrument of EU law, which is not binding per se;[22] this detracts further from the degree to which the 1995 Resolution may stabilise Member States' expectations in a crisis situation.

Both the German Draft Resolution and the 1995 Resolution relied heavily on what has been identified as a control strategy.[23] In the 1995 Resolution, however, steering principles had been watered down to a degree to which allocating capacity was lost and the whole instrument became dysfunctional.

TREATY OF AMSTERDAM

After the entry into force of the ToA, the consolidated EC Treaty contains in Title IV two articles having a bearing on burden-sharing. This implies a formal shift of these areas to the supranational First Pillar, while retaining intergovernmental Third Pillar elements and incorporating a timetable. Article 63(2) EC offers a broad entitlement to take action:

> "The Council, acting in accordance with the procedure referred to in Article 67, shall, within a period of five years after the entry into force of the ToA, adopt:
>
> . . .
>
> (2) measures on refugees and other displaced persons within the following areas:
>
> . . .

[19] Ibid., Art. 7.

[20] Ibid., Preamble.

[21] Draft, para. 11.

[22] In exceptional cases, where the Member States had expressed an intention to be bound, the ECJ has declared such instruments to have binding force. Case 22/70 *Commission* v. *Council* [1971] ECR 263, paras 34–55 (European Agreement on road transport). Nothing in the present instrument indicates that Member States indeed intended to be legally bound by it.

[23] J. van der Klaauw, "Refugee Protection in Western Europe: A UNHCR Perspective", in J.-Y. Carlier and D. Vanheule (eds) *Europe and Refugees: A Challenge?* (Kluwer Law International, The Hague, 1997), 227, 244, who criticises the EU approach to burden sharing as too narrow minded and focused on immigration control.

> (b) promoting a balance of effort between Member States in receiving and bearing the consequences of receiving refugees and other displaced persons.
>
> . . .
>
> Measures to be adopted pursuant to points 2(b) . . . shall not be subject to the five year period referred to above."

More specifically, Article 64(2) transgresses unanimity in decision-making in a carefully delimited area:

> "In the event of one or more Member States being confronted with an emergency situation characterised by a sudden inflow of nationals of third countries and without prejudice to paragraph 1, the Council may, acting by qualified majority on a proposal from the Commission, adopt provisional measures of a duration not exceeding six months for the benefit of the Members States concerned."[24]

Within the context of Title IV, these articles beg questions with regard to their precise content and their capacity to provide solutions. Before embarking on clarifications, however, it is necessary to identify the fundamentals of burden sharing within the normative architecture of the European Union.

Decision-making under Article 63

The originality of the agenda set out by the ToA lies in the fact that the named policies are formally shifted from the Third Pillar to the First Pillar. At first sight, this might be interpreted as a shift from an intergovernmental to a supranational forum, from Maastricht to Rome, or from EU to EC law. A discriminating look reveals that this is not quite the case. Pending further steps by an unanimous Council, Title IV remains a sheep in wolf's clothing, as the ToA retains an intergovernmental procedure of decision-making.

During a "transitional period" of five years,[25] the Council shall adopt measures under Title IV by unanimous vote.[26] After this period, a shift to majority voting takes place, provided that the Council takes an unanimous decision "with a view to providing for all or parts of the areas covered by this Title to be governed by the procedure referred to in Article 251 and adapting the provisions

[24] Paragraph 1 of the same article reads: "This Title shall not affect the exercise of the responsibilities incumbent upon Member States with regard to the maintenance of law and order and the safeguarding of internal security".

[25] The transitional period under Art. 67 has to be distinguished from the five-year period set out for most measures under Art. 63. To wit, burden sharing measures have been exempted from the five-year period under Art. 63, but they may still come under the ambit for a decision based on Art. 67.

[26] Decisions on visa requirement and a uniform visa format represent the sole exception to the unanimity rule. However, those areas were already exempted from unanimity under the Maastricht Treaty. Compare Art. 67(3) EC, Art. 62(2)(b)(i) and (iii) EC and Art. 100C(2) and (3) OEC.

relating to the powers of the ECJ".[27] This decision is a precondition for unanimity.[28]

Thus, there will not be an automatic transition to majority voting, which might have resolved the stalemate on burden sharing. If Member States disagree on burden sharing, they will, quite logically, refrain from shifting this issue to a procedure of majority voting. In effect, the solution chosen in Article 67 EC is structurally identical with the old "*passerelle*" in Article K.9 TEU, and the question imposes itself, whether any substantial progress has been attained.

Exemption from the temporal framework in Article 63

It emanates from the very wording of Article 63 EC that measures relating to burden sharing are not included amongst those which must be adopted within a five-year period. This implies that the Council may take as much time as necessary for reaching consensus, at the risk that consensus might never be reached. Essentially, this makes the content of Article 63(2)(b) EC a mere reminder that burden sharing should be on the agenda, without imposing an obligation to adopt measures within a certain time-frame.

The very disparity of the temporal limits set is a telling example of the new two-speed Europe. Recalling that openness towards persons in need of protection and cost distribution is interrelated, this disparity may have detrimental consequences for the level of protection offered through EU measures. As for Article 63 EC, the deliberations on cost distribution, i.e. the measure on burden sharing—are open-ended, while the degree of openness i.e., the measures relating to the granting of protection is to be determined within five years. This keeps protection costs uncertain. As long as this uncertainty prevails, a rational state will opt for a minimum level of protection. Translated back to practice, this promotes the spiral of restriction in EU asylum policies further. When adopting measures under Article 63(1) and (2)(a) EC, Member States will attempt to minimise the scope of protective burden by reinforcing deflection and seeking to lower the level of rights enjoyed by protection seekers who manage to enter their territories.

The temporal disparity has been affirmed by and fortified in the 1998 Action Plan of the Council and the Commission on how best to implement the provisions of the ToA establishing an area of freedom, security and justice.[29]

[27] Article 67(2) EC.

[28] Compare also the Declaration on Article 73O of the Treaty establishing the European Community (Declaration No. 21 annexed to the Final Act of the Inter-Governmental Conference): "The Conference agrees that the Council will examine the elements of the decision referred to in Article 73o(2), second indent, [Art. 67] of the Treaty establishing the European Community before the end of the five year period referred to in Article 73o with a view to taking and applying this decision immediately after the end of that period".

[29] Council of the European Union, Action Plan of the Council and the Commission on how best to implement the provisions of the Treaty of Amsterdam establishing an area of freedom, security and justice (OJ 1999 C19/01). The Action Plan is a non-binding instrument.

The Action Plan makes up a more detailed schedule for the adoption of measures under Article 63. In spite of the fact that Article 63 EC allows for five years, some measures are considered so important that they shall be adopted already within two years.[30] Burden sharing does not belong to these measures. It is listed amongst the measures "to be taken as quickly as possible in accordance with the provisions of the Treaty of Amsterdam".[31]

Mandate of Article 63(2)(b)

Which classes of beneficiary are covered by the provision on burden sharing in Article 63(2)(b) EC? Here, the drafters chose a comprehensive solution by including both "refugees" and "displaced persons". The importance of that choice should not be underestimated. Let us imagine for a moment that burden sharing had been limited to displaced persons, while refugees had been excluded from its ambit. That would have incited Member States to minimise the group of persons defined as refugees and to maximise the group of persons defined as displaced persons. As the precise scope of the refugee definition is a contested issue, this would be a rational and feasible strategy to avoid incalculable costs.

From a protection perspective, the inclusive wording of Article 63 EC is a positive feature. It gives the Council a base to counteract the concentration effects brought about by the Dublin Convention.[32]

THE SOLIDARITY DRAFTS: MERGING ADMISSION AND SOLIDARITY?

With the dysfunctional 1995 Resolution, the framework provisions launched with the ToA, the topic of burden sharing in the European Union is not exhausted. Initiated by the Commission, a proposal for a twin instrument regulating both admission to temporary protection and solidarity with regard to such protection has been negotiated from 1997 until early 1999.

Different stages of the negotiation process illustrate in a very graphic fashion how decisions of access, level of accorded protection, fiscal burden sharing and redistribution of physical protection responsibilities are intertwined. As this process may be of decisive value for tracking the intent of the Union as well as Community legislator, we shall deal with it at some length.

In March 1997 the European Commission launched a proposal on a Joint Action concerning temporary protection of displaced persons.[33] It was the first time ever that the Commission made use of its right to initiative in relation to

[30] OJ 1999 C19/01, para. 36.

[31] Ibid, para. 37(b).

[32] For a comprehensive analysis of the Dublin Convention. see G. Noll, above at n. 4, 405–437.

[33] European Commission, Proposal to the Council for a Joint Action based on Article K.3 2(b) of the Treaty of European Union concerning Temporary Protection of Displaced Persons (OJ 1997 C106/13) (hereinafter the 1997 Proposal).

asylum, pursuant to Article K.3(2)(b) TEU. On a strategic level, this proposal signalled a certain caution with regard to the demanding paradigm of redistribution. Rather, its drafters returned to the proven technique of harmonisation, i.e. sharing norms. The 1997 Proposal's main goal was to eliminate distortional effects[34] flowing from differences between national regimes of temporary protection.

With the proposal, the Commission sought to frame a Union-wide temporary protection regime, containing a number of minimum rights[35] and a mechanism for the common opening-up and phasing-out of such a régime.[36] Interestingly, the binding decisions on opening up and phasing out were proposed to be taken by qualified majority in the Council.[37]

Article 5 of the 1997 Proposal addressed the question of assistance to particularly affected states:

> "On the basis of the report of the Commission referred to in Article 4,[38] the Council shall examine how best to support Member States which have been particularly affected by the mass influx of persons in need of international protection."[39]

The Explanatory Memorandum attached to the 1997 Proposal underscored that:

> "One of the very purposes of the joint action is precisely to create conditions for an effective sharing of the responsibility with regard to situations of mass influx of persons in need of international protection. Article 5 reflects the content of the Council resolution on burden-sharing which foresees the possibility of taking measures based on solidarity if one or more Member States are particularly affected by mass-influx situations. Such measures may for example take the form of financial compensation and/or, if that is not sufficient, a fair allocation of the persons who are fleeing from the crisis region."[40]

Under the consultation procedure, the European Parliament introduced a number of amendments to the 1997 Proposal.[41] The readings in the Council focused, *inter alia*, on the issue of burden sharing, where Article 5 of the 1997

[34] Ibid. See also paras 7 and 8 of the Explanatory Memorandum attached to the Proposal.

[35] Ibid., Arts 6–9 Proposal.

[36] Ibid., Arts 3 and 4 Proposal.

[37] Ibid., Art. 12 Proposal.

[38] Ibid. According to Art. 4, the Commission is to prepare a yearly report on the situation in the country of origin, the application of the temporary protection regime by the Member States, and its financial implications. This report will, *inter alia*, provide the basis for decisions on the phasing-out of a temporary protection regime.

[39] Ibid.

[40] Ibid., para. 21 of the Explanatory Memorandum.

[41] European Parliament, Legislative Resolution embodying Parliament's opinion on the proposal to the Council for a Joint Action based on Article K.3(2)(b) of the Treaty on European Union concerning temporary protection of displaced persons, COM (97) 0093—C4–0247/97—97/0081 (CNS), A4–0284/97 (23 October 1997). These amendments reinforce the language of the original Proposal, stress the exceptional nature of temporary protection, and underscore the importance of complying with international law and of consulting the UNHCR in the context of temporary protection.

Proposal drew most of the fire, apparently being wholly unacceptable to certain Member States.[42]

Therefore, the Commission changed tactics. In June 1998 the Commission presented two draft joint actions for adoption by the Council. One joint action would deal with a Union-wide temporary protection regime, containing a number of minimum rights[43] and a mechanism for the common opening-up and phasing-out of such a regime.[44] Another joint action would be entirely devoted to burden sharing, or rather, according to the terminology of the Commission, "solidarity".[45] Primarily, Member States would share the burden by a system of financial compensations. First, a fixed emergency aid is proposed, limited to the first three months of a crisis and intended to cover accommodation, means of subsistence and emergency medical assistance.[46] The budgetary support for this item remains to be created. Secondly, reception projects could be financed by using an existing item in the EU budget.[47] This longer-term measure would cover accommodation, social assistance and education.

Explicitly termed a *secondary measure*, a Council decision may also define the rules allowing the beneficiaries of temporary protection to be distributed between Member States, before or on arrival in their territory.[48] This form of people sharing shall not, however, prejudice the rules laid down in the Dublin Convention, as long as Member States do not suspend the examination of asylum applications.[49] To wit, in the 1998 Solidarity Proposal, fiscal burden sharing is endowed with a rather specific framework, while people sharing remains formally on the agenda, but lacks further specification.

[42] See the Explanatory Memorandum attached to the 1998 Temporary Protection Proposal (see below at n. 43), paras 1.1.3, 2.12 and the Explanatory Memorandum attached to the 1998 Solidarity Proposal, (see below at n. 45), para 1.

[43] European Commission, Amended proposal for a Joint Action concerning temporary protection of displaced persons (presented by the Commission pursuant to Article 189a(2) of the EC Treaty), COM (98) 372, final/2 (hereinafter the 1998 Temporary Protection Proposal), Arts 6–9. If the goal of harmonisation is to be taken seriously, a deviation from these minimum rights in favour of beneficiaries is rather improbable.

[44] Ibid., Arts 3 and 4. A provision on burden sharing was retained in the 1998 Temporary Protection Proposal in a rephrased form (Art. 5). It prescribed that the future means of implementing solidarity were to be included in the reports on which a decision under Arts 3 and 4 would be based. Further, it stipulated that "[s]uch solidarity shall be implemented in accordance with the provisions of" the 1998 Solidarity Proposal (see below at n. 45).

[45] European Commission, Proposal for a Joint Action concerning solidarity in admission and residence of beneficiaries of the temporary protection of displaced persons (presented by the Commission pursuant to para 2(b) of Article K3 of the EU Treaty), COM (98) 372, final/2 (hereinafter the 1998 Solidarity Proposal).

[46] Article 4 of the 1998 Solidarity Proposal; Financial Statement attached to the 1998 Solidarity Proposal.

[47] For 1998 the proposal assumes a need for ECU 3,750,000 for these measures targeted at reception projects (financial statement attached to the 1998 Solidarity Proposal). As the reader will note, this part of the proposal was consumed by the 1998 Joint Action on improving admission.

[48] Article 4(1) of the 1998 Solidarity Proposal.

[49] Ibid., Art. 4(2). However, it cannot be excluded that single Member States might prefer to process protection seekers in a Dublin procedure (in order to shift responsibility to another Member State) rather than accord temporary protection to them.

If the Solidarity Proposal had been adopted, its efficiency would have been hampered by important limitations. Clearly, it did not contain a general authorisation to share costs. First, sharing was confined to specified items, which only cover a fraction of total reception costs. Secondly, a precondition for sharing measures was that Member States would take an unanimous decision under Article 2 of the instrument. One recalcitrant Member State had been enough to block this limited form of burden sharing. In fact, the joint action would have represented a framework mechanism, to be activated *ad hoc* by a consensus decision. As noted earlier, this makes burden sharing highly contingent upon the political situation.

The subordination of the sharing of people to the sharing of money was reversed in a revised draft presented in November 1998 by the Austrian Presidency.[50] This initiative represented a renewed approximation to a strict insurance model with highly predictable outcomes, albeit moulded in a slightly softer form than the 1994 German Draft. It is no coincidence that one of the main recipient countries of Bosnian protection seekers signed as its drafter. Article 3 read:

> "The decision [on implementing solidarity mechanisms] shall provide for beneficiaries of temporary protection to be distributed between Member States in accordance with an allocation scale established in the decision on the basis of information provided by Member States. This allocation scale should be met as far as possible with the beneficiaries' consent, for example through resettlement projects or through direct admission from the crisis area."

The observer will note that the 1994 German Draft was more radical in that it already featured a distribution key. According to the quoted Article 3 of the Austrian Draft, such a key would be established ad hoc in each single reception case. It goes without saying that outcomes are less predictable under the Austrian Draft.[51] A step forward taken by the latter was to imply that forcible reallocations are, in principle, undesirable.

In Article 4, the Austrian Draft stipulates that the decision on implementing solidarity mechanisms:

> "shall also provide for financial assistance from the Community budget to cover certain costs generated by the admission of beneficiaries of temporary protection. The assistance shall include in particular contributions towards the cost of housing, welfare and education measures"

[50] Council for the European Union, Note from the Presidency, Draft Joint Action concerning temporary protection of displaced person, Draft Joint Action concerning solidarity in the admission and residence of beneficiaries of the temporary protection of displaced persons, 9 November 1998, Doc No. 1261/98 (hereinafter 1998 Austrian Draft).

[51] It must be recalled that a Joint Action of the proposed kind is not a binding instrument at large. This should be kept in mind when judging its potential to stabilise Member States' expectations to be assisted in situations of crisis. That potential is wholly incumbent on whether or not Member States actually adopt a decision under Art. 2 of the 1998 Proposal or Art. 2 of the Austrian Proposal. Pursuant to Art. 249 EC, decisions are binding instruments of Community law.

in accordance with the norms laid down in the 1998 Temporary Protection Proposal as revised by the Council in 1998.

Another decisive difference between the Austrian Draft and the 1998 Solidarity Proposal was the introduction of an obligatory linkage between temporary protection and burden sharing by the latter. While the 1998 Solidarity Proposal *authorised* the Council to take a decision on burden sharing when temporary protection was to be phased in, the Austrian Draft *required* the Council to decide on how to share the burden.[52] The quorum for such a decision has not been fixed in the said proposal.[53] Actually, what the Austrian Presidency did was to make burden sharing a precondition to admission.[54] Without solidarity, there shall be no temporary protection regime. It is clear that those hurt most by such a blockage would be those persons in need of protection rather than other Member States.

In spite of its compromise character, the Austrian Draft did not muster the necessary support among Member States. In early 1999 the whole stream of deliberations, negotiations and drafts set off with the Commission proposals had simply got stuck. Therefore, the German Presidency proposed a fresh start. The discussions of various drafts were discontinued and replaced by a draft of principles, drawing on elements of consensus from the preceding discussions.[55]

The core elements of the 1999 discussions were:

—a linkage between the admission decision and solidarity measures;
—a pledging procedure, by which Member States would indicate the reception capacities in a given crisis situation;
—fiscal burden sharing as an incentive for reception, and;
—the harmonisation of residence rights and conditions of beneficiaries.[56]

In brief, burden sharing would take place as follows. The Council would confirm the existence of a crisis and the need for joint action. Next, the Commission would draw up a report on the number of persons already protected in Member States and the number of persons still in the crisis area. Then, the Council would:

[52] Article 2 of the Austrian Draft: "When temporary protection regimes are adopted, . . . the Council shall adopt decisions implementing solidarity mechanisms . . .".

[53] The preference of the Austrian and German Presidencies had been a majority vote, lowering the threshold for a decision on burden sharing. Obviously, other Member States bearing a lower protection burden will opt for a requirement of unanimity.

[54] The German Presidency taking over after the Austrian Presidency continued to uphold this linkage. See, e.g. Note by the Presidency, Temporary Protection of displaced persons and solidarity in the admission and residence of such persons in the EU, Doc No. 5645/99 (29 January 1999), para. 1.1.3.

[55] Table document presented by the German Presidency at the JHA Council Meeting of 11/12 February. On file with the authors.

[56] Council for the European Union, Note by the Presidency to the Asylum Working Party, Practical application of the principle of solidarity in the burden sharing with regard to the admission and residence of displaced persons, Doc No. 7157/99 (31 March 1999).

"ascertain how many refugees [sic!] Member States were prepared to admit. The Council would only decide to admit provided that enough places are made available by Member States to meet the known needs. Any possibility of taking the admission decision without coming close to covering the known admission needs would have to be ruled out, in order in particular to ensure that the number of places made available by the Member States was not restricted to the number of persons already residing in their territory."[57]

After a Council decision, the persons already protected in a given Member State would be counted against the number of reception places that state had pledged. Spare places could be occupied by beneficiaries selected in admission procedures in the region of origin. Moreover, admission could also take place at the external borders of Member States. Where the Member State in question still has spare places, persons would be admitted to its territory under a temporary protection arrangement. If it had no more spare places, "the person seeking admission" would be asked to proceed to a Member State willing to grant him/her admission.[58] Finally, financial support would depend on the number of persons admitted by a Member State. The level of social assistance guaranteed by a given state to its own nationals is proposed as a criterion for the calculation of such support. However, the note does not take a stand on whether the support percentage is to be fixed abstractly in the basic legal instrument, or contextually in the admission decision by the Council. To avoid secondary movements between Member States, the residence rights and conditions granted to beneficiaries must be harmonised throughout the Union.

Clearly, the linkage of admission and burden sharing is highly problematic. To make sense, it would require an almost perfect system of migration control. After all, the underlying idea is that Member States are free to choose whether or not to admit potential beneficiaries. This implies that the common external borders will simply be closed if Member States cannot agree on a sharing scheme in a specific crisis situation.

This begs questions. On the practical level, it is all too clear that borders cannot be sealed hermetically. Whatever Member States do to deflect flows, there will be ways and means to circumvent such measures. In the absence of a burden-sharing decision by the Council, the distribution of protection seekers would continue to be determined by geographical proximity and the availability of efficient smuggling routes.

On the legal level, the idea of voluntary admission is simply irreconcilable with the prohibition of refoulement. The note by the German Presidency veils this ugly truth in a pretty formulation, when it ponders what to do when the reception system gets numerically overstretched:

"If no Member State was willing to admit them [the persons seeking admission], the Member State at whose external border the displaced persons were waiting would check whether it could admit them on the basis of national measures."

[57] Ibid., II(A) 3.
[58] Ibid., II(B) 1.c.

To wit, the Member State hosting the external border in question has no choice. It suffices that the persons "waiting at the border" say the word "asylum", and the Member State in question has to admit them for the duration of determination procedures.[59]

There is also a moral-political dimension to the arrangement. Consider the following situation. The Council acknowledges the existence of a crisis, and the Commission has assessed the number of persons in need of protection. Now, the Member States cannot agree on a sharing scheme. In such a situation, it is politically troublesome to argue that the potential beneficiaries already counted by the Commission should not be admitted after all. If Member States go ahead and enforce non-admission, this is a slap in the face of a humanitarian interest formerly recognised by the Commission and the Council. If they do not, the linkage between admission and burden sharing is disbanded. The Council might avoid this embarrassing dilemma by never acknowledging the existence of a crisis, which is the precondition for the whole exercise outlined in the note.

In its proposal, Germany had given up for lost the prospect of a predetermined insurance mechanism involving the sharing of people, which had been at the base of its 1994 Draft. It is to be doubted whether it has won any gains in return, apart from keeping the issue of burden sharing on the table. Presently, deliberations continue and the fate of temporary protection and burden sharing on the EU level remains undecided.

PROTECTION AT THE COST OF SUSPENSION OF RIGHTS

New competences in a crucial legal context

Contemporary debates over the desirability of putting stronger emphasis on the temporary protection of refugees may often be taken to indicate that temporariness *per se* is diluting the protective quality of asylum. In this contribution, however, it is posited that the real challenge to refugee protection in Europe is not the emergent temporary aspect in itself. Rather, this new mechanism seems to be developing into a threat against refugee protection in other respects which are significantly more critical to the legal principles and underlying values of the asylum system that has been established in Western Europe and other industrialised societies in recent decades. This is intrinsically linked to the issue of *individual rights*, in terms of *access* to protection for those who need it as a result of failing protection in their country of origin, as well as the *standards* of treatment for individuals who succeed in obtaining international protection.

[59] This flows from the fact that Art. 33 of the Geneva Convention is already applicable at the border. For a comprehensive argumentation, see U. Davy, *Asyl und internationales Flüchtlingrecht* (Völkerrechtlicher Rahmen, Vienna, 1996), 93–123. A look at Art. 3 of the Dublin Convention suggests that Member States have made this view their own.

There are various, and indeed strong, reasons why temporary protection may be perceived as incompatible with the European tradition of asylum. All of these reflect the fact that an overriding feature of the temporary protection models which have been adopted in recent years, or which are now on the policy agenda at national and EU levels, is their implementation outside the framework of the 1951 Geneva Convention and the 1967 Protocol relating to the status of refugees. Thereby it is being suggested that the beneficiaries, even while vaguely defined, are presumably not refugees as defined in Article 1 of the Convention. This may, in combination with the language used in these protection models, serve as justification of the *non-Convention framework* evolving in relation to various aspects of temporary arrangements, in particular the protection standards and the criteria for cessation of protection. Such standards and criteria are indicative of lesser individual rights than those normally guaranteed within the protection system under the Convention, in both substantive and procedural terms.

By falling short of the refugee rights stipulated in the Geneva Convention, and sometimes even of those following from general human rights treaties, temporary arrangements may thus jeopardise the principles and values of the salient refugee protection system. While this is likely to be the most important challenge stemming from the emphasis on temporary models of protection, the non-Convention feature of temporary arrangements can also be seen as part of a more general trend in Europe in recent years. Temporariness may not after all, be a very new phenomenon, in so far as the residence rights of persons falling under so-called *subsidiary forms of protection* have already largely been established as non-permanent in most European states. Thus, both subsidiary protection and the more explicitly temporary arrangements distinguish themselves from the traditional asylum policies that made Convention refugee status synonymous with permanent residence rights. This may have inspired the quite widespread perception that temporary protection is—only, normally, or at least frequently—offered to persons *not* qualifying for refugee status under the Convention.

It is precisely the interaction between temporary protection policies, and the more general inclination of states to adopt *non-Convention solutions* to refugee problems, that necessitates a cautious approach to the issue of temporariness in the context of the new legal framework of EU asylum policies, established by the ToA. This is so much more called for, as temporary arrangements outside the Geneva Convention are no longer exclusively occurring in Member States faced with large-scale influx of asylum seekers. As demonstrated during the Kosovo refugee crisis in 1999, such solutions have been similarly resorted to towards very small numbers of persons in need of protection, even under circumstances where their refugee status under the Convention could hardly be questioned.[60]

[60] See the ECRE Secretariat's *Survey on Status of Kosovo Albanians in Some European Countries*, updated as of 25 May 1999.

Against this somewhat apocalyptic background, it can reasonably be assumed that the future policies concerning temporary protection may be decisive as to whether the EU Member States are effectively going to uphold the Geneva Convention as the primary legal instrument for refugee protection. This seems to be the crucial reality notwithstanding various official declarations of the intent to maintain the Convention as the "cornerstone" of EU's asylum policy.[61] The challenge thus present in Europe goes to the heart of the problem, which was eloquently pointed out in the 1999 Protection Note from the UNHCR:

> "Overall, UNHCR detected a distinct trend in an increasing number of States to move gradually away from a law or rightsbased approach to refugee protection, towards more discretionary and ad hoc arrangements that give greater primacy to domestic concerns rather than to their international responsibilities. These restrictive tendencies found their most recent manifestation in one country where legislative proposals aimed at doing away with the distinction between aliens and refugees, including dropping any requirement for specific determination of refugee status under the 1951 Convention.
>
> There is a worrying recent tendency on the part of some States to present problems as resulting more from wars and conflicts than from persecution in the classic sense of Article 1 A of the 1951 Convention, and to argue that the 1951 Convention offers an increasingly inadequate framework to address presentday challenges. Calls for an alternative refugee protection regime to that of the 1951 Convention have been made.
>
> This argument is inherently dangerous and, at best, misguided. Persecution, whether occurring in time of peace or of war, continues to be one of the major causes of refugee movements worldwide. The Convention and Protocol remain the firm and universally accepted foundation for the protection of those who have been forced to leave their country owing to serious threats to their fundamental human rights to life, security, freedoms and dignity."[62]

Development perspectives under the Treaty of Amsterdam

According to Article 63(2) EC, as amended pursuant to the ToA, the Council shall adopt measures on refugees and displaced persons within the area of:

> "(a) minimum standards for giving temporary protection to displaced persons from third countries who cannot return to their country of origin and for persons who otherwise need international protection . . ."

This new Community competence, taken together with the 1997 and 1998 Commission proposals concerning temporary protection, raises various questions against the background of the international legal protection framework and the

[61] Note from the Finnish Presidency on Preparation of the European Council of Tampere—Asylum and Immigration Issues, Doc No. 10015/99 (9 July 1999), 5; see also the Tampere Conclusions of 15–16 October 1999, para. 13.

[62] UNHCR, Note on International Protection, UN Doc A/AC 96/914 (7 July 1999), paras 10–12.

recent development tendencies, outlined above. The most important issue is to what extent such an EC legal act is likely to be respectful to the protection regime, and the inherent individual rights, established under the Geneva Convention.

An initial question in this context is whether some indication might be found in the fact that Article 63(1) EC makes express reference to the Geneva Convention, whereas the Convention is not mentioned in relation to the temporary protection measures to be adopted under Article 63(2)(a). This formal difference in phrasing the basis of future EC legal acts, however, must be considered immaterial to the issue of the Convention's substantive impact on the respective regulatory measures. Referring to "measures on refugees and displaced persons", Article 63(2) acknowledges that such measures may cover both *refugees* as defined in the Geneva Convention, a category more specifically dealt with in Article 63(1), and *displaced persons* in a broader sense. Not an internationally defined legal concept, the latter must be considered a more general category, thus potentially encompassing victims of notorious displacement whose status as refugees is unclear, or has not yet been formally determined.

Focusing more closely on Article 63(2)(a), it may cause some trouble to ascertain the exact meaning as regards the interrelation between "temporary protection" measures and the overall competence entrusted with the EU Council under this provision. The problem here is whether Article 63(2)(a) authorises legislative acts exclusively dealing with temporary protection, and aiming at "displaced persons" and "persons who otherwise need international protection" alike. If the former is considered a general, legally undefined category, as proposed above, it would seem superfluous to make reference to an additional broad(er) category of persons in need of protection. Consequently, rather than adding to the legislative competence *ratione personae*, the final part of the provision is likely to refer to an additional competence in terms of the substance of the measures which are to be adopted.[63]

As such a substance-based alternative, Article 63(2)(a) can be construed so as to provide the Council with two separate regulatory competences: one concerning minimum standards for *temporary protection* of displaced persons, another dealing with minimum standards for person who otherwise need international protection, i.e. the issue of *subsidiary forms of protection*. Taking both the wording[64] and the context of the provision into account, this seems the most logical way of interpretation. It might be argued, however, that the wording differs between various language versions, and that in some languages the

[63] This difference of interpretation may appear to have only minor practical implications. However, in as much as temporary protection measures concerning "displaced persons" will be dealing exclusively with situations of large-scale displacement, as pointed out below, it does make a difference whether the Council is separately obliged under Art. 63(2)(a) to adopt measures for the protection of persons seeking asylum in individual cases who are not considered refugees under the Geneva Convention, but who are nonetheless in need of international protection.

[64] Cf. the passages italicised here: "minimum standards *for giving temporary protection* to displaced persons from third countries who cannot return to their country of origin *and for persons* who otherwise need international protection".

provision must be construed in the opposite way, meaning that standards for temporary protection must be adopted both for "displaced persons" and for "persons who otherwise need international protection".[65] Apart from the fact that a majority of language versions of the Treaty are apparently in line with the English text quoted above,[66] the interpretation proposed here seems to be the one best in accordance with the object and purpose of the Treaty.[67]

In this connection it should also be taken into consideration that the issue of subsidiary forms of protection was on the agenda of the co-operation on asylum under the EU's Third Pillar already before the adoption of the ToA in 1997.[68] Against this background of ongoing efforts to harmonise asylum policies in this respect, it could hardly be assumed to have been the intention of the Treaty drafters to exclude such measures from the future competences under the First Pillar pursuant to Title IV EC. Hence, it is noteworthy that there seems to be consensus within the European Union and among Member States about this delimitation of the legislative competence under Article 63(2)(a),[69] as was demonstrated both by the 1998 Communication from the Commission,[70] by the 1993 Action Plan of the Council and the Commission,[71] and the 1999 Commission working document on the asylum procedures.[72]

[65] See, as a clear example, the German text: "Mindestnormen für den vorübergehenden Schutz *von vertriebenen Personen* aus dritten Länder . . . *und von Personen,* die anderweitig internationalen Schutz benötigen". The French version can be understood similarly, although it does not seem unequivocal in this respect: "normes minimales relatives *à l'octroi* d'une protection temporaire *aux personnes deplacées* en provenance de pays tiers . . . *et aux personnes* qui, pour d'autres raisons, ont besoin d'une protection internationale". See K. Hailbronner's overview of competences under Art. 63 in (1999) 1 *European Journal of Migration and Law* 12, which has possibly been influenced by the German version of this Treaty provision.

[66] This is, at least, the case for the Danish, Dutch, Spanish and Swedish versions of the Treaty text.

[67] *Cf.* Art. 33(4) of the Vienna Convention of the Law of Treaties. The object of measures under Title IV is to establish an area of freedom, security and justice, more specifically aimed at ensuring the free movement of persons in accordance with Art. 14, e.g. Art. 61(a). This provision expressly mentions Art. 63(2)(a) as part of the basis for some of the directly related flanking measures with respect to external border controls, asylum and immigration.

[68] Council Resolution of 14 October 1996 setting the priorities of cooperation on Justice and Home Affairs for July 1996—June 1998 (OJ 1996 C319/01). See also notes from the Danish delegation of 17 March 1997 on subsidiary forms of protection (Doc No. 6764/97 ASIM 52), and from the Netherlands Presidency of 28 April 1997 (Doc No. 7779/97 ASIM 89).

[69] *Cf.* G. Noll and J. Vedsted-Hansen, above at n. 3, 377.

[70] Commission of the European Communities, Communication from the Commission: Towards an Area of Freedom, Security and Justice (14 July 1998), COM (98) 459, final, 6 ("the adoption of a mechanism for giving temporary protection, thus allowing the Union to respond adequately and rapidly to situations of mass influx . . . Aside from mass-influx situations, the Union needs to develop minimum standards for asylum procedures as well as subsidiary forms of protection for people whose individual cases demonstrate a need for protection, despite the fact that they are not refugees under the Geneva Convention").

[71] Action Plan of the Council and the Commission on how best to implement the provisions of the ToA establishing an area of freedom, security and justice, 7 December 1998 (OJ 1999 C 19/01). See para. 37(a); *cf.* para. 38(b)(ii) with reference to Art. 63(2)(a), second part EC as the basis for "minimum standards for subsidiary protection to persons in need of international protection".

[72] European Commission, Working Document: Towards common standards on asylum procedures, SEC (1999) 271, final, (3 March 1999), para. 5(7); *cf.* para. 5(6), referring to Art. 63(2)(a) first part and second part EC, respectively.

This interpretation of Article 63(2)(a) EC allows us to conclude that a measure to be adopted on temporary protection cannot be based on any presupposition as to the issue of refugee status or non-status of the beneficiaries. Instead, such measures will have to be designed so as to encompass in principle all kinds of displaced persons, irrespective of their Convention refugee status, while at the same time taking heed of the possibility that among the displaced persons some may be covered by the Geneva Convention. This is bound to bear on the legal contents of the minimum standards for giving temporary protection, as further discussed below.

Taken at face value, the legal basis of the upcoming EC legislative process should therefore not raise problems of incompatibility between temporary protection measures and the Geneva Convention. Developments in policy making within this field since the Commission's 1997 Proposal for a Joint Action concerning temporary protection nonetheless give reasons for some concern. While the 1997 Proposal was respectful to the most important aspects of the Convention protection system, subsequent changes have moved away from this principled position, partly by substituting reference to refugee protection standards by those of legally resident aliens, partly by making deference to national legislation on certain crucial points. In addition to being counter-productive in terms of efficient EU harmonisation,[73] this is at variance with Member States' obligations under the Geneva Convention, and possibly also under general human rights conventions.

The definitional problem: refugees or beneficiaries?

In order to determine the likelihood of individual rights being properly secured in the future EC measures concerning temporary protection, it may be useful to briefly look at the harmonisation attempts within this field in retrospect. In its initial Proposal for a Joint Action, the Commission defined the term "persons in need of international protection" as:

> "any third country national or stateless person who has left his/her country of residence and whose safe return under humane conditions is impossible in view of the situation prevailing in that country, in particular:
>
> —persons who have fled from areas affected by armed conflict and persistent violence;
>
> —persons who have been or are under a serious risk of exposure to systematic or widespread human rights abuses, including those belonging to groups compelled to leave their homes by campaigns of ethnic or religious persecution; and
>
> —persons who for other reasons specific to their personal situation are presumed to be in need of international protection."[74]

[73] *Cf.* R. Bank, "The Emergent EU Policy on Asylum and Refugees" (1999) 68 *Nordic Journal of International Law* 2–3, 9–10. See also G. Noll and J. Vedsted-Hansen, above at n. 3, 369–70, 399.

[74] Article 1(b) of the 1997 Proposal (see above at n. 33).

This delimitation of beneficiaries of future EU temporary protection regimes were clearly influenced by the UNHCR's guidelines for the selection of persons in need of protection during the Bosnian crisis in 1992–94.[75] Similar criteria were subsequently proposed by the UNHCR with a view to establishing temporary protection in a broader context as a possible asylum strategy for Europe.[76] Likewise, as an outcome of the so-called Gap Consultations, in which UNHCR, together with a number of interested European and other states, were contemplating ways and means of securing international protection to all persons in need thereof, the beneficiaries of protection were described in largely the same terms.[77]

Even while it was made clear in connection with these previous policy initiatives that the beneficiaries thus delimited could possibly include considerable numbers of Convention status refugees, a fact of which the Commission seems to have been well aware when drafting the 1997 Proposal, a certain degree of cautiousness or reluctance in drawing the consequences of this occurs at least in the Explanatory Memorandum. Here the Commission did not limit itself to clarifying the relationship between temporary protection regimes and the traditional institution of asylum, as normally granted to refugees covered by the Convention. At the same time, in a manner that might perhaps be seen as slightly contradictory, it was suggested that beneficiaries of temporary protection would normally not be Convention status refugees.[78] In the commentary on the definition proposed in Article 1, it was stated:

> "strictly speaking, the term 'temporary protection regimes' covers all arrangements other than those involving admission as a refugee under the Geneva Convention or admission on humanitarian grounds. However, temporary protection has been deemed an appropriate response to mass influxes of persons seeking refuge abroad, *most* of whom are not Convention refugees but refugees in a wider sense. Thus, the definition of 'persons in need of international protection' has been drawn up in rather broad terms, to cover not only situations where mass influxes have occurred, but also

[75] *Cf.* the Explanatory Memorandum attached to the 1997 Proposal, para. 10. Reference is here made to the UNHCR's Note on International Protection, UN Doc A/AC.96/830 (7 September 1994), para. 47 which, with a forward-looking perspective, was based on the description of beneficiaries given in the UNHCR's Background Note: Informal Meeting of Government Experts on Temporary Protection, 23 March 1994, para. 1. The latter document contained certain adjustments, in particular concerning the third subcategory, of the criteria originally proposed by UNHCR in the Working Document to the Follow-up Committee on the Comprehensive Response to the Humanitarian Crisis in the Former Yugoslavia, UN Doc HCR/CRHC/FC/2 (4 September 1992), para. 25.

[76] *Cf.* Temporary Protection in a Broader Context, Annex to UNHCR's Background Note of 23 March 1994 (above at n. 75), para. 5, and the 1994 Note on International Protection (above at n. 75), para. 47.

[77] UNHCR, Progress Report on Informal Consultations on the Provision of International Protection to all Who Need it, UN Doc IC/47/SC/CRP/.27 (30 May 1997), Section II: Summary of Discussions on Temporary Protection, para. 4.

[78] For a similar understanding of the 1997 Proposal, see K. Kerber, "An Assessment of the Harmonisation Policies of European Union Member States" (1997) 9 *International Journal of Refugee Law* 464.

cases when it becomes clear that they cannot be avoided. This would allow anticipatory action."[79]

Similarly, the Commission described the new dimension added to European refugee crises by the conflict in the former Yugoslavia, among which it mentioned that "the people concerned do not necessarily meet the conditions to qualify for refugee status under the terms of the Geneva Convention".[80] While this assumption was indeed correct per se, it might have been useful to qualify it in order to frame the legislative process in an adequate way.

Against this background, it would seem logical that the Commission emphasised the discretionary and pragmatic nature of temporary protection regimes, most distinctly expressed in the following statement:

> "One very relevant and fundamental characteristic of temporary protection is that it is *not a right established by any international instrument*: States grant it as an autonomous act, and for the most parts national legislation is carefully worded to keep it that way. The proposed joint action does not seek to introduce a new right to seek temporary protection in addition to the existing right to seek asylum. This approach is realistic and takes into account the history of temporary protection in Europe, and stresses the exceptional character of any temporary protection regime. Indeed, if a *right to seek temporary protection* does not exist, the right to seek asylum remains essential."[81]

Having thus renounced the essentials of a legally binding framework for temporary protection, the Commission nonetheless demonstrated a great deal of preparedness to maintain the norms and principles of the Geneva Convention in designing the temporary protection regime that was proposed. As shall be described in some detail below, the refugee rights enshrined in the Convention strongly inspired the protection standards laid down in the proposed Joint Action. Furthermore, the Explanatory Memorandum referred not only to general human rights treaties such as the European Convention on Human Rights and the European Social Charter, but also to the protection against refoulement provided by Article 33 of the Geneva Convention on apparently equal terms with Article 3 of the European Convention on Human Rights, both of which protections were to be regarded as "essential".[82] In the subsequent statement, the rationale of harmonising protection standards was made clear:

> "It is, however, of great importance to restate those minimum rights in the framework of a joint action for the coordination of the regimes of temporary protection of the Member States, *so as to avoid distortions in the streams of displaced persons* who would otherwise flow to those states where they would seem to have the most rights."[83]

[79] Explanatory Memorandum attached to the 1997 Proposal, para. 10.
[80] Ibid., para. 2, second indent.
[81] Ibid., para. 8, first part (emphasis added).
[82] Ibid., para. 8, second part.
[83] Ibid., para. 8, second part (emphasis added).

Regardless of the somewhat double-sided policy objective of the standards of treatment suggested by the Commission, it should be noted that they were in fact largely in accordance with the refugee rights protected under the Geneva Convention. The overall acceptability of the protection standards was also acknowledged by the UNHCR in the comments issued by the Office on the proposed Joint Action.[84] This level of protection has, however, come under considerable pressure during the subsequent negotiations of the proposed instrument. As we shall see, the outcome of this process may eventually be determined by the prevention of "distortions in the streams of displaced persons" emerging as the primary objective of EU harmonisation.

Suspending refugee rights

Temporary protection without prejudice?

In defining "temporary protection regime", the Commission's 1998 Amended Proposal for a Joint Action concerning temporary protection of displaced persons declares "such arrangement being without prejudice to recognition of refugee status in accordance with the Geneva Convention".[85] This definitional statement, which was upheld in the revised text drawn up by the Presidency in February 1999,[86] was explained by the Commission to be bringing the provision into line with Article 10 of the proposed Joint Action, i.e. the article which stipulates that examination of asylum applications may be suspended.[87]

At first glance one may feel satisfied, then, that there should be no incompatibility between the proposed temporary protection arrangement and the obligations of EU Member States under the Geneva Convention. Further scrutiny will disclose, however, that there is more to this than the issue of prejudicing the *recognition of refugee status*. This may at least be understood as merely referring to the formal issue of subsequent status determination, thereby making it clear that neither positive nor negative inferences on the status recognition can be drawn from the fact that a person has been beneficiary of a temporary protection arrangement. In other words, the question of possibly prejudicing the *protection standards* in accordance with the Geneva Convention has not been settled by the statement quoted from Article 1 of the proposed Joint Action, notwithstanding its apparent commitment to respect the principles of the Convention.

[84] UNHCR observations on Proposal for a Joint Action concerning temporary protection of displaced persons (April 1997), in particular 5–6.

[85] Article 1(a) of the 1998 Temporary Protection Proposal, above at n. 43.

[86] Note from the German Presidency of 16 February 1999, Doc No 5682/1/99 REV 1 ASILE 3; Art. 1(a) of the revised Draft Joint Action.

[87] Explanatory Memorandum attached to the 1998 Temporary Protection Proposal, para. 7.

Suspended versus presumptive refugee status

Before focussing on some specific protection standards, we need to make a few remarks on the legal implications of the suspension of the *processing* of asylum applications. On the one hand, such suspension of procedures cannot in itself be considered a violation of the Geneva Convention, since the Convention obliges states to a certain level of refugee protection in terms of securing the entitlements of persons covered by its definition, rather than requiring formal decisions on the definitional issue as such.[88] Hence, as long as a state grants civil, economic and social rights to the beneficiaries of temporary protection, in accordance with the Convention rights regime, it has honoured its obligations under the Convention. On the other hand, these protection duties cannot be suspended on purely procedural grounds.

While this may seem rather uncontroversial as a general statement of legal principles, recent situations of *deliberate suspension* of asylum procedures raise more complex questions as to whether such practices allow states to exempt themselves from the protection standards under the Convention. Will a Convention state become more or less free to design the conditions of beneficiaries according to its own preferences, if it simply blocks beneficiaries' access to determination of their claim to refugee status? These questions may reflect the crux of the matter in terms of *individual rights* in the context of EU harmonisation of temporary protection.

For at least two reasons the answer has to be unequivocally in the negative. First, a state party to the Geneva Convention cannot evade its treaty obligations by plainly *omitting* to determine claims to refugee status submitted by individuals under its jurisdiction. A legal possibility for states to do so is inconceivable under international law, in as much as it would run counter to the fundamental duty to perform treaty obligations *in good faith*.[89] Secondly, allowing state authorities such a possibility would be incompatible with the legal nature of the refugee concept as defined in the Convention. It is generally recognised that this concept implies that the status of refugee comes into existence as soon as a person fulfils the definitional criteria laid down in Article 1 of the Convention—in other and well-known words, the recognition of refugee status is not a decisive criterion for the attainment of such status, but merely a declaratory act.[90]

[88] This does not, however, imply total freedom of procedural (in)action, especially where procedural arrangements are necessary in order to achieve substantive rights. Thus it can hardly be considered compatible with states' duty to protect individuals if they make temporary protection—at a reduced level, compared to the Convention rights regime—contingent on the withdrawal of applications for recognition of refugee status under the Convention. For an opposite view, see K. Kerber, above n. 78, 469.

[89] Article 26 of the Vienna Convention on the Law of Treaties. On the legal impact of the processing of asylum applications, see P. Hyndman, "The 1951 Convention and its Implications for Procedural Questions" (1994) 6 *International Journal of Refugee Law* 246; and J. Hathaway and J. Dent, *Refugee Rights: Report on a Comparative Survey* (York Lanes Press, Toronto, 1995), 21–2.

[90] UNHCR, *Handbook on Procedures and Criteria for Determining Refugee Status* (1979), para. 28. See also J. Hathaway and J. Dent, above at n. 89, 7; and G. S. Goodwin-Gill, *The Refugee in International Law*, 2nd ed. (Oxford University Press, Oxford, 1996), 32, 141.

It follows that by suspending the examination of claims to refugee status, a state cannot provide itself unfettered discretion as to the treatment of persons who have been offered the alternative of temporary protection as a substitute for the normal processing of their cases. Hence, the legal principle determining such situations must be that "non-access" to status determination procedures imposes the duty on a state to implement what could be termed a "presumptive refugee status" towards the affected persons. This does not, however, entail the obligation to grant immediately the full scope of refugee rights laid down in the Convention. Importantly, refugee status implies the gradual accrual of entitlements, some of which will have to be granted to all beneficiaries in any temporary arrangement, while others may be withheld for a certain period.[91]

Reference to Convention rights versus deference to national laws

As mentioned above, developments in relation to the EU harmonisation of temporary protection since the Commission's 1997 Proposal can be described as a process of partly substituting refugee protection standards, in accordance with the Geneva Convention, by lower common standards, partly abandoning any effective harmonisation by making deference to national legislation of the various EU Member States. This process, largely in contravention of the principles for temporary refugee protection under international law, as analysed above, can be illustrated by the changes that have taken place in respect of some of the core refugee rights.

Pursuant to the 1997 Proposal, Member States would have to ensure to beneficiaries of a temporary protection regime the grant of a permission to engage in gainful activity, just as there would have to be equality of treatment between such beneficiaries and "recognised refugees" regarding remuneration, social security and other working conditions.[92] In its 1998 Amended Proposal the Commission modified the first standard slightly by prescribing the grant of such permissions in accordance with the provisions of Member States' "national law regarding recognised refugees".[93] Whereas the 1998 Austrian Presidency suggested that both parts of this standard be aligned to national law provisions regarding "legally resident aliens",[94] the most recent proposal from February 1999 left the standard-setting totally open by obliging Member States to ensure only that beneficiaries have *in principle* the possibility of taking up a gainful activity, and by allowing the detailed conditions therefore to be *governed by national law*.[95]

[91] See J. Hathaway and R. Alexander Neve, "Making International Refugee Law Relevant Again: A Proposal for Collectivised and Solution-Oriented Protection", (1997) 10 *Harvard Human Rights Journal* 157.

[92] Article 8 of the 1997 Proposal.

[93] 1998 Temporary Protection Proposal, Art. 8, first part.

[94] Note from the Austrian Presidency of 9 November 1998, Doc No. 12617/98/ ASIM 230; Art. 8 of the revised draft Joint Action.

[95] Article 8(1) of the revised draft Joint action, attached to the note from the German Presidency of 16 February 1999, above at n. 86. In Art. 8(2) it was proposed to return to equality of treatment

Similar dilution of the protection standards can be found in relation to the provisions on housing and education. In this regard the 1997 Proposal's reference to the facilities offered to "recognised refugees" was largely upheld in the 1998 Amended Proposal.[96] Instead, the Austrian Presidency suggested a very vague obligation on housing, while the standard on education was differentiated remarkably between general education (with reference to "legally resident aliens") and minors of school age (same conditions as nationals of the host state).[97] These standards are substantially unchanged in the most recent Presidency text.[98]

With regard to family reunification—an issue not covered by the Geneva Convention, but which is related to the obligation to respect the right to family life under general human rights treaties such as Article 8 of the European Convention on Human Rights—the development has been much the same. The 1997 Proposal would oblige states to ensure that beneficiaries would have the "right to family reunification", modified in the 1998 Amended Proposal by making reference to the provisions of *national law*.[99] This has now been reduced into a "possibility in principle", the conditions of which shall be governed by national law.[100]

It does not require much imagination to realise that such deference to national legislation as reflected in the above-mentioned draft instruments, will lead to considerable inconsistency of treatment between EU Member States. If this is going to be the prevailing regulatory tendency one may ask to what degree harmonisation within this area of asylum policy will become effective at all.[101] In addition, the level of protection under some of the recent proposals for an EU instrument are more than likely to be at variance with the gradually increasing refugee rights under the Geneva Convention which states are bound to fulfil during deliberately suspended asylum procedures.

with that of recognised refugees, yet only regarding remuneration and other working conditions, while Art. 8(3) would refer to national law as to the conditions for social security.

[96] Article 9 of both the 1997 Proposal and the 1998 Temporary Protection Proposal. It must be noted, however, that Member States would only have to "endeavour" to provide housing facilities, in the 1998 text even only "temporary housing".

[97] Article 9(1), (4) of the revised draft Joint Action, attached to the note from the Austrian Presidency of 9 November 1998, above at n. 94.

[98] Article 9(1), (4) of the revised draft Joint Action, attached to the note from the German Presidency of 16 February 1999, above at n. 86.

[99] Article 7(1) of both the 1997 Proposal and the 1998 Temporary Protection Proposal. Furthermore, the latter limited the right to reunification to cover only spouses and minor and dependent children.

[100] Article 7(1) of the revised draft Joint Action, attached to the note from the German Presidency of 16 February 1999, above at n. 86.

[101] It may be indicative to this type of concern that in a recent discussion paper on temporary protection and solidarity, prepared by the Commission, the somewhat fundamental questions were asked: "Do Member States agree that minimum harmonisation is necessary and crucial in avoiding secondary movement? Do Member States want to harmonise the rights of the beneficiaries?" Note from the Presidency of 7 July 1999, Doc No. 8791/99 ASILE 21, P. 5.

Individual rights as a subsidiary objective

From the above description of the evolving temporary protection standards at the EU level it can be seen that there are quite good reasons to consider such arrangements as a pretext for the suspension of asylum procedures, and thus for the *de facto* transferral of significant groups of persons in need of protection to a *non-Convention status* involving lesser rights and reduced protection standards than would have resulted from the ordinary processing of their asylum cases. It must be emphasised, however, that these features are not conceptually inherent in temporary protection as such but occur as a result of policy decisions concerning the implementation of temporary protection models. Such reduction of standards appear to be part of a policy-making process in which the costs of protection are being negotiated down to the minimum acceptable to Member States, in terms of the level of individual rights, the duration of protection and, consequently, the number of beneficiaries anticipated to be present at a given point in time.

Is this a warning of the challenge to be expected from future EU measures on temporary protection? One may fear that it is going to be an exercise in solidarity between EU Member States not so much in burden sharing, but rather in the non-fulfilment of obligations under the Geneva Convention. Even while harmonisation as such is perfectly logical in the context of the objectives of Title IV EC, i.e. the abolishment of intra-Union border controls, it may well lead to the collective reinforcement of already existing tendencies towards reduced standards of refugee and human rights protection.

Just as the issue of burden sharing has been set up as a kind of conditionality for the adoption of a common model of temporary protection, the very absence of harmonised standards on temporary protection may in practice become an incentive for individual Member States to avoid developing their own responses to actual protection needs. Hence, it comes out still more clearly that the simultaneous adoption of burden sharing *and* protection measures is likely to be a condition *sine qua non* for access to protection in the most serious and challenging refugee situations.

CONCLUSION

Let us revert to the three factors determining the cost of protection systems: the numbers of beneficiaries present on state territory, the level of individual rights accorded to them and the degree of burden sharing with other states. The 1997 Proposal by the Commission mainly focused on the interrelationship of rights and burden sharing. The recent Council drafts on temporary protection have pursued a much more far-reaching slashing of rights than was originally proposed by the Commission. Simultaneously, the role of burden sharing was weakened. By way of compensation, the Council discussion moved focus to the number of beneficiaries. The German presidency proposed to involve admission as a further steering instrument: without a joint decision on temporary protection and burden sharing, there would not be any admission of beneficiaries. By this move, the geometry of the debate has changed. As states have a hard time agreeing on burden sharing, cost limitation is to be achieved not only by limiting the rights of those beneficiaries already present, but also by inhibiting the arrival of would-be beneficiaries. Briefly, the emphasis is now on the two former factors (the number of beneficiaries and individual rights), rather than on the two latter (individual rights and burden sharing).

With regard to burden sharing, we have to accept that no Rawlsian veil of ignorance facilitates the drafting of its foundational legal instrument. Therefore, the Council moves in circles, covering anything from rigid insurance solutions to the institutionalisation of cheap talk, but is careful not to commit itself. As long as there is no solution on burden sharing forthcoming, Member States will pursue their self-interest by investing additional resources to promote deflection. On top of that, the Dublin Convention continues to concentrate burdens in a number of Member States hosting external borders. For each day of inertia on the sharing of reception burdens, the actual distribution grows more and more inequitable.

9

Security of Residence and Access to Free Movement for Settled Third Country Nationals under Community Law

KEES GROENENDIJK

WHY AN IMPORTANT ISSUE?

Why is the security of residence of the third country nationals legally resident in the EU an important issue?

First, the sheer number of persons concerned makes this a major issue. In 1995 approximately twelve million nationals of third countries were legally resident, spread among the EU Member States.[1] This number will have increased since. The size of this group outnumbers the population of most of the Member States.

Secondly, Community law so far has focused primarily on granting and extending residence rights to EU citizens, explicitly excluding almost all third country nationals from the free movement of persons and the majority from its equal treatment rules. The introduction in 1992 of the concept of EU citizen has reinforced this process of distinguishing between EU citizens and others. Most nationals of third countries settled in the European Union, on the ground of their family name, mother tongue, religion or the colour of their skin are perceived as belonging to a visible minority. To these existing differences Community law adds another distinction: it explicitly withholds from third country nationals rights granted to EU citizens. In doing so Community law tends to reinforce the idea that unequal treatment of EU citizens and third country nationals is justified. Hence, Community law unintentionally is a source of legitimation of unequal treatment of ethnic minorities. This effect is clearly contrary to the new mission of the Community to combat racial discrimination, enshrined in the new Article 13 EC.

Thirdly, the majority of the third country nationals now settled in the European Union will remain there permanently or at least for most of the rest of their lives. The idea that the issue can be solved by return of the immigrants to

[1] Eurostat, *Statistics in Focus, Population and social conditions* (1998), No. 3, 6.

their country of origin is unrealistic. A large share of the first generation will, for reasons I will deal with later, not acquire the nationality of the country of residence, and hence in a legal sense will remain "aliens". As non-EU citizens resident in the country of immigration, their status will be governed primarily by the national immigration law of the Member State, defining them as aliens, *Ausländer*, *étrangers* or *vreemdelingen*. This official label tends to support the social exclusion rather than the inclusion of the individuals concerned.[2]

With regard to EU citizens, secure residence status and equal treatment ever since the establishment of the Community have been considered essential conditions for integration in the host society. Why would this be different for settled immigrants from non-EU countries?

Finally, since the European Union is and will continue to be a region of immigration, new immigrants from outside the European Union will continue to arrive in the years ahead. Thus simple lapse of time will not solve this problem.

CURRENT RESIDENCE RIGHTS AND FREEDOM OF MOVEMENT UNDER COMMUNITY LAW

Our issue would have been less of a problem if the drafters of the secondary legislation on the free movement of workers in the 1960s had not limited the Community rules to workers who are nationals of a Member State. Article 39 EC does not compel that restriction.[3] Moreover, exclusion of the third country workers admitted in one Member State from freedom of movement is contrary to the idea of one labour market in the European Community.[4] This restrictive interpretation of Article 39 is probably due to the fact that most of the migrant workers in the European Community at that time came from Italy or other EC Member States and to the desire of the Member States to retain their traditional discretion in immigration matters as much as possible.

The Council of Ministers already in 1976 recognised the need to remedy this lacuna. In the Resolution on the action programme for migrant workers the Council set as an aim: "the realisation of equal treatment with respect to living conditions and labour conditions, payment and economic rights of workers

[2] Both the Commission and the Finnish Government in their proposals for measures under Title IV EC rightly avoid the alienating term "alien" and use the more neutral term "third-country national" in Art. 2(a) of the draft Directive on the right to family reunification, COM (99) 638, and Art. 2(a) of the draft Regulation on readmission (OJ 1999 C353/6). The Dutch Parliament has been told by the Government that in the JHA Council Germany and Austria opposed replacing "alien" by "third-country national" in the draft Regulation on Eurodac, Tweede Kamer 23490, No. 146, 14. The Dublin Convention and the Schengen Implementing Agreement, both signed in 1990, use the term "alien" to indicate "any person other than a national of a Member State", a good definition of a third country national.

[3] A more literal interpretation of Art. 39 would have included non-EC workers who were admitted in one Member State and subsequently migrated to another Member State.

[4] Each of the four freedoms (free movement of goods, workers, services and capital) aimed at the creation of one market with respect to those four fields.

who are nationals of third countries and their family members legally living in the Member States".[5] Almost 25 years later this noble aim has not yet been realised. At present third country nationals under Community law have residence rights or, in certain cases freedom of movement, only on two grounds: either as derivative rights of EU citizens or on the basis of agreements concluded by the Community with third countries.

Derivative rights have been granted to third country family members of EU citizens who use their freedom of movement[6] and to the third country workers employed by a company established in one Member State that provides services in another Member State.[7] In both cases, not extending the right to move and reside to the third country nationals concerned would hamper the freedom of movement of EU citizens. As regards the third country family members, their residence right, free access to the labour market and equal treatment were also granted to enable and support their integration in the country of immigration.

Agreements with third countries are the other source of residence rights for third country nationals. The case-law of the ECJ since *Sevince* has made it clear that Turkish workers admitted to the labour market and their family members under the secondary legislation based on the Association Agreement EC-Turkey, are entitled to continuation of residence, access to the labour market and to equal treatment in labour relations and social security.[8] From the Court's judgments in *Kziber*[9] and *El Yassini*[10] it appears that admitted workers from the Maghreb countries are entitled to equal treatment in social security and, under certain circumstances, to extension of residence rights under the Co-operation Agreements concluded with the Maghreb countries. The Europe Agreements concluded with countries in Central and Eastern Europe contain the right to equal treatment for admitted workers, a right to establishment in the European Union for citizens and companies from those countries and a residence right for key workers in those companies.[12]

The present picture of Community law is rather complicated: most third country nationals only have residence or other rights in the Member State where they have been admitted but no right to move to another Member State (Turkey,

[5] Council of Ministers, Resolution on the Action Programme for migrant workers and their family members, 9 February 1976, *EC Bulletin*, Supplement 3/76.

[6] Articles 10–12 of Regulation (EC) No. 1612/68.

[7] Case C–43/93 *VanderElst* [1994] ECR I–3803.

[8] Case C–192/89 *Sevince* [1990] ECR I–3461; see, for a discussion of the case-law and the text of most relevant judgments, N. Rogers, *A Practitioners' Guide to the EC-Turkey Association Agreement*, (Kluwer Law International, London, 1999); R. Gutmann, *Die Assoziationsfreizügigkeit türkischen Staatsangehöriger*, (Nomos Verlag Baden-Baden, 2nd ed. 1999); H. Gacon, "*L'Association entre la Communauté Européenne et la Turquie*", in *Dictionnaire Permanent Droit des Etrangers* (Paris); and H. Staples, "De associatieovereenkomst EEG-Turkije, Een leidraad voor de praktijk" (1999) *Migrantenrecht* 179.

[9] Case C–18/90 [1991] ECR I–199.

[10] Case C–416/96 (unreported) 3 March 1999.

[12] E. Guild, *A Guide to the Right of Establishment under the Europe Agreements* (BS&G/ILPA, London, 1996).

Maghreb, CEEC); some have a limited right to free movement within the European Union (third country family members and workers employed by service providers); others have the full right of establishment anywhere in the European Union (self-employed persons from the CEEC).

Considering that in the European Union there are actually living more than two-and-a-half million citizens of Turkey, approximately two million citizens of the three Maghreb countries and about one million citizens of CEEC countries, the legal status of more than five-and-a-half million, i.e. almost half of all resident third country nationals, is in one way or another regulated by Community law. This sets clear limits on the freedom of the Community legislator in using its new competence to make rules on the legal status of third country nationals under Title IV EC. With respect to them the new rules cannot be below the level of protection presently granted by Community law.

PATCHWORK OR SYSTEM?

The residence rights or other rights of third country nationals under Community law depend on their relationship with an EU citizen or an EU company, on their nationality, on the conditions under which they have been admitted in an EU country, on present or past performance of an economic activity, or a combination of these factors. For each category different rights and conditions apply. Moreover, these rights are codified in a range of different instruments. The exact meaning of the relevant provisions is to a large extent specified in the rapidly growing case-law of the ECJ on this issue.

Is there a system in this apparent patchwork? Basically, in granting residence rights, access to employment, equal treatment or free movement to certain categories of third country nationals, the Community used two approaches: either the nationals of third countries were granted the same rights as EU citizens with a few exceptions, or one or more specific rights of EU citizens, having used their freedom of movement, were granted to certain third country nationals.

The first approach was used with respect to the third country spouses and children of EU citizens. They have the same residence rights, free access to employment and are entitled to national treatment in the country of immigration as their EU spouse or parent. The main exceptions are the obligation to apply for a visa prior to first entry,[13] no freedom of movement to other Member States independent from their EU family member and no right to vote in local elections.

The second approach, granting only certain specific rights, has been used in the Association Agreement with Turkey and the Decisions of the Association Council EEC-Turkey, in the Co-operation Agreements with the Maghreb coun-

[13] The extent of this exception is the subject of a recent reference to the ECJ by the Belgian Raad van State in Case C–459/99 *MRAX*.

tries and in the Europe Agreements. Both the text of the instruments and the case-law of the Court reflect this approach. From a detailed analysis of the relevant provisions of those instruments it appears that they have been drafted after the model of similar provisions in the EC Treaty, in EEC-Regulation 1612/68 and the two preceding regulations on free movement during the transitional period between 1957 and 1968.[14] The Court has made a considerable contribution to the coherence of Community law by giving provisions in the EC-Turkey Council Decisions 1/80 and 3/80 and in the Maghreb Agreements as far as possible the same meaning as the analogous provisions on the free movement of EC citizens.[15] The Court in four cases pending before it, three references by UK courts and one by a Dutch court, will have the opportunity to extend this approach of analogous interpretation to the provisions on the right of establishment in the Europe Agreements concluded with the Central European countries.[16]

USING THE NEW COMPETENCES AFTER AMSTERDAM: FIVE APPROACHES

After Amsterdam the EC Treaty provides in three places a specific competence of the Council to make rules concerning the residence status and other rights of third country nationals. The Council has the power to make rules on:

- conditions of entry and residence, and standards on procedures for the issue by Member States of long term visa and residence permits, including those for the purpose of family reunion (Article 63(3)(a) EC);
- the rights and conditions under which nationals of third countries who are legally resident in a Member State may reside in other Member States (Article 63(4) EC);
- conditions of employment for third country nationals legally resident in Community territory (Article 137(3) EC).

Together these three provisions create the competence to make rules on entry and residence status, access to the labour market, conditions of employment of third country nationals in the Member States and freedom of movement to other Members States of third country nationals legally resident in a Member State. Moreover, the Council under the new Article 13 EC has a general competence to "take appropriate action to combat discrimination based on . . . racial or ethnic origin, religion or belief".

[14] E. Guild, *The European Community From a Migrant's Perspective* (Nijmegen, 2000) (forthcoming); S. O'Leary, "Employment and Residence for Turkish Workers and their Family Members: Analogies with the Case-Law of the ECJ on Article 48 EC", in *Scritti in onore di Guiseppe Federico Mancini*, Vol. II (Il Giuffre, Milan, 1998), 731; and Gutmann, above at n. 8.

[15] Case C–18/90 *Kziber* [1991] ECR I–199; Case C–1/97 *Birden* [1998] ECR I–7747; Case C–262/96 *Sürül* (unreported) 4 May 1999; Case C–340/97 *Nazli* (unreported) 10 February 2000; Case C–329/97 *Ergat* (unreported) 16 March 2000.

[16] Case C–63/99 *Glosczuk* (EC-Poland) (OJ 1999 C121/12), Case C–235/88 *Kondova* (EC-Bulgaria) (OJ 1999 C246/15); Case C–257/99 *Barkoci* and *Malik* (EC-Czech Republic) (OJ 1999 C265/2); and Case C–268/99, *Jany and others* (EC-Poland/Czech Republic) (OJ 1999 C265/4).

In using the new competence the Council and the Commission, which under all four provisions has the right of initiative,[17] may choose between at least five different approaches. In each approach the drafting of the new rules is oriented by another model of existing rules.

In the *first* approach the relevant *national immigration rules of the Member States* are taken as a starting point. This approach of rule making has been the prevailing one in the Third Pillar between Maastricht and Amsterdam. The Resolution on the status of third country nationals residing on a long-term basis in the territory of the Member States, adopted by the Council in 1996 is a good example of the approach.[18] The Resolution was proposed by the French Presidency and the fingerprints of French immigration legislation are evident. This approach tends to produce instruments that are close to the lowest common multiple of the relevant national rules. Each Member State attempts to avoid a Community rule that will oblige it to change its national law or policy.[19] This approach also makes it hard to reach the required unanimity among the Member States, because the debate does not start from a common position with respect to central issues.

In other areas of Community law, e.g. environmental protection, we see that one of the large Member States makes great efforts to have its liberal national standards adopted as Community rules, in order to protect its national industries against unfair competition.[20] It is doubtful whether a similar mechanism will work in the same direction (more liberal rules) with respect to new rules on the status of settled immigrants.

The *second* approach takes *existing international standards developed outside the European Union* as a starting point. The UN instruments are of little help here. The rules codified by the United Nations in its Convention on the Rights of All Migrant Workers and the Members of their Families 1990 are of little use, if only because that Convention has not been ratified by a single EU Member State so far.[21] The opinions of the Human Rights Committee on the provisions of the ICCPR with special relevance for immigrants are less numerous and less specific than the Strasbourg case-law on the relevant provisions of

[17] After 1 May 2004 the Commission will have the exclusive right of initiative with respect to measures under Articles 62 and 63 EC; before that date the Member States also have the right of initiative under Art. 67 EC.

[18] Council Resolution of 4 March 1996 (OJ 1996 C80/2).

[19] For some common trends in the national legislation of several Member States with respect to long-term residents, see K. Groenendijk, E. Guild and H. Dogan, *Security of Residence of Long-term Migrants, A Comparative Study of Law and Practice in European Countries* (Council of Europe, 1998).

[20] D. Vogel, *Trading up, Consumer and environmental regulation in a global economy* (Harvard University Press, Cambridge, 1995); V. Eichener, in B. Unger and F. van Waarden (eds), *Convergence or diversity? Internationalization and economic policy response* (Avesbury, Aldershot, 1995).

[21] The European Commission commissioned an eminent German expert to write an opinion on the Convention, but so far has not made that document public: H. Rittstieg and Weber, "The Significance of the UN Convention on Migrant Workers for the Member States of the European Union", referred to in K. Barwig *et al.*, *Neue Regierung—neue Ausländerpolitik?* (Nomos, Baden-Baden, 1999), 231, n. 4.

the European Convention on Human Rights (ECHR). Two clauses from the ILO Convention on Migrant Workers 1949 may be helpful: the clause on equal treatment and the clause on protection against expulsion in case of permanent disablement.[22]

The Council of Europe has produced several instruments containing rules intended to protect settled immigrants: the European Convention on Establishment 1955, the European Convention on Social and Medical Assistance 1953 and the European Social Charter 1962.[23] Moreover, the case-law of the European Court of Human Rights has made it clear that the right to family life in Article 8 and the anti-discrimination-clause in Article 14 ECHR do protect the rights of aliens with long legal residence in a European country.[24] However, most of the Council of Europe instruments provide minimum rules only. They do set outer limits to the implementation of Title IV. As soon as the Member States agree to go beyond the required minimum, these Conventions will have limited relevance.

The *third* approach would be to *extend an existing set of Community rules applicable to one category of third country nationals* to all legally resident nationals of third countries irrespective of their nationality. Here an extension of the most elaborated set of rules, the one adopted under the Association Agreement with Turkey,[25] comes to mind.

The *fourth* approach would be to take the *existing rules of Community law on free movement of persons* (workers and others) as a model for the rights of certain categories of third country nationals and make exceptions or special additional rules only where necessary. Such exceptions might be unavoidable because of the limits of Community competence (e.g. no voting rights for nationals of third countries in the absence of a competence in Title IV or elsewhere in the EC Treaty) or because of the fact that the relevant persons are not nationals of a Member State and hence the international law obligation of a state to readmit its nationals does not apply. This approach is the one presently applied with respect to third country family members of EU citizens using their freedom of movement. In this approach most of the free movement rights of EU citizens could be extended to third country nationals with long legal residence in a Member State.

The Commission has opted for this approach in its proposals on family reunification with EU citizens who have not used their freedom of movement: both in its 1997 draft Convention and in its 1999 proposal for a directive on the right to family reunification it proposes that their third country family members will

[22] Articles 6 and 8 of ILO Convention on Migrant Workers no. 97 of 1949.

[23] K. Groenendijk, "Long-Term Immigrants and the Council of Europe" (1999) *European Journal of Migration and Law* 275–292.

[24] P. van Dijk, "Protection of 'Integrated' Aliens Against Expulsion under the European Convention on Human Rights" (1999) *European Journal of Migration and Law* 293; for the right to equal treatment of lawfully resident third country nationals under the ECHR, see the ECtHR in *Gaygusuz v. Austria* [1997] 23 EHRR 413.

[25] See n. 8 above.

have the same rights as third country family members of an EU citizen who has used the freedom of movement.[26]

There is a *fifth* approach possible: to *extend EU citizenship to third country nationals with long legal residence in a Member State*. During the IGC that produced the Treaty of Amsterdam several non-governmental organisations (NGOs) proposed that union citizenship should be extended to include third country nationals with five years' lawful residence in a Member State.[27] This proposal would be the most far-reaching approach short of the acquisition of the nationality of a Member State. It would extend EU citizenship without changing the nationality legislation of the Member States. This approach was widely discussed in the legal press,[28] but it did not win great support among governments of the Member States. This approach, however, exceeds the competence granted to Community in Title IV. It would require amending Article 17 EC.

TAMPERE: A DUAL APPROACH—EQUAL RIGHTS WITH EU CITIZENS AND THE ACQUISITION OF NATIONALITY

In a document drafted under the German Presidency and presented under the Finnish Presidency in summer 1999 in preparation for the European Council in Tampere in October the paragraph on the legal status of resident third country nationals also touches on the issue of acquisition of nationality. According to that document an integration policy:

[26] See Article 25 of the draft Convention (see below at n. 40). Article 4 of the draft Directive, of 1 December 1999 OJ 2000 C 116/E provides that the reunification of third country family members with an EU citizen will be governed by Arts 10–12 of Regulation (EC) No. 1612/68 and eight pieces of secondary Community legislation on free movement listed in an Annex.

[27] Standing Committee of experts in international immigration, refugee and criminal law, *Proposals for the amendment of the Treaty on European Union at the IGC of 1996* (Utrecht, March 1995); reprinted in H. Meijers *et al.*, *Democracy Migrants and Police in the European Union: the 1996 IGC and Beyond* (FORUM, Utrecht, 1997), 123–32, 130; the European Council's Consultative Commission on Racism and Xenophobia, *Final Report* (May 1995), 6909/1/95 RAXEN 24, 45; Migrants Forum, *Proposals for the Revision of the Treaty on European Union at the IGC of 1996* (May 1995), 6; the UK's Immigration Law Practitioners' Association in D. B.Winn, *Third Country Nationals in the European Union, The Right to Equal Treatment* (ILPA, London, 1995), 13. JUSTICE, in a paper on the 1996 Inter-Governmental Conference (London, November 1996), 22 proposed that "third country nationals who are duly registered as belonging to the labour force of a Member State shall be accorded all rights conferred under Articles 48 to 66 [EC] on nationals of the Member States". The European Commission, in its 1994 *White Paper on Social Policy*, COM (94) 33, had cautiously stated: " improving the situation of third-country nationals legally resident within the Union by taking steps which will go further towards strengthening their rights relative to those of citizens of the Member States".

[28] For a survey of this literature, see H. Staples, *The Legal Status of Third Country Nationals Resident in the European Union* (Kluwer Law International, The Hague/London, European Monograph Series No. 22, 1999), 347; and A. Oliveira, "The position of resident Third-Country Nationals: Is it too early to grant them union citizenship"? in M. La Torre (ed.), *European Citizenship: An Institutional Challenge* (Kluwer Law International, The Hague/London, 1998), 185–99.

"requires . . . further assimilation of the rights of legal immigrants with those of citizens of the Member States . . . Concrete steps should be taken with a view to improving the legal situation of legally resident third country nationals and their families. . . . This could in turn lead to a common approach for access to nationality and citizenship."[29]

This last sentence comes as a surprise. In the Action Plan on the implementation of Title IV of the EC Treaty agreed in December 1998 the issue of acquisition of nationality is not mentioned.[30] The Community has no competence to legislate with respect to the nationality legislation of the Member States.[31]

In their common contribution to the European Council in Tampere France, Germany and the United Kingdom stated their "wish to indicate without any ambiguity that third country nationals residing legally and long-term in a Member State are entitled to be fully integrated . . . This integration must be carried out in conformity with the principle of non-discrimination with own nationals". The three states were "convinced that a more vigorous harmonisation in integration policies of the Member States is possible". Moreover:

"Irrespective of such a harmonisation, it is desirable that exchanges take place between Member States on the way in which they define their nationality, on procedures for acquiring nationality and on access to citizenship. For in reality as soon as good integration has been achieved and confirmed, it is natural and desirable that the foreigners defined above should acquire the nationality of their state of residence."[32]

Apparently nationality in this paper is presented as the natural conclusion of a "confirmed" integration in the country of residence, not as a support in the integration process. The governments of the three largest Member States consider nationality law to be a suitable topic for discussion among the Member States.

The three Benelux countries in their common position paper for the Tampere Council stated that in order to assist their integration, the legal status of long-term resident third country nationals should gradually be made as far as possible equal to that of EU citizens. The Commission was invited to present proposals to that end in the short term under Article 63(4) EC. The Benelux countries did not touch the issue of nationality law.[33]

[29] Note of the Presidency, "Preparation of the European Council of Tampere—Asylum and Immigration Issues", 10015/99 ASIM 31 (9 July 1999).

[30] Adopted by the Justice and Home Affairs Council on 3 December 1998 (OJ 1999 C19/1).

[31] The solemn declaration that Denmark succeeded in wresting from the European Council in Edinburgh in 1992 that nationality law would remained fully in the sovereign domain of the Member States, may have temporarily allayed some fears, but it was an unmistakable indication that in practice the developments would go in the opposite direction in the not too distant future.

[32] Contribution from France, Germany and the United Kingdom for the European Council of Tampere, undated paper circulated at the JHA Council of 4 October 1999. It may be indicative for the changing relationship between the three largest Member States that it was a tripartite rather than a French-German paper.

[33] Benelux Priorities for Tampere, adopted by the three Prime Ministers on 6 October 1999, Tweede Kamer 215501–20, No. 96.

Two weeks later the European Council, in its conclusions, went one step further. The Council concluded:

> "A common approach must also be developed to ensure the integration into our societies of those third country nationals who are lawfully resident in the Union . . . The legal status of third country nationals should be approximated to that of Member States nationals. A person who has resided legally in a Member State for a period of time to be determined and who holds a long-term residence permit, should be granted in that Member State a set of uniform rights which are as near as possible to those enjoyed by EU citizens: e.g. the right to reside, receive education, and work as an employee or self-employed person, as well as the principle of non-discrimination vis-à-vis the citizens of the State of residence. The European Council endorses the objective that long-term legally resident third country nationals be offered the opportunity to obtain the nationality of the Member State in which they are resident."[34]

The European Council subscribes to the position that a secure legal status assists the integration process. Naturalisation is no longer presented as the crown on a successfully completed integration. Long-term residents should "as near as possible" have equal rights to EU citizens. This also covers residence status. These equal rights, however, are restricted in the conclusions to the Member State of residence. Free movement within the European Union is not mentioned. The Council has chosen the fourth approach mentioned above. Moreover, it considers offering the opportunity to obtain nationality (not the obligation to naturalise) as a serious alternative.

A *press communiqué* is not a legal document. It does not create legal obligations for the Member States and even less enforceable rights for individuals. But the Council in Tampere sent an important political signal: the highest political body of the Union publicly recognised that the European Union has become an area of immigration and that long-term immigrants, irrespective of their nationality, should not be treated as second class citizens, but are entitled to equal treatment, secure residence rights and the option of full citizenship.

During the last decade of the twentieth century a convergence of nationality law in the European Union can be observed. The amendments of the German nationality legislation, which entered into force on 1 January 2000, granting children of settled immigrants German nationality at birth, represents an important step in that convergence.[35] At the beginning of the new century in all but three EU Member States (Austria, Greece and Luxembourg) second generation immigrants have the right to acquire nationality either at birth or through simple declaration or another simplified procedure.[36] However, first generation

[34] Presidency Conclusions on the Tampere European Council of 15 and 16 October 1999, Press Document 220/99, sub. 4 and sub. A(II)(4).

[35] Gesetz zur Reform des Staatsangehörigkeitsrecht of 15 July 1999, Bundesgesetzblatt 1999-I, 1618. For the tumultuous parliamentary history of this Act, see Innenausschuss der Deutschen Bundestages, *Reform des Staatsangehörigkeitsrecht*, Zur Sache 1/99 (Deutscher Bundestag, Bonn, 1999).

[36] P. Weil and R. Hansen, "*Citoyenneté, immigration et nationalité: vers la convergence européenne?*", in P. Weil and R. Hansen (eds), *Nationalité et citoyenneté en Europe* (La Découverte, Paris, 1999), 9–28.

immigrants can acquire nationality of the country of residence only through naturalisation. Many first generation immigrants either are or feel unable to fulfil the conditions for naturalisation (e.g. the obligation to give up their first nationality), or are unwilling to apply on financial or emotional grants. For this large group reinforcement of their residence status is the only alternative.

PROPOSALS BY NGOS AND THE EUROPEAN COMMISSION

Some Member States have changed their position on resident third country nationals after Amsterdam. In Amsterdam the German Government under Kohl succeeded at the last moment to have the words "and work" deleted from Article 63(4) EC. Apparently, the German intention was to withhold competence from the European Community to make rules on the access of third country nationals established in one Member State to employment in another Member State. The German Government, in a letter to the Presidency, even gave its own interpretation of Article 63(3) and (4).[37]

In my view the German amendment did not reach its goal. First, the current text of the provision does not forbid the Council to make rules on access of third country nationals to employment. The words "conditions under which . . . may reside in other Member States" do not contain any restriction as to the purpose of the residence. Secondly, access to employment for third country nationals since Maastricht was explicitly included among the issues of common interest of the Member States in the Third Pillar (Article K.1(3)(b) TEU). It is difficult to argue that whilst all other issues concerning third country migrants after Amsterdam were transferred to the First Pillar, only this issue returned to the exclusive domain of the Member States. Moreover, the Council has the competence to make rules on the conditions of employment for legally resident third country nationals under Article 137(3) EC.

No time limit was set in the ToA for the adoption of measures under Article 63(3)(a) and 63(4) EC. In the Action Plan of December 1988 a time limit was set.[38] In Tampere the new German Government (SPD-Grüne) agreed on how the Council should use its new competence: to make specific rules creating equal rights. Moreover, offering access to the nationality of the country of residence was defined as a common objective. Possibly concrete proposals made by NGOs

37 K. Hailbronner, "European Immigration and Asylum Law After the Amsterdam Treaty" (1998) *CML Rev* 1047, 1052, and S. Peers, *EU Justice and Home Affairs Law* (Longman, London, 1999), 101 both rightly express doubts on the legal effect of this kind of unilateral interpretation. However, making secondary rules under Art. 63 EC requires unanimity in the Council.

38 The Action Plan of the Council and the Commission on the best implementation of the provisions of the Treaty of Amsterdam on the Area of Freedom, Security and Justice (OJ C19/1) sets a two-year time limit for a document on the status of legal immigrants and a time limit of five years for the conditions for free movement and the residence rights of third country nationals in the European Union outside their Member State of residence; K. Groenendijk, "*Aktionsplan, Strategiepapier und Task Force Asyl und Migration—Eine neue europäische Migrationspolitik nach Amsterdam*", in Barwig *et al.*, *Neue Regierung—neue Ausländerpolitik?* (Nomos, Baden-Baden, 1999), 557–71.

and by the European Commission in the previous years have contributed to this change of position.

Since 1997 several NGOs have advanced concrete and detailed proposals concerning the legal status of settled third country immigrants. The active role of NGOs can be seen as a small contribution to the democratisation of decision-making in the European Union. Most of these proposals dealt with two issues: (1) free movement within the European Union; and (2) legal status in the Member State of residence.

The first issue was the subject of a proposal for a regulation drafted by a group of academics in 1996 at the request of the Dutch Centre for Immigrants. The authors chose to extend the present rules concerning the free movement of workers to third country nationals with five years' residence in a Member State.[39]

The same issue was dealt with, though in a less detailed way, in a proposal for a directive on third country nationals published by Starting Line Group and the UK Commission for Racial Equality in 1998. This proposal was not limited to workers; it also covered the right of establishment and the provision of services.[40] According to this proposal, the right to work in another Member State would be acquired after three years' employment in the first Member State.

In 1999, three NGOs (ECRE, ENAR and MPG) published a proposal for a directive which would allow free movement of third country nationals within the European Union, where the right to work derived from the length of legal residence and the workers enjoyed the same treatment as EU citizens. [41]

The Commission, in 1997, before the ToA had been signed, proposed a draft Convention on rules for the admission of third country nationals to the Member States of the European Union. In this draft it is proposed to grant third country nationals recognised as long-term resident in one Member State (generally, after five years' residence) the right to look for employment, work and study in the other Member States.[42]

[39] D. Curtin, C. Denys, M. Geurts, C. A. Groenendijk, A. Roos and H. Staples, "Draft Regulation on Freedom of Movement for Workers within the European Community for Third-Country Nationals with Long Term Residence in One Member State", *in Free Movement for non-EC-Workers within the European Community* (NCB, Utrecht, 1997), 29–64.

[40] Articles 16–19 of a draft Directive on Third Country Nationals, published in: I. Chopin and J. Niessen (eds), *Proposals for Legislative Measures to Combat Racism and to Promote Equal Treatment in the European Union* (Refugee Council and Starting Line Group, London, 1998), 37–52.

[41] ECRE/ENAR/MPG, *Guarding Standards—Shaping the agenda* (Brussels/London 1999), 23; this proposal explicitly refers to the Starting Line proposal where the right to free movement is linked not to long residence but to employment in the first Member State.

[42] Articles 32–35 of the proposal for a Convention concerning the admission of third country nationals to Member States of 30 July 1997 (OJ 1997 C337/9). For an analysis of this proposal, see S. Peers, "Raising Minimum Standards or Racing to the Bottom?: The Commission's Proposed Migration Convention", in E. Guild (ed.), *The Legal Framework and Social Consequences of Free Movement of Persons in the European Union* (Kluwer, The Hague/London, Law International, 1999).

The main legal questions with respect to this issue are:

- the transfer of residence rights and "responsibility" from the first Member State to the second and the maintenance or loss of the residence rights acquired by the migrant in the first Member State;
- the right of family members to follow the migrant to the second Member State;
- the consequences of the loss of residence rights in the second Member State.

The Commission draft Convention dealt only with the first of these questions. The second question was indirectly addressed by the proposal for general rules on admission of third country nationals for family reunion.[43]

The main political problem confronting all these proposals is the fear within the governments of some Member States, that many third country nationals will migrate to their country and compete with unemployed workers in that state. This fear is not supported by available empirical evidence on the effects of extension of freedom of movement in the EU so far,[44] but is perceived as real nevertheless.

The second issue dealt with in most of these proposals is the status of long-term immigrants in the Member State of residence.

The Commission's draft Convention on this issue follows the line of the Council Resolution of 1996. It is precise on the definition of long-term immigrants (five years' legal residence or a residence permit valid for ten years) and the right of these immigrants to a residence document valid for at least ten years, access to employment and the right to equal treatment as EU citizens with regard to employment and self-employment, training, trade union rights, the right of association, access to public and private housing and schooling.[45] However, these rights and the issue of increased protection against expulsion are not specified and are deferred to implementing measures to be adopted by the Council.[46]

The Commission in its draft Convention on the legal status of long-term immigrants, adopted a mixture of the first and the second approach: elements from both national immigration rules and minimum rules of Council of Europe conventions are used.

In my view it is surprising that the Commission felt unable to propose that third country nationals after five years' legal residence should have the same protection against expulsion that is granted by Directive 64/221?EEC to EU citizens already after a few months of employment in another Member State.[47]

[43] Articles 24–31 of the draft Convention.

[44] P. Muus, "A Study on the Expected Effects of Free Movement for Legally Residing Workers form Third Countries within the European Community", in *Free Movement for non-EC-Workers within the European Community* (NCB, Utrecht, 1997), 5–28.

[45] Articles 32 and 33 of the draft Convention.

[46] Article 34(2) of the draft Convention.

[47] A recent overview of this protection and the relevant case-law to the Court is to be found in the European Commission's Communication on the special measures concerning the movement and

Belgium codified a similar rule for all settled third country nationals in its Aliens Act long ago.[48] The same protection is already in place for all Turkish citizens with residence rights under Decision No. 1/80.[49]

On the issue of security of residence the 1998 Starting Line/CRE proposal adopted the third approach: in essence the proposal follows the model of Decision No. 1/80. However, with respect to the right to continue residence and employment in the Member State of admission, this proposal is far more liberal than Decision No. 1/80; free access to the labour market should be granted after two years' employment rather than the four years required under Decision No. 1/80.[50]

In January 1999 a group of senior officials from seven Member States and Switzerland, (including the Finnish Ombudsman for Foreigners, the German Beauftragte der Bundesregierung für Ausländerfragen, the Luxembourg Commissaire du Gouvernement aux Etrangers and the UK Commission for Racial Equality) entrusted by their governments with furthering the interests of immigrants, in reaction to the Commission's draft Convention published a plea to reinforce the legal status of third country nationals. Next to freedom of movement in the European Union and equal rights, these public officials specifically demanded that the protection against expulsion "should be of a high level and could be based on the same conditions which are applicable in situations of expulsion of EU citizens. Nationals of third countries born or raised in a Member State should never be subject to expulsion".[51] A few months later five academics published a manifesto with a view to the Tampere Council in which the same points were specified in more legal detail.[52]

Possibly the efforts and proposals of the Commission and the NGOs over several years, combined with the change of government in Germany, have contributed to the new wind in Tampere. Maybe in some Member States it was recognised that it is hard to justify the privileged treatment given to Turkish citizens (equal treatment and security of residence) and withhold that treatment from established nationals of other third countries who have the same links with the country of residence.[53]

residence of citizens of the Union which are justified on grounds of public policy, public security or public health, COM (99) 372, 19 July 1999.

[48] See K. Groenendijk, E. Guild and H. Dogan, above at n. 19, 24–6.

[49] See the recent judgment of the ECJ in Case C–340/97 *Nazli* (unreported) 10 February 2000.

[50] The ECRE/ENAR/MPG paper supports this proposal but is far less detailed on this issue.

[51] Proposition regarding an European Union agreement and future standards for regulation on the rights of nationals of third countries within the territory of the Member States, letter of 18 January 1999 to European Commissioner Gradin.

[52] AGIT, "Efficient and encompassing approaches to a European Immigration and Asylum Policy", Amsterdam, 9 June 1999, 22, to be published in the *Journal of Refugee Law*.

[53] This point is made by H. Rittstieg, "*Vom Gastarbeiter zum deutschen Staatsbürger*", in K. Barwig (ed.), *Neue Regierung—neue Ausländerpolitik?* (Nomos, Baden-Baden, 1999), 237.

CONCLUSIONS

In my view with respect to the first issue (freedom of movement within the European Union) the fourth approach discussed above should be used: extension of existing rights of EU citizens to established third country nationals. The Commission has chosen this approach in other proposals, e.g. the proposal to bring third country workers or self-employed persons under the coverage of Regulation (EC) No. 1408/71.[54] The European Council in Tampere did not take a position on this issue.

With respect to the second issue (legal status in the Member State of residence) the European Council appears to have chosen the fourth approach: equal treatment with EU citizens—"a set of rules as near as possible to those enjoyed by EU citizens". Here the third approach could be an appropriate first step, i.e. to extend the rights of Turkish workers and their family members under the Association rules to all admitted third country nationals. I hold the extension of that set of rules to be more urgent than a liberalisation of those rules.

This choice is based on both practical and moral reasons. It will produce a coherent system of rules, avoiding further complexity by reducing the present six classes of residents in the European Union, from top to bottom: nationals, EU and EEA citizens, residents from Turkey, the CEEC countries, the Maghreb countries, and finally, at the bottom, settled residents from countries of the world, each class due to Community law having less rights than the previous one. Members of the class at the bottom are predominantly migrants from Africa and Asia.

With both sets of rules, those for EU citizens and the rules for Turkish immigrants, there is now considerable experience in practice. These rules have been applied for many years to large groups of migrants without creating major problems, other than in the heads of certain politicians and civil servants.

Short of the fifth approach, only the third one and, to a lesser extent, the fourth are apt to send a clear signal to the population in the EU Member States that established nationals of third countries are entitled to equal treatment.

Hedemann-Robinson, in 1996, wrote:

> "It is vital, both economically and morally, for the EU institutions to realise the arbitrariness and dangers of making the institution of EU citizenship the exclusive property of nationals of Member States. . . . granting simply economic free movement rights to third country national residents is not enough, only a genuine level equality will do."[55]

I consider granting genuine free movement rights an important first step. Granting equal treatment, a secure residence status and free movement within

[54] Proposal of 12 November 1997, COM (97) 561 (OJ 1998 C 5/4).

[55] M. Hedemann-Robinson, "Third-Country Nationals, European Union Citizenship, and Free Movement of Persons: a Time for Bridges rather than Divisions" (1996) *Yearbook of European Law* 321, 361.

the European Union to migrants from third countries with long legal residence in a Member State may not solve the discrepancies in the labour market situations between the Member States (high unemployment in some Member States and high demand for labour in neighbouring states), nor will it end discrimination against migrants, but it will prove to be a far more effective way to combat racial discrimination than the Directive the Council of Ministers has adopted in July 2000 under the new Article 13 EC.

10

Family Reunion, Third Country Nationals and the Community's New Powers

GISBERT BRINKMANN*

BACKGROUND

Since the entry into force of the ToA on 1 May 1999 the European Community enjoys comprehensive powers in the field of immigration, *inter alia*, of family reunion. The European Council of Vienna of December 1998 identified family reunification as one field in which action should be taken. The Special Meeting of the European Council of Tampere on the creation of an area of freedom, security and justice in the European Union of October 1999 stressed, "the European Union must ensure fair treatment of third country nationals who reside legally on its territory. A more vigorous integration policy should aim at granting them rights and obligations comparable to those of Union citizens"[1] In particular, the European Council accords to the integration of third country nationals lawfully resident in Member States on a long-term basis high priority; according to it, policies should be designed to promote integration of such third country nationals by according to them "a set of uniform rights which are as near as possible to those enjoyed by EU-citizens; e.g. . . . the principle of non-discrimination vis-à-vis the citizens of the State of residence".[2]

In the context of the European Union, family reunification could be described as a situation in which the authorities of one Member State allow a third country national already residing in this Member State to be reunited with another third country family member residing either in a third country or in another

* This chapter represents exclusively the personal opinions of the author.

1 Action Plan on how best to implement the provisions of the Treaty of Amsterdam in an area of freedom, security and justice (OJ 1999 C19); 9, and see, e.g. Guidelines for a European migration strategy, Council Document 11162/99, ASIM 38 JAI 68 (24 September 1999).

2 http://europa.eu.int. Although Tampere calls for fair treatment of third country nationals in the Union by awarding them rights and duties comparable to Union citizens, this appears to apply primarily to long-term residents. The examples for equal treatment of long-term residents (right to reside, receive education, and work) mentioned in the conclusions of Tampere refer mainly to the situation once third country nationals are installed in the host Member State but do not appear to refer to equality in transnational situations, such as family reunification.

Member State. Family reunification is to be distinguished from family formation which could be defined as the founding of a family by marriage, cohabitation or adoption either where the family members reside or wish to reside.[3]

There is no universally accepted definition of the family, because cultural, social and religious norms influence the way families are constituted in different societies. In the narrow sense, the family covers persons related by blood and living together as one household. In a wider sense it covers all persons with the same ancestry. Thus the word "family" covers relatives in a direct line, whether the relationship is legal or natural, spouses, brothers and sisters, uncles, aunts, nephews and nieces, but also less closely related relatives, or even unrelated persons, belonging to it because of a shared life or emotional ties (cohabitation, engaged couples, etc.). In short, all those who consider themselves and are considered by each other to be part of a family, and who wish to live together, are deemed to belong to that family.[4] In Member States of the European Union the meaning of "family" in terms of family reunification has somewhat converged. Depending on the instrument in question, "family" ranges from the nuclear family, consisting of the spouse and minor children, to relatives in the ascending and descending lines and even colateral lines.

Family reunification cases involve people who wish to join "first-generation" aliens; other cases involve "second-generation" aliens, i.e. aliens either born in the respective host country or who had immigrated to their respective host country as minors. In the meantime family-based migration to "third-generation" immigrants takes place. Family-based admissions might lead to a "chain-migration" process which occurs when each immigrant petitions for his/her qualifying relatives, each of whom petitions for their relatives in turn.

In the aftermath of the oil crisis, in the early 1970s, all Member States restricted labour-based immigration. Before this, many states had been short of human resources and thus had encouraged a steady, regular flow of immigrant workers and their settlement in the Community. During this earlier period, immigration policy was largely determined by labour market demands, only later coming to include cautious attempts to foster integration. Family reunification was at that time encouraged by both employers and the host countries. While some first-generation migrants brought their families with them, still more sent for their families later. After the end of recruitment in the first half of the 1970s migrant workers realised that movement in and out of the Member States was about to become much more difficult since they could no longer count on being able to re-enter the host country after returning home. This inevitably changed the structure of migration. While initially migrant workers

[3] Academic Group on [Im]migration—Tampere (AGIT), "Efficient, effective and encompassing approaches to a European Immigration and Asylum Policy (9 June 1999), 9 Family unity.

[4] Red Cross, "Commentary to the Additional Protocols, Geneva Convention of 1949, Article 74 of Protocol I"; quoted in Secretariat of the Inter-Governmental Consultations on Asylum, Refugee and Migration Policies in Europe, North America and Australia, *Report on family reunification: Overview of policies and practices in IGC participating States* (IGC, Geneva, 1997), 357.

had adhered to the concept of staying temporarily, they then either had to stay or to leave the country with hardly any chance to return. Once reunited, the families of migrant workers settled in their receiving countries and had children, most of whom have little or no contact with their parents' native land. In many countries today, family reunification remains—apart from asylum—the single category of immigration which leads to the most substantial numbers of third country nationals gaining long-term residence.[5]

The treatment of family reunification questions reflects many fundamental assumptions underlying immigration and citizenship laws, in particular assumptions about the value of individual rights, the importance of its consequences for the social equilibrium and the economic well-being of the community. Therefore, family reunification could be seen, on the one hand, as a humanitarian or human rights issue, and, on the other hand, as an immigration matter which might place a strain on the labour market and social facilities, such as housing, education and medical facilities. Such basic assumptions and considerations will be decisive to the various questions which have to be answered in treating family reunification, such as which family relationships will count, whether there will be a quota for family-based immigration, whether EU nationals or own citizens will be preferred over third country nationals, what the conditions for family reunification should be, what the procedure is for deciding eligibility and how family-based immigration is likely to affect the society.

Family reunification is regarded by the EC Commission as "a necessary way of making a success of the integration of third country nationals residing lawfully in the Member States. The presence of family members makes for greater stability and deepens the roots of these people since they are enabled to lead a normal family life".[6] The right to family reunification is of considerable importance to third country nationals legally resident in the Union and the success of integration policies is likely to be affected by the policies which apply in this field. Measures for the integration of immigrants in host countries are essential in order to promote social cohesion, to avoid exclusion and to prevent racism and xenophobia. Legal certainty is essential in order to generate respect for the right to family life.[7] The rationale for family reunification was described by an International Labour Organisation report:

> "Uniting migrant workers with their families living in the countries of origin is recognised to be essential for the migrants' well-being and their social adaptation to the host country. Prolonged separation and isolation lead to hardships and stress situations

[5] For information on family reunification policies and practice relating to traditional migrant-receiving states, see Secretariat of the Inter-Governmental Consultations on Asylum, Refugee and Migration Policies in Europe, North America and Australia: *Report on family reunification: Overview of policies and practices in IGC participating States* (IGC, Geneva, March 1997).

[6] COM (99) 638, final, 3.

[7] *Cf.* Commission Document SEC (91) 1855, 6: "security of stay and permanent residence for all those satisfying the stability criteria constitute the fundamental prerequisite for any successful integration."

affecting both the migrants and the families left behind and prevent them from leading a normal life. The large numbers of migrant workers cut off from social relations and living on the fringe of the receiving community create many well-known social and psychological problems that, in turn, largely determine community attitudes towards migrant workers."[8]

Article 6(2) EU stipulates that the Union "shall respect fundamental rights, as guaranteed by the (ECHR) . . . as general principles of Community law". This provision, introduced in 1992 into European primary legislation by the Treaty of Maastricht as Article F(2) TEU, only reflects the already existing standard of the protection of human rights by the (former) EEC, as developed mainly through the long-standing case-law of the ECJ. The ToA introduced several new provisions relating to human rights and thus strengthened the dimension of human rights in the European Union, such as that the ECJ has the competence to check the compliance of acts of the institutions with human rights (Article 46 TEU); social rights were explicitly referred to in the Preamble to the EU and Article 136 EC.

Article 6(2) EU further refers to "fundamental rights . . . as they result from the constitutional traditions common to the Member States". As regards family reunification, although it can be observed that the protection of the family is enshrined in the constitutions of several Member States, none of them guarantees a right to family reunification.[9] Although in Germany the Federal Constitutional Court[10] deduced from the constitutionally guaranteed principle of protection of the family a right to family reunification in certain cases, such right cannot be regarded as "common to the Member States".

The relevance of human rights in the Union is going to be further enhanced through the implementation of a decision of the European Council in Cologne (June 1999) which agreed to set up a "body" in order to draw up a Charter of Human Rights of the European Union which eventually could become part of primary law. The Charter should cover human rights not only applying to Union citizens but also to third country nationals. In defining the content of the Charter in general terms the European Council referred explicitly to the human rights, *inter alia*, enshrined in the European Convention on Human Rights (ECHR) and European Social Charter.

Thus, human rights encompassed in international, regional or national instruments are of utmost relevance to the European Union.[11] According to the Commission "family reunification is a matter of fulfilling international

[8] ILO, Migrant workers, Report VII(1), International Labour Conference, 59th Session (Geneva, June 1974), 27.

[9] COM (99) 638, final, 5.

[10] Decisions of the Federal Constitutional Court, judgment of 12 May 1987, Vol. 76, 1.

[11] The ECJ draws inspiration from the guidelines supplied by international treaties for the protection of human rights on which the Member States have co-operated or of which they are signatories, e.g. Case C–260/89 *ERT* [1991] ECR I–2925, para. 41.

obligations and implementing individual rights to which all the Member States subscribe".[12]

Family reunification will be analysed, first, regarding existing standards (international and regional standards, in particular EC/EU standards), and, secondly, regarding the prospect for a binding standard in the European Union, in particular as regards the proposal of the Commission for a Council Directive on the right to family reunification.[13] Although family reunification is relevant both in migration and asylum policies, the context of the latter will not be covered in this chapter.[14]

THE RIGHT TO FAMILY PROTECTION IN INTERNATIONAL AND EC/EU STANDARDS

Public international law used to be regarded exclusively as a system of rules governing the relations between sovereign and independent states. This meant, *inter alia,* that every sovereign nation had the power, inherent in sovereignty, and essential to its preservation, to forbid the entry of foreigners into its territory, or to admit them only in such cases and on such conditions as it may have seen fit to describe. The state's right, especially as embodied in the principle of sovereignty, became a serious obstacle to the international protection of human rights.

During the second half of the twentieth century, in the aftermath of World War II, rules and principles of international law governing the rights and obligations of the individual were developed. The inspiration for these obligations of the state lies in "morality", "justice", "ethics" or just regard for humankind. The law of human rights became an exception to the absolute and exclusive power which a state otherwise possesses. The right to a family and to family life has become a human right which finds expression in international, regional and national instruments and thus in legal obligations and not just in moral principle. Although the right to exit one's country is generally recognised as a human right,[15] the corresponding right of a person to enter a country other than his own has not developed since no state allows the unrestricted crossing of its borders. Primarily, human rights law operates to prevent a state from causing injury to its own nationals and by extension to non-nationals on its territory.

Although international law has established a strong humanistic and moral basis for countries to allow family reunification, international instruments have failed to appropriate the state's rights and establish a universal right to family

[12] Explanatory Memorandum, Proposal of the European Commission for a Convention on Rules for the Admission of Third Country Nationals, COM (97) 387, final.

[13] COM (99) 638, final, 1 December 1999.

[14] The situation of family reunification in case of refugees is different from that of other migrants. Refugees are in a more vulnerable situation than the latter which might ask for more favourable treatment of family reunification.

[15] Article 13 of the Universal Declaration of Human Rights.

reunification since the international system still grants states a considerable degree of latitude to define their interests. This can be seen from existing international standards, such as those of the United Nations and its agencies, and regional standards, such as those of the Council of Europe and of the European Community; European standards, however, reflect the integration efforts of European states which caused immigration policies to be most developed in the sense that they have explicitly addressed family reunification.

Standards of international law

UN standards

UN instruments, although protecting the family, do not entail a right to family reunification which, however, is an important element in the application of the right to family life. The Universal Declaration of Human Rights of 1948 and the International Covenant on Civil and Political Rights of 16 December 1966 emphasise only that "The family is the fundamental group unit of society and is entitled to protection by society and the State". The protection of all members of the family and particularly children is enshrined in the UN Convention on the Rights of the Child. Even the UN's far-reaching Convention on the Protection of the Rights of All Migrant Workers and Members of Their Families of 1990[16] stipulates only that ratifying states should "take measures that they deem appropriate and that fall within their competence to facilitate . . . reunification".

The International Labour Organisation (ILO), a UN specialised agency, has been dealing with migrant workers almost since its foundation in 1919.[17] However, none of its instruments confer an obligation of international law to guarantee family reunification. While Convention No. 97 of 1949 on Migration for Employment does not mention family reunification at all, the accompanying Recommendation No. 86 stipulates only that a permanent migrant worker should be allowed to be accompanied or joined by the members of his family. Convention No. 143 of 1975 on Migrant Workers no longer differentiates between permanent and temporary migrant workers and only stipulates that "a Member *may* take all necessary measures which fall within its competence and collaborate with other Members to facilitate the reunification of the families of all migrant workers legally residing in its territory" (emphasis added). Convention No. 143 and the accompanying Recommendation No. 151 define the family as "the spouse and dependent children, father and mother". Recommendation No. 86 goes beyond the nuclear family and states that "favourable consideration should be given to requests for the inclusion of other members of the family dependent upon the migrant".

[16] Not (yet) in force; ten ratifications.

[17] The first instrument relating to migration was adopted in 1926.

Council of Europe instruments

Article 8 ECHR protects, *inter alia*, the right to respect for private and family life, and in several cases the European Court of Human Rights (ECtHR) has considered that expulsion of a non-national may constitute a violation of the right to respect for family life.[18] The Convention does not create any right to enter a country of which one is not a national. From the case-law it remains unclear to what extent a state is obliged to permit family members to join someone already permitted to reside within its territory; such an issue may arise where established residence of one close member of the family exists.[19] In two cases, the Commission found that the refusal to allow family reunification violated Article 8, but the ECJ considered that there was no violation.[20] In addition, Article 12 ECHR enshrines the right to marry and to found a family. This right, however, does not entail a right to family reunification or family formation.

The European Social Charter of 1961[21] and the Revised European Social Charter of 1996[22] are concerned with the right of migrant workers and their families to protection and assistance. Article 19 of both instruments contain binding obligations. Article 19(6) provides for family reunification, according to which the contracting parties undertake "to facilitate as far as possible the reunification of the family of a foreign worker permitted to establish himself in the territory". The Appendix to the Charter of 1961 defines the term "family of a foreign worker" as meaning "at least his wife and dependent children under the age of 21 years", while the Appendix to the Revised Charter of 1996 provides that the rule on family reunification applies to the spouse (and no longer just to the "wife", by which the scope of the Charter has been extended) and to unmarried children, provided they are regarded as minors by the relevant legislation of the host state and are dependent on the worker (by this change a restriction is introduced since the children have to be unmarried and must now be considered as minors, which means that the age limit has been lowered to 18 years).

[18] See, e.g. *Berrehab* v. *Netherlands*, Court judgment, Vol. A 138 (1988); *Moustaquim* v. *Belgium*, Court judgment, vol. A 193 (1991); *Beldjoudi* v. *France*, Vol. 234 (1992); *Nasri* v. *France*, No. 19465/92, Rep. 10 March 1994, and judgment 13 July 1995.

[19] See *A. and others v. the Netherlands*, No. 14852/89, Dec 29 June 1992. The application was declared partly admissible, but was subsequently rejected under Art. 29 of the Convention. *Cf. K.D.* v. *Finland*, No. 23065/93, Dec 10 March 1994, where the application was struck off the list of cases on the basis that the Finnish authorities had indicated that they would issue a residence permit allowing the applicant to join her family in Finland, where they had been granted residence permits for humanitarian reasons.

[20] See *Gül* v. *Switzerland*, No. 23218/94, Rep. 4 April 1995, and judgment 19 February 1996; and *Ahmut* v. *The Netherlands*, No. 21702/93, Rep. 17 May 1995, and judgment 28 November 1996.

[21] The Charter has been ratified by 17 EEA Member States, including all 15 EU Member States.

[22] Entry into force: 1 July 1999; so far, the Revised Charter has been ratified by three EU Member States—France, Italy and Sweden.

The European Convention on the Legal Status of Migrant Workers of 1977 came into force in 1983.[23] It is designed to supplement the protections afforded by the ECHR and the European Social Charter; it is based on the principle of equality of treatment between migrant workers and nationals of the host country. In the matter of family reunification a migrant worker resident in a state is entitled to be joined by his spouse and dependent children; a waiting period of not more than twelve months may be prescribed (Article 12). The migrant worker is obliged to have available for his family housing considered as normal, while the requirement of sufficient resources is optional.

EC/EU standards

In contrast to international law, which becomes binding on states only once they have ratified an instrument intended to be binding, EC law takes priority over national law and—in case of regulations and directives—is binding on Member States (Article 249 EC). Other instruments, such as resolutions, however, are not legally binding.

(a) Economically active EU citizens

Articles 39–41 EC provide for free movement of EU workers within the European Union. These persons enjoy the right to look for work and take up employment in another Member State. For self-employed persons, Articles 43–48 EC provide for freedom of establishment and Articles 49–55 for freedom to provide services. In addition, according to these Treaty provisions, EU nationals cannot be discriminated against on grounds of nationality. The Treaty provisions have been elaborated through regulations and directives, adopted mainly between 1964 and 1972, and through the jurisprudence of the ECJ. Recital 5 of Regulation (EEC) No. 1612/68 establishes that freedom of movement constitutes a fundamental right of workers and their families; in addition, recital 7 states that "obstacles to the mobility of workers shall be eliminated, in particular as regards the worker's right to be joined by his family and the conditions for the integration of that family into the host country".

Article 10 of Regulation 1612/68[24] gives EU workers and their spouses the right to take with them certain family members once they are employed in another Member State: (1) descendants (children, grandchildren . . .) provided they are either under 21 or dependent on the worker; and (2) ascendants (parents, grandparents . . .) provided they are dependent on the worker. Member States are also required to "facilitate" the entry of other family members (siblings, aunts, uncles . . .) if they are either dependent on the worker, or live with the EU worker in the country they are living in prior to taking up employment

[23] The Convention has been ratified by Italy, France, the Netherlands, Norway, Portugal, Spain, Sweden and Turkey. It has been signed by another four states—Belgium, Germany, Greece and Luxembourg.

[24] OJ 1968 L257/2.

in another Member State. The family reunification rights of nationals of Member States are irrespective of the nationality of their family members. The same circle of family members applies to self-employed persons (Article 1 of Directive 73/148 EEC[25]).

According to Article 10(3) of Regulation 1612/68 "the worker must have available for his family housing considered as normal for national workers in the region where he is employed". According to the ECJ,[26] this provision applies solely as a condition under which each family member is to come to live with the worker and not for the entire duration of their residence. After family reunification has taken place the housing requirement can be applied only on a strictly non-discriminatory basis *vis-à-vis* nationals of the Member State.

According to Article 11, the spouse and children of a worker and self-employed person enjoy the right to take up any activity as an employed person (however not as a self-employed person) without any waiting period and without giving priority to nationals of the Member State.

The Commission has proposed[27] to reinforce such rights of these family members in several ways: (1) by removing completely the dependency and age criteria for immediate family members (ascendants and descendants); (2) by upgrading the current provisions requiring Member States to "facilitate" the entry of other family members by giving EU workers the right to take with them other family members provided they are either dependent on the EU worker, or already live with the EU worker in the country of origin; (3) unmarried partners are equated to married partners, if national law provides so;[28] (4) the circle of family members who enjoy the right to take up employment, including self-employment, is extended to all family members who are admitted for family reunification; (5) family members admitted for family reunification shall enjoy an independent right to tax, social, cultural, economic and other advantages; (6) in the case of family members who are not nationals of a Member State, they shall retain the right of residence in the Member State of residence if the marriage is dissolved, on condition that they have lived in that country for a period of three consecutive years.

The rationale for these proposals is expressed in recitals 6 and 7 of the proposed amended Regulation:

> "(6) Whereas freedom of movement for workers means full and effective integration of migrant workers exercising their right to freedom of movement, and that of their families; whereas family reunification must be enhanced to ensure that the migrant worker's family is not broken up as a result of free movement;

[25] OJ 1973 L172/14.

[26] Case 249/86 *Commission* v. *Germany* [1989] ECR 1263.

[27] OJ 1998 C344/9; see Opinions of the European Parliament of 4 May 1999, and of the Economic and Social Committee (OJ 1999 C169/24).

[28] This is a clarification arising from an ECJ ruling: Case 59/85 *Reed* [1986] ECR 1283; the ECJ regarded this right as a "social advantage" (Art. 7(2) of Regulation 1612/68) and not as part of family reunification.

(7) Whereas the integration of family members will not be complete without true *de jure* integration; whereas it is therefore necessary to grant rights to family members directly, so that they can themselves assert their entitlement to equal treatment directly, while maintaining the link between those rights and their status as family members;"

(b) Economically non-active EU nationals

For economically non-active EU nationals, family reunification is also acknowledged as a right: "whereas this right [of residence] can only be genuinely exercised if it is also granted to members of the family" (Directives 90/364/EEC[29] and 90/365/EEC[30]), or, as the case may be, "to the spouse and their dependent children" (Directive 93/96/EEC[31]). As regards Directives 90/364 and 90/365 the right to family reunification is similar to the one under Regulation 1612/68: descendants benefit from the right to family reunification if they are dependent irrespective of age, as well as dependent relatives in the ascending line, while under Directive 93/96 dealing with students the circle of family members is restricted to the nuclear family. The right to family reunification is subject to sufficient financial means[32] and to sickness insurance.

(c) Third country nationals

Although Member States used to regard the admission of third country nationals as the embodiment of their sovereignty in the mid-1980s they started on a purely intergovernmental plane outside the structures of the (then) EEC to discuss matters of immigration. Since then they have devoted much time and energy to taking stock of their national immigration policies and to analysing the differences between them. Member States' legislation in this field used to vary greatly. National interests and attitudes, however, have become increasingly compatible. Immigration policies of one country have echoes in other European countries. Both with regard to policy developments, and policy outcomes, or numbers, national disparities appear to be narrowing. The process could best be described as approximation rather than harmonisation of immigration policy in the field of family reunification.

Unlike admission for employment, differences between Member States' legislation regarding family reunification are not significantly influenced by pull factors towards certain Member States. Third country nationals outside the European Union go to that Member State which either needs their specific skills or generally has low unemployment and therefore where they are most likely to

[29] Council Directive 90/364/EEC of 28 June 1990 on the right of residence (OJ 1990 L180/26).

[30] Council Directive 90/365/EEC of 28 June 1990 on the right of residence for employees and self-employed persons who have ceased their occupational activity (OJ 1990 L180/28).

[31] Council Directive 93/96/EEC of 29 October 1993 on the right of residence for students (OJ 1993 L317/59).

[32] Observe, however, the differences between, on the one hand, Directives 90/364 and 90/365, and, on the other, Directive 93/96. While under the former two Directives possession of resources has to be proven, under the latter Directive only a declaration of resources is required.

gain admission. It appears only of secondary relevance that, as regards family reunification, differences between the Member States exist. In this respect measures adopted in one Member State do not affect, either directly or perhaps at all, migratory movements towards certain Member States. Family reunification has never been of high importance to the Member States since there has been no competition between them and Member States have not experienced major difficulties in controlling family reunification through national instruments.

As regards family reunification of third country nationals, Member States adopted the Resolution on harmonisation of national policies on family reunification at the meeting of immigration ministers of 1 and 2 June 1993 at Copenhagen:[33] This Resolution reflects the principle that family reunification is intrinsically linked to the right of family life as recognised by Article 8 ECHR. The resolution is not of a legally binding nature; it is, however, a politically binding instrument. A mechanism to monitor its implementation has been created by a decision of the Council in order to "reveal the practical effect of the Council's work in this matter and provide useful lessons for its future work".[34]

The Resolution does not concern EC nationals, people with refugee status, or non-EC family members of EC nationals who are exercising a right of free movement of persons. Since Member States were unable to agree on a common policy, most of the provisions are vague and Member States are free to give their own interpretation to them. This Resolution does not cover all the questions associated with the subject matter, such as family formation, unmarried partners, polygamous marriages, second degree relatives and employment rights.

According to the Resolution Member States will, in general, admit the spouse of a third country national, the children of the resident and his or her spouse, and adopted children under more specific conditions. These family members may be admitted only for the purpose of living together with the resident. Member States are free to introduce waiting periods for family reunification. Children who are to be admitted in the course of family reunification must be below a certain age which the Member States agreed should be between sixteen and eighteen. Other family members may also be given leave to enter and stay in the territory for compelling reasons. Family members may be given an independent right of residence within a reasonable period of time.

This resolution is the only EU instrument in force dealing with family reunification of third country nationals. Although since its foundation in 1958, the European Community has concluded numerous treaties with third countries (Turkey, the Maghreb and Machrek countries, Israel, the African, Caribbean and Pacific countries, and the countries of Central and Eastern Europe), some of which cover co-operation in field of workforce or the movement of workers, including the corresponding rules of co-ordination of the social security laws of

[33] SN 2828/1/93 WGI 1497 REV 1; E. Guild, *The Developing Immigration and Asylum Policies of the European Union* (Kluwer, The Hague/London, 1996), 251.

[34] OJ 1996 C11/1; *cf.* Analysis of replies to the questionnaire on family reunification, Council Documents 8491/98 of 12 May 1998, and 8491/98 ADD 1 of 8 June 1998.

the Member States, none of these agreements confer on persons the right to family reunification. Competence in respect of family-based admission of immigrants lies still with the respective Member State.

PROPOSAL OF THE COMMISSION ON FAMILY REUNIFICATION

On 30 July 1997 the Commission submitted a "Proposal for a Council Act establishing the Convention on rules for the admission of third country nationals to the Member States".[35] Although this Proposal was submitted shortly after the adoption of the ToA which transferred the power for immigration from the Third Pillar (ex Title VI TEU) to the First Pillar (Title IV EC) it based its proposal on ex Article K.3(2)(c) TEU—the proper legal base at the time of submitting it.[36] The proposal of the Commission was designed to be rather comprehensive by covering most aspects of migration, such as admission of third country nationals for employment, self-employment and for study purposes. Chapter VII of the proposal (Articles 24–30) contains provisions on family reunification. The first reading in the Migration Working Party (Admission) of the proposal for a Convention showed that obstacles would have to be overcome before an agreement could be reached.[37]

In complying with its own commitment to table a proposal for an EC measure once the ToA entered into force[38] the Commission proposed a Directive on family reunification on 1 December 1999 and introduced it into the Council the next day, thus demonstrating its commitment to make use of new Title IV EC.

The Commission based its proposal on Article 63(3)(a) EC which provides for Council measures relating to conditions of entry and residence, and standards for the issue of long-term visas and residence permits, including those for purposes of family reunification. Given the content of the proposal, this article is—in the words of the Commission[39]—the "natural legal basis" for the proposed Directive. Although Article 63(3)(a) EC does not explicitly provide for access to the labour-market, such provision should be regarded a condition of residence.[40]

[35] COM (97) 387, final.

[36] Both the Member States and the Commission were aware that the Convention was not going to be adopted before the entry into force of the ToA. The object of the Commission was "to preserve the benefit of discussions on the substance of the text when producing a Community legal instrument" (COM (99) 638, final, 8).

[37] The discussion among the Member States on the proposed provisions on family reunification (chapter VII) is reproduced in Council Document 6488/98 ADD 1 of 1 September 1998.

[38] Council Document 12027/1/98 REV 1 of 23 October 1998.

[39] COM (99) 638, final, 10.

[40] While only the earlier drafts and not the adopted version of Art. 63(4) EC included a reference to access to employment, as regards Art. 63(3)(a) there was never a discussion on this point. Since ex Art. K.1(3)(b) TEU expressly included "access to employment" and since the powers of the EC according to the ToA include the powers under the old Third Pillar, the right to work for family members can be regarded as included. Otherwise it would mean a step backwards in the integration process.

Although Title IV EC contains a commitment to adopt measures relating to immigration, including family reunification, and although the Vienna Action Plan of 1998 set a five-year time limit for adoption of such measures, the proposed directive cannot escape the requirement of Article 5 EC on subsidiarity and proportionality. While there may be doubts as regards the statement that "the objectives of the proposed action cannot be sufficiently achieved by the Member States and can therefore . . . be better achieved by the Community" (Article 5(2) EC), and while the relevant reasoning of the Commission appears to be rather weak (that a directive will improve certainty and that it will establish common criteria because of the divergences of the law between the Member States)[41] from the perspective of the overall context of the admission of third country nationals to the Member States of which the present Directive is only the first part[42] the conditions of the subsidiarity test can be regarded as met.[43]

The completion of the internal market (Article 14 EC) according to which checks at internal borders are to be abolished appears to necessitate family reunification. Although control of the migratory flows is essential to the Member States because of the abolition of checks at the internal borders, the alignment of the conditions governing the entry of third country nationals into the Member States serves to make control on migration possible.

Since family reunification is not only governed by legislation but also by decrees, circulars, etc., and since the law on family reunification is sometimes redrafted when there is a change of government or of political philosophy, only a legally binding instrument, such as a directive, could guarantee legal certainty.

The proposal of the Commission follows the concept of harmonisation of rules relating to family reunification.[44] Although some provisions prescribe minimum standards, such as Article 13 on an autonomous right of residence ("At the latest after four years of residence . . ."), or allow discretion of Member States, such as Article 10 on a waiting period ("Member States may require . . ."), or certain fields are outside the proposed Directive and are left to the Member States, such as seasonal workers, the proposed Directive in fields regulated by the proposed Directive does not appear to allow for the continuation of more favourable provisions of Member States since Article 3(4) states only that.

[41] *Cf.* COM (99) 638 final, 11. Such reasons do not really satisfy the subsidiarity test, nor is the added reason that it "will also help to ensure that third country nationals are less likely to select their country of destination purely on the basis of the more generous conditions available to them" sufficient. In addition, the validity of the latter reason can be questioned since a third country national is not likely to select the country of work or study on the basis of conditions of family reunification but on the basis of which country accepts him in the first place.

[42] COM (99) 638 final, 3: "In the medium term it will tackle all aspects of entry and residence of third country nationals in turn, and particularly entry and residence for the purposes of study, of salaried and self-employed occupations and unpaid activities".

[43] According to K. Hailbronner, "The Treaty of Amsterdam and Migration Law" (1999) 1 *European Journal of Migration Law* 9, 14, "the principle of subsidiarity . . . may also be used as a limitation clause once the unanimity requirement in asylum and immigration matters has been abolished or reduced following the five year period".

[44] COM (99) 638, final, 9: "Ultimately, the proposed directive seeks to harmonise the legislation of the Member States".

"This directive is without prejudice to more favourable provisions of bilateral and multilateral agreements"; it does not, however, mention national provisions.

Although, at first sight, the proposal uses language such as sickness insurance or the public order proviso, which might be considered vague and thus leaving ample scope of interpretation to the host Member State such latitude does not actually exist since most of the terms have already been given a precise meaning in primary or other secondary Community legislation or through the jurisprudence of the ECJ.

The proposed Directive addresses some—not all—differences in the policies of the Member States. The proposal includes provisions in particular on eligibility for family reunification and family formation, exclusion grounds, conditions for the exercise of the right to family reunification, entitlements to other rights, autonomous status, measures to deter abuses and legal remedies.

Eligibility: person in the country of reception (principal)

The proposed Directive confers a right to family reunification on the person in the host country. Awarding a *right* contrasts to the 1993 Resolution where, at principle 2, it states that "Member States will normally grant admission . . .". Although during the first reading of the proposed Convention objections from some Member States against enshrining a right had been voiced, the proposal of the Commission corresponds to the legal situation of third country nationals who are family members of a Union citizen and who enjoy rights under Regulation 1612/68 or Directives 73/148, 90/364, 90/365 and 93/96.

Awarding a *right* to family reunification, however, could conflict with numerical limitations on family-based immigration, as exist in one Member State (Austria) which has a system of annual quotas. While the existence of numerical limitations reflects basic attitudes towards immigration in so far as it is a recognition that family reunification is an ordinary part of an immigration flow which itself is ordinary, broader family reunification categories could be set up in order to limit and shape the immigration process than if there is only qualitative control.

According to Article 3 the holder of the right to family reunification is the person already legally resident in a Member State. This corresponds with Article 7 according to which the application must be submitted by the person already on the territory, in order to be reunited. Although the Commission refers to practical reasons for this solution (it is easier for the resident third country national to provide evidence for the conditions required by Article 9), the laws of some Member States provide that the holder of the right is the person still living abroad. This corresponds to the relevant provisions of EC law on freedom of movement. According to Article 10 of Regulation 1612/68 the family members "have the right to install themselves with a worker", not that the worker has the right to be joined by his/her family members. Thus, the question who is the holder of the right could be left to the Member States, while it should be ensured that, if the holder of the right is not the principal already residing in the host country, he/she should not be deprived of legal remedies since otherwise the right could become meaningless.

Article 3, dealing with the personal scope of the Directive, is almost comprehensive in so far as it covers all those third country nationals who have a residence permit valid for at least one year regardless of the reasons for the residence in the host country.[45] The proposal does not prescribe a compulsory waiting period before the principal can exercise his/her right to family reunification. Article 10 leaves the requirement of a waiting period for up to one year to the discretion of the Member States.

Such proposal excludes third country nationals with a residence permit valid for less than one year, i.e. temporary migrant workers, from family reunification which would be left to the Member States, which some admit. This exclusion could be justified by the consideration that in cases of temporary, seasonal or project-tied work, family reunification may be inappropriate since the admission of the families of migrant workers who are to be in the country only for a limited period of time may cause practical problems of accommodation, schooling, adaptation, etc.

Concerning the eligibility of the person in the host country, a basic issue arises whether to treat differently the family reunification interests of resident migrants and citizens not exercising or not having exercised the right to freedom of movement. Presently, there is no family reunification right regarding members of families of EU citizens not exercising their right to freedom of movement. The case-law of the ECJ has confirmed that this competence rests with the Member States;[46] thus, so-called reverse discrimination is outside the domain of the European Community. Article 4 addresses this problem by providing for family reunification with the same group of family members as specified in Article 10 of Regulation 1612/68. Spouses and children will enjoy the right to employment contained in Article 11, and children the right under Article 12 to be admitted to the state's general educational, apprenticeship and vocational training courses on a non-discriminatory basis. The proposal does not extend other rights of Regulation 1612/68 to family members, such as the right to social and tax advantages which, though according to the wording are only meant for the worker him or herself, can be claimed by the family members if they are an advantage to the worker him or herself.[47] Therefore, this question is left to national law.

[45] Although the proposal includes refugees and persons enjoying subsidiary protection, the special situation of such persons will not be dealt with in this chapter; concerning persons enjoying subsidiary protection there is not even yet any definition on European level: Council Document of 19 November 1999, 13167/99.

[46] Joined Cases 35 and 36/82 *Morson and Jhanjan* [1982] ECR 3723.

[47] Case 32/75 *Cristini* [1975] ECR 1085.

Since some Member States are less generous to their own nationals than they have to be to nationals of other Member States who can rely on Community law, during the discussion of the proposed Convention some delegations had raised objections to this proposal on the grounds that severe changes to national law would be necessary or that this might widen the differences *vis-à-vis* family members of third country nationals or that it might increase considerably the number of third country nationals admitted to Member States.

The proposal does not specifically consider the position of long-term residents; the Commission will deal with their position at a later stage.[48] Although Article 32 of the proposal of the Commission for a Convention granted persons extended rights after legal residence of at least five years and the prospect of at least a further five years' residence, the proposal did not provide for extended rights relating to family reunification. Article 15 of the proposed Convention, however, indicates that the longer the residence the better the protection; according to this provision in case of rejection or withdrawal of a residence permit "the duration of his/her residence" has to be taken into account. This might lead to the conclusion that long-term residents should benefit from more favourable rights.

Eligibility: categories of persons entitled to family reunification

One major family reunification question concerns which family ties should be taken into account. Article 5 mentions the categories of persons entitled to be reunited. Although Article 5 does not require, as does Article 10(1) of Regulation 1612/68, that the purpose of family reunification is the family member installing himself with the principal, it can be assumed that under the proposed Directive such requirement is self-evident since the prime purpose of family reunification is to make family life possible. Various provisions of the proposed Directive indicate the purpose of family reunification, such as Article 14(1)(b), according to which Member States may refuse an application for entry where it is shown that the marriage or adoption was contracted for the sole purpose of enabling the family member to enter or reside in a Member State. Since there is still a gap, such as when there was a proper marriage (and not a marriage of convenience) which broke down later and the principal petitions for family reunification but without any intention to lead a normal family life, the requirement might be added that family reunification is permitted only for the purpose of living together with the principal, as is included in Principle 2 of the 1993 Resolution.

Eligibility to immigrate based on family ties depends on the relationship between the parties and on the family member's age and marital status. The circle of persons entitled to be reunited is primarily limited to the nuclear family, spouses and minor children, and secondarily, under certain circumstances, to relatives in the ascending line and children of full age.

[48] COM (99) 638, final, 3.

In case of polygamous marriages, Article 5(2) provides that, although family reunification of several spouses and their children is prohibited, the reunification of one spouse and her children, however, is possible. The reason behind this restriction is the contention that the fundamental principles of the Member States' legal orders are not compatible with polygamous marriages (the extend to which this is in fact the case is unclear, particularly as regards the United Kingdom).

In case of non-married couples such as cohabitants (same-sex or opposite-sex spouses, and fiancé(e)s) the proposal does not generate harmonisation since it refers only to national rules. If national law treats the situation of unmarried couples as corresponding to married couples, only then is there a right to family reunification for third country nationals. This proposal corresponds to that of the Commission on amendments to Regulation 1612/68.[49] The requirement of a "durable relationship", however, being a subjective element which was included in order to avert the risk of abuse[50] could lead to different interpretations in the various Member States.[51] Despite the requirement that the situation of unmarried couples corresponds to married couples, family reunification on other grounds, such as humanitarian ones, does not appear to be excluded since such reasons could be regarded as being outside the scope of the Directive.

Article 5(1)(b)(c) provides for family reunification as regards children. It is required that the child is a minor, meaning younger than the age of legal majority in the Member State where the unification should take place, and is not married. Both conditions mean that only those children qualify for reunification who are legally dependent on their parents; in the case of a married child, though he/she might be economical dependent, family reunification is not possible since the proposed Directive does not allow more generous national provisions. It is obviously assumed that married children are no longer dependent or no longer have such close family ties as require family reunification. The child could be a child of the principal and/or of his spouse or unmarried partner.

Article 5 also provides for adopted children, provided the adoption is "in accordance with a decision by the authority responsible in the Member State or a decision recognised by that authority". Because of fears of possible abuse, the requirement of principles 2 and 7 of the 1993 Resolution, "where the adopted child has the same rights and obligations as the other children and there has been a definitive break with the family of origin", might be included.

For reasons of family reunification most Member States set the age limit for family reunification at the age of legal majority, i.e. 18 years, though Portugal is higher (21 years) and two Member States are lower (Austria (14 years);

[49] *Cf.* above at n. 28.

[50] COM (99) 638, final, 14. According to the Commission the durable relationship must be "backed up by evidence of cohabitation or by reliable testimony". Such requirement, however, is not mentioned in the proposed Directive.

[51] Since the instruments applicable to EU citizens do not cover this situation there is no requirement of a "durable relationship". It is entirely left to national law whether a cohabitant is entitled to reunification.

Germany (16 years as a rule, 18 years in exceptional cases)). Legal majority as an upper-age limit as proposed by the Commission would be in line with international instruments, such as Article 1 of the UN Convention on the Rights of the Child according to which "a child means every human being below the age of eighteen years unless under the law applicable to the child, majority is attained earlier". Although the higher the age limit the more difficult integration of children is likely to be, the criterion of legal dependency appears to be appropriate.

Although most children who have reached legal majority will no longer be dependent on their parents, problems may well arise for children after majority who are handicapped or continue their studies beyond the age of majority, or are unable to find employment in the home country, for instance because of the weakness of the labour market. In all such cases there is continuing dependency. Article 5(1)(e), however, permits family reunification only if the children are "objectively unable to satisfy their needs by reason of their state of health".

According to Article 5(1)(d), reunification of relatives in the ascending line is possible where they have no family support in the country of origin and are dependent on the applicant. Although this provision could leave ample scope for discretion to the Member States, comparable rights for EU-citizens, however, are to be applied. The concept of dependency as used in Article 10 of Regulation 1612/68, however, means that the family member is supported by the principal while there is no need to determine the reasons for recourse to the principal's support or whether the worker is able to support him or herself.[52]

If the principal is a student according to Article 5(5) he may not be joined by relatives of the ascending line but only by the spouse or unmarried partner and dependent children. This restriction could be justified on the ground that the residence right of the principal, the student, is usually time-limited and therefore the extension of residence rights only to those persons considered absolutely essential to enable the effective exercise of the right was considered appropriate.[53] Regarding students, most Member States allow family reunification only on a discretionary basis.

The Commission states that its concept of family reunification covers both "family reunification *strictu sensu* and family formation". The latter is to be understood as meaning "(the principal) decides after entering a Member State to form a family with a third country national who does not reside in that Member State and wishes to have this person to join him".[54] While it leaves to national law the appreciation whether a third country national wishes to enter a Member State to marry a third country national already residing there, it is, only a ques-

[52] *Cf.* D. Martin and E. Guild, *Free Movement of Persons in the European Union* (Butterworths, London/Edinburgh, 1996), para. 8.64; according to the ECJ (Case 316/85 *Lebon* [1987] ECR 2811) dependency does not depend on a right to support but solely on the factual situation of support.

[53] Concerning EU students according to Directive 93/96/EEC the right to family reunification also excludes family members in the ascending line; *cf.* Martin and Guild, ibid., para. 10.6.

[54] COM (99) 638, final, 12.

tion of who petitions for family reunification (formation) since if the right-holder does so it falls within the scope of the proposed Directive.

Once a Member State has approved an application for family reunification, according to Article 11(2) it shall issue residence authorisations to the family members to be reunited, which shall be valid for the remaining duration of the current residence authorisation of the person with whom they are being reunited. If the principal already holds an unlimited residence permit the first residence permit of the admitted family member can be limited to one year; this exception "serves to prevent abuse and, where appropriate, to check whether family life is still pursued when the renewal is applied for".[55] Such exception does not apply to family members joining an EU citizen (*cf.* Article 4(4) of Directive 68/360). Where a visa for the family member to enter the Member State or transit through another Member State is necessary, Member States must facilitate the issue of the visa without delay and free of charge.

Exclusion grounds

According to Article 8, states have a discretionary power to decide on the entry and residence of family members wherever considerations of public policy, domestic security and public health come into play. Since the public order reservation can also be found in other EC policy fields, e.g. on the free movement of goods (Article 30 EC), the free movement of workers (Article 39 EC), and the right to establishment (Article 43 EC), it could be inferred that such exception is inherent at least in relation to the movement of persons. It should, however, be noted that as regards the security reservation the aforementioned relevant EC provisions refer to public security, which appears to cover both a Member State's domestic security and its external security.[56]

Article 8(2) prescribes that the public policy and domestic security considerations that can be taken as a basis for refusing entry or residence must be based on the family member's personal conduct. Thus, factors extraneous to personal conduct must not be taken into account. This criterion is similar to Article 3(1) of Directive 64/221. Although the proposed Directive does not explicitly refer to Directive 64/221 it can be taken that there are other limitations of the use of the public order proviso, such as that it cannot be employed other than for its appropriate purpose, i.e. it cannot be "invoked to service economic needs" (Article 2(2) of Directive 64/221).[57] The Commission refers only to the obligation of Member States "to consider the proportionality relationship between the alleged offence and respect for the right to family reunification".[58]

[55] Ibid., 19.

[56] *Cf.* C–367/89 *Richardt* [1991] ECR I–4621. Although this decision relates to Art. 30 EC the ECJ's conclusions also apply to Art. 39 EC in so far as in the two provisions the public security proviso has the same objective; *cf.* Martin and Guild, above at n. 52, para. 3.120.

[57] *Cf.* Case 36/75 *Rutili* [1975] ECR 1219 for an application of this proviso.

[58] COM (99) 638, final, 17.

According to Article 8(3), the exclusion ground of "public health" must not be invoked as the sole ground if the family member suffered an illness or disability after the issue of a residence permit. This proviso may be used only in case of a renewal of a residence permit. At the same time it means that it allows a Member State to make the entry and the issue of the first residence permit subject to a medical examination to determine whether the family member suffers from an illness or a disability. This provision corresponds to Article 4 of Directive 64/221 and Article 10 of Directive 68/360.

Conditions for the exercise of the right to family reunification

Most Member States make family reunification dependent upon conformity with a number of conditions, most commonly the provisions of suitable accommodation and financial means to cover living expenses. In line with this, Article 9 details the material conditions in terms of "adequate accommodation", "stable and sufficient resources" and sickness insurance; these conditions, however, are only optional. Although the conditions appear to leave scope for national interpretation, they have already found a fairly precise meaning in other Community legislation.

EU citizens not engaging in economic activities are required to give proof of resources or, in case of Directive 93/96, to declare that they have sufficient resources; sufficiency is defined as "to avoid becoming a burden on the social assistance system of the host state", which means being above the level which entitles a person to social assistance in the host Member State.[59] As regards the financial resources requirement the proposed Directive mentions the same criterion or, in case this form of support does not exist in the host Member State, requires at least the level of a minimum social security pension in that Member State. In addition, family members have to be covered by sickness insurance in respect of all risks in the host Member State; the scope of sickness insurance coverage is determined by Regulation (EEC) No. 1408/71 on the co-ordination of social security systems of migrant workers. Concerning "adequate accommodation" the Commission refers to the criteria of size, hygiene and safety which may not be stricter than for accommodation occupied by a comparable family living in the same region. Its interpretation may be by reference to Article 10(3) of Regulation 1612/68 which stipulates a "normal housing" requirement.

By these conditions, the risk of a burden on public funds of the host country is largely eliminated. However, they may result in a situation where only migrants who are highly qualified and highly skilled, and thus able to meet the expenditure incurred on their families in the country of employment from their salaries, will qualify for family reunification, while low-paid, low-skilled workers will not be able to meet the cost.

[59] *Cf.* Martin and Guild, above at n. 52, para. 10.60.

These conditions must be met at the time of entry of the family members. There is, however, no provision that in case these conditions are no longer fulfilled after their admission the residence permit of admitted family members could be withdrawn or its renewal refused.

Entitlements to other rights

Article 12 is designed to grant family members the same rights as citizens of the Union as regards access to education, employment and self-employed activity, and vocational guidance, initial and further training and retraining. While the right of access to education, meaning general and vocational education (Articles 149 and 150 EC), can be enjoyed by all admitted family members, the latter two rights are limited to the nuclear family (spouse and children under age). This means that such family members have immediate and unrestricted access to the labour market and to all forms of vocational training without any waiting period. Since the proposed Directive does not allow more favourable treatment, Member States cannot, as some presently do, extend such rights to other family members.

Some Member States, however, require a waiting period for access to employment and since employment rights of family members were a stumbling block on the 1993 Resolution (which stated that no employment rights were included in that Resolution[60]) it might be that, once again, such proposed rights could hinder the adoption of the Directive. Because of great divergences in the law of the Member States[61] there should be an optional requirement of a minimum duration of legal residence before family members have access to work and vocational training; such waiting period, however, should avoid rendering the rights nugatory.

Although, according to Article 12, the right to employment seems to be unrestricted, this right cannot be construed as conferring on third country nationals a more favourable treatment than EU citizens enjoy. Article 39(4) EC excludes from the right to free movement employment in the public service. In doing so, EC law takes account of the legitimate interests which Member States have in reserving for their own nationals a range of posts connected with the exercise of powers conferred by public law and with the protection of general interest.[62]

[60] The only excepton is principle 12, according to which family members who after "a reasonable period of time" have obtained an independent status "may . . . if appropriate, be authorised to work".

[61] For example, in Germany family members of a third country national student have access to the labour market after a waiting-period of only one year while, in addition, the priority of German and Union citizens has to be observed (section 3 Arbeitsgenehmigungsverordnung).

[62] *Cf.* the relevant jurisprudence of the ECJ which limits the exception clause to posts which involve direct or indirect participation in the exercise of powers conferred by public law and in the discharge of functions whose purpose is to safeguard the general interests of the state or of other public authorities and which therefore require a special relationship of allegiance to the state on the part of the persons occupying them and reciprocity of rights and duties which form the foundation of the bond of nationality; *cf.* Martin and Guild, above at n. 52, para. 3.122.

Autonomous (independent) status

An autonomous right of residence shall be given no later than after four years' residence (Article 13(1)). The period of up to four years, however, could be too long.[63] Although as a general rule, the residence permit of family members is closely tied to the principal's, it might lead to a situation where a person has to leave the country where he or she has legally lived for up to four years, or where a woman who suffers domestic violence is afraid of filing for divorce or leaving home for fear of losing her residence right.

According to Article 13(3), if family members are widowed, divorced or legally separated, or lose their parents through death, they may apply for a residence permit if they have been resident for at least one year. This provision is designed to meet circumstances which could happen to any person regardless of his or her nationality. In particular, it avoids the situation where migrants are required to have more conventional or successful marriages than resident citizens, or avoid fatal accidents more successfully. This provision, however, means that there is no automatic right to an independent status; it is a matter for national law to determine this unless "by reason of a particularly difficult situation" Member States shall issue a residence permit after one year's residence.

Although a provision similar to Article 13(3) has been included in the Commission's proposal on Regulation 1612/68—unlikely to be adopted—an autonomous right does not exist for family members of EC nationals unless there is a right to remain according to Regulation 1251/70.[64]

Measures to deter abuses

In following the Resolution of 4 December 1997 on measures to combat marriages of convenience[65] Article 14 stipulates that if fraud or forgery has been used in obtaining family reunification an application may be refused or an authorisation withdrawn. This applies also where the marriage or adoption was contracted "for the sole purpose" of enabling such person to be admitted to a Member State. The reference to the *sole* purpose could lead to different interpretations in the Member States since it is a subjective element; but, as it is an exception, it should be interpreted narrowly. In order to avoid arbitrary inter-

[63] For example in Germany, section 19 of the Act on foreigners presently provides for a four-year period (in certain cases of extreme hardship there is no such requirement). The two parliamentary parties forming the present German Government, however, have introduced a bill into Parliament to reduce the period from four to two years and to relax the hardship clause (Bundestags-Drucksache 14/2368).

[64] OJ 1970 142/24. Family members acquire an independent residence right once the principal has acquired a right to remain, i.e. if the principal has reached the age of retirement and has worked previously at least one year and has lived there previously for more than three years, in case of death of the principal the right can be acquired earlier (*cf.* Article 3 of Regulation (EEC) No. 1251/70).

[65] OJ 1997 C382/1.

ference of public authorities in private and family life, systematic controls are prohibited; checks are to be made only where there are grounds for suspicion.

Although Community law appears to treat legal relationships at face value, e.g. a marital relationship cannot be regarded as dissolved as long as it has not been terminated by the competent authority,[66] it can be questioned, however, whether Article 14 is really necessary since, according to established case-law of the ECJ, no rights can be claimed if abuse is involved.[67] On the basis of the ECJ's jurisprudence it would constitute an abuse of the right to family reunification if its sole purpose was to enable the person concerned to enter or reside in a Member State.

Legal remedies

Article 16 grants the right to appeal to the courts where family reunification is rejected or a permit is not renewed or withdrawn. Article 13 ECHR requires an effective domestic remedy before a national authority (not necessarily a court) when an individual has an arguable claim that his rights have been (or are about to be) violated. A review procedure within the administration before persons concerned go to the law, as exists in several Member States, is certainly not excluded by Article 16 which only guarantees access to the courts. The right to appeal to the courts of law as contained in Article 16 goes beyond the rights of Union citizens who, in the absence of a right to appeal to the courts,[68] only have the right to a review procedure (Article 9 of Directive 64/221/EEC).

The right to go to the law includes the jurisdiction of the ECJ. According to Article 68 EC, which is a derogation of the general rule of Article 234 EC, national courts against which there is no judicial remedy under national law are obliged to make a request for a preliminary ruling if they consider that a decision on the question is necessary to enable to give judgment (see chapter 12 below).

CONCLUSION

As it will have become clear, the position of third country nationals under the proposed Directive is weaker than that of EU citizens. Although the principle of non-discrimination is at the heart of the protection of human rights according to the proposal of the Commission, third country nationals will not enjoy the

[66] *Cf.* Case 267/83 *Diatta* [1985] ECR 567.

[67] *Cf.*, e.g. Case 39/86 *Lair* [1988] ECR 3161, para. 21; Case C–206/94 *Paletta II* [1996] ECR I–2357, para. 24.

[68] The right to appeal to the courts, however, must be on a non-discriminatory basis (*cf.* Art. 8 of Directive 64/221). The conditions under Art. 9(1) of Directive 64/221 must not be less favourable to the person concerned than the conditions applicable to proceedings before other national authorities of the same type (Joined Cases 115 and 116/81 *Adoui and Cournaille* [1982] ECR 1665).

same rights as Union citizens, nor will they enjoy equality of opportunities and treatment with nationals. Since efforts to curtail immigration have taken place in all European states in the wake of global recession and stagnation, it may lead to the conclusion that it has become more difficult to support the proposition that family reunification is a requirement of fundamental human rights.

The prospect for the adoption of the proposed Directive in the present form is rather weak. This can be assumed because of several reasons. The first is the requirement of unanimity of Article 67 EC for its adoption.[69] One of the reasons behind the reluctance of some Member States to agree to the proposal is the current level of unemployment in all Member States; any additional immigration could mean a strain on the labour market and public funds. Since there appears to be a lack of data on how much family-based immigration could be reasonably expected under the proposed Directive, Member States could be tempted to exaggerate the number of family members entitled to move into the Union.

In addition, the proposed Directive grants certain rights to third country nationals which Union citizens do not enjoy. Although the Commission justifies its approach,[70] Member States are unlikely to accept more favourable treatment of third country nationals unless the proposed amendments to Regulation 1612/68 and Directive 68/360 are adopted, which is unlikely.[71]

Furthermore, the proposed Directive grants to family members of third country nationals more favourable rights than the principal himself is likely to enjoy. The Directive on family reunification forms only the first part of a package covering all aspects related to migration of third country nationals, so far proposals of the Commission on other aspects have not yet been tabled. Given, however, the provisions of the draft Convention proposed by the Commission in 1997, which grant fewer rights to the principal, leaving apart the resolution of 1994 which is even more restrictive than the proposed Convention, it cannot be expected that third country principals should enjoy rights similar to those of EU citizens. For example, as regards admission for the purposes of paid employment according to Article 7(1) of the proposed Convention, a third country national may be admitted only "where a job vacancy cannot be filled in the short term (a) by citizens of the Union"; in addition, according to Article 8 of that Convention, on their initial admission they "must already have obtained a work contract of not less than one year's duration". On the other hand, according to Article 12 of the proposed Directive, family members of third country nationals enjoy the same employment rights as citizens of the Union. The difference

[69] According to Art. 69 EC, Title IV is subject to the special situation as regards Denmark, Ireland and the United Kingdom (*cf.* the relevant Protocols annexed to the TEC). While Denmark does not take part at all in measures falling under Title IV EC, Ireland and the United Kingdom can decide for an opting-in. Thus, in any case, unanimity does not include Denmark.

[70] COM (99) 638, final, 20.

[71] Although the Commission presented its proposals in 1998 (see above at n. 27) it has not yet introduced them into the Council and no discussion in the relevant Working Party of the Council has taken place. After their publication the proposals have already been rejected by some Member States.

between the rights of the principal and those of his family members becomes even more obvious in the case of students. While, according to Article 17 of the proposed Convention, a student is not authorised to engage in gainful occupation, his family members may enjoy this right.

The Commission's aim of harmonisation, usually understood to mean the development of common rules and policies, is unlikely to be achieved under the proposed Directive. Although the Commission does not attempt a comprehensive harmonisation of family reunification rules, a minimum standards approach which guarantees a core of rights while each Member State remains free to grant more rights would be more appropriate. Since Member States are likely to negotiate on the basis of their specific legal situation which can be both more restrictive and more generous than the proposed Directive, a minimum standards approach would be more appropriate to allow Member States to accommodate to a large extent their own national legislation with a directive. Unlike the Resolution on limitations on admissions of third country nationals in the Member States for employment of June 1994,[72] which does not allow Member States to be more generous ("the principles may not be relaxed"), Member States should be allowed to enlarge the circle of family members to be admitted for family reunification and/or to attach to it less stringent conditions. The concept of minimum standards is widely used in Community legislation; it can be found in other migration matters, such as asylum (Article 63(1) EC), and in the social policy field (Article 137(2) EC).

It is not, however, clear whether Article 63 EC would allow a minimum standards approach. According to the penultimate sentence of this provision a directive shall not prevent any Member State from maintaining or introducing in asylum and migration matters national provisions which are compatible with the Treaty and with international agreements. This provision appears rather ambiguous. After the signing of the ToA, Germany declared that under the conditions of this provision it would be possible to deny third country nationals a right of residence if they were looking for admission to the labour market or dependent on social assistance.[73]

In addition, in order to prevent Member States from using the Directive entailing minimum standards to reduce their existing standards more favourable to third country nationals, the Directive could include a standstill clause, i.e. that in no case shall the Directive be deemed to affect any law which ensures more favourable conditions to the third country national concerned than those provided for by the Directive. In the beginning of the (then) EEC, standstill clauses were an instrument used to protect the emerging Community from the threat of continuing divergence of national law in the areas of new Community competence. Until the entry into force of the ToA the EC Treaty had included such clauses, e.g. Articles 12, 31, 53, which were already part of the

[72] OJ 1996 C274/3; Guild; above at n. 33, 311.

[73] The declaration, included in a letter of the German Chancellor to the President of the Council, is reproduced in Hailbronner, above at n. 43, 14.

Treaty of Rome 1957. The situation in 1957, when fields (customs duties, imports and right of establishment) originally falling within the sovereign power of the Member States became communautarised, is similar to the present situation regarding immigration which was included in the First Pillar only with the entry into force of the ToA. Standstill provisions concerning national migration law in force at the date of adoption of the Community measure are to be found, *inter alia*, in Article 4(3) of Directive 64/221 and Article 13 of Decision 1/80 of the Association Council EC/Turkey.

Although family reunification is absolutely vital for the integration of third country residents, in order to achieve real integration—apart from equality of treatment and opportunities—more is needed. There appears to be a need for measures to facilitate the integration of family members of migrants, such as measures to inform the family of social policy, as well as their rights and duties in the host country. In addition, the cultural aspects of integration should not be overlooked, such as language training, since learning the language of the host country is essential to ensuring that migrant workers and members of their families make a smooth transition to the host country, and are not marginalised either in the workplace or in society at large.[74]

[74] According to Directive 77/486/EEC on the education of children of migrant workers (OJ 1997 L199/32) Member States shall ensure free tuition of the official language of the host state and promote teaching of the mother tongue.

11

Deference or Defiance? The Court of Justice's Jurisdiction over Immigration and Asylum

ELSPETH GUILD AND STEVE PEERS

The Court of Justice is no stranger to protracted disputes with powerful national ministries. In areas as diverse as tax, employment law and social security law, the Court has a complex, often conflicted, relationship with the officials whose tasks include national implementation of Community rules. The Court's confidence in its solutions reached a high point in 1991 with the *Francovich*[1] judgment, establishing the principle of state liability for breach of Community law. Its integrationist ideology, structured on the principle of Rule of Law, made an imperative of the completion of the internal market which informed the outcome of disputes in most fields of Community law.[2] The exception to the rule is free movement of persons. The Court's relationship with national interior ministries as regards movement of natural persons, particularly where they are third country nationals, became increasingly tense through the 1980s and reached a decisive standoff in 1991 with the Maastricht Treaty. The policies of the interior ministries towards the Court have been perhaps more restrictive in the field of third country nationals than in almost any other. The Court's exclusion from competence in the field of immigration and asylum by the Maastricht Treaty marked a turning point in these relations, taking place as it did within the wider context of a changing balance between democratic and political legitimacy and judicial power within the structure of the Union. The Court's reaction as evidenced by its consideration of issues relating to immigration after Maastricht was to circumscribe its jurisdiction and temper its judgments, even where this results in internal inconsistencies between the treatment of persons and, for instance, goods. The most recent step in this exchange is the limited inclusion of the Court in the field as spelt out in the ToA. [3] The Court's

[1] Joined Cases C–6 and 9/90 [1991] ECR I–5357.

[2] For a fuller discussion, see C. Harlow, "Francovich and the problem of the Diobedient State" (1996) *ELJ* 199.

[3] A detailed analysis of the Court's jurisdiction over these issues as such is beyond the scope of this chapter. See S. Peers, "Who's Judging the Watchmen?: The Judicial System of the Area of Freedom Security and Justice" (2000) 18 *YEL* 337.

answer is found in its submissions on its jurisdiction to the Inter-Governmental Conference (IGC) to be concluded by the end of 2000.

In this chapter we will examine the evolving role of the Court in the field and its implications for individual immigrants and asylum seekers in the Union. To do so, we will consider in turn: first, the Court's jurisdiction prior to May 1999, including its judgments within the scope of that jurisdiction; secondly, the Court's expanded jurisdiction under the ToA; and, thirdly, the future of the Court's jurisdiction, including, most immediately the IGC.

THE COURT'S JURISDICTION AND JUDGMENTS PRE-MAY 1999

Jurisdiction: 1957–91

The EC Treaty made no particular arrangements for immigration to be dealt with differently by the Court from any other aspect of Community law. The rights of free movement of persons—originally limited to workers, the self-employed and service providers (which the Court itself extended to service recipients) were subject to same rules of the EC Treaty without differentiation. The Court did not differentiate as regards its jurisdiction, though in the field of expulsion a certain latitude was provided to the Member States as regards national appreciation of public policy. Nonetheless, the Court found that it had jurisdiction to determine the meaning of public policy and only within that ambit were the Member States entitled to a certain margin.[4] Similarly, as regards the jurisdiction of the Court to determine various concepts within the field, a consistent approach was taken that this task was for the Court, not the national level, for instance in respect of the concept of a "worker".[5]

From 1985 the interior, justice and home affairs ministries in the Member States had begun their deliberations on what the Single Market was going to mean for them.[6] In various venues discussion began on the consequences of integration for movement of third country nationals.[7] The 1986 SEA's introduction of the objective of abolition of intra-Member State border controls on persons (Article 14 EC) was framed as a challenge to sovereignty (particularly in the United Kingdom) and security in a number of other Member States. Accordingly, the UK's Home Office ensured that on its signing, the then Prime Minister insisted on the inclusion of a declaration about the non-effect of the abolition of border controls on national sovereignty regarding movement of third country nationals.

[4] Case 36/75 *Rutili* [1975] ECR 1219.

[5] Case 53/81 *Levin* [1982] ECR 1035.

[6] D. Papademetriou, *Coming Together or Pulling Apart? The European Union's Struggle with Immigration and Asylum* (Carnegie Endowment for International Peace, New York, 1996).

[7] D. Bigo, *Police en Reseaux* (Press de Sciences-Po, Paris, 1996); A. Cruz, *Schengen, Ad Hoc Immigration Group and other European Intergovernmental Bodies in view of a Europe without internal borders*, Briefing Paper No. 12 (Churches Committee for Migrants in Europe, Brussels, 1996).

In other Member States interior/justice ministry concerns about maintaining control over movement of persons, in particular third country nationals, took a different expression: security. The declaration of President Mitterand and Chancellor Kohl in Saarbrucken in July 1994 that they would work faster to abolish border controls between Germany and France was a response to pressure from the road haulage industry through the transport ministries.[8] However, by the signing of the first Schengen Agreement 1985 the interior and justice ministries had already taken over the process on the grounds of security.[9] The consequence, *inter alia*, of the Schengen Agreement was to diffuse pressure to achieve the abolition of border controls under Article 14 EC from the exclusive responsibility of the Community to a responsibility shared between the Community and Schengen.

The timing indicates that the intergovernmental approach preceded the Community obligation. The first Schengen Agreement was signed in 1985 introducing the intention to abolish border control checks between the signatories; the SEA, in 1986, introduced the same principle into the EC Treaty with a transitional period ending on 31 December 1992; in 1990 the Schengen Implementing Agreement provided the nuts and bolts of the system, and the EC transitional period ended at the start of 1993 with no nuts and bolts having been decided. The effect of the Schengen arrangement was thus to move the issue of movement of persons within the European Union into the central sphere of the interior and justice ministries and out of the Community sphere with its mandatory control by the Court of Justice. The interests of the interior and justice ministries in this field had the benefit of co-ordination over a number of years through first informal networks from 1985 to more and more formalised ones up to 1991. The twin concerns over national sovereignty and national security met at the question of borders.

The determination of a contest between the Commission and the Member States on the Community's competence over third country nationals in general in the mid-1980s was important to the perception by these ministries of the Court of Justice. In 1985 the European Commission introduced a Decision to establish a notification procedure whereby the Member States would be required to notify it of intended and actual changes to national immigration legislation. Five Member States, including the largest Member States with the most substantial numbers of third country nationals, at the instigation of their interior and justice ministries, begun an annulment action before the Court against the Commission. They argued that the legal base of the decision could not support the activity. The Court of Justice found in favour of the Commission in all respects except on one minor point (relating to cultural integration), on the grounds that the access to employment and working conditions of third

[8] D. Bigo, above at n. 7.

[9] Ibid. See the lengthy provisions in the agreement on police co-operation, drugs, firearms, etc., all security concerns of the interior and justice ministries.

country nationals affected the Community employment market and thus the Community's social policy.[10]

Within only a few months of this decision, the Court went on to claim jurisdiction over the provisions addressing workers in treaties between the Community and third states, holding that such provisions could be directly effective and interpreting them relatively liberally. This has become the most important leg of the Court's jurisdiction over third country nationals. Although it first established jurisdiction over treaties with third states in the 1970s the early cases concerned mostly movement of goods (squarely within the Community exclusive jurisdiction over commercial policy), rather than the movement of persons. However, starting with *Demirel* in 1987,[11] the Court has asserted the direct effect and a relatively liberal interpretation of the relevant provisions in treaties with Turkey and the Maghreb states, and measures implementing those treaties.[12] In the period under consideration here, two other judgments shocked the Member States' interior and social affairs ministries: *Sevince*[13] in 1990, where the Court held that Turkish workers under the subsidiary legislation of the EC–Turkey Agreement could benefit from direct effect and gave a Community law right to extension of a work and residence permit; and *Kziber*[14] in 1991 where the Court held that the provision of the EC–Morocco Agreement providing for equal treatment of Moroccan workers with own nationals as regards social security was directly effective.

The interior ministries, already concerned that the accommodation of their sovereignty and security interests could not be found within the existing Community structure, were further convinced of the need for a dramatic change of the Community into a Union and the virtual exclusion of the Court of Justice from extra Community immigration and asylum.

The interface between jurisdictional and jurisprudential issues is so intertwined that their separation is somewhat fraught. However, we will deal with them separately in order to highlight the different considerations involved. There is, nonetheless, unavoidable cross-over between the two areas.

Jurisprudence 1957–91

From the end of the transitional period on free movement of workers in 1968, the Court had taken a robust approach to the Community content of movement

[10] Joined Case 281 and 283–287/85 *Germany and others* v. *Commission* [1987] ECR 3203.

[11] Case 12/86 [1987] ECR 3719.

[12] To date there are 20 judgments regarding Turkish nationals (with three cases pending), eight judgments on Maghreb nationals (with two cases pending), and a further initial five pending cases on the Europe Agreements with ten applicant states. Similar issues arise with respect to the European Economic Area agreement and the recent Treaty on Free Movement of Persons with Switzerland. The Court has extended its powers to implementing measures agreed by the Association Council set up by the EC-Turkey Agreement.

[13] Case C–192/89 [1990] ECR I–3461.

[14] Case C–18/90 [1991] ECR I–199.

of persons for economic purposes. Indeed, the Court did not even exclude the inclusion of third country nationals in the concept of worker in Article 39 EC until 1998.[15] However, its judgments over this period were almost exclusively in respect of Community nationals. The few judgments before 1990 which dealt with non-Community nationals were either as regards third country national family members of Community nationals[16] or the right of service providers to send their personnel (which individuals themselves did not have a right of free movement) to other Member States for service provision.[17] The jurisdictional judgment of 1987 on the Commission's powers to require advance notice of national legislation on third country nationals did not result in any practical change as regards the rights of third country nationals. However, the third country agreement jurisdiction did. The Court's judgments in *Sevince* and *Kziber* were both opposed by some Member States. The German Government in particular would continue to argue against the Court's jurisdiction on workers in the third country agreements for at least three years.

Jurisdiction 1991–99

The Maastricht Treaty constituted the Member States' verdict on the Court's jurisdiction and judgments as regards immigration. The extent to which this reaction was conditioned by the Court's treatment of the field of immigration as opposed to its action in other areas is unclear. Certainly the impact of the Court's jurisprudence on state liability for failure to implement Community law was more substantial across the interests of many ministries within Member States. This wider concern over the Court's jurisdiction may have made the proposals of the interior ministries regarding the severe restriction of the Court from their field more palatable to other ministries, such as the justice ministries which traditionally had been defenders of supranational judicial supervision. The addition of an optional power to include the Court may well have satisfied the concerns of some justice ministries.

When the Member States agreed the Maastricht Treaty in 1991 the whole structure of the European Community was fundamentally changed. A brand new Treaty was created with permanent life[18]—the TEU—which, in particular, demonstrated a determination to limit the status of the European Court of Justice.[19] The change in the fundamental structure of the Community could

[15] Case C–230/97 *Ayowemi* [1998] ECR I–6781.

[16] Joined Cases 35 and 36/82 *Morson & Jhanjhan* [1982] ECR 3723; Case 267/83 *Diatta* [1985] ECR 567; Case 131/85 *Gul* [1986] ECR 1573; Case C–297/88 *Dzodzi* [1990] ECR I–3763.

[17] Case C–113/89 *Rush Portugesa* [1990] ECR I–1417.

[18] Previously, the SEA had no "independent" life as its role was almost exclusively to amend the existing treaties.

[19] For a full discussion of the aspects of the Maastricht Treaty, in particular some of its protocols which evidence this lack of confidence, see R. Dehousse, *The European Court of Justice* (Macmillan,

hardly have been more dramatic. The original treaties were subsumed into a new structure likened to a Greek temple. This analogy, devised by the Community institutions to seek to make the changes comprehensible, describes the new structure as one where the roof is the European Union (a new concept introduced by the TEU), which is supported by and encompasses as its First Pillar the original treaties and the *acquis communautaire* (everything which previously had the character of Community law). The Second Pillar (Common Foreign and Security Policy) was intended to support the roof—the new concept of the European Union—but only according to its own *sui generis* rules which allowed it a fundamentally inter-state diplomatic character, albeit circumscribed by more constraining rules than are generally accepted in public international law.

The Third Pillar was perhaps the most anomalous. It was entitled "Co-operation in the Fields of Justice and Home Affairs" and provided for co-operation in the fields of immigration and asylum as well as civil and criminal judicial co-operation, drugs and terrorism. Under the provisions of the new TEU (before its amendment by the ToA) the Third Pillar was intended to share a single institutional framework with the other Pillars, ensuring the consistency and continuity of the activities carried out in order to realise the objectives of the Union.[20] However, this common institutional framework was perhaps not so common as the statement of intention indicated. To start with, the European Commission, while "fully associated"[21] with the Third Pillar, did not have the exclusive right of initiative. Instead, it had to share that right with the Member States. The European Parliament's role was also more limited than had been the case in the EC Treaty: while it was entitled to be informed, that right went no further and did not include participation on the legislative process.[22] The most particular aspect of the common institutional framework of the Union's Third Pillar was the exclusion of the jurisdiction of the Court of Justice unless explicitly specified in a convention under it. Whether or not to confer such jurisdiction was entirely up to the Member States' discretion.[23] For Third Pillar measures other than conventions (joint actions, joint positions and common positions), the Court had no jurisdiction.

Throughout the Maastricht era of the Third Pillar, the Commission made only two proposals for a convention in the field of immigration and asylum. These both proposed inclusion of jurisdiction for the Court of Justice, but both were doomed. The first proposal in December 1993 (on external borders and never agreed) was a late competitor to the Schengen Implementing Agreement

Basingstoke, 1998); and D. Curtin, "The Constitutional Structure of the Union: A Europe of Bits and Pieces" (1993) 30 *CML Rev* 17.

[20] Ex Art. A second indent and ex Art. C, first indent TEU.

[21] It was in fact excluded from any right of initiative in judicial co-operation in criminal matters, customs co-operation and police co-operation (ex Art. K.3(2) TEU).

[22] Ex Art. K.6 TEU.

[23] Ex Art. L TEU.

1990. The Member States could not agree on the inclusion of the jurisdiction of the Court of Justice which was one of the few changes the Commission had made to the earlier intergovernmental version of the draft agreement. The reluctance of the Member States was undoubtedly influenced by the increasingly seductive intergovernmentalism of the Schengen arrangements which permitted interior ministries to settle arrangements with only vestigial national democratic and judicial control. The second (on migration) was introduced just after the ToA had been agreed and therefore must be seen as something of a show case by the Commission of what it proposed to do with the new powers which the Member States had extended to it.[24] The Member States themselves did make one proposal for a convention in the asylum field in respect of which unresolved discussion about the possibility of the Court's jurisdiction took place.[25]

This *de facto* exclusion of a Community institution from a field of activity is unusual. The Member States' choice to co-ordinate the areas of immigration and asylum indicated a desire to use the occasion of the completion of the internal market to co-operate in this area, not least what the abolition of intra-Member State border controls on persons would mean for movement of third country nationals.[26] The Treaty negotiators' virtually complete exclusion of one of the fundamental institutional actors of the Community is a particularly strong statement of disaffection.

Immigration and asylum were not the only fields in which this reassessment of the Court's role was taking place. Dehousse states of the Maastricht compromise as regards the Court in another context:

> "[e]vidently national governments, which were aware of the crucial part taken by the ECJ in the development of the European Community, did not want similar dynamics to develop in areas perceived as belonging to the hard core of national sovereignty."[27]

We would go further and suggest that it is insufficient to view "governments" as monolithic. To understand the Maastricht Treaty and the exclusion of the Court one must look at the interests and strength of the interior ministries working together against the involvement of the Court. It is their framing of the concepts of "hard core" national sovereignty which permitted them to resist the integrationist force of the Community. However, the golden apple of the Maastricht Treaty to them was the power and duty to co-ordinate action in

[24] OJ 1994 C11/8 and OJ 1997 C337/9.

[25] The proposed Eurodac Convention regarding the fingerprinting of asylum seekers, subsequently extended to illegal entrants, was integrally connected to the Dublin Convention (see chapter 3 above). Originally it was proposed without reference to jurisdiction of the Court but subsequent proposed amendments included such jurisdiction. The draft Convention was presented by the Commission in the form of a regulation after the entry into force of the ToA (COM (99) 260 (26 May 1999), revised in COM (2000) 100 (15 March 2000)).

[26] By third country nationals, here we mean nationals of countries outside the territory of the Union and whose nationals do not enjoy free movement rights identical with Community nationals as a result of agreements between their states and the Community (in essence the non-Community contracting parties of the EEA Agreement 1991).

[27] R. Dehousse, above at n. 1, 164.

the field themselves. It was not just their failure to achieve results between 1993 and 1997 which ended the Third Pillar experiment in immigration and asylum, but their inability to contain their own disagreements over the meaning and intent of their actions.

Jurisprudence 1991–99

The Court's jurisprudence after the Maastricht expression of Member States' distrust of it has been rather more deferential to interior ministries. This can be seen notably in *Commission* v. *Council* (airport transit visas) and *Awoyemi*.[28] The first case concerned a dispute between the EU institutions over whether the subject of airport transit visas fell within the First Pillar (pursuant to the former Article 100c EC, which allowed the Community to adopt a list of countries whose nationals needed visas to cross the external borders of the Member States) or the intergovernmental Third Pillar. The Community had already exercised its jurisdiction to adopt a Regulation[29] on nationals of third countries for whom mandatory visa requirements applied (itself subject to a challenge by the Parliament). The Member States acting in the Council of the Third Pillar adopted a Joint Action on airport transit arrangments[30] based on former Article K.1 TEU which, in fact, set out a second list of countries whose nationals were required to have visas for the purpose of transiting through Member States' airports. The Commission brought an action against the Council arguing that the subject matter could be dealt with only under the EC Treaty provision. The Court claimed jurisdiction to "police the borderline" between the First and Third Pillars, and to annul any Third Pillar acts that "encroached" upon the First Pillar on the ground that express provision in the TEU (ex Article M) specifically protected the integrity of the EC Treaty from incursions into its jurisdiction by the Third Pillar. In order to give effect to that protection the Court therefore must accept the policing responsibility. However, it ruled for the Council on the merits. The Court, in reaching its decision in favour of the Council, held:

> "Entry into and movement within the internal market by a national of a third country necessarily implies that that person is not only present on the territory of a Member State but has also been duly authorised to move within that territory. As regards entry into a Member State through an airport, that authorisation means that the person concerned is authorised to pass the border control point in the international area of the airport in that Member State."

By so finding the Court appeared to hand to the interior ministries in effect the right to determine who is and who is not within the internal market. If this

[28] Respectively Case C–170/96 [1998] ECR I–3655 and Case C–230/97 [1998] ECR I–6781.
[29] Regulation (EC) No. 2317/95 (OJ 1995 L234/1).
[30] 96/197/JAI (OJ 1996 L63/8).

judgment still applies after enter into force of the ToA, a third country national who is present in the territory of the Union but whom an interior ministry claims has not been duly authorised to move is not within the internal market for the purposes of Community law. The implications of such a position may be wide indeed. For instance, if a third country national is on the Union's territory but not duly authorised to move, does that mean that he or she is excluded from the benefit of all Community law in respect of the internal market?

When the judgment is compared to the later ruling in *Polo/Lauren*,[31] where the Court upheld the validity of a *First Pillar* act which governs customs treatment of *goods* at the EC external borders when in transit to third states, it can be seen that the Court has adopted a wholly contradictory approach to imports of people and imports of goods.

For *people* who *de facto* enter the territory of the Community in transit between third countries, the Court believes that the concept of entry into the internal market implies not only physical presence but authority to cross a border crossing point.[32] This is so even though the stated purpose of the airport transit visa Joint Action was to avoid illegal immigration into the Member States,[33] and such illegal immigration undoubtedly affects the internal market (for the same reasons which the Court had outlined back in 1987 in *Germany and others* v. *Commission*). Contrast this with *goods* which enter *de facto* in transit between third states. In *Polo/Lauren*,[34] the Court observed that:

> "After all, the external transit of non-Community goods is not completely devoid of effect on the internal market. It is, in fact, based on a legal fiction . . . In reality, [such goods] are imported from a non-member country and pass through one or more Member States before being exported to another non-member country. This operation is all the more liable to have a direct effect on the internal market as there is a risk that counterfeit goods placed under the external transit procedure may be fraudulently brought on to the Community market . . ."

It seems that the Court has a completely different view of persons in transit as compared to goods in transit, even where the procedures in question are equally legal fictions,[35] and where the purposes of each procedure both aim at prevention of illegal activity affecting the Community. This suggests again that interior ministries enjoy an extra degree of judicial deference from the Court where persons are involved.

In *Awoyemi* a Nigerian national was stopped by the Belgian police while driving in Belgium with a UK-issued licence. The police charged him with driving a motor vehicle without being in possession of a Belgian driving licence of which

[31] Case C–383/98 (unreported) 6 April 2000.

[32] See *Commission* v. *Council*, para. 22. The Court found it necessary to define the "internal market" because it took the view that the scope of Art. 100c EC was linked to entry onto the internal market.

[33] See paras 36 and 37 of the Advocate-General's Opinion.

[34] Paragraph 34 of the judgment.

[35] See para. 29 of the Opinion in *Commission* v. *Council*.

charge he was convicted by the national court and fined. He challenged the conviction on the basis that he was entitled to rely on his UK-issued licence in accordance with Community legislation on driving licences. The Court confirmed that Mr Awoyemi was entitled to rely on Community legislation on driving licences adopted under Community transport policy. However, as the legislation made no provision for penalties in the event of a breach of the duty to exchange driving licences, this remained a matter for national law. For Community nationals, however, in respect of exactly the same offence, Community law prohibits Member States from imposing criminal penaltes so disproportionate to the gravity of the offence as to become an obstacle to the free movement of persons. Thus, in the case of *Skanavi*[36] the Court was willing to consider the question of equal treatment with own nationals and the gravity of the penalty. But for Mr Awoyemi the Court held:

> "A national of a non-member country who finds himself in the same position as Mr Awoyemi may not effectively rely on the rules governing free movement of persons, which, in accordance with settled case law only apply to a national of a Member State . . ."

Because the right to non-discrimination is attached to nationality of a Member State and free movement rights, Mr Awoyemi was not protected. The effect of excluding third country nationals from free movement law is that the Community principle of proportionality applies only weakly, if at all, within the sphere of, for instance, transport law. The end result is that third country nationals, consisting of substantial numbers of racial, ethnic and religious minorities, might be prosecuted and face severe fines for "driving without a licence", while Community nationals would be wholly exempt from prosecution in such circumstances. Again, the Court's choice not to seek a basis for a Community law right to equal treatment for lawfully resident third country nationals—which should lie in the "respect for human rights and fundamental freedoms, and the rule of law, principles which are common to the Member States" upon which Article 6 TEU states that the Union is founded—indicates an apparent blindness to third country nationals.

Finally, the Court has similarly shown increasing deference to national concerns even in the area of migration of Community nationals and their families. It has been generally unwilling to give much substantive meaning to Union citizenship, or any coherent interpretation of the concept.[37] While it has in one case interpreted more specific free movement provisions in light of the concept of citizenship (concerning linguistic rights as criminal defendants), it has rejected such an approach in other cases (concerning driving licences and expulsion).[38]

[36] [1996] ECR I–929.

[37] See, further, S. Peers, "Dazed and Confused: Family Members' Residence Rights and the Court of Justice", (2001) *EL Rev*, forthcoming.

[38] Compare Case C–274/96 *Bickel and Franz* [1998] ECR I–7637, with Case C–193/94 *Skanavi* [1996] ECR I–929 and Case C–348/96 *Calfa* [1999] ECR I–11.

It has seemingly deferred to a conservative interpretation of the intent of the Maastricht Treaty drafters, under which the concept of citizenship adds nothing to the more specific rights set out in the Treaty or secondary legislation.[39] In *Martinez Sala*,[40] it showed itself willing to defend a link between citizenship and equality, holding that any EC national legally resident in a Member State should be entitled to a "social advantage" that a Member State offered its own nationals. But it then ignored this development in *Kaba*,[41] holding that a Member State could deny a residence status which was arguably a "social advantage" to family members of EC nationals who were legally resident in another Member State. In the *Wijsenbeek* case the Court has similarly deferred to interior ministries as regards the abolition of internal border controls.[42]

Although this decision of the Court post-dates the entry into force of the ToA it deserves mention as it indicates an internalisation of the interior ministries' criticisms of the Court. Mr Wijsenbeek refused to show his passport on his return from Strasbourg to Rotterdam after 31 December 1992 on the ground that the transitional period for the application of the control-free territory of the Union had passed; thus he should be entitled under Community law to cross the internal borders without a check on his identity. The Court did not agree; it held that the deadline for application of the control-free area did not have automatic legal effect. The fact that the flanking measures regarding external border controls had not been adopted meant that the conditions for the abolition of internal controls had not been met.

THE COURT'S JURISDICTION POST-MAY 1999

The role of the Third Pillar in the field of immigration and asylum has turned out to be transitory. With the ToA, these two areas of competence (together with civil judicial co-operation) have been inserted into the EC Treaty as a new Title IV, concerning visas, asylum, immigration and other policies related to free movement of persons. The Third Pillar has been renamed "Provisions on Police and Judicial Co-operation in Criminal Matters" and restructured to resemble the First Pillar more closely.

The purpose of the new Title's provisions is to establish progressively an area of freedom, security and justice. This time, "justice" in the form of a supranational judicial instance responsible for the interpretation of the area has been included. The Title includes the requirements for the achievement of free

[39] Joined Cases C–64 and C–65/96 *Uecker and Jacquet* [1997] ECR I–3171; implicitly Joined Cases C–65 and 111/95 *Shingara and Radiom* [1997] ECR I–3343; *Calfa*, above at n. 38; Case C–378/97 *Wijsenbeek*, 21 September 1999; and Case C–356/98 *Kaba* (unreported) 11 April 2000.

[40] Case C–85/96 [1998] ECR I–2691.

[41] Case C–356/98 (unreported) 11 April 2000. *Kaba* did not turn on distinctions between family members and EC nationals for, according to the Court's case-law, "social advantages" must be accorded equally to third country national family members of EC nationals.

[42] *Wijsenbeek*, above at n. 39.

movement of persons as part of the internal market objective contained in Article 14 EC, which it clearly describes as applying both to Community nationals and third country nationals.[43]

In short, the ToA awarded the Court some jurisdiction, with the possibility of further extensions of its power later. In all other parts of the EC Treaty consistent provisions regarding the jurisdiction and scope of the Court apply, with the exception of minor derogations regarding the application of the infringement procedure. But for Title IV *sui generis* arrangements have been made. We will set them out here in full:

> "*Article 68*
>
> (1) Article 234 shall apply to this Title under the following circumstances and conditions: where a question on the interpretation of this Title or on the validity or interpretation of acts of the institutions of the Community based on this Title is raised in a case pending before a court of a tribunal of a Member State against whose decisions there is no judicial remedy under national law, that court or tribunal shall, if it considers that a decision on the question is necessary to enable it to give judgment, request the Court of Justice to give a ruling thereon.
>
> (2) In any event, the Court of Justice shall not have jurisdiction to rule on any measure or decision taken pursuant to Article 62(1) relating to the maintenance of law and order and the safeguarding of internal security.
>
> (3) The Council, the Commission or a Member State may request the Court of Justice to give a ruling on a question of interpretation of this Title or of acts of the institutions of the Community based on this Title. The rulings given by the Court of Justice in response to such a request shall not apply to judgments of courts or tribunals of the Member States which have become res judicata."

Considering this provision element by element, what are the differences between the regime of judicial control by the Court of Justice in this field in comparison with other parts of Community law? First is the issue of Article 234 EC. This is the provision of the Treaty which permits any national courts or tribunals to ask questions on the interpretation or validity of Community law from the Court of Justice. It sets out two critical aspects of the Court's role: first, the scope of its interpretation jurisdiction and, secondly, the procedure by which it is seized of questions from the national courts or tribunals. On the first point there is no substantial change as regards the new Title in comparison with the rest of the Treaty. The Court's role as contained in Article 234 is as follows:

(1) the interpretation of the Treaty: this power is unchanged as regards the new Title;

(2) the validity and interpretation of the institutions of the Community and of the ECB: again, this power is unchanged;

(3) the interpretation of the statutes of bodies established by an act of the Council, where those statutes so provide: it is unclear whether this aspect will have consequences in the field of the new Title.

[43] Article 62(1) EC.

Clearly, the Member States approved of the mechanism of interpretation and the scope of the Court's powers. The introduction of a new field of activity within the EC Treaty in the sensitive field of immigration and asylum did not, in the Member States' opinion, justify a change to these powers.

However, Article 68(2) does place a limitation on the Court's interpretative power: as regards any matter taken pursuant to Article 62(1), which concerns ensuring the absence of any controls on persons when crossing internal borders, the Court shall not have jurisdiction to rule on any measure or decision relating to the maintenance of law and order and the safeguarding of internal security. This clause is obviously intended to "carve out" a sphere of action which is reserved to interior ministries, and which cannot be touched by the Court. Such a limitation is not entirely new. A similar proviso appeared in the former Article 100c(5) EC, before the abolition of Article 100c by the ToA, but there it governed the exercise of Community powers over visas, not the jurisdiction of the Court. Further, the obvious successor to Article 100c(5) is Article 64(1), not Article 68.

Two questions arise as regards the restriction: the first is, who is responsible for interpreting its scope? Here we are in the territory of the *kompetenz-kompetenz* debate about which the concerns of the Bundsverfassungsgeright,[44] and German commentators[45] have received the most attention. The central issue of the discussion is to what extent the Court itself has the power to determine the limits of its power. The formulation of Article 68(2) by placing the restriction specifically in the context of the Court's jurisdiction makes the *kompetenz-kompetenz* problem unavoidable. Who other than the Court itself is in a position to determine the scope of the jurisdiction as regards this question? However, by determining its scope as regards this question the Court must unavoidably open itself to attack on the *kompetenz-kompetenz* debate. Either the Court accepts any determination by a Member State's national court (if it has competence or, if not, the Member State's interior ministry) that an aspect of intra-Member State border crossing is outwith its jurisdiction on the new grounds, or its must enter the lion's den. This is a particularly difficult issue for the Court to manoeuvre. The second question then is how should the concepts of "maintenance of law and order and the safeguarding of internal security" be interpreted? In the context of the former Article 100c EC they were never the subject of a case before the Court of Justice. Thus it remains uncertain what they meant in that context. In any event, this is quite a different formulation than that which appears in Article 39(3) EC, the limitation on free movement of workers on grounds of "public order, public security and public health", though clearly a link could be made.

[44] BvR 2134 and 2159/92, 12 October 1993.

[45] For instance, T. Schilling, "The Autonomy of the Community Legal Order—An Analysis of Possible Foundations" (1996) 37 *Harvard International Law Journal* 389; and the discussion in J. H. H. Weiler, *The Constitution of Europe* (Cambridge University Press, Cambridge, 1999), 286–323.

The right which is being exercised in respect of Article 62(1) to cross the internal borders is a fundamental one attached to the completion of the internal market. The fact that the necessary flanking measures have not been adopted and as a result border controls on movement of persons among Member States remained lawful, at least before the application of the Schengen Convention,[46] does not change the nature of the internal market right. Accordingly, the scope of the restriction should, in parallel with the meaning given to Article 39(3), be limited. If a similar approach is adopted, the paramount concern should be the right of the individual, whether a national of a Member State or third country national, to cross the internal borders without being subject to any controls.

Turning then to the mechanism of reference from the national court to the Court of Justice Article 234 provides that "where [a question involving one of the three considerations within the Court's interpretative scope] is raised before any court or tribunal or a Member State, that court or tribunal may, if it considers that a decision on the question is necessary to enable it to give judgment, request the Court of Justice to give a ruling thereon". It is here that the greatest difference is to be found between Article 234 and Article 68. While any tribunal may ask a question of the Court of Justice in other fields of Community law, in this field only courts of final instance may do so.

There are several possible explanations for this restriction, which will obviously slow down the rate of references to the Court of Justice and probably also reduce the overall numbers. Perhaps the most important aspect of the modification of the jurisdiction of the Court of Justice in this area is what it means for the national courts, the middle men between national interior ministries, and the Court of Justice. Weiler and Shapiro have both recently examined this role. The latter argues that the Court of Justice has largely completed its tasks as regards freedom of movement of persons, and can focus on less controversial, detailed aspects of the relevant issues without scrutinising national administrations too closely: "[t]he main point is that the Court's relative quiescence in free movement is in large part the natural result of success not retreat".[47] This argument does not work when applied to free movement of third country nationals, for, of course, those issues were arguably kept from the review of the Court not least as a result of the defeats which the Court previously inflicted upon national administrations.

Weiler seeks to analyse the mechanism of compliance of the Member States with Community law.[48] He notes that the story is one of double acceptance: on the one hand the development of Community law doctrine, and on the other integration of the doctrine at national level whereby it becomes a "processual

[46] See *Wijsenbeek*, above at n. 40.

[47] M. Shapiro, "The European Court of Justice", in G. de Burca and P. Craig, *The Evolution of EU Law* (Oxford University Press, Oxford, 1999), 341.

[48] J. H. H. Weiler, *The Constitution of Europe* (Cambridge University Press, Cambridge, 1999), 188–218.

reality". For the purposes of this chapter, the interest of the analysis is as regards the role of the lower courts in the dialogue. He notes:

> "[a]lthough the pattern of usage differs from Member State to Member State and even within Member States, it would be a reasonable generalisation to suggest that on the whole since the early 1960s, cases which established the utility of the preliminary procedure in this context, national courts, typically lower courts, have been willing partners in this use of Article [234] 'against' national public authorities."[49]

There are several important features in the development of the role of lower courts as regards relations with national authorities. First, higher courts have a tendency to be slower to take advantage of the preliminary reference procedure. Weiler argues that this may be the result of a concern not to disadvantage their national system and their governments in their dealings with other Member States. If his argument is correct, or indeed if the reasoning were accepted by the Member States as correct, it may be that the exclusion of the lower courts from Article 68 jurisdiction is founded on the belief that the higher courts are more sensitive to the concerns of the interior and justice ministries and less likely to make radical references.

Weiler also suggests that there is another explanation for the increased engagement of lower courts with the Court of Justice in comparison with higher courts: "Lower courts and their judges were given the facility to engage with the highest jurisdiction in the Community and, even more remarkable, to gain the power of judicial review over the executive and legislative branches even in those jurisdictions where such judicial power was weak or non-existent. Has not power been the most intoxicating potion in human affairs?". Again, such active engagement was not exactly what the interior and justice ministries in the Member States particularly wanted for the field of immigration and asylum. In the compromise to bring the jurisdiction of the Court to the field, the reluctance of the Member State actors to a wide scope for the Court is self-evident.

It would appear then that the limitation of the Court's jurisdiction to preliminary questions from courts of final instance will have a number of consequences not limited to a delay in the period of time before which the first references will arrive before the Court. There is also the expectation that the type of questions and their frequency when limited to courts of final instance will be more conservative as regards immigration and asylum.

It might also still be argued that there has been an internalisation of the interior ministries' criticism by the Court as regards Article 68: the restriction on references is in the Court's own good, for it will prevent it being "deluged" by references. It is true that the ToA, unlike the SEA and the TEU, made no change to the judicial architecture of the Community. But there was nothing to preclude the Treaty negotiators from considering such a change. Indeed, their failure to address this issue only exacerbated the pressure on the EC court system, and so

[49] Ibid., 193.

reform of the EC judicial system inevitably became part of the agenda of the next Inter-Governmental Conference to amend the Treaties (see below).

There are a number of other aspects of the limitation of preliminary reference jurisdiction which merit consideration as regards the Court's relationship with interior ministries. First, it will be necessary to determine what a "judicial remedy under national law" means.[50] Problems related to the status of "leave to appeal" applications in the United Kingdom are already arising: do they qualify as judicial remedies? In the field of immigration and asylum another very important consideration is whether a judicial remedy in national law, which does not ensure or provide for suspensive effect during the procedure, qualifies as such. The problem here is most dramatic in respect of asylum cases where the lack of suspensive effect means that although the individual may be entitled to introduce an appeal he or she will be removed to a country where he or she fears persecution or torture before the determination of the appeal, thus rendering the appeal procedure highly unattractive to the individual. In such cases, judicial control over interior ministry decisions is to a large extent only nominal.[51]

Secondly, in practice what is the situation? In increasing numbers of Member States there has been a limitation of instances of appeal as regards decisions particularly in the field of asylum but also immigration, the court of final instance against which there is no judicial remedy has become lower and lower. In some Member States for some types of asylum appeals the final court is also the first instance court.[52] This tendency in some Member States means that in effect first instance courts will be the ones with the power to make references to the Court of Justice. Interior ministries' desire to restrain *national* court control over their discretion will thus have the paradoxical effect of *increasing* access to (and therefore control by) the *Court of Justice*.

In any event, the dividing line between the Title IV "ghetto" and other aspects of Community law is not very clear. For example, migration competence is divided between Title IV of Part 3 of the EC Treaty and Title III of Part 3 (along with Part 2). Title III relates to Community nationals, their third country national family members,[53] and, if they are enterprises, their third country

[50] On the definition of "top" courts, see now Case C–99/00 *Lyckeskog*, pending. Also, the European Court of Human Rights (ECtHR) is regularly faced with this problem from the perspective of its jurisdiction in the light of Art. 35 of the European Convention on Human Rights (ECHR). Here the Court "may only deal with the matter after all domestic remedies have been exhausted, according to the generally recognised rules of international law". Its resolution is by no means straightforward, particularly in cases of immigration and asylum where a fundamental right, such as protection from torture or the right to family life, is at stake. The Court of Justice will now be faced with similar problems as regards this limitation, so the assistance which the ECtHR jurisprudence may provide deserves attention.

[51] It is certainly arguable that under the Joined Cases C–6 and 9/90 *Francovich* [1991] ECR I–5357 doctrine a lack of suspensive effect in itself would be contrary to Community law.

[52] See, for instance in the Netherlands as regards refusal of an asylum application on the grounds that there is a safe third country.

[53] Article 10 of Regulation (EC) No. 1612/68.

national personnel at least as regards service provision.[54] The Commission has recently proposed legislation to extend the right of service provision to third country nationals established within the territory of the Union as provided for in Article 49, second paragraph.[55] Article 63(4) provides for a right to define the rights and conditions under which nationals of third countries who are legally resident in a Member State may reside in other Member States. While any court or tribunal may ask a preliminary question of the Court as regards Article 49, only a court against which there is no judicial remedy may do so in respect of Article 63. This question becomes even more complicated when one takes into account the rights of certain third country nationals under agreements between their state and the Community, as discussed above. The plans of interior ministries to restrict Court jurisdiction may come partly unstuck as a result.

Another aspect of the jurisdictional issue of Article 68, however, also deserves attention: the possibility of the Court and the institutions and Member States directly pursuant to Article 68(3).[56] For the first time in the EC Treaty there is a power for two of the institutions (the Commission and Council) and for Member States to request a ruling on a question of interpretation of Community law. This power will give the possibility to the Member States (no doubt at the urging of their interior ministries) to seek clarification, for example, of their responsibilities as regards asylum seekers, assuming that a measure to replace the Dublin Convention is adopted within Title IV as required by Article 63(1)(a). A creative use of this power by the Commission may be particularly important to the interpretation of the new Title. One advantage of this new power is that it is, at least in principle, non-confrontational. The Commission is not, under this power, seeking an enforcement action against a Member State as provided for under Article 226. The Court is invited to clarify what the scope and meaning of a provision is without a specific case necessarily before it. Further the interpretation which it gives "shall not apply to judgments of courts or tribunals of the Member States which have become *res judicata*" (i.e. decided in law). Exactly how this limitation is to apply in practice remains less certain.

Should the clarification indicate that the national court's (and previously the national administration's) decision is incorrect the lack of a remedy for an aggrieved individual is particularly repugnant, most obviously in cases where the individual was returned to a country where he or she feared torture on the basis of a misconstruction of the Community rule.

[54] Case C–43/93 *Vander Elst* [1994] ECR I–3803; the Commission has now proposed a Directive to clarify this right: (COM (99) 3 (27 January 1999), since amended by COM (2000) 271 (8 May 2000)).

[55] Proposal of 27 January 1999 for a Council Directive extending the freedom to provide services to third country nationals established within the Community (COM (99) 3 (27 January 1999), since amended by COM (2000) 271 (8 May 2000)).

[56] This is a distinct issue from the relationship between Community law and international law, which can be the subject of special proceedings brought by the same parties pursuant to Art. 300 EC.

THE INTER-GOVERNMENTAL CONFERENCE 2000 AND THE COURT OF JUSTICE

The ToA, like the Maastricht Treaty, was a messy compromise destined to be considered again shortly. As regards the Court of Justice, Article 67(2) EC requires the Council to take a decision altering the Court's jurisdiction in all or part of Title IV five years after the ToA entered into force (so by 1 May 2004). But there is an earlier chance to reconsider this matter, because the agenda of the IGC due to conclude by the end of 2000 has expanded to include the issue of reform of the Court of Justice. Also, the 2000 IGC has proved an opportunity to consider the voting procedure applied to Title IV measures in the Council even before the five-year deadline.[57] So it might seem an opportune time to reconsider the restrictions in Article 68 EC.

In fact, the IGC seems instead likely to prove a missed opportunity. Most remarkably, the restrictions on the Court's jurisdiction in Article 68 EC have been *backed by the Court itself*. The Court's May 1999 report, *The Future of the Judicial System of the European Union*, set the tone for the subsequent debate. In this document, the Court backtracked on its previous strong insistence that all Union matters should be covered by identical judicial rules: "to limit access to the Court would have the effect of jeopardising the uniform application on interpretation of Community law throughout the Union, and could deprive individuals of effective judicial protection and undermine the unity of the case-law".[58]

Instead, while "the specific nature of the rules contained in Title IV . . . justif[y] derogations from the principle that all courts and tribunals are to have the power to make references to the Court of Justice, that solution cannot be directly transposed to the rules concerning the internal market and to joint policies and actions".[59] The Court does not explain what the "specific nature" of Title IV is, and how it differs so profoundly from other Community rules. While the Court refers to the need "for the rights of individuals to be safeguarded", it defines the purpose of the preliminary ruling procedure as "a key factor in the proper functioning of the *internal market*".[60]

The Court describes Title IV as a set of rules "relating to the external aspects of freedom of movement for persons", rather than as an aspect of the internal market (or a flanking policy).[61] This is a perplexing description, because Article 61 expressly links much of the new Title to the completion of the internal market, and Article 62 refers expressly to the key internal market principle set out

[57] See Council document 4776/00, 28 Sept. 2000, suggesting qualified majority voting for Arts 62, 63, 65 and 66 EC.

[58] 1995 report, cited in Chapter IV, part 3 of the 1999 teport.

[59] Ibid.

[60] Ibid. Chapter I, part 1.

[61] Ibid. Chapter I, part 2.

in Article 14 EC.[62] The rules on internal border crossings and external border checks also affect Community nationals. Moreover, Article 63 is inconsistent as to whether the asylum rules the Community must adopt cover only third country nationals.[63] Freedom to travel pursuant to Article 62(3) and freedom to move pursuant to Article 63(4) will also inevitably affect the internal market. Third country nationals who enter the Community may become family members of Community nationals or employees of Community companies which may post them to other Member States.

In any event, it is not logical to regard *any* aspect of the entry and movement of third country nationals within the Community as a matter distinct from the internal market. Their presence obviously affects the employment market in Member States, as the Court recognised back in *Germany and others* v. *Council* (above) in 1987, and they obviously function as market participants in other senses for the duration of their presence. Why should a special jurisdictional regime for external entry of persons be justified, when there is no such special regime for the external entry of goods, services and capital, and where indeed the Court has bent itself in extreme contortions to claim jurisdiction over TRIPs rules?[64]

The Court gives excellent reasons for maintaining the possibility for lower courts and tribunals to refer other types of cases. Early references are needed because "the uniform application of Community law frequently depends on the answer to a question of interpretation raised before a national court not having to await the outcome of appeal proceedings but being given by the Court of Justice at the outset, so that the case-law can become established at an early stage in the Member States of the Union". Moreover, barring references from lower courts "would result in proceedings being brought before supreme courts in the Member States solely in order to enable the parties to seek a referral to the Court of Justice". These two considerations obviously apply with equal force to immigration and asylum matters. In fact, the Court's paper admits the importance of quick decisions in some Title IV cases at least, because it singles out Title IV cases (among others) as examples of judgments which might have to be delivered under accelerated procedures.[65] But as a result of the structure of Title IV, months and years might have passed before the case is referred to the Court in the first place. Finally, even though the Court's paper is about the future of

[62] Although this issue is beyond the scope of this chapter, the Court seems entirely unaware of Art. 65 EC, on civil co-operation. It refers to conventions on this subject instead, even though the Council was already planning to replace them by EC legislation. Moreover, Art. 65 measures must expressly concern "the proper functioning of the internal market".

[63] Although the Protocol to the EC Treaty on asylum claims by EC nationals severely restricts claims from such nationals, they are not completely excluded.

[64] Case C–53/96 *Hermes International* [1998] ECR I–3603.

[65] 1999 report, Chapter II, part 1. The Court suggested changes to its Rules of Procedure to allow for such procedures later in 1999, in force after Council approval OJ 2000 L122/43. The amendments also set out provisions concerning the new "request for interpretation" power set out in Title IV.

the EU judicial system, nowhere does the Court acknowledge that Article 68 is in principle transitional: the Council *shall* alter the Court's role in Title IV by May 2004.

It seems that the Court's reticence about Title IV affected later discussions. The subsequent experts' report on the Court makes no reference to potential changes to Title IV jurisdiction, other than to suggest the possible transfer of civil co-operation cases to the Court of First Instance.[66] Following this report, the Commission's submission to the IGC regarding the Court only raises the reform of Article 68 very tentatively.[67] The Court's own formal submission to the IGC makes no mention of the topic and the issue was only raised in Spring 2000 by IGC negotiators.[68]

A constant theme in the justification of the restrictions on references to the Court in this field has been the "swamping", "flooding" or overwhelming" arguments which contaminate, at every level, discussion in the area. They are the staple of the tabloid press and, to their shame, of Home Affairs ministers whenever new restrictions on access to the territory for asylum seekers, in particular, is at stake. Their parallel as regards the Court's jurisdiction over immigration and asylum takes the form of a discourse on "deluge" of cases. But if the reason for the restriction of the Court's jurisdiction over immigration and asylum was really a concern about a "deluge" of cases, the planned reform of the judicial system offers the opportunity to solve the problem.

The proposals to the IGC by the Court, which have been welcomed by the IGC negotiators, in part concern the possibility of creating specialist EU courts to deal with certain issues. While the present intention is to consider specialist courts for staff disputes and intellectual property matters in particular, there is nothing in the proposals under discussion to prevent the creation of a special tribunal for immigration and asylum matters. This could accompany the abolition of Article 68 EC, or as a compromise the creation of such a new court could be agreed to accompany a Council decision to amend the Title IV jurisdictional regime in 2004. The much threatened "flood" of third country national cases following the Court's assertion of jurisdiction over free movement of people in treaties concluded by the Community has only been a trickle so far.[69] Therefore it would be preferable to extend normal Treaty rules to Title IV first, to see whether a "deluge" of cases really is going to happen, or whether the prospect is as mythical as the long-threatened deluge of Community trade mark cases which has not yet arrived (and may never arrive). Creation of an expensive new tribunal would be justified only if there is genuine evidence of a build-up of immigration and asylum cases before the Court.

[66] *Report by the Working Party on the Future of the European Communities' Court System* (January 2000).

[67] COM (2000) 109 (1 March 2000).

[68] Respectively, *Contribution by Court of Justice and the Court of First Instance to the Intergovernmental Conference*; and Council document 4747/00 (31 May 2000).

[69] See above at n. 12.

However, any such tribunal will have to be closely linked to the existing EC courts, given the close connections between Title IV and the internal market and the problems caused by "mixed jurisdiction" disputes (cases that fall within more than one jurisdictional regime of the Court). At present, a Turkish resident of the European Community who wishes to return after a trip back to Turkey, but finds herself barred from entry to her Member State of residence because she is listed in the Schengen Information System (SIS), would be covered by three different ECJ jurisdictional rules.[70] It would be worse still if it were unclear which of three different EU courts (to say nothing of the European Court of Human Rights) could decide her fate.

CONCLUSIONS

The story of the Court's jurisdiction over immigration and asylum matters shows distinct historical development. At first, the Court was keen to assert Community competence, along with its own jurisdiction over international agreements and the direct effect of those agreements. Interior ministries reacted by fighting hard for the exclusion of immigration and asylum matters not only from Community competence but also from the mandatory jurisdiction of the Court.

The two positions have since been partly reconciled. The Court has shown itself willing to defer to national concerns about the possible effect of Union citizenship and has carefully and continually reassured Member States that they still control the initial entry of persons, for instance, from Turkey. It has claimed in both its judgments and its discussion papers that immigration and asylum matters are not linked to the internal market, in the process reversing its initial case-law, ignoring the clear wording of Title IV, and overlooking the obvious links between these matters. It has also given a green light to the continued maintenance of a distinct jurisdictional regime for immigration and asylum matters and has not taken the opportunity provided by the current discussion on the EU's future judicial system to address the alleged risk of a "deluge" of immigration and asylum cases in any way. It appears at present that an alliance has developed between national interior ministries anxious to preserve maximum discretion over entry and movement of third country nationals, and Community judges with protracted concerns over their workload. In this alliance, the role of the "deluge" argument as a justification is central. Without it, the legitimacy of the *sui generis* jurisdictional rules is severely weakened. But what are the basic assumptions implicit in the "deluge" argument?

[70] She would have a right of re-entry pursuant to the EC–Turkey Agreement subsidiary legislation, falling within the "mainstream" ECJ jurisdiction; an issue under the entry control provisions of the Schengen *acquis*, allocated to Title IV jurisdiction; and an issue under the SIS provisions of that *acquis*, at present falling under the Court's "Third Pillar" jurisdiction because of the failure to allocate the SIS provisions of the *acquis*.

First, the "deluge" argument is clothed in the language of threat. In the terminology of boundaries and borders, "deluges", "floods" and "overwhelming" invoke the dual fear of blind, unstoppable natural forces, such as water or enemy attack. In either case this is an alleged type of external security risk. The underlying assumption is of a Europe under threat from the movement of persons. In the popular press, there is some divergence on the source of the threat. In most Member States asylum seekers are the ones who are "deluging" and "flooding" into the Member States. However, recently in Germany and Austria in particular it is the "deluge" of migrant workers from Central and Eastern Europe which is the focus of attention.

What is the validity of these arguments? As regards the "deluge" of asylum seekers, it is worth noting that the majority of third country nationals staying in the Member States are not asylum seekers, but are in fact admitted workers, family members of Community nationals or of third country nationals authorised to remain there.[71] For the moment in Europe there does not seem to be a discourse of "deluge" as regards work permit holders or family members. As regards nationals of the Central and Eastern European countries (CEECs), under the Europe Agreements, all their nationals have the right of self-employment within the territory of the Member States. This right has existed for the nationals of the most populous CEEC, Poland, since February 1994. But the collection of statistics regarding the exercise of this establishment right in the Member States is not particularly exact. According to the statistics available for the United Kingdom in 1998, the "deluge" of persons exercising this right was at most 160 people.[72]

Will this translate into a "deluge" of cases? If we continue drawing an analogy with family members, Community law rules on family reunion with third country national family members, on average, give rise to one case before the Court of Justice every two or three years (maximum). As regards the rights of CEEC nationals, from 1994 until the present—there have been only five references from national courts to the Court of Justice—one Dutch, one German and three from the United Kingdom. The "deluge" argument plays well with the tabloid press, defining new categories of threat from which "we", the "indigenous people" of Europe, deserve protection, but in the supposedly cool light of juridical reality it finds little foundation.

The final comment we would make about the legitimacy of the "deluge" argument is its characteristic as a constant in the discourse surrounding enlargement

[71] For instance, in 1992, the year when more than 430,000 persons applied for asylum in Germany alone, Germany admitted over 400,000 persons as foreign workers (OECD, *SOPEMI Trends in International Migration, Annual Report* (1994), 197. This is without the addition of family members, who traditionally form the majority of inward migration in Europe (J. Salt, *Migration and Population Change in Europe* (UNIDIR Research Paper No. 19, New York, 1993), 16–17).

[72] Extract from "Control of Immigration Statistics UK, Cm 4431, 1998, Table 5.1: in the UK statistics by category of extension including independent means and business (which covers the self-employed) and by nationality: extensions were granted to 80 Bulgarians, 70 Poles, 10 Romanians. Some of these persons might have qualified under provisions other than the establishment right; thus, the figure of 160 is a maximum.

of the Union. In the first enlargement to the United Kingdom, Ireland and Denmark, Bohning points out that there were press reports in some continental countries about the impending flood of immigrants from the United Kingdom.[73] The second and third enlargements to Greece, Spain and Portugal, traditional sources of migration to northern European Member States, also gave rise to "deluge" threats which never materialised. However, the "deluge" argument is distasteful not only from the perspective of its complicity in the description of the movement of third country nationals (rather than Community nationals) as a security threat, but also because of the consequences as regards the commitment of the Community to human rights standards.

For this reason, we do not accept that even a significant number of references concerning immigration and asylum matters would justify the extreme restrictions upon the Court's jurisdiction imposed by Article 68 EC. In the past, the Member States were willing to find the funds to set up the Court of First Instance, created largely to deal with commercial firms' complaints against the Community institutions, and trade-mark appeal boards, created to ensure effective review over the creation of new Community intellectual property rights. Any "deluge" of references would concern persons who are seeking protection from torture and persecution, or the creation or maintenance of family life. It is hard to see how a Union "founded on the principles of liberty, democracy, respect for human rights and fundamental freedoms, and the rule of law" can justify extensive judicial resources for the protection of multinational companies, while dedicating marginal judicial resources for the protection of immigrants and asylum seekers.

[73] R. Bohning, *The Migration of Workers in the United Kingdom and the European Community* (OUP, Oxford, 1972).

12

Aliens, Workers, Citizens or Humans? Models for Community Immigration Law

STEVE PEERS

INTRODUCTION

Any entrant into any EU Member State (bar persons crossing internal Schengen borders) is faced with one passport line for EU nationals and one line for non-EU nationals. It is tempting to transpose this distinction to EU immigration law, and conclude that there are (or should be) two different systems of law for these two groups, with two different sets of substantive rules. But in light of the EU's extensive patchwork of treaties granting rights to nationals of various third countries, this conclusion would be misleading. Therefore, with the entry into force of the ToA, the European Union has the choice between several possible models when adopting its immigration law. It can base its immigration law rules on: the "alien" model of the restrictive pre-Amsterdam "soft law"; the "worker" model of the rules in agreements with third states (particularly Turkey); or on the "citizen" model of the rules applying to EU citizens. Finally, the EU could improve the rules applying to European Union citizens and develop a "human" mode of immigration law.

OUTLINING THE MODELS

The "citizen" model: EC nationals

The present immigration rules applying to EU citizens are very liberal compared to most national immigration laws, but still contain restrictive elements if compared to the rules which apply to movements within states. The EU's well-known system, like most immigration laws, divides immigrants into different categories of persons. In the EU's case, some of these categories mirror some of the freedoms guaranteed by the EC Treaty. *Workers* have rights to enter and stay, and to search for and take up employment without discrimination, under the directly effective Article 39 EC, implemented by further Regulation (EC) No. 1612/68 on employment and benefit status of workers and status of their family members and Directive 68/360/EEC (on immigration law status of workers and their family members.[1] Family reunion rights include rights to bring in a substantial extended family. In addition, Commission Regulation No. 1251/70, foreseen by Article 39(3)(d) EC, allows workers and their family members to stay after retirement or disability, and their family members to stay after a worker's (or ex-worker's) death.[2] The *self-employed* have rights to enter and stay, to enter professions and take up other forms of self-employment without discrimination and to claim benefits for themselves and family members under the directly effective Article 43 EC, implemented further by Directive 73/148/EEC on immigration law status of the self-employed and their family members.[3] In addition, Directive 75/34/EEC grants rights to the self-employed and their family members on retirement, disability or death.[4] Service providers and recipients have rights to enter and stay, to pursue employment and professions temporarily, and to certain benefits, under Article 49 EC, in part implemented by Regulation No. 1612/68 and Directive 73/148.

Students in vocational training have directly effective rights to enter and reside and to non-discrimination in education during their studies as a result of Articles 12 and 150 EC, as implemented further by Directive 93/96/EEC, which also grants rights to family members.[5] This applies to publicly funded vocational training; students taking private vocational training can claim rights as service recipients under Article 49 EC.[6] It is also arguable that students in other types of education have directly effective rights to enter and reside and to non-discrimination in education since 1993 by conjunction of Articles 12 and 149 EC. *Pensioners* have rights to enter and reside along with their family members by virtue of Directive 90/365/EEC.[7] *Other persons* who have all-risk sickness insurance and income above the level for granting social assistance in the host state can enter and reside pursuant to Directive 90/364/EEC.[8] In addition, it is arguable that the "citizenship" right to "move and reside freely" pursuant to Article 18 EC grants further rights beyond those described above.[9] Certainly the formal status of "citizen", in conjunction with the right to equal treatment pursuant to Article 12 EC, entitles persons to equal treatment in benefits even if they do not fall within other categories of migrants.[10] Workers, the self-employed,

[1] OJ Special Edition (1968) L257/2 and L257/13.

[2] OJ Special Edition (1970) L142/24.

[3] OJ 1973 L172/14; and see ECJ judgment in Case C–337/97, *Meeusen* [1999] ECR I–3289.

[4] OJ 1975 L14/10.

[5] Case C–357/89 *Raulin* [1992] ECR I–1027 (OJ 1993 L317/59).

[6] C–109/92 *Wirth* [1993] ECR I–6447; see now ECJ judgment of 28 October 1999 in Case C–55/98 *Vestergaard* [1999] ECR I–7641.

[7] OJ 1990 L180/28.

[8] OJ 1990 L180/26.

[9] See ECJ judgment of 21 September 1999 in Case C–378/97 *Wijsenbeek* [1999] ECR I–6207 and Case C–413/99 *Baumbast* (pending).

[10] Case C–85/96 *Martinez Sala* [1998] ECR I–2691.

service providers and students can derive social security rights from Regulation (EC) No. 1408/71, which co-ordinates national social security systems where persons have exercised free movement,[11] and the former three groups (along with students after graduation) also benefit from legislation on recognition of qualifications.

The distinction between these various categories is not as critical for EC nationals as it is for third country nationals, because EC nationals are not prevented from switching between the various categories. Therefore an "ex-student" (graduate) can stay and look for work in the host Member State pursuant to Article 39 EC; an "ex-worker" or "retired professional" can enter or stay as a pensioner pursuant to Directive 90/365 even if he/she does not meet the conditions for remaining after employment or self-employment applied under Regulation 1251/70 or Directive 75/34; and migrants can move freely between various categories whenever they wish. They can even hold more than one status at the same time (student and worker, for instance). Furthermore, the rules on expulsion or refusal of entry pursuant to Directive 64/221/EEC apply to all categories.[12] However, there are certain differences as regards access to benefits, with the self-employed and workers enjoying extended rights to social security benefits and "social advantages" and other groups enjoying less access.[13]

The EU rules, while liberal, have been criticised because: they do not generally allow persons dependent upon state benefits to move to another Member State; they discriminate against women, because they do not provide adequately for protection of persons after divorce; and they do not recognise the status of unmarried partners.[14] These criticisms need to be qualified. First, some persons dependent on benefits *can* move: a pensioner dependent on benefits from state A *can* reside in state B as long as he/she meets the criteria of Directive 90/365.

Secondly, not all ex-spouses will face an immigration problem. All third country national divorcees will, unless they have acquired rights under one of the EC's international agreements or under national law, claim the right to stay with their children pursuant to Article 8 of the European Convention on Human Rights (ECHR). However, a divorcee with nationality of the host state will obviously face no migration problem at all, and a divorcee with the nationality of another EC Member State will be able to stay if he/she falls within one of the formal categories of migrant mentioned above. Even persons who do not fall within one of the formal categories, because they are looking after children

[11] As last consolidated by Regulation (EC) No. 118/97 (OJ 1997 L28/1).

[12] OJ Special Edition 1964, No. 850/64, 117.

[13] However, this position is unclear as a result of the *Martinez Sala* judgment (see above at n. 10). A full discussion of the possible implications of the *Martinez Sala* is beyond the scope of this chapter.

[14] For example, see T. Hervey, "Migrant Workers and their Families in the European Union: The Pervasive Market Idealogy of European Law", in J. Shaw and G. More (eds), *New Legal Dynamics of European Union* (Oxford University Press, Oxford, 1995). Spouses still retain rights after separation, as distinct from divorce (Case 267/83 *Diatta* [1985] ECR 567) but only if the separated spouse remains within the host state.

and/or other family members without pay, can arguably claim benefit rights pursuant to *Martinez Sala* and may have a right to stay under the citizenship provisions of the EC Treaty, under Article 8 ECHR, or as a corollary of their child's or children's right to finish education in the host state.[15] In any event, the treatment of divorcees is not necessarily sexist, since ex-husbands can equally face difficulties under immigration law, although fewer ex-wives may qualify as "workers" in Member States with lower female participation in the workforce.

Thirdly, unmarried partners can enter another Member State where that Member State allows its own citizens the right to bring in unmarried partners.[16] If both are EC nationals, they can both claim independent rights to enter and remain if they can come within the categories discussed above. Even if one is financially dependent upon the other, the dependent partner (if an EC national) should be able to rely on Directive 90/364.[17] But although some critiques of EC free movement law may overstate the extent to which that law excludes the poor, divorced women and unmarried partners, these critiques are essentially valid, since those groups as a whole are either not able to take full advantage of free movement rights or are prejudiced by exercise of those rights.

One of these difficulties would also be ameliorated if the Commission's proposals to amend Directive 68/360 and Regulation 1612/68 are adopted.[18] These proposals would allow divorcees to stay automatically if the divorce took place more than three years after entry and to retain the right to work automatically if the divorce took place more than five years after entry. Obviously, the latter right would only be relevant to third country nationals, but the former right would benefit EC nationals and third country nationals alike. The proposals would improve the existing situation but would apply only to divorcees of workers, not other categories of EC nationals. There would still be problems for divorcees who got a divorce within three years of entry into the host state, and even afterwards for those third country national divorcees who would lose their right to employment (unless they had been resident for five years) and for all divorcees who could not meet the conditions of remaining after divorce (equivalent to those applying under Directive 90/364). At the time of writing, Member States were not interested in discussing these proposals and so any final amendments to the current legislation, if agreed at all, may well be less liberal than the Commission's proposal.

[15] Case C–85/96 *Martinoz Sala* [1998] ECR I–2691. By analogy with Joined Cases 389 and 390/87 *Echternach and Moritz* [1989] ECR 723; and see particularly Case C–413/99 *Baumbast* (pending). On the connection between Art. 8 ECHR and EC law, see the Commission's Communication on the application of Directive 64/221, COM (99) 372 (9 July 1999).

[16] Case 59/85 *Reed* [1986] ECR 1283.

[17] Of course, this would not solve problems of access to benefits, for the dependent partner would be able to claim benefits as a "family member" of the EC national worker of self-employed person unless the host state's law was more generous to unmarried partners with the benefits system than it was as a matter of immigration law.

[18] OJ 1998 C344. The Commission also proposes a change relevant to unmarried partners, but this would essentially only formalise the *Reed* judgment (see above at n. 16).

It can be seen that the current rules largely entrench the concept of "market citizen" within the EC legal order.[19] Rights to free movement are very liberal for persons who can wholly or largely "pay their way" from employment, professional or other non-benefit income in the host state. Migrants may have access to state benefits of various types on the same basis as nationals, but only if they initially entered without claiming benefits or have at least some non-benefit income.[20] The position might change, depending on the Court's approach to cases following *Martinez Sala*. But at present it appears that free movement, rather than political community, forms the core of EU citizenship and that the full exercise of free movement rights is financially contingent. While the majority of the EU national population is eligible to benefit from free movement, a significant proportion of the population is excluded or faces difficulties if they divorce after moving. So EU citizenship extends beyond "workers", but it does not extend fully to all groups of people whatever their situation in life. While the jurisprudence of the Court reflects a generous interpretation of the EC Treaty, the Treaty's inbuilt limitations lead to a concept of citizenship that still excludes many.

The "alien model": pre-Amsterdam "soft law"

At the other end of the spectrum from the rules applying to EC nationals are the various resolutions on third country nationals adopted by immigration ministers prior to 1993 and by the EC Council from 1993 to 1999.[21] It will probably be these rules, rather than the rules applying to EC nationals, to which the Commission and Council will turn when considering the adoption of post-Amsterdam migration legislation. Indeed, the migration convention proposed by the Commission in 1997 was clearly based on the pre-Amsterdam soft law, albeit with some important changes.[22]

[19] On this concept, see M. Everson, "The Legacy of the Market Citizen", in Shaw and More, above at n. 14.

[20] See Case 139/85 *Kempf* [1986] ECR 1741.

[21] Council document 2828/1/93 (1 June 1993) (not published in the *Official Journal*; see T. Bunyan, (ed.), *Key Texts on Justice and Home Affairs in the European Union* (1997), Vol. 1, 98); OJ 1996 C274/3 (workers); OJ 1996 C274/7 (self-employed); OJ 1996 C274/10 (students) and OJ 1996 C80/2 (long-term residents). For detailed comments on the soft law, see Hedemann-Robinson, "Third-Country Nationals, European Union Citizenship and Free Movement of Persons: A Time for Bridges Rather than Divisions" (1996) 16 *YEL* 321; K. Hailbronner, "Migration Law and Policy Within the Third Pillar of the Union Treaty", in T. Bieber and J. Monar (eds), *Justice and Home Affairs in the European Union: The Development of the Third Pillar* (European University Press, Brussels, 1995); and S. Peers, "Building Fortress Europe: The Development of EU Migration Law" (1998) 35 *CML Rev.* 1235.

[22] COM (97) 387 (30 July 1997). For an analysis of the proposed Convention, see Hedemann-Robinson, "From Object to Subject? Non-EC Nationals and the Draft Proposal of the Commission for a Council Act Establishing the Rules for the Admission of Third Country Nationals to the Member States" (1998) 18 *YEL* 289; S. Peers, "Raising Minimum Standards, or Racing for the Bottom? The Commission's Proposed Migration Convention", in E. Guild (ed.), *The Legal Framework and Social Consequences of Free Movement of Persons in the European Union* (Kluwer, The Hague/London, 1999).

Both the substance of the soft law and its institutional context classifies third country nationals as "aliens". Institutionally, the soft law has been adopted outside the EC legal system. These resolutions were proposed by Council Presidencies, not the Commission, and without any participation of the European Parliament and the ECJ has no jurisdiction over them. As soft law, the resolutions lack not only the distinct legal effect attributed to EC law by the ECJ, but also any binding effect as public international law. There is no system to settle disputes between Member States or Member States and the Commission over interpretation or application of the soft law, or for individuals to complain about their enforcement. So measures designed to govern important aspects of individuals' lives cannot in any way be pleaded by those individuals. Furthermore, there was no effective parliamentary involvement in the adoption of these measures.

Substantively, entry into the European Union is limited and the right to continued residence is highly contingent. There is no single set of rules on entry and residence, but different rules for different categories of person, set out in different resolutions. These follow the categorisation already described as regards EC nationals. First, the Resolution on workers does not apply to persons with rights under EC free movement law or pursuant to EC agreements with third states, persons admitted for family reunion or entering under "au pair" or similar schemes, or Geneva Convention refugees, other displaced persons and asylum applicants. In principle, no other third country nationals can be admitted to the European Union. However, their requests may be considered where a job cannot be filled by EC nationals or third country nationals already part of a Member State's "regular labour market". Without prejudice to these two criteria, third country nationals can be admitted on a temporary basis in one of the following situations: they are specific employees of a specific firm with special qualifications; there is a temporary labour shortage which is significantly affecting the operation of the undertaking; or they are seasonal workers, trainees, frontier workers or intra-corporate transferees being posted as key personnel of a company. If such workers are admitted, they must fulfill procedural requirements including possession of a work permit and possibly acquisition of a visa or residence permit. The Resolution permits Member States to allow entry to business visitors and to preserve certain existing agreements with third states.

The Self-employment Resolution has initial exclusions from its scope similar to the exclusions from the scope of the Workers' Resolution. However, it does not exclude refugees, asylum seekers or displaced persons. It has a more liberal underlying approach than the Workers' Resolution, accepting that in principle self-employed persons might benefit the EU's economy. Therefore, they may be admitted where they "add value (investment, innovation, transfer of technology, job creation)" or are "artists exercising an independent activity of significance". However, if they are applying in conjunction with setting up a company in the European Union, only associates actively involved with the company whose presence is necessary to establishing it may be authorised for entry. The self-employed are barred from admission if they seek employment or if their position in a company "amounts to disguised paid employment". Once admitted, they cannot look for or accept a job on the labour market, although they may be allowed to do so eventually, and conversely persons admitted on other grounds should not be allowed to establish themselves as self-employed. There are a number of procedural requirements to fulfill, including compliance with national immigration law and provision of detailed information regarding the planned activity. The rules regarding the validity of the initial permit and later renewal of the permit are more liberal than those applying to workers. Member States are allowed to "roll out the red carpet" and exempt very wealthy investors from the rules in the Resolution.

The Students' Resolution exempts persons with EC law rights, or persons admitted for family reunion. It applies only to post-secondary education, not to school pupils or apprentices. Entry is restricted to the period for completion of the course, and students cannot switch to another status either after dropping out of studies or after graduation. Students might be allowed to take short-term or subsidiary employment. Entry of family members and their employment is left to national law.

The Family Reunion Resolution applies only to third country nationals with the expectation of permanent or long-term residence in a Member State (although this concept is not defined). It requires Member States to admit the spouses and children of a long-term resident, subject to many conditions. Member States can impose an indefinite waiting period before entry and can impose accommodation and financial conditions before allowing entry at any time. Children must be under an age limit which permits the Member States a discretion to set the upper limit at between 16 and 18 to qualify for admission. Other family members should be allowed entry only if there are "compelling reasons". Family members "may" be authorised to stay on an independent basis "and if appropriate, be authorised to work" after a "reasonable period of time following their admission".

Finally, the Long-term Residents' (LTR) Resolution does little to facilitate integration into a host Member State's society or workforce. It excludes persons covered by EC law and persons admitted as students, and does not affect the rights of Geneva Convention refugees or those admitted under a bilateral agreement with a Member State. Persons should be accepted as long-term residents after a period specified in national law, and after ten years at the latest. This status should result in a long-term or permanent residence permit. Member States can apply vague conditions for grant of the residence authorisation, including the "level and stability of the means of existence" of the applicant. Long-term residents "should be able to obtain authorisation to engage in gainful activities", without any specific right of access to employment or self-employment, and they (with their family) should receive access to national territory and equal treatment in certain specified fields.

The text of each Resolution makes clear that the rights of entry and all subsequent rights are discretionary, even where the relevant provisions establish an apparently clear and unconditional rule. This reflects Member States' intention of retaining full control over the status of third country nationals without in any way creating a clear floor of rights which they could rely upon. In addition, it is obvious that the substantive rights in the soft law are hugely different from those applying to EC nationals.

The "worker" model: third country agreements

The third type of model applied by EU law is the "worker" model, as best exemplified by treaties with third states. Many of the EC's agreements with third states create no rights for individuals, but several do. On a spectrum, the first (most favourable) agreements are the European Economic Area (EEA) Agreement with Norway, Iceland and Liechtenstein and the Agreement on Free Movement of Persons with Switzerland.[23] Both of these Agreements essentially grant the full rights of EC free movement law (except citizenship rights) to the nationals of the contracting parties.[24] Second on the spectrum is the agreement with Turkey, supplemented by a Protocol of 1970 and Decisions 1/80 (on workers) and 3/80 (on social security) of the EC–Turkey Association Council established by the Agreement.[25] These rules grant no rights to Turkish nationals to enter the Member States, but they grant rights to employment, education and corollary rights of residence, along with the right to social security equality, to Turkish workers and their families. The 1970 Protocol obliges Member States to impose a "standstill" in new restrictions on establishment and services, to the benefit of self-employed Turks and Turkish service providers and recipients. Thirdly, the EC's treaties with ten Central European applicant states (the Europe Agreements) grant rights to self-employment as well as equality in working conditions and access to employment for family members (if the latter are admitted) and entry of "key personnel" of companies.[26] Fourthly, the EC's treaties with Maghreb states grant equal treatment in social security and working conditions to nationals of the signatory states.[27] Fifthly, the EC's Lome

[23] OJ 1994 L1/1 and COM (99) 229 (4 May 1999), currently being ratified in the European Union and Switzerland.

[24] In fact, to return to the analogy used at the outset of this chapter, many passport lines in the Member States distinguish between EEA nationals and non-EEA nationals.

[25] OJ 1973 C113/2 (Ankara Agreement); OJ 1972 L293/2 (protocol); *EC–Turkey Association Agreement and Protocols and Other Basic Texts* (Council of the EC, Brussels: 1992) (Decision 1/80); OJ 1983 C110/60 (Decision 3/80).

[26] OJ 1993 L347 (Poland); OJ 1993 L348 (Hungary); OJ 1994 L357 (Romania)); OJ 1994 L358 (Bulgaria); OJ 1994 L359 (Slovak Republic); OJ 1994 L360 (Czech Republic); OJ 1998 L26 (Estonia); OJ 1998 L51 (Latvia); OJ 1998 L68 (Lithuania); OJ 1999 L51 (Slovenia).

[27] OJ 1978 L263 (Algeria); OJ 1978 L264 (Morocco), replaced by a new treaty (OJ 2000 L70); OJ 1978 L265 (Tunisia), replaced by OJ 1998 L97. The new treaties contain essentially the same rules as the 1978 treaties.

Convention with seventy African, Caribbean and Pacific states requires identical treatment to the Maghreb treaties, but it is not yet clear whether this provision is binding, because it is only contained in an Annex to the relevant Convention.[28] Finally, the EC's Partnership and Cooperation Agreements (PCAs) with eleven of the twelve former Soviet republics require the Member States to allow in key personnel of companies formed in the ex-Soviet states.[29]

There is extensive case-law on association agreements. The ECJ has ruled in principle that these agreements (including measures implementing them) form part of EC law and that it has jurisdiction to interpret them, even the provisions concerning the free movement of persons.[30] Such provisions can be directly effective, like internal EC law, depending upon the nature and purpose of the relevant agreement and upon whether the rules in question are clear, precise and unconditional.[31] Even if they contain identical clauses to provisions of EC rules, they need not necessarily be interpreted in the same way (the "*Polydor*" principle[32]). Interpretation instead depends on the context and purpose of the relevant agreement. So far the ECJ has found that provisions of EC–Turkey Association Council Decisions 1/80 and 3/80 and the treaties with Maghreb states are directly effective. It hinted that the EEA was not directly effective, but the Court of First Instance (CFI) subsequently ruled that it could be.[33] The Court has not yet had occasion to rule on the PCAs or the Lome Convention, and cases on the Europe Agreements are pending.[34]

While the EEA and the EC–Switzerland Agreement copy the strengths and weaknesses of the "market citizen" model of EC free movement law, albeit without including the formal notion of citizenship, the EC's other agreements are more limited. The EC–Turkey Association Agreement, which covers the largest single group of third country nationals in the European Community, is the classic example of the "worker" model. The Agreement and its implementing measures give liberal rights to admitted workers and their family members, but its effects are largely confined to persons with access to the workforce.[35] So,

[28] OJ 1991 L229. Early in 2000, the European Community and the Lome states reached agreement on a new Convention (COM (2000) 324), which includes a right to equal treatment in working conditions (Art. 13(3)). This provision clearly meets the conditions for direct effect.

[29] OJ 1997 L327 (Russia); OJ 1998 L49 (Ukraine); OJ 1998 L181 (Moldova); OJ 1999 L196 (Kazahkstan); OJ 1999 L196 (Kyrgyz Republic); OJ 1999 L205 (Georgia); OJ 1999 L229 (Uzbekistan); OJ 1999 L239 (Armenia); OJ 1999 L246 (Azerbaijan); COM (97) 693 (6 February 1998) (Turkmenistan), being ratified; COM (95) 44 (22 February 1995) (Belarus), ratification frozen. The only ex-Soviet state without a PCA is Tadjikistan.

[30] Case 181/73 *Haegemann* [1974] ECR 449 and Case 12/86 *Demirel* [1987] ECR 3719.

[31] See particularly *Demirel*, ibid.

[32] Case 270/80 *Polydor* [1982] ECR 329.

[33] Opinion 1/91 [1991] ECR I–6079 and Case T–115/94 *Opel Austria* [1997] ECR II–39. These cases did not directly concern the provisions on free movement of people.

[34] For example Case C–63/99 *Gloszcuk* (pending); Opinion of 14 Sept. 2000.

[35] Persons other than workers and their family members can claim some rights. To obtain equality in social security rights under Decision 3/80, Turkish nationals need only be insured under a national scheme, not necessarily a worker under Decision 1/80 (Case C–262/96 *Surul*, [1999] ECR I–2685. This follows EC social security law (see above at n. 13). Also, the "standstill" on new restrictions on establishment in the 1970 Protocol creates directly effective rights (see

for example, the agreement does permit Turkish workers (at least after four years' employment in a Member State) to leave their jobs voluntarily and to stay in the host Member State and look for another job for a reasonable period, as long as they register with the host state's employment services.[36] However, while the definition of "Turkish worker" follows the same broad definition as found under EC law,[37] this means that Decision 1/80 borrows both the strengths and the drawbacks of EC free movement law. So persons who quit a job in order to look after their children and/or other family members full time will lose any rights they have accrued under Article 6 of the Decision, because they will have departed from the formal workforce.[38] Similarly, the Court has ruled that persons who have definitively left a host Member State's workforce because of retirement or permanent disability have also lost all rights under Decision 1/80.[39]

The Decision also imposes restrictions upon family members. According to Article 7(1) of the Decision, family members who have been "authorised to join" a Turkish worker may have access to employment after three years' residence, subject to EC nationals' priority, and may take up any job after five years' residence. During the first three years' residence, the Court has ruled that a family member must be residing with the worker in order to claim rights to reside under Article 7(1), unless there are "objective circumstances" such as work or education at another location which justify the departure of the person concerned from the marital home.[40] It was up to the national court to determine whether leaving an abusive husband constituted an "objective" reason for leaving the household.[41] So while Turkish workers may leave their job for *subjective* reasons, their family members must show *objective* reasons for leaving their marriage. The Court essentially argued in *Kadiman* that the rights of family members should not exceed those of workers on whom the rights are based.[42]

Therefore, the "worker" model for EC immigration law also has significant strengths and weaknesses. The Court's relatively liberal interpretation of the

judgment of 11 May 2000 in Case C–37/98 *Savas* (not yet reported)). Presumably the standstill on services is also directly effective.

[36] Case C–171/95 *Tetik* [1997] ECR I–329.

[37] See Case C–36/96 *Gunaydin* [1997] ECR I–5143; Case C–98/96 *Ertanir* [1997] ECR I–5179; and Case C–1/97 *Birden* [1998] ECR I–7749. This follows from the obligation to interpret the Decision consistently with EC free movement law "as far as possible", in accordance with the obligation in the Ankara Agreement to be "guided by" the EC rules when adopting the rules governing Turkish workers (Case C–434/93 *Bozkurt* [1995] ECR I–1475).

[38] Of course, they may be able to rely on Art. 7 instead as a family member of a worker (see particularly the judgment of 16 March 2000 in Case C–329/97 *Ergat* (not yet reported)), but this status may be less secure.

[39] See *Bozkurt*, above at n. 27. However, such persons will still retain social security rights under Decision 3/80.

[40] Case C–351/95 *Kadiman* [1997] ECR I–2133. This contrasts with the right of spouses of EC nationals to retain the right to reside and work after separation (see *Diatta*, above at n. 14).

[41] Apparently the national court in *Kadiman* subsequently decided that spousal assault *was* an objective reason justifying retention of rights under Art. 7(1), but this does not bind other courts faced with the same circumstances.

[42] Above at n. 40, paras 38–40.

Decision has allowed many Turkish workers and their family members to fall within its scope. In addition, the direct effect of the Decision gives effect to the principle that immigration law should guarantee individual rights rather than allow unfettered discretion by national authorities. However, Decision 1/80 only allows Turkish workers rights within one Member State,[43] and because its scope is confined to persons currently participating in the labour market and their families, it excludes an even broader range of persons than does EC free movement law. In effect, Turkish nationals in the EC are "market denizens", with their status not merely financially contingent (like EC national "market citizens") but inextricably connected to workforce participation.

While there is as yet no case-law on the Europe Agreements, one can tentatively reach similar conclusions about them. They arguably allow entry into the Member States in order to take up self-employment, and indeed they arguably allow continued free movement to other Member States in order to continue self-employment.[44] The definition of "self-employment" (as compared to "employment") is not yet known. Even if the Court rules that the definition of "self-employment" must be taken from EC free movement law, the EC law definition is not yet known.[45] But the agreements in no way suggest entry rights for other categories of persons, or the right to reside after completing self-employment or failing at self-employment and drawing upon public funds. Therefore, the Europe Agreements have created an alternative type of "market denizenship", inextricably connected to professional activity, rather than workforce participation.

COMPARING THE DIFFERENT MODELS

There is obviously no prospect of allowing unlimited initial entry of third country nationals into the Member States. Rightly or wrongly, immigration is connected in the public mind with increased levels of unemployment, and the EC Member States have been willing to allow rights of entry only to nationals of other Member States and of very wealthy and relatively small third countries. Therefore, while EC free movement law is essentially concerned with only two connected questions (how to eliminate obstacles to free movement and ensure equality for nationals of Member States who move to another state), EC immigration law will have to address three questions. First, what rules should apply to determine whether a third country national should be allowed entry into a

[43] See case-law beginning with *Tetik*, above at n. 36.

[44] See E. Guild, "The Europe Agreements: The Rights of Establishment in the Central and Eastern European Agreements", in Guild, above at n. 22; S. Peers, "Towards Equality: The Actual and Potential Rights of Third-Country Nationals in the European Union" (1995) 35 *CML Rev* 7, 37–9.

[45] There is a brief definition in *Factortame II* (Case C–221/89 [1991] ECR I–3905). The reason for the dearth of case-law is probably that there is little need to distinguish between "employment" and "self-employment" for EC nationals (see above).

Member State? This question does not arise for EC nationals, who have rights to enter automatically as long as they can bring themselves within the categories described above. Secondly, to what extent should third country nationals, once allowed entry into a Member State, be allowed to integrate into the regular workforce and society? Here, EC nationals are entitled to full equality immediately and can be removed after entry only in limited circumstances.[46] Thirdly, how should the Community deal with illegal entry and illegal residence? This situation rarely arises for EC nationals because the rights which they enjoy are so broad.

Of these three questions, only the second has a parallel in EC free movement law, or indeed in the EC–Turkey Agreement. The rest of this chapter will therefore focus on the issue of employment equality and broader social integration in the European Union. It will compare the detailed rules currently applying to the "alien" model with the alternative "[Turkish] worker", "[market] citizen" and (so far theoretical) "human" models of immigration law.[47]

Employment of workers

"Aliens", according to the EU Resolution on admission for employment, can be admitted only on a "temporary basis and for a specific duration" and (as employees) only if they fall within six separate sub-categories of employee (see above). This authorisation will "normally be restricted to a specific job with a specific employer". Seasonal workers can be admitted only for a maximum of six months within each twelve-month period; trainees for a year at first with extensions only to complete their training; and others for four years maximum at first. There are two levels of "anti-switching" rules. First, visitors, students and the self-employed must leave first if they want to apply for admission for employment. Secondly, trainees, service providers and employees of service providers cannot switch and obtain the right to stay as another type of employee. "Regular" workers can ask for an extension of their permission to reside and work, but they may only be permitted an extension if the initial criteria applying to admission are still met, at least at the time of the first extension. There are no rules on when full access to the labour market must or even *might* be granted, but if it is granted, Member States "will examine the desirability of issuing a permanent residence permit".

[46] For reasons of public policy, public security or public health, in accordance with the rules in Directive 64/221 (see above at n. 12); if they are unemployed or have ceased occupational activity at time of first renewal of their residence permit (Directives 68/360 and 73/148, see above at nn. 1, 3); upon graduation unless they switch categories (Directive 93/96, see above at n. 6); or if the conditions which pensioners or "others" must meet are no longer met (Directives 90/365 and 90/364, see above at nn. 6, 7).

[47] In the following text, whenever the words "alien", "worker", "citizen" and "human" appear in inverted commas, they refer to the specific legal models discussed above.

Clearly, "citizens" cannot be restricted to temporary entry or, entry for a specific duration, forced to stay with a specific employer (never mind a specific job), classified as a sub-category of employee, or "checked" to see whether they still meet the initial criteria for entry (because no such criteria may be imposed).[48] A "human" model of immigration law would not seek to draw any distinction between workers and other types of migrants in the first place. The "worker" model also has a number of important differences from the "alien" model, which can be appreciated by examining Decision 1/80 and the relevant case-law in more detail.

Article 6(1) of Decision 1/80 states that Turkish workers "duly registered as belonging to the labour force of a Member State" are entitled to renewal of their work permit for the same employer after one year's "legal employment", to renewal to stay in the same occupation (subject to EC nationals' priority) after three years' "legal employment", and renewal of their work permit for any job in the host Member State after four years' "legal employment". Article 10 of the Decision also requires Member States to secure equality in working conditions. Each indent of Article 6(1) is directly effective, but the Court has not yet ruled on the meaning and legal effect of Article 10. The Court has held that Member States are free to control the initial entry onto the workforce of a Turkish national, and so it seems that a Member State is free, in accordance with the Resolution, to allow seasonal workers entry for only six months a year or to authorise entry for other strictly limited periods, as long as those periods are less than one year. Having said that, such restrictions are subject to the ban on employment discrimination in Article 10, and any fresh restrictions are banned by the directly effective Article 13 of the Decision, which precludes Member States from any new restrictions on access to employment by resident Turkish workers and family members.[49]

After that first year is over, any Turkish worker who is still legally employed by the same employer is free of the Resolution's restrictions.[50] First, while the Turkish worker must stay with the *same* employer for three years to retain the right to take another job in the same occupation,[51] there is no requirement that the worker remain in the same *job* with that employer, as the Resolution requires. So Turkish workers are entirely free to do different jobs for their employer over those three years.[52] Secondly, Member States are banned from creating any type of "special" employment for Turks with the effect that their

[48] Of course, an unemployed EC national worker still faces possible removal at the time of renewal of the first residence permit (see above at n. 45).

[49] On the legal effect of Art. 13, see Case C–192/89 *Sevince* [1990] ECR I–3641. The Court has not yet had the opportunity to give a detailed interpretation of this article, but see now the *Savas* judgment on the standstill on establishment rules (above at n. 34).

[50] However, the worker must have been employed by the *same* employer throughout the first year: see Case C–386/95 *Eker* [1997] ECR I–2697.

[51] Case C–355/93 *Eroglu* [1994] ECR I–5113.

[52] However, it seems open to Member States to restrict the Turkish worker to a specific job with the employer during the first year, subject to Arts 10 and 13.

employment can be limited in time to any period over one year.[53] Thirdly, and similarly, Member States cannot create a special category of "trainees" who are distinct from regular workers, and who are therefore not entitled to qualify for rights under the Decision and are obliged to leave at the end of their training. Trainees are entitled to rights under Article 6 of the Decision if they are entitled to the same conditions of work and pay as workers performing identical or similar activities within the same undertaking.[54] It must logically follow that Member States cannot prevent Turkish workers from "switching" between other types of employment. So a Turkish worker authorised to work in a Member State because he/she has special qualifications, is an intra-corporate transferee, or is an employee of a service provider also has the right to take other jobs with the employer after one year and then move to other employers after three years and other occupations after four years. It should not be relevant whether an employee of a service provider has been posted from Turkey, another third state, or another Member State pursuant to EC companies' right under Article 49 (ex Article 59) EC to post their third country national employees to other Member States during the provision of services.[55]

Fourthly, Member States are precluded not only from adopting such bans on "switching" between types of *employment*, but also from adopting bans on "switching" from classification as another type of *migrant* to classification as a worker. Therefore, persons who were originally admitted as students can qualify under Article 6 if they otherwise meet the criteria of that article,[56] as can persons initially admitted for the purposes of family reunion.[57] For the latter group, this provides a separate route to secure employment and residence status in addition to the route under Article 7(1), which requires a three-year wait and continued residence with a partner during those three years.[58] Furthermore, Turkish graduates have full access to the workforce upon graduation pursuant to Article 7(2), regardless of whether they were admitted as students or family members, if one of their parents worked in that Member State for three years.[59] It is also strongly arguable, based on the case-law of the Court, that persons allowed to stay as Geneva Convention refugees, under temporary protection

[53] See particularly *Ertanir* and *Gunaydin*, above at n. 36.

[54] *Gunaydin*, ibid. The Court did not comment on the effect of Art. 10 of the Decision, which requires Turkish workers to be placed in such an equal situation.

[55] Case C–43/93 *Vander Elst* [1994] ECR I–3803. However, *quaere* whether Turkish nationals can retain their rights under the Decision within the first Member State if they switch to another one. It is strongly arguable that they retain such rights *during* the posting if they do not switch to the other Member State, since threatening the home state immigration status of *any* person posted pursuant to *Vander Elst* would breach Art. 49 EC by creating a huge obstacle to the free movement of services.

[56] *Eroglu*, above at n. 51.

[57] Case C–237/91 *Kus* [1992] ECR I–6781.

[58] *Kadiman*, above at n. 40. In that case, Mrs Kadiman had not accrued enough time with one employer to qualify under Art. 6.

[59] *Eroglu*, above at n. 51, Case C–210/97 *Akman* [1997] ECR I–7519. It is unlikely that many such graduates are initially admitted as workers, but if they are, logically they can still take advantage of Art. 7(2).

schemes, or under national forms of subsidiary or complementary protection, have rights under the Decision. On the other hand, asylum applicants probably cannot accrue rights under the Decision, even if authorised to work, since their right to reside is contingent, not definite, with the result that their employment cannot be considered "legal employment" for the purposes of the Decision.[60] Also, visitors will probably not be able to derive any rights to switch to "employee" status as a result of the Decision, since, in accordance with the Resolution, Member States will probably bar visitors from accruing any employment at all without authorising a change in their status to another category of migrant.[61]

Family members

"Alien" family members, as noted above, might have to wait indefinitely to enter the Member States, and then will not necessarily obtain the right to independent residence or employment. "Citizens" can bring in a wide array of family members, who have immediate rights to enter and take up employment (though not self-employment, if they are family members of workers or self-employed persons). If they are "citizens" themselves, the family members can rely on their "citizenship" to gain independent status, presuming that they can fit within a permitted category of "citizen". If they are not "citizens", their status is jeopardised if they get divorced or if the "citizen(s)" to whom they are linked leave the Member State in question. A "human" model of immigration law would not draw distinctions between categories of migrant, and so migration would no longer be financially contingent.

The "worker" model leaves it to Member States to decide whether and when to allow entry of family members into the host Member State, and which family members to admit, but it does require the Member States to grant important rights to family members once they have been admitted. All family members have directly effective rights to reside with the family member for three years, then employment rights after three years and wider such rights after five years. Students have the right to equal treatment in education, if they are residing with their parents.[62] Graduates have full employment rights upon graduation. In either case, employment rights carry with them a corollary right of residence. As noted above, the family members of "workers" can qualify for "worker" status (and thus independent rights to work and reside) if they have the nationality of the worker; otherwise, they are required to reside with the worker initially and then gain fully independent rights after three years.[63]

[60] See *Sevince*, above at n. 49; *Kus*, above at n. 56; and Case C–285/95 *Kol* [1997] ECR I–3069.

[61] See by analogy the Court's endorsement of Member States' restrictions on switching from visitor to self-employed status (*Savas*, above at n. 34).

[62] Article 9 of Decision 1/80. From the Court's case-law on other provisions of the Decision, this clause should confer directly effective rights to reside during the student's education.

[63] *Ergat*, above at n. 38.

Students

"Alien" students may be permitted entry in order to study, although they have no *right* to do so. They must leave as soon as study is completed and cannot "switch" to another category. They may only be permitted employment in "short-term or subsidiary jobs". Their family members *might* be permitted to enter and take up employment. "Citizen" students have the right to enter and study, but must leave subsequently unless they can "switch" to another category, which they have every right to do. Their family members have the right to enter and work, but must leave when the "citizen" leaves after graduation, unless of course they are the type of "citizens" with independent rights or the "citizen" exercises the right to stay under a different category. A "human" model of immigration law would not insist upon placing students in a particular category distinct from other categories. Finally, under the "worker" model, students have rights as family members of workers (see above), and then rights as graduates, and Member States cannot preclude them from gaining "worker" status via graduation even if they have been admitted as students, rather than as workers. Furthermore, arguably they may even gain worker status while working part time as students, since part-time work will classify them as a worker under Article 6 of Decision 1/80 if they meet the conditions of that article.[64]

Self-employed persons

The "alien" model allows self-employed persons to enter and stay, subject to initial and later checks on their status, and restrictions on changing to "worker" status. Self-employed "citizens" have the right to enter and take up any profession and then switch status if they wish. A "human" model of immigration law would allow the take-up of a profession along with, or instead of, any other activity by migrants. Finally, the two versions of the "worker" model on offer either impose a standstill on national rules or (arguably) allow for full rights of entry, or at least equal treatment after entry.

APPRAISAL OF EU IMMIGRATION LAW

Which model of immigration law should the European Union adopt for third country nationals? First, the "alien" model of integration, which was followed until 1999 within the EU Third Pillar, is both substantively and institutionally deficient. The latter deficiency has, in principle, been cured by the "transfer" of immigration and asylum law matters to the First Pillar of the European Union.

64 This follows logically from the definition of "worker" under Decision 1/80 (see above at n. 36). See also the second Opinion of Advocate-General La Pergola in Case C–262/96 *Surul*, above at n. 34.

As Community law, future immigration measures will inherently be directly effective. But it will still be open to Member States to press for highly discretionary legislation which would not require them to grant any specific rights to third country nationals. Such essentially advisory legislation would breach the principles of the EC Resolution on the quality of drafting of Community legislation,[65] but Member States might be more concerned about restricting the rights of third country nationals than the principles of that Resolution. It can only be hoped that they accept instead that the "discretion and control" approach must give way to the "security and equality" approach, with firmly binding guarantees for their residents. Only such an approach can ensure that third country nationals, mostly of minority racial and religious groups, can indeed be certain of legal integration into the European Union, in the same way that EC nationals can. It should be noted that the Tampere European Council, in October 1999, endorsed equal treatment for long-term resident, third country nationals compared to EC nationals "as near as possible", so at least the principle of equality has been recognised at the level of a summit meeting.

Substantively, the "alien" model also failed to meet the test of ensuring equality for the Community's minorities. A lengthy restriction on the occupations which a third country national can engage in or the employers which a third country national can contract with will obviously hinder that person's integration into the workforce and social mobility. A restriction to the same job with a particular employer will even prevent promotion and deter acquisition of skills, and leave the third country national particularly vulnerable to economic changes. Lengthy restrictions upon family members' access to the workforce mean that third country nationals' family income is below that of many other families, leading to an increased risk that their children will grow up in poverty.

Similarly, the "alien" model damaged the EC's internal market and, if still applied, would damage its recently developed labour market policies. First, barring third country nationals from settling in other Member States restricts EC companies from choosing between all potential employees on the EC labour market. Secondly, banning family members from the labour market, restricting persons from becoming employees or even a different *type* of employee, and "freezing" many individuals into certain occupations, certain employers or certain jobs, severely damages labour market flexibility.

For those reasons, the "alien" model for integration of third country nationals must be wholly rejected, and the Community must reject the principles underlying the Third Pillar immigration rules. Of the remaining models, which is preferable? It is not politically realistic at present to expect a full move to a "human" model of immigration law, because the wealthier Member States fear an influx of nationals of the poorer Member States seeking to draw benefits.[66] Therefore the choice is between the "worker" model and the "citizen" model.

[65] OJ 1999 C73.

[66] However, it remains to be seen whether the Court's post-*Martinez Sala* case-law will nudge EC free movement law in this direction.

It might be objected that the "worker" model as found in the EC–Turkey relationship and the Europe Agreements is too generous a model to extend to nationals of all third countries in the Community, for those "worker" models are premised upon the eventual EU membership of the relevant third state. Similarly, it may be argued that the full rights of EC free movement law should be reserved for EC nationals only, because of the fundamental link between the Member States and their citizens. On the first point, the Europe Agreements are rather vague about future membership of the signatory states; the EU's "pre-accession policy" is instead a political process that has developed largely outside the contractual commitments in the Europe Agreements. Turkish membership is an explicit goal of the EC–Turkey Association Agreement, but seems unlikely to be agreed in the foreseeable future. On the second point, the European Community has already extended full free movement rights, including rights of initial entry, to nationals of four non-EC states, so it has already broken the exclusivity of free movement. In response to both objections, it is suggested that the choice between the different models should depend upon the goals which the Community seeks to achieve with its immigration law, not the original source of the relevant model.

It is the "citizen" model, applied to EU citizens and citizens of four adjacent states which is the most appropriate for EC immigration law. Only the extension of relevant EC free movement law as far as possible to third country nationals, as called for by the Tampere European Council as regards long-term residents, will give effect to the principle of equality between the EC's minority and majority groups. It would be open to the Community to phase in the application of the "citizen" model gradually, with the adoption of the "worker" model as a transitional stage and extension of the formal concept of EU citizenship with related political rights as a final stage for consideration during a future Inter-Governmental Conference. But to adopt the "worker" model as the final stage of EC immigration law would be to entrench its considerable flaws across the entire Community.

Endpiece

CAROL HARLOW

On the wall of the Palazzo Publico in Siena, was rendered, for the edification of the medieval citizenry, Ambrogio Lorenzetti's *Allegory of Good Government*. The effect is enormously pleasing. We do not at first notice if some features of the landscape are left vague and inchoate, or that some of the figures are decidedly ambivalent. Lorenzetti's ravishing figures of peace and justice, for example, are allegedly based on professional male entertainers. The hidden properties of other characters are, on closer investigation, somewhat less than pleasant. For, intruding into Lorenzetti's pleasant landscape, we find the image of "Securitas", an ambiguous personage holding as his insignia a gallows and hanged man as a fearful warning.

The sibylline language used by the Treaty of Amsterdam to deal with the acutely sensitive issues of migration and freedom of movement is reminiscent of this allegory. Its proclamation of an area of "freedom, security and justice" is vague and inchoate. A pronouncement from the Council and Commission cited by Pieter Boeles characteristically suggests the utopian character of the European Union, a society where there is apparently:

> "freedom to live in a law abiding environment in the knowledge that public authorities are doing all in their power to combat and contain those who seek to deny or abuse freedom."

But does this have any real meaning? And, as Boeles asks in the introduction to this collective book, what is the area for and who is entitled to enjoy it? Key questions as to its landscape remain deliberately unasked and unanswered, while the image of "Securitas" lurks unpleasantly in the background.

The contributors to this book, all liberal by instinct, would argue strongly for a positive interpretation of the concept of "freedom, security and justice". Liberty is a central concept of western political philosophy, implying rights of self-determination seen as fundamental. "Man is born free" and every human being is the holder of inalienable fundamental rights and freedoms. These are seen as illimitable, save where they cause harm to the rights of others or of the community. Modern human rights law insists that even then the response should be proportionate; liberty should be curtailed and limited to the least possible extent.[1] Similar reasoning must be applicable to the core Treaty principles

[1] J. Rawls, *A Theory of Justice* (OUP, Oxford, 1972).

of liberty, democracy, respect for human rights and fundamental freedoms, and the rule of law for, if liberty is equated with freedom, then the rule of law must be synonomous with justice. It would also seem to follow that the protections of the area of freedom, justice and security should extend to all within the boundaries, whatever their origin. It is this ideal, squarely based on liberal democratic values, which he calls the "human model" of treatment of outsiders, that Steven Peers[2] believes the European Union should aspire to.

Amsterdam, and Tampere therafter, spawned fine words; to the talk of freedom, security and justice at Amsterdam, Tampere added the discourse of rights, to be established in an EU charter of rights, presently being drafted[3]. As we now know, the draft Charter contains several articles which, while not new, have a bearing on Title IV. Article 1, for example, asserts, without obvious limitation, that "Human dignity is inviolable. It is to be respected and protected". Article 24 asserts the rights of the child. More specifically, Article 18 guarantees a right to asylum in accordance with the Geneva Convention. Article 7 confirms respect for private and family life. Article 15 states that "Third-country nationals working lawfully in member states are entitled to equal treatment", while Articles 20–23 greatly strengthen protection against discrimination on gender, ethnic and cultural grounds.

This would endorse an optimistic reading of the Tampere formula according to which "freedom" should not be regarded as the prerogative of EU citizens. Freedom is a fundamental human right and this perception should form the basis of the treatment of non-citizens in every state.

But as Pieter Boeles points out, freedom may, in the context of Title IV EC, simply mean "crime-free", while justice may be equated with criminal justice and law enforcement, in which case the area of freedom, security and justice might degenerate into an open prison. John Crowley similarly regards the formula of "freedom, security and justice" as capable of a contingent and negative interpretation, a view which gains some credibility from the secondary phrases of Article 73j ToA (now Article 62 EC). These firmly limit the parameters of the promises by reference to free movement of persons and then move sharply on to the defensive with mention of "appropriate measures to deal with immigration, asylum and the prevention and combating of crime". We have come down to earth with a vengeance, landing abruptly on the familiar land of Fortress Europe.

We can link this directly to Peers' choice of four possible models of migration policy in the European Union. In ascending order, these are: (i) the "alien model", which treats all nationals of third party countries as aliens, whose permission to stay inside the EU borders is a privilege regulated by discretion and soft law; (ii) the "worker model", theorised by Michelle Everson as a legacy of the EU's origins in the Common Market;[4] (iii) the "citizen model", related to the

[2] See Chapter 12 above.

[3] Draft of Charter of Fundamental Rights of the European Union Charte 4487/1/00, REVI, 10 October 2000.

[4] M. Everson, "The Legacy of the Market Citizen", in J. Shaw and G. More (eds), *New Legal Dynamics of European Union* (Clarendon Press, Oxford, 1995).

Article 18 EC right for all Union citizens to "move and reside freely within the territory of the Member States"; (iv) the "human model", already mentioned, deriving ultimately from the duties of common humanity imposed by international law. Peers presents his "aliens model", in which soft law and discretion replace principles, entitlements and rules[5] and are used to preclude challenge, rather as a historical survival, and the development of modern administrative law might certainly suggest this progression.[6] Peers sees the "citizen model" as the most probable outcome for the European Union. Thus, the "goodies" on offer at Amsterdam, positively designed to buttress the concept of EU citizenship, were negatively reserved, as this book makes clear, for the citizenry.

To others this would be an optimistic assessment. In many areas, such as treatment of third country nationals, EU law clings to the less progressive "worker model", as Peers himself concedes. Indeed, the principles concerning the rights of third country workers suggest that Everson's analysis is more appropriate. Family rights depend upon the "worker", yet third country nationals cannot freely enter the labour market in other states. Companies from one Member State providing services in another may, on the other hand, import their labour.[7] Surely this is Everson's "market model"?

Again, as Guild points out, a sharply contrasted attitude to economic activity exists and is reflected in attitudes to migrants. Inside the cosy borders of the European Union, as outside within the club of the world's rich trading nations, we find commitment not only to the dismantling of internal barriers, but also to equality of economic opportunity, creating a framework within which personal freedom of movement for economic purposes has emerged as a "human right" vested in individuals. This is the original rhetoric of the Four Freedoms, which have obtained the mantra and status of constitutional rights, entrenched in an "economic constitution"[8] enshrining competition and economic freedom as fundamental rights. Even here, if internal freedom of movement has been easily accepted and has produced relatively few problems, this may be because it is a right which, as Guild reminds us,[9] is comparatively rarely exercised. There is

[5] This is, of course, Davis' famous model of discretionary justice: see K.C. Davis, *Discretionary Justice: a preliminary inquiry* (Louisiana State University Press, 1969). For discussion, see C. Harlow and R. W. Rawlings, *Law and Administration* (Butterworths, London, 2nd ed. 1997), ch. 4; K. Hawkins (ed.), *The Uses of Discretion* (Clarendon Press, Oxford, 1991); D. Galligan, *Discretionary Powers, A Legal Study of Official Discretion* (Clarendon Press, Oxford, 1990).

[6] C. Harlow, "European Administrative Law and the Global Challenge", in P. Craig and G. de Burca (eds), *The European Union in Perspective* (OUP, Oxford, 1999).

[7] Case C–43/94 *Vander Elst* v. *Office des Migrations Internationales* [1994] ECR I–3803. And see G. More, "The Principle of Equal Treatment", in P. Craig and G. de Burca (eds), *The European Union in Perspective* (OUP, Oxford, 1999), 527 *ff*.

[8] See M. Streit and W. Mussler, "The Economic Constitution of the European Community: 'From Rome to Maastricht'", in F. Snyder (ed.), *Constitutional Dimensions of European Economic Integration* (Kluwer, London, 1996); and E,-J. von Mestmacker, "On the Legitimacy of European Law" (1994) 58 *RabelsZ* 617.

[9] Guild states (at p.65) that around five million EU citizens reside in another state and less than 2% of the working age population in the European Union consists of workers from one Member State working in another. R. Hansen, "A European citizenship or a Europe of citizens? Third

much evidence that the Member States prefer to keep it that way; the proposal for a right of residence divorced from the exercise of economic activities[10] has never yet, for example, found its way into law.

Despite high levels of unemployment, migrant labour remains an essential feature of EU economies, while international commitments (e.g. to the GATS) provide further impetus for a liberal regime of labour migration. Yet as they cross borders, economic migrants are transmuted into "bogus asylum seekers". The rights of third country nationals for the most part remain inferior to those of Member State citizens, despite a helping hand from the Court of Justice.[11] There is a niggardly attutude to peripheral rights, evident in the provisions on family reunion described by Gisbert Brinckmann. Yet filling of gaps in the present protection of third country nationals would be relatively simple. Association agreements stand as models, and regulations based on them could standardise treatment of third country nationals, while unfavourable national laws of citizenship and nationality could be amplified by recourse to a concept of EU citizenship. A general "levelling-up" towards the standard set for EU nationals could commence. Notably, however, none of this is on offer or even on an agenda, giving further grounds for pessimism.

Where Peers suggests progression, other contributors point sharply to regression. Guy Goodwin-Gill warns that states sign up to international covenants on human rights in the expectation that implementation will never be expected of them; strong on grandiose rhetorical statements of intention, they are in the event short on action, compliance being difficult to monitor. Behind promises of non-refoulement, for example, we find a fairly widespread practice of refoulement. Similarly, a new Convention to Protect the Rights of the Child is put in place while, alongside, commitment to the 1951 UN Convention on Asylum Seekers is acquiring an increasingly restricted interpretation. Arguments are that it is outdated, intended only to deal with individual cases of political asylum, long recognised in extradition law. The principles are inapplicable in the circumstances of mass exodus and steady economic migration of today's world.

Jens Vedstedt-Hansen and Gregor Noll show both the European Union and the component Member States as slipping back from international commitments, a gap deepened and widened by transfer of police and immigration functions to the Third Pillar and, after Amsterdam, in part to the European Community. This point is developed by Nicholas Blake, whose national case study of UK immigration practice shows the way in which the Dublin Convention and Schengen *acquis* can be used as vehicles for retreat from liberal practice. Member States are also quietly using the co-operation machinery to

country nationals in the EU" (1998) 24 *Journal of Ethnic and Migration Studies* 751, 753, tells us that of 300 million European citizens, 4.9 million are intra-EU migrants and that 12–13 million third country nationals reside in the EU.

[10] OJ 1979 C207/14.

[11] Especially Case 14/78 *Demirel* [1987] ECR 3719. The jurisprudence is more fully analysed in other chapters, especially Guild and Peers, in ch. 13 above.

develop novel and less generous concepts. Refugee status, for example, is overlapped by the concept of temporary protection, originating in a concession or discretionary extension of asylum law for "hard cases". These authors suggest a different and less humane use to embrace some who might be entitled to claim refugee status and would formerly have been designated refugees. Temporary permission to stay—on the face of things a discretionary concesssion designed to extend help to persons outwith the rules—is in fact being used to offer temporary shelter to people who might well deserve permanent protection. Again, the "burden-sharing" agreement between Member States works against potential asylum seekers, producing a situation in which incomers cannot choose where they want to be, nor settle in countries with which they have connections. A quota system could evolve in which "rights" to enter are rationed by limiting the correlative duties to accept. In just this way, a rejected "aliens model" can operate behind the scenes to limit the more generous legal provisions of a "human" or "citizen" model" (in this case, the 1951 UN Convention on the Status of Refugees).

How can we fight retrenchment? A majority of our contributors might accept as a starting point that, since international responsibility lies on states, it is for states to ensure compliance. On the other hand, greater commitment to the intermediate building-block which is the European Union is also necessary. Perhaps everyone would agree on abolition of the Third Pillar, demanded before but not conceded at Amsterdam. But would they also agree on full integration of present responsibilities for migration into the competence of the European Union? This is, after all, a common position amongst migrants' organisations, which tend "to see *more* not *less* Europe as a corrective to lowest common denominator Council-based decision making".[12]

The problem is, as Juliet Lodge warns, that the European Union has opened up a "democracy deficit". The European Parliament lacks the capacity to fill gaps left by national parliaments; national parliaments are losing what control they had over national executives:

> "What was and remains ill-understood is the degree to which the European Parliament has not won powers forfeited to national governments by national parliaments: neither can exercise effective control over either what national governments do in the EU or what the EU executive does."[13]

Johannes van der Klaauw sees the process of "harmonisation" inaugurated by Schengen and carried steadily through Maastricht and Amsterdam as the underlying principle of an EU migration policy, as escalating the process of erosion. Because the emphasis has been on identifying a common position, harmonisation has meant in practice description and concretisation of the current immigration situation in Member States, with each state able to protect its particular

[12] A. Favell and A. Geddes, *European Integration, Immigration and the nation State: Institutionalising transnational Political Action?*, RSC WP 99/32 (EUI, Florence, 1999), 19.

[13] J. Lodge, "The European Parliament", in S. Andersen and K. Eliassen, *The European Union: How Democratic Is It?* Sage, London, 1996 188.

fetishes. In this way, minimum standards of protection or procedures have elided into maximum standards. The consequence is an amazingly complex and detailed maze of rules, devised ad hoc to deal with, and applicable to, specific situations. This is illustrated in the area of family reunification through which Gisbert Brinckmann tries to guide us. The exercise reveals a complex tangle of rules, discretions, soft law and exceptions which operate against transparency. This is why the Council of Europe calls the "ever more intensive efforts by the European Union to harmonise asylum and immigration procedures" a threat to human rights.[14] If codification means simplification, as the Community has itself acknowledged,[15] then there is a need to return to basic principles. But, as all contributors argue, this is rendered impossible by the absence of agreement on what that principle should be.

Pessimists—amongst whom the present author is to be numbered—might justifiably draw the conclusion that on the present evidence, the transfer, albeit less grudging and niggardly than that actually conceded, of plenary competence to the European Union under the First Pillar was never likely to cure any problems. To the contrary, the compromise solution adopted at Amsterdam is not a step forward. It is likely to add to existing problems, by stimulating further co-operative ventures, such as development of and access to the SIS system, without providing adequate controls. It is therefore best to keep migration policy clearly as a national responsibility, for which national governments must accept full responsibility to national institutions. Yet it is precisely the mixed record of national governments on questions of migration, asylum and racism which—as Blake's contribution to this collection suggests—create the demand for a transfer of responsibility to the European level. Hence, Blake himself, on the ground that states act largely without adequate democratic or judicial supervision, argues for a European agency with adequate powers to monitor and enforce asylum law within EU borders. This solution, however, conflicts not only with the present pattern of EU agencies,[16] but is also likely to compound the problems by adding the difficult question of how to secure agency accountability.[17]

The landscape of the Third Pillar has never been either democratic or transparent. Lack of transparency was indeed one reason why it was so easy to transform high visibility, political problems into low visibility decisions by

[14] Goodwin Gill, above at p. 162, n. 88.

[15] See Edinburgh Resolution of 11/12 December 1992; and Council Resolution of 8 June 1993 (OJ 1993 C166/1), discussed by T. Burns, "Better Lawmaking? An Evaluation of Law Reform in the European Community", in P. Craig and C. Harlow (eds), *Lawmaking in the European Union*, (Kluwer International, London, 1998).

[16] On which, see A. Kreher, "Agencies in the EC—A Step Towards Administrative Integration in Europe" (1997) 4 *Journal of European Public Policy* 225; and A. Kreher (ed.), *The EC Agencies Between Community Institutions and Constituents: Autonomy, Control and Accountability* (EUI, Florence, 1997).

[17] For example G. Majone, "The New European Agencies: Regulation by Information (1997) 4 *Journal of European Public Policy* 262; M. Shapiro, "The Problems of Independent Agencies in the United States and European Union" (1997) 4 *Journal of European Public Policy* 276.

transferring them from national to European level. The Third Pillar was space used deliberately by Member State governments to develop:

> "an array of non-binding immigration and asylum conclusions, recommendations and the like, that reflected a degree of new political activity and demonstrated routinised co-operation. These seemingly muddled and messy intergovernmental compromises have allowed member states to use European cooperation to slip domestic political and judicial constraints."[18]

Curtin, a leading contributor to the debate which surrounds the European "democratic deficit",[19] insists that transparency of decision and policy making is essential. As Curtin has always argued, the importance of transparency lies in its relation to popular democracy. There is a need for a democratic debate on citizenship and migration at both national and European levels and, for this debate to be of any value, an informed public is essential. But whether greater transparency would really go as far as Curtin hopes to stimulate "deliberative democracy" is, I think, dubious. The problem is not and never has been entirely one of lack of transparency—although Curtin is of course right to deplore this as anti-democratic;—it is rather the lack of interest in European affairs on the part of press and public. This is a side of Europe's notorious "democratic deficit" for which political scientists have been unable to devise either explanation or cure.[20] The problem is not a simple one of "cause and effect", but a dangerous interplay between lack of transparency and apathy, circular in so much as apathy as often accounts for lack of transparency as vice versa. For the more liberal states, then, a move to the First Pillar may present more of a threat than an opportunity. Several serious complaints of secrecy involve Third Pillar matters.[21] There is a very real fear of lessened control and democratic subversion—hence the pressure by these states in the Council and through the Community

[18] Favell and Geddes, above at n. 11, 17. See, to similar effect, E. Guild, "The Constitutional Consequences of Lawmaking in the Third Pillar of the European Union", in P. Craig and C. Harlow (eds), *Lawmaking in the European Union* (Kluwer International, London, 1998).

[19] D. Curtin, *Postnational Democracy: The European Union in Search of a Political Philosophy* (Kluwer, The Hague, 1997). See also P. Craig, "Democracy and Rulemaking within the EC: An Empirical and Normative Assessment", in P. Craig and C. Harlow (eds), *Lawmaking in the European Union* (Kluwer International, London, 1997); J. Weiler, "European Neo-constitutionalism: in Search of Foundations for the European Constitutional Order" (1996) 44 *Political Studies* 517; and "The Reformation of European Constitutionalism" (1997) 35 *JCMS* 97.

[20] See S. Andersen and K. Eliassen, *The European Union: How Democratic Is It?* (Sage, London, 1996); C. Lord, *Democracy in the European union* (Academic Press, Sheffield, 1998).

[21] Case T–194/94 *Carvel and Guardian Newspapers* v. *Council* [1995] ECR II–2769; Case T–174/95 *Svenska Journalistiförbundet* v. *Council* [1998] ECR II–2289 and Case T–14/98. *Hautral* v. *Council* (19 July 1999). See also the Statewatch complaints to the European Ombudsman: Complaints 1054/25.11.96/STATEWATCH/UK/IJH against the Council, AR 1997, 179; and 1087/10.12.96/STATEWATCH/UK/IJH against the Council, AR 1998, 41. To their credit, both the CFI and EO ruled that the Code of Conduct on access (Decision 93/731/EC) (OJ L340/41 of 31 December 1993, adopted by the Commission in Decision 94/90/EC applied to Third Pillar documents.

Courts for a more open system of European government. It is depressing to note that currently events are moving in the opposite direction, The Commission's attempt at redrafting the Code as a regulation is in some ways more restrictive than the Code. The Council Decision at the COREPER meeting in July, and adopted by written procedure, which provides for the classification of security and defence material, is a decisive step in the wrong direction.[22]

In one key respect, however, Amsterdam does provide the basis for a new start. Article 6(a) ToA (now Article 13 EC) contains a far-reaching equality clause which, for the first time, explicitly empowers "appropriate action to combat discrimination based on . . . racial or ethnic origin". This could make a very positive contribution, affording a significant way forward through steady and consistent action plans if the institutions chose to use it.[23] The obstacle lies in what Gearty has vividly called the "hard seed of hate"[24] which is emerging from European soil, manifesting itself in the resurgence of seriously right-wing politicians with racist and xenophobic policies high on their agenda. While substantial sections of the European electorate support anti-migrant policies, it is difficult for even the most liberal politicians entirely to avoid the effects of the so-called race card, and the minority representation in the European Parliament has already been noted. At national level, politicians unashamedly seek to capitalise on the xenophobic spirit abroad, using it to raise alarm about "bogus" asylum seekers and to curtail the welfare benfits—allegedly the goal of "economic" migrants. National politicians (liberal and illiberal) may seek to evade and depoliticise the race problem by transferring it to the European level. This can usefully be accompanied by reassuring noises concerning the need for co-operation and burden sharing in dealing with incomers and security against the incursions of those who traffic in drugs. Perhaps this explains why Vedstedt-Hansen and Noll see Community law as *legitimating* the unequal treatment of ethnic minorities contrary to Article 14 ECHR.

Let us grant that liberal sentiments and a general commitment to anti-racism are widespread among the groups which at present make up the European elite. The Commission has a respectable record, and European bureaucracy by and large forms a comfortable liberal terrain in which racism and xenophobia are unlikely to flourish.[25] (Cynics might remark that a greater interest in and tolerance towards a personal freedom to migrate is likely to be found among this

[22] See Council Decision 10702/00 amending Decision 93/731/EC on public access to Council documents and Decision 2000/23/EC on the improvement of information on the Council's legislative activities and the public register of Council documents.

[23] See Draft Communication from the Commission, to the Council, the European Parliament, the Economic and Social Committee and the Committee of the Regions on certain Community measures to combat discrimination.

[24] C. Gearty, "The Internal and External 'Other' in the Union Legal Order: Racism, Religious Intolerance and Xenophobia in Europe", in P. Alston (ed.), *The European Union and Human Rights* (OUP, Oxford, 1999).

[25] S. O'Leary, "The Free Movement of Persons and Services", in P. Craig and G. de Burca (eds), *The Evolution of EU Law* (OUP, Oxford, 1998), 378.

peripatetic elite than among the rest of us.[26]) The same is not entirely true of the European Parliament, where right-wing parties have found a secure foothold.[27] Yet paradoxically it is the European Parliament which has perhaps to date shown greatest commitment to anti-racism through a series of reports and resolutions which call for determined action.[28]

It is questionable, however, whether genuine commitment to anti-racist policy is present in a majority of Council members. Thus, O'Leary somewhat pessimistically suggests that:

> "Forty years after the signing of the Treaty of Rome it appears that the Member States still cling to a mindset reminiscent of the days when sovereignty meant that aliens could be expelled or excluded at the discretion of the host state. In certain respects, the Court has not opposed Community secondary legislation which translates this mindset into Community law."[29]

The anxiety of Member States to preserve national rights of veto reflects more than the usual concern over national sovereignty which many see as the true motor of EU policy making.[30] It reflects also fear and the transfer of national tension over "outsiders" to European level. As Crowley reminds us, identity is normally defined in terms of "otherness" and Europe, a repository of multiple cultures and identities,[31] has traditionally protected itself against "its internal 'differentness' "[32] by focussing on the otherness of others. The Cold War gave material shape to "otherness". It also established definite and virtually impermeable barriers, protecting us from otherness. The parameters have changed with the destruction of the barriers and disintegration of the corporate "other". The disastrous failure of EU foreign policy in ex-Yugoslavia, with the consequential flood of refugees, has provoked a foreseeable though dangerous rise in nationalist feelings.

The substantial enlargement of the European Union presently under consideration will not help this development. States of the previous buffer zone will be brought inside the European Union and, if expansion outstrips economic performance, the sanctity of the free movement principle could itself come into question. At the same time, abolition of internal borders will transfer

26 Ibid.

27 On the make-up of the extreme right in European politics, see S. Hix and C. Lord, *Political Parties in the European Union* (Macmillan, London, 1997), 42–4.

28 For example, Report of the Committee of Inquiry into the Rise of Fascism and Racism in Europe 1985 (the Evrigenis Report); Report of the Committee of Inquiry on Racism and Xenophobia 1991 (the Ford Report); a series of reports from the Parliament's Committee on Civil Liberties and internal Affairs; and a series of resolutions on racism, xenophobia and related matters.

29 Above at n. 24, 9.

30 A. Moravscik, "Preferences and Power in the European Community: A Liberal Intergovernmentalist Approach" (1993) 31 *JCMS* 473.

31 The consequences of which are discussed notably by J. Weiler, "Does Europe Need a Constitution? Reflections on Demos, Telos and the German Maastricht Decision" (1995) 1 *European Law Journal* 219.

32 A phrase borrowed from J. Derrida, *The Other Heading: Reflections on Today's Europe* (Indiana University Press, Indiana, 1992).

responsibility for frontier control from inside the European Union to its external borders. The erstwhile buffer states will form the border between the European Union and its neighbours. In effect this entails a transfer from long-standing and trusted European partners (the Schengen six) to new states with which Europe is unaccustomed to co-operate. Minimum procedural standards for the protection of refugees will then, as van der Klaauw argues, become essential. It is, however, doubtful that they could be guaranteed. Research has shown that even when border control is in the hands of states with relatively sophisticated administrations and immigration systems, there is substantial national variance in implementation;[33] this variance will inevitably increase in states whose traditions of civil liberty are less well-established and where administration itself may be precarious.

As external borders become more porous, "Securitas" will become an increasingly important actor. It is Securitas who nurtures the "hard seeds of hate", legitimating reliance on the "model of aliens" epitomised in the mantra of "national security", "general interest" and "police powers". The insignia of Securitas today consist of a battery of immigration and police controls, bringing with them division between citizens and non-citizens. The power of Crowley's good/bad dichotomy will not easily be extinguished by borders. Even after entry into the "area of freedom, security and justice", the citizens of outside states will remain, as they are today, infected by their provenance. We are afraid of the insecurity and injustice experienced by societies which have not, like us, confirmed their attachment to the principles of liberty, democracy, respect for human rights and fundamental freedoms, or where the rule of law has failed. Fear of foreigners not only defines our identity but has become our security blanket. On the walls of Sala della Pace at Siena, Lorenzetti's second allegory of bad government is fragmentary and in bad repair. We should not set about restoring it.

[33] S. Peers, *Mind the Gap! Ineffective Member State Implementation of European Union Asylum Measures* (ILPA and Refugee Council, London, 1998).

Index